ENQUIRY CONCERNING
POLITICAL JUSTICE

Enquiry Concerning Political Justice

BY

WILLIAM GODWIN

With selections from
Godwin's other writings

ABRIDGED AND EDITED
BY

K. CODELL CARTER

OXFORD
AT THE CLARENDON PRESS
1971

Oxford University Press, Ely House, London W. 1

GLASGOW NEW YORK TORONTO MELBOURNE WELLINGTON
CAPE TOWN SALISBURY IBADAN NAIROBI DAR ES SALAAM LUSAKA ADDIS ABABA
BOMBAY CALCUTTA MADRAS KARACHI LAHORE DACCA
KUALA LUMPUR SINGAPORE HONG KONG TOKYO

PRINTED IN GREAT BRITAIN

THIS BOOK IS
RESPECTFULLY DEDICATED
TO MY PARENTS

EDITOR'S PREFACE

WILLIAM GODWIN'S *Enquiry Concerning Political Justice* has been generally neglected since shortly after its publication at the end of the eighteenth century. This is doubtless due in part to a widespread and persisting notion that the fundamental doctrines of the *Enquiry* are excessively Utopian and naïvely optimistic. In recent years, however, some writers have advanced more sympathetic interpretations of Godwin's views and, at the same time, there has been a general re-awakening of interest in the kind of libertarian theories that Godwin advocated. These two factors are occasioning a revival of interest in the *Enquiry*.

Unfortunately Godwin's writings abound in antique examples and illustrations, and in redundant reiterations of the principal conclusions. The only modern edition of the *Enquiry*, a photographic reproduction of Godwin's two-volume third edition, does not reduce the bulk of superfluous material. In this abridgement I have cut the text of the *Enquiry* to less than two-thirds of its original length, mostly by eliminating unnecessary illustrations and repetitions. Godwin's minor political works are difficult to obtain, and, because they are much inferior to the *Enquiry* and contain even more material which is of little interest to the modern reader, they are not likely ever to be widely circulated. Some of the minor political works, however, contain passages which elucidate the principal conclusions of the *Enquiry*. For this reason I have included, as an appendix, excerpts from three of the minor works. By abridging the *Enquiry* and by including the selections from Godwin's other writings, I hope to have provided a comprehensive presentation of Godwin's main political and philosophical conclusions that will be convenient for students.

The text of this abridgement is from the third edition, published in 1798. Godwin's arguments are most fully stated in that final edition and his major conclusions do not differ materially from those of the earlier editions.[1] With a few exceptions Godwin's punctuation has been retained. I have silently corrected a few misprints, modernized the spelling, and standardized Godwin's footnote references to other works. My footnotes are placed within square brackets to distinguish them

[1] First edition 1793; second edition 1796.

from Godwin's. When quoting material translated from non-English sources Godwin regularly gives the passage in the original language as a footnote; these I have omitted. Textual omissions less than a paragraph in length are indicated by three dots in the text, omissions of one or more paragraphs by four dots centred on the page. There is no special indication in the text where entire chapters or appendices have been deleted, but such deletions are indicated in the full table of Contents on p. 7.

I would like to thank the Cornell University library for making available a copy of the third edition of the *Enquiry*, and the staff of the Rutgers University library system for helping me to obtain original editions of Godwin's writings from which the excerpts were taken. Thanks go to Joseph A. Graves and to Elizabeth Hankey for help with the proofs and to the Rutgers University Research Council for a grant which defrayed some necessary expenses. I greatly appreciate the suggestions of Dr. Clifford Brown, Mr. Clyde Snyder, and a Clarendon Press adviser; especially the Introduction is much better because of their efforts. Most of all I owe thanks to my wife, Barbara, for her extensive help in preparing the typescript and checking the proofs, and especially for her encouragement and optimism during the entire undertaking.

CONTENTS

EDITOR'S INTRODUCTION

WILLIAM GODWIN was born 3 March 1756. Following his father he became a nonconformist minister. Early in his life Godwin read Rousseau and the French materialists, Holbach and Helvétius; this led him gradually to lose faith in religion, and after a few years he withdrew from the ministry. By 1793 when the *Enquiry Concerning Political Justice* was first published, Godwin was an atheist. Through a large part of his early life Godwin supported himself by writing fiction, newspaper articles, and political pamphlets. Godwin was always acutely interested in contemporary political issues and several times he risked his own safety writing in defence of radical friends who were under attack from the government. As he matured, his own political views grew more radical and developed into the anarchistic theories advocated in the *Enquiry*. Godwin never gave up the fundamental political theses of that work.

The *Enquiry* was warmly received by English liberals and it enjoyed a wider distribution than Godwin himself anticipated. One contemporary essayist wrote of Godwin and his book: 'No work in our time gave such a blow to the philosophical mind of the country as the celebrated *Enquiry Concerning Political Justice*. Tom Paine was considered for the time as a Tom Fool to him; Paley an old woman; Edmund Burke a flashy sophist.'[1] A year after the *Enquiry* appeared Godwin published his most successful novel, *Caleb Williams*. This brought him to the zenith of popular esteem and recognition. At this time Godwin met and subsequently married Mary Wollstonecraft who has an independent reputation as the first woman to publish a demand for the emancipation of her sex. The relation between Godwin and Mary Wollstonecraft was an extremely happy one, but it ended tragically after about a year when Mary died following the birth of their only child, Mary Godwin.

The success of the *Enquiry* was short lived. It had been published in the face of growing reactionary sentiments prompted by post-revolutionary political developments in France. As the reaction mounted Godwin, who refused to abandon the principles espoused in the *Enquiry*, was vehemently denounced by conservatives and even by his former

---

[1] William Hazlitt, 'William Godwin', *Treasury of Modern Biography*, ed. Robert Cochrane (Edinburgh: William P. Nimmo and Company, 1881), p. 59.

liberal friends. To support himself he was obliged to write miscellaneous plays, novels, histories, and even children's stories. His subsequent serious political works were neither as interesting nor as popular as the *Enquiry*. His fame waned under the torrent of abuse and in his old age he gradually descended into the oblivion which enshrouds him still. He died 7 April 1836.

Godwin exerted a faint but real influence upon those who followed him. Godwin's relation to Shelley—his son-in-law and most important disciple—is well known even if only in caricature. Godwin also influenced other English poets including Wordsworth and Coleridge. Through Coleridge Godwin may have influenced the formation of some of John Stuart Mill's ethical and political views. Malthus wrote his first *Essay on Population* in reaction against Godwin and then, after Godwin responded by pointing out various mistakes in his position, he wrote the second *Essay* in which his doctrines are altered to accommodate some of Godwin's criticisms. Through William Thompson and other early socialists Godwin's influence extended, faintly but perceptibly, to Owen and beyond to Proudhon and Marx.

Godwin begins the preface to the *Enquiry* by observing that politics, like every other science, ought to make advances from time to time. He explains that political events in America and France had exposed errors in contemporary political theory, thereby pointing out the need for a new study in which the science of politics could be advanced by correcting these errors. It was, Godwin explains, his awareness of this need that led him to undertake writing the *Enquiry*. In a diary entry Godwin observes that his 'original conception proceeded on a feeling of the imperfections and errors of Montesquieu, and a desire of supplying a less faulty work'. The entry continues: 'In the just fervour of my enthusiasm I entertained the vain imagination of "hewing a stone from the rock", which by its inherent energy and weight, should overbear and annihilate all opposition and place the principles of politics on an immovable basis.'[1] Godwin's interests and objectives in writing the *Enquiry* were, therefore, to develop political theory; however, Godwin himself insists that politics be conceived as an extension of ethics,[2] and that many of the shortcomings of contemporary political theory could be attributed to a failure to see the intimate relation between ethics and politics.[3] Consistent with this general view, Godwin derives most of

[1] H. N. Brailsford, *Shelley, Godwin, and Their Circle* (reprinted, Hamden, Conn.: Anchor Books, 1969), p. 90.
[2] p. 67.   [3] p. 68.

his important political conclusions from ethical presuppositions. One should consequently begin one's study of the *Enquiry* by considering Godwin's ethics.

Godwin is, in the first place, a utilitarian. He appeals repeatedly to considerations of utility both in his arguments and in his analyses of the meaning of ethical terms. He defines 'duty', for example, as 'that mode of action on the part of the individual, which constitutes the best possible application of his capacity to the general benefit'.[1] For the most part Godwin seems to feel that right behaviour is to be determined by applying the criterion of utility to each individual act rather than to classes of acts and he is, therefore, an act-utilitarian rather than a rule-utilitarian.[2] Godwin seems to have arrived at utilitarianism at about the same time as, yet independently from, Jeremy Bentham. His views on ethics differ in detail from those both of Bentham and of John Stuart Mill, and they are, perhaps, more similar to Mill's than to Bentham's.[3]

Godwin appears occasionally to depart from strict utilitarianism. F. E. L. Priestley argues persuasively that these departures reflect his indebtedness to Plato and to the English Platonists.[4] While many of Godwin's doctrines do reflect this influence, what seem to be departures from utilitarianism are frequently more apparent than real. His treatment of the meaning of 'virtue' is a good example. Both actions and agents can be referred to as virtuous.[5] Godwin insists that the agent's intentions leading to any act must be appraised before either act or agent can be regarded as virtuous.[6] This conforms to the way we ordinarily use the term—an agent may perform a selfish act that happens to yield the greatest utility for humanity as a whole, but in such a case neither the act nor the agent is virtuous. But while Godwin's analysis appears accurate in this respect, it seems to entail that virtue cannot be accounted for simply on the basis of utility. In reality, however, it does not.

Godwin recognizes that people who are not virtuous occasionally perform right acts while virtuous people occasionally perform wrong ones. Virtue is a dispositional quality and cannot be ascribed to individuals on the basis of single acts right or wrong. A good clue to disposition is intention—it is reasonable to assume that a person who acts

---

[1] p. 83. [2] e.g., p. 104, but cf. p. 222.

[3] For example, Godwin recognizes the existence of qualitatively different kinds of pleasures. p. 78.

[4] William Godwin, *Enquiry Concerning Political Justice*, ed. F. E. L. Priestley (Toronto: University of Toronto Press, 1946), iii. 8–26 *passim*.

[5] p. 79. [6] pp. 79, 83.

with benevolent intentions will more frequently perform beneficent acts than will a person who acts with selfish ones. Consequently, while motives in themselves may be unrelated to the utility—and hence to the rightness—of any specific act, they are one criterion for establishing who has a benevolent disposition—who is virtuous. Thus, Godwin observes, in evaluating one's behaviour, utility is the principal consideration, and the agent's intention is important 'merely as it tends to insure to us a continuation of benefit or injury'.[1] 'In deciding the merits of others', Godwin continues, 'we are bound, for the most part, to proceed in the same manner, as in deciding the merits of inanimate substances. The turning point is their utility. Intention is of no further value than as it leads to utility: it is the means, and not the end.'[2] Similarly, we think of an act as virtuous if it is both right itself and indicative of utilitarian tendencies of the agent, i.e. the product of beneficent intentions.

The first object of virtue is to contribute to the welfare of mankind. The most essential attribute of right conduct therefore is, that it shall have a beneficent and salutary tendency. One further characteristic it is usual to add. Men, in the exercise of their rational faculties, are influenced by motives and inducements apprehended by the intellect. The more a man is incited to an action by reflecting on the absolute nature of that action, the more ground of expectation he affords of a repetition of such actions. We do not therefore consider ourselves as authorized to denominate an action virtuous, unless it spring from kind and beneficent intentions.[3] These two circumstances taken together, constitute everything that can reasonably be included in the term virtue. A beneficent action to which a man is incited by a knowledge of its beneficent tendency, is an act of virtue. The man who is in the frequent practice of such actions, is a worthy, virtuous and excellent man.[4]

This account raises immediate questions. For one thing it presupposes the possibility of benevolent, disinterested intentions. Many of Godwin's contemporaries stoutly denied this possibility. Furthermore it presupposes the contingent premiss that the intention to produce the greatest good is the intention which, when acted upon, usually does produce the greatest good. This premiss is not obviously true and could be denied. But whatever the shortcomings of this account of virtue, it is beyond a doubt consistently utilitarian. In general, Godwin

[1] p. 81.   [2] p. 83.
[3] At this point Godwin has a footnote reference to the *Enquiry*, II. iv. As is illustrated in the preceding three sentences, Godwin uses 'intention' and 'motive' interchangeably.
[4] *The Enquirer* (Dublin: J. Moore, 1797), pp. 252 f.

persists in his utilitarianism even when it carries him to conclusions that many utilitarians would be hesitant to accept, e.g., that we are bound by a particular promise only in so far as obeying that promise yields the greatest utility,[1] and that innocent men ought to be made to suffer, even to die, if such suffering produces the greatest good for the community.[2]

Godwin's utilitarianism also leads to his theory of rights. In Godwin's day there had been a good deal of discussion about natural law and about its consequences. One consequence of natural law is inalienable rights—rights that accrue to humans because of their very nature and that cannot, therefore, be given up or taken away. Godwin recognizes that utilitarianism is incompatible with the existence of rights that are inalienable in this strong sense. One can never have a moral right to do something that is morally wrong; any of the supposed inalienable rights (e.g. to life, liberty, or happiness) can be exercised only to the extent tolerated by the demands of utility. From Godwin's definition of 'duty' it follows that in any situation one has a duty to discharge and that it is always unjust to do more or less than one's duty.[3] Thus one can have rights to do only those things that are prescribed by duty.[4] But if this is true then rights are either reduced to duty or are non-existent, and there appears to be no reason to talk about them as separate entities. This is as far as Godwin carried the discussion in the first edition of the *Enquiry*. In the second and third editions, however, he considers and gives approval to a different theory of rights. He begins by distinguishing between active and passive rights.[5] Active rights are the inalienable rights which he rejects. Passive rights, however, are defeasible claims to the non-intervention or to the assistance of one's neighbour.[6] Godwin insists that such rights are always operative and that they flow from the very nature of man.[7] The difference between these rights and the active or inalienable ones which he rejects is that passive rights are claims that, while always relevant and appropriate, are to be honoured only so long as justice demands. As a human being, for example, I can always claim 'a sphere of discretion' within which my own judgement will be respected,[8] but this claim is to be honoured only so long as it is sanctioned by utility. There may be occasions on which this, or any other right I may claim, will be overridden. Such rights, then, are inalienable only in the sense that as claims they must always be considered.

[1] p. 104.   [2] p. 74.   [3] p. 83.   [4] pp. 86 f.   [5] p. 84.
[6] pp. 89 f.   [7] p. 89.   [8] p. 89.

In addition to utilitarianism, Godwin also endorses hedonism.[1] But Godwin's hedonism, while as explicitly affirmed, is not as consistently maintained as is his utilitarianism. Godwin frequently asserts that pleasure and only pleasure is ultimately desirable and that pain is the only evil. He suggests, furthermore, that this is true by virtue of the meaning of the terms involved in making the assertion.[2] Godwin's first deviation from classical hedonism is in admitting that some pleasures are more 'exquisite' and thus more desirable than others.[3] There is, moreover, a more serious departure from hedonism which may be important enough to void completely Godwin's official endorsement of that doctrine. In many places Godwin uses 'happiness' interchangeably with 'pleasure'. There are other passages, however, in which he seems to presuppose a distinction between happiness and pleasure such that the latter appears to be nothing more than a means to the former. In the Summary of Principles at the beginning of the Enquiry, for example, he writes that 'the most desirable state of man, is that, in which he has access to all . . . sources of pleasure, and is in possession of a happiness the most varied and uninterrupted'.[4] If ultimately only pleasure is desirable this would come to saying that the greatest pleasure is having access to all (other?) pleasures. This may be a viable theory but it is certainly not Godwin's. Over and over again Godwin insists that disinterested beneficence is the greatest source of pleasure, and his most important arguments against egoism presuppose that this is the case. His view is that such a state of happiness, not the pleasures that lead to it, is the ultimate good for which we ought to seek. This view becomes most clear in his discussion of the various levels of happiness which man attains.

Godwin distinguishes four levels of happiness;[5] the level that any particular person occupies is a function of the pleasures to which he has access. The lowest level is that of the labourer who has a minimum of pleasure because his work leaves him time in which to pursue only the more readily available forms. Such an individual has a kind of happiness, Godwin explains, for 'he is happier than a stone'.[6] On the next level is the man of 'rank, fortune and dissipation'.[7] He enjoys the pleasures of the senses, is never bored, 'tastes the pleasures of liberty', and 'is familiar with the gratifications of pride'. Each of these is an addition to the pleasures of the labourer, but the dissipated man falls far short of the ideal because 'he is a model of ignorance'.[8] The next kind of man

---

[1] p. 184.   [2] p. 185.   [3] p. 78.   [4] p. 13.
[5] pp. 186-8.   [6] p. 187.   [7] p. 187.   [8] p. 187.

enjoys the beauties of nature and of the arts. He enjoys learning and understanding the sciences. 'There is', however, 'a rank of man, more fitted to excite our emulation than this, the man of benevolence.'[1] The most exquisite pleasures of which man is capable are found in disinterested benevolence; there are no pleasures of sense or intellect that can compare with them.[2] Furthermore, the man of benevolence has access to all those pleasures experienced by the members of the lower levels and he enjoys, therefore, not only the most desirable but also the most diverse pleasures.

The advantage of raising people out of the lower levels into the higher ones is obvious: in that way the balance of happiness in the universe will become greater. Godwin's analysis of duty, therefore, comes to the following: each person ought to do all that is in his power 'to endeavour to raise each class, and every individual of each class, to a class above it'.[3] Godwin believes that social organization—government in a broad sense—exerts the most profound influence upon men's capacity for happiness. Consequently, if one wishes to help men to be happy he must know what form of social organization will be most conducive to this end. Godwin sets out to explain and to argue for the form of organization that he believes best.

In order to appreciate Godwin's conclusions we must begin by considering more carefully some of the salient features of the benevolent man. In the first place he will be independent. Every virtuous act is performed on the basis of one motive only—to produce the greatest happiness of mankind in so far as it is within the agent's capacity to do so. This entails that other motives such as fear of punishment or desire for reward—irrespective of the good that such motives may occasionally engender—never lead to virtuous behaviour. Thus the beneficent man will have a kind of independence from threats, fears, enticements, and personal ambitions.[4] Each decision being made on the basis of utility, these other factors will be ignored except in so far as the goods promised or the evils threatened (whether to the agent or to anyone else) enter into the general utility of the act in question. Godwin believes, moreover, that the beneficent man will be independent in an even stronger sense. Consider two men, the first capable of deciding for himself which course of action is the right one, the second without this

---

[1] p. 188.   [2] p. 50.

[3] p. 188. Professor Clifford Brown pointed out that this seems to commit Godwin to saying that the labourer's path to benevolence is by way of dissipation.

[4] p. 299.

capacity but willing, perhaps, to defer to the judgement of the first. Both may have the desire to do only what is right. Which will be the more reliable and consistent in doing his duty? The first, obviously. Situations frequently arise in which it is not practical to consult advisers and in such situations only the first will be reliable. The other may sometimes do the right thing—just as the selfish man may occasionally do what is good for others—but in the long run the first will be right more often than the other. Hence, Godwin feels that the beneficent man will strive to be independent in the sense that, as far as possible, each decision will be made on the basis of his own judgement. He will be open to (and even seek) advice on difficult matters,[1] but he will, to the greatest possible extent, make final decisions for himself.

Closely related to independence is the second quality of the beneficent man: intelligence. The utilitarian analysis of duty can be given along either of two lines: the agent may be obliged to do that which will yield the greatest good, or he may be obliged only to do that which he believes will yield the greatest good. The first entails that one has failed to discharge his duty if he does something which he believes to be right but which is, in fact, wrong. Most utilitarians find this conclusion unacceptable, and, therefore, reject the analysis of duty upon which it rests. Godwin, however, consistently and emphatically endorses both the first analysis and its implications.[2] Consequently, he insists that it is not enough to have beliefs about what one ought to do— one must have a good deal of knowledge as well. One must understand, in special cases, exactly how one's behaviour will affect others; one must also have a thorough grasp of the general principles of morality.[3] Only by having these kinds of knowledge can one possibly hope to be consistently correct in one's judgements about what is right and what is wrong.

Finally, the beneficent man will be rational. Godwin was widely misunderstood on this point; his contemporary critics took him to mean that one must rely upon cold reason and never allow sentiments of love to sway one's decisions. In a sense Godwin's point is just the opposite. Far from advocating that his reader be unmoved by compassion and sympathy, Godwin thinks that every act one performs should be accompanied by these feelings. The point is that we should not, as we now inevitably do, feel love for some individuals and not for others. No one person is innately more deserving of our love and compassion than any other; in particular, no one becomes more deserving of love

[1] p. 300. [2] pp. 83 f. [3] p. 148.

and sympathy by virtue of his relation to the agent. Part of being
rational is being disinterested, and only the disinterested person can
recognize that special relationships do not create special obligations of
love and compassion. There is, Godwin maintains, only one consideration by which competing claims of different individuals can be adjudicated—utility. Some persons are more useful to humanity than are
others. Other things being equal, our obligation to the more useful
individual is the greater. This, of course, does not remove my obligation
to feel love and sympathy towards everyone, including those who have
little chance of improving mankind.

To illustrate and support this point Godwin provides the famous case
of the Bishop Fenelon and his valet.[1] The essence of the illustration is
this: if one is forced to choose between saving the life of a person who
will promote a great deal of good for humanity (Fenelon) and the life
of one who will promote very little (his valet), one is obliged to save
the former; and this does not cease to be true when the second individual—the one whose life is to be sacrificed—is the agent's near
relative or friend. Godwin is considering an incredibly hard moral
choice, one to which there is no happy solution. He fully grasped the
depth of personal affection and understood that whoever would pursue
the right course would suffer a tragic loss. Fenelon and the valet both
have the right to life, and the personal friends and relations of each
have the right to be spared the grief occasioned by the death of either.
Fenelon, however, has an additional and overriding claim in that he is
more able to promote the happiness of humanity than his valet. If this
analysis is correct—and the act-utilitarian seems, by the very nature
of the case, obliged to concede that it is—then the right thing for anyone to do would be to save Fenelon. Godwin recognizes that anyone
who takes the other alternative is acting understandably and perhaps
even excusably.[2] However, for the benevolent man, for the man who is
motivated in all cases by the desire to do the right thing and that only,
there is just one available choice. Furthermore, and this is important
to Godwin, one is not to save Fenelon from a 'cool, phlegmatic,
arithmetical' calculation of utility.

No great and honourable deed can be achieved, but from passion. If I save
the life of Fenelon, unprompted to do so by an ardent love of the wondrous
excellence of the man, and a sublime eagerness to achieve and secure the welfare
and improvement of millions, I am a monster, unworthy of the appellation of a
man, and the society of beings so 'fearfully and wonderfully made', as men are.[3]

---

[1] pp. 70 f.   [2] p. 325.   [3] p. 326.

A variety of hypothetical situations, in some respects similar to Godwin's, have been conjured up by contemporary critics of act-utilitarianism. There is, for example, the case of the two starving explorers, one of whom volunteers to give up his share of the rations and so die in order to save the life of his colleague, but only on the condition that the latter will educate the former's children. Later the survivor discovers, first, that he does not have money enough to educate both his own children and those of the deceased colleague, and secondly, that while his own children show great intellectual potential, the colleague's children show very little. Here the act-utilitarian seems obliged to say that the agent should break his promise and educate his own children; this, the critics maintain, is counter to what we all know to be right. In this situation, as in Godwin's, someone comes under competing obligations, all of which cannot be satisfied, and such that our feelings about what is right and wrong do not coincide with the demands of utility. We cannot here decide upon the adequacy of act-utilitarianism, but we can see that whatever is wrong with Godwin's conclusion in the Fenelon case is not due to an insistence on cold and passionless reason or to a misapplication of utilitarianism in a special situation. In so far as anything is wrong, the mistake flows from the same source as does the reputed mistake in the explorer case: from the inadequacies of act-utilitarianism as a general account of moral obligation.

We now have a fair idea of the kind of individual that Godwin is interested in fostering. At this point, however, Godwin appears to be vulnerable to the following kind of criticism: It is reasonable to say that we ought to make people benevolent only if people can be made benevolent; as a matter of fact, there are limits as to how benevolent people can be made. Therefore, it is pointless to talk about making people better. There were several doctrines widely espoused among Godwin's contemporaries that seemed to entail this view and Godwin devotes considerable space in the *Enquiry* to answering them. He argues, for example, that human behaviour is not instinctive; people have no congenital traits or 'innate principles' by which their behaviour is regulated and their potential for benevolent actions restricted.[1] Godwin also animadverts against a particular doctrine of free will and concludes that each voluntary act is completely determined by the agent's desires and opinions.[2] Once we provide men with the proper desires we can be confident that they will be benevolent; capricious behaviour will not

---

[1] pp. 28–34.   [2] pp. 160–6.

thwart our attempts to improve ourselves. Godwin also argues against Montesquieu's thesis that the social organization of any group of people is determined by climate and topography.[1] If this were the case it would seem to restrict our ability to improve our social institutions. Finally, Godwin rejects the view, which Malthus later adopted, that any attempt to improve mankind would entail a coincident growth in the population and would, therefore, be self-stultifying.[2] All these arguments are intended to clear the ground for a key theory to which Godwin was heavily committed and in which he firmly believed— the theory of the progressive nature of man.

Eight years after the *Enquiry* was first published Godwin wrote about that work:

> The great doctrine of the treatise in question is what I have there called (adopting a term I found, ready coined in the French language) the perfectibility, but what I would now wish to call, changing the term, without changing a particle of the meaning, the progressive nature of man, in knowledge, in virtuous propensities, and in social institutions.[3]

There are two parts to Godwin's doctrine of the progressive nature of man. The first is that the human species, as a whole, is gradually improving morally and intellectually; this belief was very popular among Godwin's contemporaries. On the basis of a cursory investigation of the *Enquiry* various authors have concluded that Godwin was firmly committed to this belief.[4] It is no longer fashionable to subscribe to the doctrine of human progress, and because he seems to have done so, Godwin is often dismissed as Utopian and naïvely optimistic. However, it is unfair and short-sighted to dismiss Godwin in this way. In the first place there are grounds for doubting that Godwin believed humanity to be progressing significantly.[5] Secondly, this belief bears no necessary relation to the more important and the more plausible part of Godwin's theory of perfectibility. At one point Godwin describes the important part of his theory as follows:

> By perfectible, it is not meant that he [man] is capable of being brought to perfection. But the word seems sufficiently adapted to express the faculty of being continually made better and receiving perpetual improvement; and in this sense it is here to be understood. The term perfectible, thus explained, not only does not imply the capacity of being brought to perfection, but stands in

---

[1] pp. 60–2.   [2] pp. 303 f.   [3] p. 326.
[4] e.g. J. B. Bury, *The Idea of Progress*, ed. Charles A. Beard (New York: Dover Publications, Inc., 1955), ch. xii.
[5] p. 191.

express opposition to it. If we could arrive at perfection, there would be an end to our improvement.[1]

Godwin does not carefully distinguish between these two parts of the theory, but it is important to see clearly that there is no logical relation between them. Godwin believed, much in advance of his time, that each person is largely a product of his environment and culture.[2] This led him to the conclusion that the only consistent and reliable way of improving individual men is by making adjustments in the society in which they live. We can put this by saying that the perfectibility of men presupposes the malleability of society. But of course all this says nothing whatsoever about whether or not society is actually progressing; that is a doctrine which Godwin probably did, but need not have, espoused. The perfectibility of man is presupposed in saying that we have an obligation to help men improve themselves. Godwin's arguments against free will and against instincts are intended to support the claim that man is perfectible. The malleability of society is presupposed in saying that men are perfectible. Godwin's arguments against Montesquieu and against the view later taken up by Malthus are intended to show that society is adequately malleable. These are the crucial doctrines to which Godwin is committed and for which he argues. The other is logically extraneous.

Given that people can be made more benevolent, the question of how we are to make them so remains. A good starting-place for finding Godwin's answer to this question is his classification of human actions as voluntary, imperfectly voluntary, and involuntary.

That action is involuntary, which takes place in us, either without foresight on our part, or contrary to the full bent of our inclinations. . . . Voluntary action is, where the event is foreseen previously to its occurrence, and the hope or fear of that event forms the excitement, or, as it is most frequently termed, the motive, inducing us, if hope be the passion, to endeavour to forward, and, if fear, to endeavour to prevent it.[3]

In addition there are habitual (i.e. imperfectly voluntary) acts. Habits may begin with acts whose motivation is clear to the agent and which are therefore voluntary; but as the act is repeated we give less and less attention to the reasons for it and it becomes similar to involuntary behaviour. Habitual acts are necessary for expedience; they make little or no demand upon the mind, thus leaving us free to concentrate upon other things while we walk, eat, dress, etc. However, since we, together

[1] pp. 58 f.   [2] pp. 34–8.   [3] pp. 40 f.

with the situations to which we must respond, are constantly changing, acts that were at one time right may be so no longer. For this reason we cannot rest in habit; the grounds underlying habitual acts must be scrutinized frequently to ensure that such acts are still right. Rational independent men will strive to make as many as possible of their acts purely voluntary.[1]

The definition of 'voluntary act' entails that every such act is intended either to achieve an object of desire or to avoid an object of aversion. Godwin believes that under normal circumstances one cannot have an opinion that something is desirable without desiring it; the more desirable one deems a thing to be, the stronger he will desire it.[2] Prior to any voluntary act one judges which available course of action is the most desirable; that course thereby becomes the most desired one. If the agent recognizes that the course chosen is within his physical capacity the action follows immediately.[3] Godwin summarizes this by saying that the 'voluntary actions of men in all cases originate in their opinions'.[4] Hence, all that is necessary to ensure that normal men will do their duty is to bring them to understand clearly that it is most desirable that they do so. Vice is due to ignorance or to misunderstanding; the person who knows the truth will always be beneficent. 'Vice and weakness are founded in ignorance and error; but truth is more powerful than any champion that can be brought into the field against it; consequently truth has the faculty of expelling weakness and vice, and placing nobler and more beneficent principles in their stead.'[5] Therefore to make men benevolent it is necessary only to bring them to understand that it is most desirable for them to be so.

This view becomes more plausible as one comes to appreciate what Godwin takes to be entailed by understanding a proposition. Godwin feels strongly that understanding something requires more than simply recognizing, intellectually, the general principles involved. To understand something truly one must grasp all the specific details of the situation so intimately and so concretely that one cannot avoid being caught up emotionally. Feeling appropriate emotions towards a situation is part of fully understanding it. D. H. Monro has given an apposite illustration:

> I may readily agree that it is a bad thing that millions of Asiatics should be starving, and that I ought to do something about it. But in practice I probably won't. We are inclined to say that this is because my purely intellectual apprehension of the facts is not reinforced by any emotional apprehension of them.

[1] p. 46.   [2] p. 35.   [3] pp. 41 f.   [4] p. 42.   [5] p. 58.

But now suppose that an Asiatic comes and starves on my doorstep. Almost certainly I shall be moved to feed him. Again it seems reasonable to say that the sight of his sufferings touches my emotions as the mere abstract knowledge of them does not. But more than this is involved. When I see a man starving before my eyes, the proposition: 'starvation ought to be relieved' takes on a new meaning for me. I can now see in detail precisely how and why starvation is bad; I can see exactly how the generalization applies to the particular instance. It is not a question of perfect knowledge being reinforced by emotion; my knowledge before was imperfect. When it becomes perfect, it necessarily brings the emotion with it: it is no longer possible for desire and emotion to conflict.[1]

Now Godwin is probably willing to admit that there are (or could be) individuals who are morally 'blind' such that even after being exposed to all the facts they are unable to feel the proper emotions.[2] Furthermore, one can certainly have the proper emotions, for example, a feeling of benevolence towards a deserving person in need, without a knowledge of all the relevant facts. Having the proper emotions is not logically equivalent to knowing the facts. Godwin's point is only that normal people are built in such a way as to ensure that the more they know about a situation the more likely they are to have emotions (and to form judgements) which are correct, i.e. sanctioned by utility.

Given that this is what is involved in understanding a situation, does it follow that one will always do one's duty once he understands it? Do people always do what they think is right? Godwin would respond with the following argument: In any voluntary act the agent will do what he desires most to do. A person will always desire most to do that which he believes is the most desirable thing to do. Therefore, in any voluntary act a person will do that which he believes is the most desirable thing to do. This is the heart of Godwin's scheme. His whole theory for increasing men's happiness rests upon the presupposition that people do that which they believe is right. If he cannot establish the truth of this proposition, the whole scheme becomes less plausible. Let us begin by considering the second premiss. This premiss may initially appear to involve the mistake of advancing from 'X is desirable' to 'X is desired'. Godwin does not make this mistake, however. He moves instead from 'X is believed to be most desirable' to 'X is most desired'. Furthermore, Godwin regarded this move as justified, not because of the meaning of the terms involved, but because it reports a contingent fact about people; people normally do desire that which

    [1] *Godwin's Moral Philosophy* (London: Oxford University Press, 1953), pp. 31 f.
    [2] William Godwin, *Thoughts on Man* (London: n.p., 1831), pp. 48–52.

they believe to be desirable. One might attempt to construct a counter-example along the following lines: I may understand that it is right or most desirable that I help the poor, but I may succumb, nevertheless, to other wants which I recognize to be less desirable, and so end up desiring most something that I know to be less desirable. To obviate this kind of objection Godwin appeals to his account of understanding. If a normal person really understands that X is the right thing to do, he will have the right emotions towards X. If we grant this account of what is entailed in knowing or understanding something, the premiss is reasonable. There remains, however, a serious defect in the argument.

Consider the first premiss: in any voluntary act a person does that which he desires most to do. Godwin believed this to be true by defini-tion—he insists that it is nonsense to talk of someone's voluntarily doing something other than that which he most desires to do.[1] Godwin thinks, in other words, that 'strongest desire' and 'desire acted upon' are equivalent in meaning. This seems to be a departure from ordinary usage. The following proposition is intelligible; 'More than anything else I desired to go, but I stayed as you asked me to do.' People fre-quently do things voluntarily that they do not strongly desire to do but that are expected or requested of them. But if this is the case—if the desire that leads to a voluntary action is not always the strongest desire—then Godwin has not proved that people always do that which they find most desirable. Furthermore, if the first premiss is false, either the second premiss or the conclusion itself must be false. Both the second premiss and the conclusion entail their own converses: given that people desire most that which they believe most desirable, it follows that a person will always believe to be most desirable that which he desires most. Similarly it follows from 'people do what they believe is most desirable' that 'people believe that which they do is most desirable'. But these two converses together entail the first premiss. Consequently, if the first premiss is false, one of the converses must be false as well; this, in turn, entails that either the second premiss or the conclusion is false. Godwin could not have given up the conclusion, and he seems obliged to admit, therefore, that people do not always most desire that which they know to be most desirable.

It remains to consider the thesis for which Godwin has unsuccessfully argued, viz. that men always do that which they believe to be correct. Godwin's critics have rejected his thesis as obviously counter to the facts of experience. His view, however, is not that unreasonable.

[1] p. 42.

Suppose one encountered someone doing something that was clearly wrong and asked him why he did so. One might get a variety of answers: 'I didn't have time to think but just reacted to my initial impression of the situation', 'Things turned out other than I'd expected', 'I promised to do what I did and one ought to honour one's promises', 'I was ordered to do so', 'It gives me pleasure', etc. In the first case the act was not voluntary. In the second the agent did wrong because he was ignorant of the full consequences of his act. In the other cases he seems not to understand the principles of morality—he may, for example, be mistaking lesser obligations for greater ones. Each of these cases is compatible with Godwin's account. On the other hand, suppose the agent responded: 'Yes, you are quite right; what I did was wrong. Furthermore I performed the act voluntarily, fully expecting the evil consequences which followed, knowing at the time that what I did was immoral.' Such a response would be difficult to comprehend; when challenged, people normally accept the responsibility of attempting to justify their behaviour. If the agent in question refused to go further in explaining himself one would perhaps be inclined to take his response as evidence of some psychological disorder. This does not exclude the possibility that the agent is rationalizing; Godwin realizes how frequently one deceives oneself in evaluating one's own motives.[1] Nor does this view ignore the common situation in which one decides that some earlier act was not adequately justified. The point is that when one does something voluntarily one must have reasons for his act; the reasons may turn out to be bad ones, but at the time of the action the agent feels that his reasons justify his behaviour.

> The actions of men . . . originate in the state of their minds immediately previous to those actions. Actions therefore which are preceded by a judgement 'this is good', or 'this is desirable', originate in the state of judgement or opinion upon that subject. It may happen that the opinion may be exceedingly fugitive; it may have been preceded by aversion and followed by remorse; but it was unquestionably the opinion of the mind at the instant in which the action commenced.[2]

As a generalization about how normal people behave this view is, perhaps, at least plausible.

We come now to Godwin's theories about politics. The foundations for his political conclusions are clear: his ethical theory entails that it is our duty to make men more benevolent. That it is always possible to do so follows from his doctrine of the progressive nature of man. We

[1] p. 43.   [2] p. 42.

have seen that giving men the proper understanding of their duty is sufficient to make them beneficent. The only question, therefore, is how we can best bring people to understand what justice demands of them. Godwin believes that one's society and culture exert a profound influence upon one's beliefs and it is to society, therefore, that we must look if we wish to find the most expedient means of educating people about duty. The most important step is to find that form of social organization that will stimulate men to be rational, independent, and intelligent.

Godwin begins by distinguishing three kinds of obedience and, corresponding to them, three kinds of authority.[1] The first is obedience to one's own understanding and judgement. This, Godwin insists, is always the highest kind of authority. So long as I do that which my own reason prescribes I will behave rationally and will be independent. But there are, as one would expect, situations in which my own understanding is not adequate to guide me: this leads to the second kind of obedience.

I want, for example, to build a house, or to sink a well. It may happen that I have not leisure or means to acquire the science necessary for this purpose. Upon that supposition I am not to be blamed, if I employ a builder for the first, or a mechanic for the second; . . . This sort of obedience is distinguished by the appellation of confidence; and to justify, in a moral view, the reposing of confidence, the only thing necessary is, that it should be fitter and more beneficial, all things considered, that the function to be performed should be performed by another person, than that it should be performed by me.[2]

This kind of obedience presupposes ignorance—only when I lack knowledge adequate to performing some task will I have occasion to rely upon another person's judgement. Furthermore, it renders me dependent upon him to whom I appeal for assistance. Therefore, there is a sense in which this second kind of authority is incompatible with virtue. To be virtuous is to do something because it is the right thing to do, not because someone advises me to do it. Thus, while this kind of authority may be necessary to accomplish various things requiring a specialized knowledge, every man is obliged to have and to exercise for himself the kind of knowledge which leads to virtuous behaviour, and confidence can, therefore, never have application here.

Finally there is obedience 'where I do that which is not prescribed to me by my private judgement, merely on account of the mischievous consequences that I foresee will be annexed to my omission, by the

[1] pp. 118–21. [2] p. 119.

arbitrary interference of some voluntary being'.[1] Godwin is here considering the case in which punishment or reward is associated with some act and in which I perform or refrain from performing the act either to avoid the punishment or to obtain the reward rather than because of the positive or negative utility of the act itself. This kind of authority, too, must be submitted to on some occasions, 'you may run south, to avoid a wild beast advancing in that direction, though you want to go north'.[2] This, Godwin insists, is the only kind of authority to which government has a valid claim.

Predictably, Godwin argues that the third kind of authority is generally pernicious and ought to be eliminated as far as possible.

I have an opportunity of essentially contributing to the advantage of twenty individuals; they will be benefited, and no other persons will sustain a material injury. I ought to embrace this opportunity. Here let us suppose positive institution to interfere, and to annex some great personal reward to the discharge of my duty. This immediately changes the nature of the action. Before, I preferred it for its intrinsic excellence. Now, so far as the positive institution operates, I prefer it, because some person has arbitrarily annexed to it a great weight of self-interest. But virtue, considered as the quality of an intelligent being, depends upon the disposition with which the action is accompanied. Under a positive institution then, this very action, which is intrinsically virtuous, may, so far as relates to the agent, become vicious. The vicious man would before have neglected the advantage of these twenty individuals, because he would not bring a certain inconvenience or trouble upon himself. The same man, with the same disposition, will now promote their advantage, because his own welfare is concerned in it.[3]

Godwin is willing to admit that this kind of authority is occasionally necessary, and since we live in a society in which it is widely employed and obeyed, it must always be taken into account in calculating utility—'an action, . . . which for its own sake might be right to be performed, it may become my duty to neglect, if I know that by performing it I shall incur the penalty of death'.[4] The use of this kind of authority can be expected to decline only as men become rational and benevolent and need no longer be forced to do their duty. Nevertheless, the perniciousness of this authority is evident, and its use is to be minimized and eliminated whenever possible.

It is the second kind of authority, however, which Godwin regards as most insidious and corrupting. One can act to obtain reward or to avoid punishment without either sacrificing one's independence or

[1] p. 119.   [2] p. 121.   [3] pp. 91 f.   [4] p. 120.

renouncing the right to decide for oneself which course of action would be the right one were the reward or punishment withdrawn. One cannot, however, defer one's moral judgements to another without becoming dependent, lethargic, and contemptible.

> Where I make the voluntary surrender of my understanding, and commit my conscience to another man's keeping, . . . I then become the most mischievous and pernicious of animals. I annihilate my individuality as a man, and dispose of my force as an animal to him among my neighbours, who shall happen to excel in imposture and artifice, and to be least under restraint from the scruples of integrity and justice. I put an end, as to my own share, to that happy collision of understandings, upon which the hopes of human improvement depend. I can have no genuine fortitude, for fortitude is the offspring of conviction. I can have no conscious integrity, for I do not understand my own principles, and have never brought them to the test of examination. I am the ready tool of injustice, cruelty and profligacy; and, if at any time I am not employed in their purposes, it is the result of accident, not of my own precaution and honesty.[1]

Godwin recognizes that this kind of authority has its appropriate uses. The important thing is that it be vested only in those who actually are superior in knowledge and wisdom and then only in those cases in which I have no positive obligation to judge for myself. Under these circumstances the persons from whom we obtain counsel deserve not only confidence and obedience but also respect.[2] The danger is in confusing the kind of authority and obedience which derives from superior force alone with this kind which is due to persons with superior knowledge. When that occurs one follows blindly him to whom only submission is due and the consequences cannot be other than disastrous.[3]

The application of these conclusions to government is obvious. Society was originally organized to provide security to the individual.[4] Godwin admits that we still need some kind of social organization to defend our security, otherwise society would degenerate into chaotic anarchy.[5] One way of organizing society is by giving government control of the accumulated force of the community. However, government never restricts itself to ensuring the security of its citizens; rather it insinuates itself into every phase of their existence[6] and attempts to regulate behaviour which ought to be left to individual discretion. In this way government robs men of their independence and rationality,

---

[1] p. 122.   [2] p. 123.   [3] p. 124.   [4] p. 113.   [5] pp. 262 f.
[6] p. 19.

and, by instituting rewards and punishments, denies them the privilege of disinterested benevolence. Government, therefore, which started out as a relative good—as an alternative to anarchy—has become a positive evil. Government can only persist when it has the support of a major part of the community.[1] But people will always do that which they perceive to be right; if they once become aware that government is pernicious they will withhold their support and government will fall. Consequently, in order to maintain hegemony those in whom the power is vested must succeed in convincing the governed that they, the rulers, are more wise and better able to direct the affairs of state than are the citizens themselves; that is, they must hide the fact that their authority is only the authority of force and attempt to gain the confidence of their subjects. But confidence presupposes ignorance and dependence. Therefore, government, by its very nature, requires that people remain dependent and ignorant. 'The true supporters of government are the weak and uninformed, and not the wise. In proportion as weakness and ignorance shall diminish, the basis of government will also decay.'[2]

There can be no doubt that Godwin's criticism of government is trenchant and full of insight. The analysis of authority upon which the critique rests, however, is vulnerable to criticism. For one thing, in deprecating the second and third kinds of authority Godwin is either presupposing questionable contingent premises or departing from utilitarianism. Godwin recognizes that there are instances in which a man is obliged to sacrifice his life in the interest of the community.[3] But if this is possible then it is difficult to see why men cannot come under an obligation to sacrifice their rationality and independence for the good of the community. Godwin emphatically denounces slavery.[4] But suppose one could prove that institutionalized slavery would have the greatest utility. From a purely utilitarian point of view one would be compelled to conclude that slavery ought to be instituted. Godwin, and any rational person, would reject this conclusion as outrageous; the sense of outrage, however, is based on considerations not of utility but of fairness (or justice). Godwin's rejection of the obedience of ignorance and weakness depends either upon the dubious assumption that one man's ignorance can never be good for humanity as a whole or upon a tacit appeal to non-utilitarian ethical principles.

Another criticism is that Godwin's list of the kinds of authority is not exhaustive, and it may well be possible for government to claim as its

[1] p. 77.   [2] p. 125.   [3] p. 74.   [4] p. 186.

basis some kind of authority that he has not considered. There are numerous types of authority which bear no overt relation to any of Godwin's classes. Consider, for example, the authority of an agent who is legally authorized to conclude contracts on behalf of his employer. In this case the employer has delegated authority to the agent but the authority is not *over* anyone and, in particular, the agent is not in authority over someone who is ignorant or intimidated. It may be that the employer followed 'the authority of his own judgement and reason' in empowering the agent to close contracts—this may be an explanation of why he did what he did—but that does not explain the legality of the agent's acts on behalf of his employer. The employer may judge that a certain man would be a good agent but that in itself does not give the man authority. The agent's authority is possible because of antecedently existing rules and conventions that define and regulate the process of delegating authority. There are many respects in which the authority of government is more analogous to this kind of authority than to any of the kinds which Godwin considers. But if government can claim some other kinds of authority, until Godwin proves that these too are pernicious, his argument is seriously impaired.

The social organization that Godwin proposes to establish in place of government is predictable. Men should form small completely voluntary federations in order to secure social benefits and to facilitate co-operative projects. As occasion demands they may select temporary representatives to deal with issues that do not lend themselves to open group debates, but no one is to be bound by the decisions of the representatives.[1] Anyone can join or withdraw from any federation at will.[2] If disputes arise they are to be adjudicated by juries.[3] Godwin feels that any organization beyond these rudiments would be super-fluous if not positively deleterious. He even hopes that these vestiges of government will one day be removed.[4] Violence is to be avoided in all but the most extreme cases;[5] Godwin believed that neither society nor individuals could be improved by force, that revolution and physical punishments invariably produce more evil than good. Hence, education and expostulation are the proper means both of instituting the new society and of regulating it once it is adopted. Among the various topics to which Godwin gives attention in the course of explaining how society ought to be organized, two deserve special consideration: the punishment of criminals, and the institution of private property.

[1] p. 115.   [2] p. 217.   [3] p. 217.   [4] p. 222.   [5] pp. 95 f.

Historically there have been two ways in which moralists have attempted to justify punishing criminals. The first, which is referred to as the retributive theory, is simply to insist that those who make people suffer ought to be made to suffer themselves; that there is an appropriateness or fitness in returning like for like and that no additional justification or argument is necessary. The second way, the utilitarian theory, is to claim that, in one way or another, punishing malefactors will ultimately yield results that, if not actually beneficial, will be the least evil of the alternatives. Godwin has arguments against each of these theories.

The retributivist defines 'punishment' as 'the voluntary infliction of evil upon a vicious being, not merely because the public advantage demands it, but because there is apprehended to be a certain fitness and propriety in the nature of things, that render suffering, abstractedly from the benefit to result, the suitable concomitant of vice'.[1] But this, Godwin quickly explains, presupposes free will.[2] We all recognize the futility and pointlessness of attempting to punish an animal or an inanimate object. This is because we recognize that such things have no free choice in what they do and always act in response to determining circumstances to which they are subject. But the same thing is true of man. A man has no more control over what he does than a knife,[3] consequently the inappropriateness of the suffering inflicted upon him is apparent and this theory of punishment is seen to be untenable. A further objection to the retributive theory can be derived from the utilitarian account of obligation. Once it is granted that one's obligation is always to do that which will yield the greatest utility, then any talk of 'fitness' or 'propriety', apart from considerations of utility, is nonsense. Thus Godwin concludes:

Whether we enter philosophically into the principle of human actions, or merely analyse the ideas of rectitude and justice . . . in the . . . sense in which that term has frequently been employed, there is no such thing as desert; . . . it cannot be just that we should inflict suffering on any man, except so far as it tends to good.[4]

Godwin moves on to define 'punishment' as the term is used by the utilitarians.

Having thus endeavoured to show what denominations of punishment justice, and a sound idea of the nature of man, would invariably proscribe, it belongs to us, in the further prosecution of the subject, to consider merely that

---

[1] pp. 244 f.   [2] p. 245.   [3] p. 170.   [4] p. 245.

coercion, which it has been supposed right to employ, against persons convicted of past injurious action, for the purpose of preventing future mischief.[1]

There are three ways in which punishment could conceivably reduce future mischief: by reforming a criminal, by restraining the criminal from repeating his crime, or, through the example established by the criminal's suffering, by dissuading others from performing his misdeed. Godwin considers each of these alternatives and much of what he says is vivid and germane. His arguments, however, suffer from the same defect that vitiates his argument against government: either Godwin presupposes the contingent premiss that inflicting punishment does not yield the greatest utility, or he appeals to non-utilitarian principles of justice and fairness. The only way in which one can prove that some specific act or kind of act does not yield the greatest utility is by an empirical investigation; there is no such investigation in the *Enquiry*. Consequently, while many of Godwin's conclusions are plausible and interesting, they are not adequately supported by his arguments.

Godwin believed that an essential step in improving social institutions is dissemination of the true theory of property.

> The subject of property is the keystone that completes the fabric of political justice. According as our ideas respecting it are crude or correct, they will enlighten us as to the consequences of a *simple form of society without government*, and remove the prejudices that attach us to complexity. There is nothing that more powerfully tends to distort our *judgement* and *opinions*, than erroneous notions concerning the goods of fortune.[2]

Godwin's theory of property is an extension of his ethics: he begins by inferring from the principle of utility that each article of property ought to belong to that individual whose possession of the article will yield the greatest good for the greatest number. The remainder of the discussion is an elucidation of what Godwin takes to be the consequences of this general thesis.

Godwin distinguishes between several kinds of property: things essential for subsistence, 'the means of intellectual and moral improvement', sources of 'unexpensive gratifications', and those things which produce gratification but which 'cannot be purchased but with considerable labour and industry'.[3] Items of the fourth class are sought, not for the pleasures which they produce in themselves, but for the admiration and respect that their possession generates in one's neighbours.[4] These things, however, almost invariably require the bestial subjection

[1] p. 246.   [2] p. 278.   [3] p. 279.   [4] p. 280.

of the poor; the labouring class is obliged to produce these luxuries without deriving any significant advantage from them. If men awarded their deference and respect to superior virtue rather than to superior wealth, the desire for admiration would compel men to abandon the quest for luxuries and the exploitation that quest entails, and to seek instead the happiness of their neighbours.[1]

Godwin also distinguishes three kinds of claims to property.[2] The first and strongest claim is his whose use or consumption of an article of property will yield the greatest total utility. Second is the claim each man has to 'the produce of his own industry'. The third and weakest claim comes from the man who, through renting land, exercising patents or monopolies, or through governmental control of manufacture and distribution, is legally empowered to dispose of the products of other men's labour. These three claims are currently in constant competition. The first claim is directly sanctioned by utility. The second, however, is to be tolerated in most cases since its violation infringes upon men's 'sphere of discretion'; men cannot be forced to be just. The last kind of claim, which is counter to both the preceding, lacks any basis in utility and ought to be rejected in every case.[3] Here again Godwin's utilitarianism will not yield the desired conclusions without support from empirical investigations. The economic theory is interesting, however, and has earned Godwin credit as the first to write systematically on the competing claims of need, production, and capital.[4]

It is fairly clear what kind of economy Godwin favours: independent home industry in which the manufacturer is also the distributor, free distribution of goods subject only to the rights of the producer to distribute and of the needy to consume, and complete absence of governmental control or supervision of any part of the production, distribution, or consumption of goods.[5] As one would expect, Godwin emphatically rejects state socialism as inimical to the very nature of man.[6]

We have now examined some of Godwin's major criticisms of existing social practices and political institutions as well as some of his suggestions for alternative ways of doing things. As we have seen, Godwin feels that most of these conclusions are logical consequences of utilitarianism. However, his arguments seem frequently to depend upon unwarranted empirical presuppositions or non-utilitarian moral

[1] p. 281.   [2] pp. 282 f.   [3] pp. 283 f.
[4] Priestley, iii. 67.   [5] pp. 286 f.   [6] p. 285.

principles, and many are not, therefore, particularly persuasive. Furthermore, as his critics have been quick to point out, in the two centuries since he wrote, government has grown continually more pervasive and more powerful, and, as a result, many of Godwin's positive proposals now appear Utopian and unrealistic. These factors have doubtless contributed to the general neglect that the *Enquiry* has suffered since shortly after its publication. On the other hand, as government assumes more and more responsibility for and control over private citizens, individual men lose independence, dignity, and worth. Consequently, the very facts that have made Godwin's proposals sound unrealistic have also made his criticisms of political organization singularly apt. To the modern reader, Godwin's conclusions regarding political authority, the use of violence and force, criminal punishment, and economic inequality are provocative and timely and of much greater interest than his recommendations for a small benevolent social federation to replace government. Further, Godwin's attempts to derive these conclusions from utilitarianism—in spite of the shortcomings of the attempts—are resourceful and imaginative. Godwin's lasting importance and his contemporary relevance derive primarily from these criticisms and from the arguments upon which they rest. With government becoming increasingly more dominant there has never been a time when Godwin's animadversions against political organization and its concomitant abuses were more justified and more germane and more relevant than today. Godwin and the kind of libertarianism that he represents need serious consideration in the twentieth century as never before.

ENQUIRY CONCERNING
POLITICAL JUSTICE

PREFACE

FEW works of literature are held to be of more general use, than those which treat in a methodical and elementary way of the principles of science. But the human mind in every enlightened age is progressive; and the best elementary treatises, after a certain time, are reduced in value by the operation of subsequent discoveries. Hence it has always been desired by the intelligent, that new works of this kind should from time to time be brought forward, including the improvements, which had not yet been realized when former compilations upon the subject were produced.

It would be strange if something of this kind were not requisite in the science of politics, after the concussion that the minds of men have suffered upon this subject, and the materials that have been furnished, by the recent experiments of America and France. A sense of the value of such a work, if properly executed, was the motive which gave birth to these volumes.

Authors who have formed the design of supplying the defects of their predecessors, will be found, if they were in any degree equal to the task, not merely to have collected the scattered information that had been produced upon the subject, but to have enlarged the science by the effect of their own meditations. In the following work principles will occasionally occur, which it will not be just to reject without examination, upon the ground of their apparent novelty. It was impossible perseveringly to reflect upon so comprehensive a science, and a science which may be said to be yet in its infancy, without being led into ways of thinking that were in some degree uncommon.

Another argument in favour of the utility of such a work, was frequently in the author's mind, and therefore ought to be mentioned. He conceived politics to be the proper vehicle of a liberal morality. That description of ethics will be found perhaps to be worthy of slight estimation, which confines itself to petty detail and the offices of private life, instead of designing the combined and simultaneous improvement of communities and nations. But, if individual correction ought not to be the grand purpose of ethics, neither ought it by any means to be overlooked. It appeared sufficiently practicable to make of such a treatise, exclusively of its direct political use, an advantageous vehicle for this subordinate purpose. The author was accordingly desirous of producing a work from the perusal of which no man should rise, without being strengthened in habits of sincerity, fortitude and justice.

Having stated the considerations in which the work originated, it is proper to mention a few circumstances of the outline of its history. It was projected in the month of May 1791: the composition was begun in the following September, and has therefore occupied a space of sixteen months. This period was for the most part devoted to the purpose with unusual ardour. It were to be wished it had been longer; but the state of the public mind and of the general interests of the species, operated as a strong argument in favour of an early publication.

The printing of the following treatise, as well as the composition, was influenced by the same principle, a desire to reconcile a certain degree of dispatch with the necessary deliberation. The printing was for that reason commenced, long before the composition was finished. Some disadvantages have arisen from this circumstance. The ideas of the author became more perspicuous and digested, as his enquiries advanced. The longer he considered the subject, the more clearly he seemed to understand it. This circumstance has led him into some inaccuracies of language and reasoning, particularly in the earlier part of the work, respecting the properties and utility of government. He did not enter upon the subject, without being aware that government by its very nature counteracts the improvement of individual intellect; but, as the views he entertains in this particular are out of the common road, it is scarcely to be wondered at, that he understood the proposition more completely as he proceeded, and saw more distinctly into the nature of the remedy. This defect, together with some others, might, under a different mode of preparation, have been avoided. The judicious reader will make a suitable allowance. The author judges upon a review, that the errors are not such as essentially to affect the object of the work, and that more has been gained than lost by the conduct he has pursued.[1]

In addition to what is here stated it may not be useless to describe the progress by which the author's mind was led to its present sentiments. They are not the suggestions of any sudden effervescence of fancy. Political enquiry had long held a considerable place in the writer's attention. It is now twelve years since he became satisfied, that monarchy was a species of government essentially corrupt. He owed this conviction to the political writings of Swift and to a perusal of the Latin

---

[1] The defects here alluded to, have been attempted to be rectified in the second edition. It is impossible perhaps so to improve a crude and unequal performance, as to remove every vestige of its original blemish.

historians. Nearly at the same time he derived much additional stimulus
from several French productions on the nature of man, which fell into
his hands in the following order, the *Systême de la Nature*,[1] the works of
Rousseau, and those of Helvétius. Long before he projected the present
work, his mind had been familiarized to several of the speculations
suggested in it respecting justice, gratitude, the rights of man, promises,
oaths, and the omnipotence of opinion. Of the desirableness of a government in the utmost degree simple he was not persuaded, but in consequence of ideas suggested by the French revolution. To the same
event he owes the determination of mind which gave birth to the
present work.

The period in which it makes its appearance is singular. The people
of England have assiduously been excited to declare their loyalty, and
to mark every man as obnoxious who is not ready to sign the Shibboleth of the constitution. Money is raised by voluntary subscription
to defray the expense of prosecuting men who shall dare to promul-
gate heretical opinions, and thus to oppress them at once with the
authority of government, and the resentment of individuals. This
was an accident unforeseen when the work was undertaken; and it will
scarcely be supposed that such an accident could produce any alteration
in the writer's designs. Every man, if we may believe the voice of
rumour, is to be prosecuted, who shall appeal to the people by the
publication of any unconstitutional paper or pamphlet; and it is added,
that men are to be punished for any unguarded words that may be
dropped in the warmth of conversation and debate.[2] It is now to be
tried whether, in addition to these alarming encroachments upon our
liberty, a book is to fall under the arm of the civil power, which,
beside the advantage of having for one of its express objects the dissuading from tumult and violence, is by its very nature an appeal to
men of study and reflection. It is to be tried whether an attempt shall
be made to suppress the activity of mind, and put an end to the disquisitions of science. Respecting the event in a personal view the
author has formed his resolution. Whatever conduct his countrymen
may pursue, they will not be able to shake his tranquillity. The duty he
conceives himself most bound to discharge, is the assisting the progress

[1] [By P. H. D. d'Holbach, 1770.]

[2] The first conviction of this kind, which the author was far from imagining to be so
near, was of a journeyman tallow-chandler, January 8, 1793, who, being shown the
regalia at the Tower, was proved to have vented a coarse expression against royalty to the
person that exhibited them. [The case was that of Daniel Crichton. Godwin himself
wrote newspaper articles in Crichton's defence.]

of truth; and, if he suffer in any respect for such a proceeding, there is certainly no vicissitude that can befall him, that can ever bring along with it a more satisfactory consolation.

But, exclusively of this precarious and unimportant consideration, it is the fortune of the present work to appear before a public that is panic struck, and impressed with the most dreadful apprehensions respecting such doctrines as are here delivered. All the prejudices of the human mind are in arms against it. This circumstance may appear to be more essential than the other. But it is the property of truth to be fearless, and to prove victorious over every adversary. It requires no great degree of fortitude, to look with indifference upon the false fire of the moment, and to foresee the calm period of reason which will succeed.

London: January 7, 1793[1]

[1] [Godwin's Preface to the Second Edition, and Advertisement to the Third Edition, are omitted here.]

CONTENTS

BOOK I

OF THE POWERS OF MAN CONSIDERED IN HIS SOCIAL CAPACITY

BOOK II

PRINCIPLES OF SOCIETY

BOOK III

PRINCIPLES OF GOVERNMENT

[1] [Chapters and Appendices omitted from this edition are indicated by square brackets.]

BOOK IV

OF THE OPERATION OF OPINION IN SOCIETIES AND INDIVIDUALS

BOOK V

OF LEGISLATIVE AND EXECUTIVE POWER

BOOK VI

OF OPINION CONSIDERED AS A SUBJECT OF POLITICAL INSTITUTION

BOOK VII

OF CRIMES AND PUNISHMENTS

BOOK VIII

OF PROPERTY

SUMMARY OF PRINCIPLES

ESTABLISHED AND REASONED UPON
IN THE FOLLOWING WORK

THE reader who would form a just estimate of the reasonings of these
volumes, cannot perhaps proceed more judiciously, than by examining
for himself the truth of these principles, and the support they afford to
the various inferences interspersed through the work.

I

The true object of moral and political disquisition, is pleasure or
happiness.

The primary, or earliest, class of human pleasures, is the pleasures of
the external senses.

In addition to these, man is susceptible of certain secondary pleasures,
as the pleasures of intellectual feeling, the pleasures of sympathy, and the
pleasures of self-approbation.

The secondary pleasures are probably more exquisite than the
primary:

Or, at least,

The most desirable state of man, is that, in which he has access to all
these sources of pleasure, and is in possession of a happiness the most
varied and uninterrupted.

This state is a state of high civilization.

II

The most desirable condition of the human species, is a state of
society.

The injustice and violence of men in a state of society, produced the
demand for government.

Government, as it was forced upon mankind by their vices, so has it
commonly been the creature of their ignorance and mistake.

Government was intended to suppress injustice, but it offers new
occasions and temptations for the commission of it.

By concentrating the force of the community, it gives occasion to wild projects of calamity, to oppression, despotism, war, and conquest.

By perpetuating and aggravating the inequality of property, it fosters many injurious passions, and excites men to the practice of robbery and fraud.

Government was intended to suppress injustice, but its effect has been to embody and perpetuate it.

III

The immediate object of government, is security.

The means employed by government, is restriction, an abridgement of individual independence.

The pleasures of self-approbation, together with the right cultivation of all our pleasures, require individual independence.

Without independence men cannot become either wise, or useful, or happy.

Consequently, the most desirable state of mankind, is that which maintains general security, with the smallest encroachment upon individual independence.

IV

The true standard of the conduct of one man towards another, is justice.

Justice is a principle which proposes to itself the production of the greatest sum of pleasure or happiness.

Justice requires that I should put myself in the place of an impartial spectator of human concerns, and divest myself of retrospect to my own predilections.

Justice is a rule of the utmost universality, and prescribes a specific mode of proceeding, in all affairs by which the happiness of a human being may be affected.

V

Duty is that mode of action, which constitutes the best application of the capacity of the individual, to the general advantage.

Right is the claim of the individual, to his share of the benefit arising from his neighbours' discharge of their several duties.

The claim of the individual, is either to the exertion or the forbearance of his neighbours.

The exertions of men in society should ordinarily be trusted to their discretion; their forbearance, in certain cases, is a point of more pressing necessity, and is the direct province of political superintendence, or government.

VI

The voluntary actions of men are under the direction of their feelings.

Reason is not an independent principle, and has no tendency to excite us to action; in a practical view, it is merely a comparison and balancing of different feelings.

Reason, though it cannot excite us to action, is calculated to regulate our conduct, according to the comparative worth it ascribes to different excitements.

It is to the improvement of reason therefore, that we are to look for the improvement of our social condition.

VII

Reason depends for its clearness and strength upon the cultivation of knowledge.

The extent of our progress in the cultivation of knowledge, is unlimited.

Hence it follows,

1. That human inventions, and the modes of social existence, are susceptible of perpetual improvement.

2. That institutions calculated to give perpetuity to any particular mode of thinking, or condition of existence, are pernicious.

VIII

The pleasures of intellectual feeling, and the pleasures of self-approbation, together with the right cultivation of all our pleasures, are connected with soundness of understanding.

Soundness of understanding is inconsistent with prejudice: consequently, as few falsehoods as possible, either speculative or practical, should be fostered among mankind.

Soundness of understanding is connected with freedom of enquiry: consequently, opinion should, as far as public security will admit, be exempted from restraint.

Soundness of understanding is connected with simplicity of manners, and leisure for intellectual cultivation: consequently, a distribution of property extremely unequal, is adverse to the most desirable state of man.

[Godwin's Index, which in the third edition follows here, is omitted in the present edition.]

ENQUIRY CONCERNING
POLITICAL JUSTICE

———

BOOK I

OF THE POWERS OF MAN CONSIDERED IN HIS SOCIAL CAPACITY

———

CHAPTER I

INTRODUCTION[1]

THE object proposed in the following work is, an investigation concerning that form of public or political society, that system of intercourse and reciprocal action, extending beyond the bounds of a single family, which shall be found most to conduce to the general benefit. How may the peculiar and independent operation of each individual in the social state most effectually be preserved? How may the security each man ought to possess, as to his life, and the employment of his faculties according to the dictates of his own understanding, be most certainly defended from invasion? How may the individuals of the human species be made to contribute most substantially to the general improvement and happiness? The enquiry here undertaken has for its object to facilitate the solution of these interesting questions.

In entering upon this investigation nothing can be more useful, than to examine into the extent of the influence that is to be ascribed to political institutions; in other words, into the powers of man, as they

———

[1] [Godwin's chapter summaries, which stood at the head of each chapter and were then repeated in the margins of the text, would have led to confusion in chapters abbreviated for this edition, and so they have been omitted throughout.]

have modified, or may hereafter modify his social state of existence. Upon this subject there has been considerable difference of opinion.

The most usually received hypothesis is that which considers the effects of government or social institutions, whether acting by express regulations or otherwise, as rather of a negative than positive nature. No doubt the purposes for which government was established, are in their strictest sense negative; to maintain us in the possession of certain advantages against the occasional hostility either of domestic or foreign invaders. But does the influence of government stop, at the point for the sake of which mankind were first prevailed on to adopt it?

Those who believe that it does or can stop at this point, necessarily regard it as a matter of subordinate disquisition, or at most only co-ordinate with several others. They survey man in his individual character, in his domestic connections, and in the pursuits and attachments which his feelings may incline him to adopt. These of course fill the principal part of the picture. These are supposed, by the speculators of whom we now speak, to be in ordinary cases independent of all political systems and establishments. It is only in peculiar emergencies and matters that depart from the accustomed routine of affairs, that they conceive a private individual to have any occasion to remember, or to be in the least affected by the government of his country. If he commit or is supposed to commit any offence against the general welfare, if he find himself called upon to repress the offence of another, or if any danger from foreign hostility threaten the community in which he resides, in these cases and these only is he obliged to recollect that he has a country. These considerations impose upon him the further duty of consulting, even when no immediate danger is nigh, how political liberty may best be maintained, and maladministration prevented.

Many of the best patriots and most popular writers on the subject of government, appear to have proceeded upon the principles here delineated. They have treated morality and personal happiness as one science, and politics as a different one. But, while they have considered the virtues and pleasures of mankind as essentially independent of civil policy, they have justly remarked, that the security with which the one can be exercised and the other enjoyed, will be decided by the wisdom of our public institutions and the equity with which they are adminis-tered; and have earnestly pressed it upon the attention of mankind, not to forget, in the rectitude or happiness of the present moment, those precautions and that 'generous plan of power',[1] which may tend to

---

[1] [Joseph] Addison [1672–1719], *Cato*, Act iv.

render it impregnable to the stratagems of corruption or the insolence of tyranny.[1]

But, while we confess ourselves indebted to the labours of these writers, and perhaps still more to the intrepid language and behaviour of these patriots, we are incited to enquire whether the topic which engaged their attention, be not of higher and more extensive importance than they suspected. Perhaps government is, not merely in some cases the defender, and in other the treacherous foe of the domestic virtues. Perhaps it insinuates itself into our personal dispositions, and insensibly communicates its own spirit to our private transactions. Were not the inhabitants of ancient Greece and Rome indebted in some degree to their political liberties for their excellence in art, and the illustrious theatre they occupy in the moral history of mankind? Are not the governments of modern Europe accountable for the slowness and inconstancy of its literary efforts, and the unworthy selfishness that characterizes its inhabitants? Is it not owing to the governments of the East, that that part of the world can scarcely be said to have made any progress in intellect or science?

When scepticism or a spirit of investigation has led us to start these questions, we shall be apt not to stop at them. A wide field of speculation opens itself before us. If government thus insinuate itself in its effects into our most secret retirements, who shall define the extent of its operation? If it be the author of thus much, who shall specify the points from which its influence is excluded? May it not happen, that the grand moral evils that exist in the world, the calamities by which we are so grievously oppressed, are to be traced to political institution as their source, and that their removal is only to be expected from its correction? May it not be found, that the attempt to alter the morals of mankind singly and in detail is an injudicious and futile undertaking; and that the change of their political institutions must keep pace with their advancement in knowledge, if we expect to secure to them a real and permanent improvement? To prove the affirmative of these questions shall be the business of this first book.

The method to be pursued for that purpose, shall be, first, to take a concise survey of the evils existing in political society;[2] secondly, to show that these evils are to be ascribed to public institutions;[3] and

----

[1] These remarks will for the most part apply to the English writers upon politics, from [Algernon] Sydney [1622–83] and Locke to the author of the *Rights of Man*. The more comprehensive view has been strikingly delineated by Rousseau and Helvétius.

[2] Ch. ii, iii.   [3] Ch. iv.

thirdly, that they are not the inseparable condition of our existence, but admit of removal and remedy.[1]

CHAPTER II

HISTORY OF POLITICAL SOCIETY

THE extent of the influence of political systems will be forcibly illustrated by a concise recollection of the records of political society.

It is an old observation, that the history of mankind is little else than a record of crimes. Society comes recommended to us by its tendency to supply our wants and promote our well-being. If we consider the human species, as they were found previously to the existence of political society, it is difficult not to be impressed with emotions of melancholy. But, though the chief purpose of society is to defend us from want and inconvenience, it effects this purpose in a very imperfect degree. We are still liable to casualties, disease, infirmity and death. Famine destroys its thousands, and pestilence its ten thousands. Anguish visits us under every variety of form, and day after day is spent in languor and dissatisfaction. Exquisite pleasure is a guest of very rare approach, and not less short continuance.

But, though the evils that arise to us from the structure of the material universe are neither trivial nor few, yet the history of political society sufficiently shows that man is of all other beings the most formidable enemy to man. Among the various schemes that he has formed to destroy and plague his kind, war is the most terrible. Satiated with petty mischief and the retail of insulated crimes, he rises in this instance to a project that lays nations waste, and thins the population of the world. Man directs the murderous engine against the life of his brother; he invents with indefatigable care refinements in destruction; he proceeds in the midst of gaiety and pomp to the execution of his horrid purpose; whole ranks of sensitive beings, endowed with the most admirable faculties, are mowed down in an instant; they perish by inches in the midst of agony and neglect, lacerated with every variety of method that can give torture to the frame.

. . . . .

War has hitherto been found the inseparable ally of political institu-

[1] Ch. v, vi, vii, viii.

tion. The earliest records of time are the annals of conquerors and heroes, a Bacchus, a Sesostris,[1] a Semiramis[2] and a Cyrus. . . .

No sooner does history become more precise, than we are presented with the four great monarchies, that is, with four successful projects, by means of bloodshed, violence and murder, of enslaving mankind. The expeditions of Cambyses against Egypt, of Darius against the Scythians, and of Xerxes against the Greeks, seem almost to set credibility at defiance by the fatal consequences with which they were attended. The conquests of Alexander cost innumerable lives, and the immortality of Caesar is computed to have been purchased by the death of one million two hundred thousand men.

. . . . .

. . . Let us examine Europe, the most civilized and favoured quarter of the world, or even those countries of Europe which are thought the most enlightened.

France was wasted by successive battles during a whole century, for the question of the Salic law, and the claim of the Plantagenets. Scarcely was this contest terminated, before the religious wars broke out, some idea of which we may form from the siege of Rochelle, where, of fifteen thousand persons shut up, eleven thousand perished of hunger and misery; and from the massacre of Saint Bartholomew, in which the numbers assassinated were forty thousand. . . .

In England the war of Cressy and Agincourt only gave place to the civil war of York and Lancaster, and again after an interval to the war of Charles the first and his parliament. No sooner was the constitution settled by the revolution, than we were engaged in a wide field of continental hostilities by king William, the duke of Marlborough, Maria Theresa and the king of Prussia.

And what are in most cases the pretences upon which war is undertaken? What rational man could possibly have given himself the least disturbance, for the sake of choosing whether Henry the sixth or Edward the fourth should have the style of king of England? . . .

The usual causes of war are excellently described by Swift. 'Sometimes the quarrel between two princes is to decide which of them shall dispossess a third of his dominions, where neither of them pretends to any

[1] [A king of Egypt. See Herodotus ii. 102–11. Three kings with the same name reigned successively during the Middle Kingdom.]

[2] [A mythical queen of Assyria who, according to legend, led campaigns against Persia, Libya, Egypt, and Ethiopia, and was finally defeated and killed on the Indus leading an army of nearly four million men.]

right. Sometimes one prince quarrels with another, for fear the other should quarrel with him. Sometimes a war is entered upon because the enemy is too strong; and sometimes because he is too weak. Sometimes our neighbours want the things which we have, or have the things which we want; and we both fight, till they take ours, or give us theirs. It is a very justifiable cause of war to invade a country after the people have been wasted by famine, destroyed by pestilence, or embroiled by factions among themselves. It is justifiable to enter into a war against our nearest ally, when one of his towns lies convenient for us, or a territory of land that would render our dominions round and compact. If a prince sends forces into a nation where the people are poor and ignorant, he may lawfully put the half of them to death, and make slaves of the rest, in order to civilize and reduce them from their barbarous way of living. It is a very kingly, honourable and frequent practice, when one prince desires the assistance of another to secure him against an invasion, that the assistant, when he has driven out the invader, should seize on the dominions himself, and kill, imprison or banish the prince he came to relieve.'[1]

If we turn from the foreign transactions of states with each other, to the principles of their domestic policy, we shall not find much greater reason to be satisfied. A numerous class of mankind are held down in a state of abject penury, and are continually prompted by disappointment and distress to commit violence upon their more fortunate neighbours. The only mode which is employed to repress this violence, and to maintain the order and peace of society, is punishment. . . .

Add to this the species of government which prevails over ninetenths of the globe, which is despotism: a government, as Locke justly observes, altogether 'vile and miserable,' and 'more to be deprecated than anarchy itself.'[2]

Certainly every man who takes a dispassionate survey of this picture, will feel himself inclined to pause respecting the necessity of the havoc which is thus made of his species, and to question whether the established methods for protecting mankind against the caprices of each other are the best that can be devised. He will be at a loss which of the two to pronounce most worthy of regret, the misery that is inflicted,

---

[1] *Gulliver's Travels*, IV. v.

[2] *Two Treatises of Government*, I. i. 1, and II. vii. 91. Most of the above arguments may be found much more at large in [Edmund] Burke's [1729–97] *Vindication of Natural Society* [1756]; a treatise, in which the evils of the existing political institutions are displayed with incomparable force of reasoning and lustre of eloquence, while the intention of the author was to show that these evils were to be considered as trivial.

or the depravity by which it is produced. If this be the unalterable allotment of our nature, the eminence of our rational faculties must be considered as rather an abortion than a substantial benefit; and we shall not fail to lament that, while in some respects we are elevated above the brutes, we are in so many important ones destined for ever to remain their inferiors.

CHAPTER III

SPIRIT OF POLITICAL INSTITUTIONS

ADDITIONAL perspicuity will be communicated to our view of the evils of political society, if we reflect with further and closer attention upon what may be called its interior and domestic history.

Two of the greatest abuses relative to the interior policy of nations, which at this time prevail in the world, consist in the irregular transfer of property, either first by violence, or secondly by fraud. If among the inhabitants of any country there existed no desire in one individual to possess himself of the substance of another, or no desire so vehement and restless as to prompt him to acquire it by means inconsistent with order and justice, undoubtedly in that country guilt could scarcely be known but by report. If every man could with perfect facility obtain the necessaries of life, and, obtaining them, feel no uneasy craving after its superfluities, temptation would lose its power. Private interest would visibly accord with public good; and civil society become what poetry has feigned of the golden age. Let us enquire into the principles to which these abuses are indebted for their existence.

First then it is to be observed, that, in the most refined states of Europe, the inequality of property has risen to an alarming height. Vast numbers of their inhabitants are deprived of almost every accommodation that can render life tolerable or secure. Their utmost industry scarcely suffices for their support. The women and children lean with an insupportable weight upon the efforts of the man, so that a large family has in the lower orders of life become a proverbial expression for an uncommon degree of poverty and wretchedness. If sickness or some of those casualties which are perpetually incident to an active and laborious life, be added to these burdens, the distress is yet greater.

. . . .

. . . The consequences that result are placed beyond the reach of contradiction. A perpetual struggle with the evils of poverty, if frequently ineffectual, must necessarily render many of the sufferers desperate. A painful feeling of their oppressed situation will itself deprive them of the power of surmounting it. The superiority of the rich, being thus unmercifully exercised, must inevitably expose them to reprisals; and the poor man will be induced to regard the state of society as a state of war, an unjust combination, not for protecting every man in his rights and securing to him the means of existence, but for engrossing all its advantages to a few favoured individuals, and reserving for the portion of the rest want, dependence and misery.

A second source of those destructive passions by which the peace of society is interrupted, is to be found in the luxury, the pageantry and magnificence, with which enormous wealth is usually accompanied. Human beings are capable of encountering with cheerfulness considerable hardships, when those hardships are impartially shared with the rest of the society, and they are not insulted with the spectacle of indolence and ease in others, no way deserving of greater advantages than themselves. But it is a bitter aggravation of their own calamity, to have the privileges of others forced on their observation, and, while they are perpetually and vainly endeavouring to secure for themselves and their families the poorest conveniences, to find others revelling in the fruits of their labours. This aggravation is assiduously administered to them under most of the political establishments at present in existence. . . .

A third disadvantage that is apt to connect poverty with discontent, consists in the insolence and usurpation of the rich. If the poor man would in other respects compose himself in philosophic indifference, and, conscious that he possesses everything that is truly honourable to man as fully as his rich neighbour, would look upon the rest as beneath his envy, his neighbour will not permit him to do so. He seems as if he could never be satisfied with his possessions, unless he can make the spectacle of them grating to others; and that honest self-esteem, by which his inferior might otherwise attain to tranquillity, is rendered the instrument of galling him with oppression and injustice. In many countries justice is avowedly made a subject of solicitation, and the man of the highest rank and most splendid connections almost infallibly carries his cause against the unprotected and friendless. In countries where this shameless practice is not established, justice is frequently a matter of expensive purchase, and the man with the longest purse is proverbially victorious. A consciousness of these facts must be expected to render the rich little cautious of offence in his dealings with the poor, and to inspire him with a temper overbearing, dictatorial and tyrannical. Nor does this indirect oppression satisfy his depotism. The rich are in all such countries directly or indirectly the legislators of the state; and of consequence are perpetually reducing oppression into a system, and depriving the poor of that little commonage of nature, which might otherwise still have remained to them.

The opinions of individuals, and of consequence their desires, for desire is nothing but opinion maturing for action, will always be in a great degree regulated by the opinions of the community. But the manners prevailing in many countries are accurately calculated to impress a conviction, that integrity, virtue, understanding and industry are nothing, and that opulence is everything. . . .

Such are the causes, that, in different degrees under the different governments of the world, prompt mankind openly or secretly to encroach upon the property of each other. Let us consider how far they admit either of remedy or aggravation from political institution. Whatever tends to decrease the injuries attendant upon poverty, decreases at the same time the inordinate desire and the enormous accumulation of wealth. Wealth is not pursued for its own sake, and seldom for the sensual gratifications it can purchase, but for the same reasons that ordinarily prompt men to the acquisition of learning, eloquence and skill, for the love of distinction and the fear of contempt. . . . If admiration were not generally deemed the exclusive property of the rich, and contempt the constant lackey of poverty, the love of gain would cease to be an universal passion. Let us consider in what respects political institution is rendered subservient to this passion.

First then, legislation is in almost every country grossly the favourer of the rich against the poor. Such is the character of the game-laws, by which the industrious rustic is forbidden to destroy the animal that preys upon the hopes of his future subsistence, or to supply himself with the food that unsought thrusts itself in his path. Such was the spirit of the late revenue-laws of France, which in several of their provisions fell exclusively upon the humble and industrious, and exempted from their operation those who were best able to support it. Thus in England the land-tax at this moment produces half a million less than it did a century ago, while the taxes on consumption have experienced an addition of thirteen millions per annum during the same period. This is an attempt, whether effectual or no, to throw the burden from the rich upon the poor, and as such is an example of the spirit of legislation. Upon the same principle robbery and other offences, which the wealthier part of the community have no temptation to commit, are treated as capital crimes, and attended with the most rigorous, often the most inhuman punishments. . . .

Secondly, the administration of law is not less iniquitous than the spirit in which it is framed. Under the late government of France the office of judge was a matter of purchase, partly by an open price advanced to the crown, and partly by a secret douceur paid to the minister. He, who knew best how to manage his market in the retail trade of justice, could afford to purchase the goodwill of its functions at the highest price. To the client justice was avowedly made an object of personal solicitation; and a powerful friend, a handsome woman, or a proper present, were articles of much greater value, than a good cause. In England the criminal law is administered with greater impartiality so far as regards the trial itself; but the number of capital offences, and of consequence the frequency of pardons, open a wide door to favour and abuse. In causes relating to property the practice of law is arrived at such a pitch as to render its nominal impartiality utterly nugatory. The length of our chancery suits, the multiplied appeals from court to court, the enormous fees of counsel, attorneys, secretaries, clerks, the drawing of briefs, bills, replications and rejoinders, and what has sometimes been called the 'glorious uncertainty' of the law, render it frequently more advisable to resign a property than to contest it, and particularly exclude the impoverished claimant from the faintest hope of redress.

Thirdly, the inequality of conditions usually maintained by political institution, is calculated greatly to enhance the imagined excellence of wealth. In the ancient monarchies of the east, . . . an eminent station could scarcely fail to excite implicit deference. . . . The same principles were extensively prevalent under the feudal system. The vassal, who was regarded as a sort of live stock upon the estate, and knew no appeal from the arbitrary fiat of his lord, would scarcely venture to suspect that he was of the same species. This however constituted an unnatural and violent situation. There is a propensity in man to look further than the outside; and to come with a writ of enquiry into the title of the upstart and the successful. By the operation of these causes the insolence of wealth has been in some degree moderated. Meantime it cannot be pretended that even among ourselves the inequality is not strained, so as to give birth to very unfortunate consequences. If, in the enormous degree in which it prevails in some parts of the world, it wholly debilitate and emasculate the human race, we shall see some reason to believe that, even in the milder state in which we are accustomed to behold it, it is still pregnant with the most mischievous effects.

CHAPTER IV[1]

THE CHARACTERS OF MEN ORIGINATE IN THEIR EXTERNAL CIRCUMSTANCES

THUS far we have argued from historical facts, and from them have collected a very strong presumptive evidence, that political institutions have a more powerful and extensive influence, than it has been generally the practice to ascribe to them.

But we can never arrive at precise conceptions relative to this part of the subject, without entering into an analysis of the human mind,[2] and

---

[1] In the plan of this work it was originally conceived that it was advisable not to press matters of close and laborious speculation in the outset. It appeared as if moral and political philosophy might assume something more than had been usual of a popular form, without deducting from the justness and depth of its investigation. Upon revisal however, it was found that the inferences of the First Book had been materially injured, by an over-scrupulousness in that point. The fruit of the discovery was this and the following chapter, as they now stand. It is recommended, to the reader who finds himself deterred by their apparent difficulty, to pass on to the remaining divisions of the enquiry. [In the second edition this footnote concluded with the following two sentences: 'The doctrine of the present chapter, with some variations, has been powerfully enforced by Helvétius. Rousseau has also treated it, so far as relates to the moral habits of the human mind, with great success in his *Emile* and his *Discourse on the Inequality of Mankind*.']

[2] Some persons have of late suggested doubts concerning the propriety of the use of the word mind. An accurate philosophy has led modern enquirers to question the existence of two classes of substances in the universe, to reject the metaphysical denominations of spirit and soul, and even to doubt whether human beings have any satisfactory acquaintance with the properties of matter. The same accuracy, it has been said, ought to teach us to discard the term mind. But this objection seems to be premature. We are indeed wholly uncertain whether the causes of our sensations, heat, colour, hardness and extension (the two former of these properties have been questioned in a very forcible manner by Locke, [*An Essay Concerning*] *Human Understanding*, the two latter by Berkeley and Hume) be in any respect similar to the ideas they produce. We know nothing of the substance or substratum of matter, or of that which is the recipient of thought and perception. We do not even know that the idea annexed to the word substance is correct, or has any counterpart in the reality of existence. But, if there be any one thing that we know more certainly than another, it is the existence of our own thoughts, ideas, perceptions or sensations (by whatever term we may choose to express them), and that they are ordinarily linked together, so as to produce the complex notion of unity or personal identity. Now it is this series of thoughts thus linked together, without considering whether they reside in any or what substratum, that is most aptly expressed by the term mind; and in this sense the term is intended to be used throughout the following work.

endeavouring to ascertain the nature of the causes by which its operations are directed. Under this branch of the subject I shall attempt to prove two things; first, that the actions and dispositions of mankind are the offspring of circumstances and events, and not of any original determination that they bring into the world; and, secondly, that the great stream of our voluntary actions essentially depends, not upon the direct and immediate impulses of sense, but upon the decisions of the understanding. If these propositions can be sufficiently established, it will follow that the happiness men are able to attain, is proportioned to the justness of the opinions they take as guides in the pursuit; and it will only remain, for the purpose of applying these premises to the point under consideration, that we should demonstrate the opinions of men to be, for the most part, under the absolute control of political institution.

First, The actions and dispositions of men are not the offspring of any original bias that they bring into the world in favour of one sentiment or character rather than another, but flow entirely from the operation of circumstances and events acting upon a faculty of receiving sensible impressions.

There are three modes in which the human mind has been conceived to be modified, independently of the circumstances which occur to us, and the sensations excited: first, innate principles; secondly, instincts; thirdly, the original differences of our structure, together with the impressions we receive in the womb. Let us examine each of these in their order.

First, innate principles of judgement. Those by whom this doctrine has been maintained, have supposed that there were certain branches of knowledge, and those perhaps of all others the most important, concerning which we felt an irresistible persuasion, at the same time that we were wholly unable to trace them through any channels of external evidence and methodical deduction. They conceived therefore, . . . that there was a general propensity in the human mind, suggesting them to our reflections, and fastening them upon our conviction. Accordingly, they established the universal consent of mankind as one of the most infallible criteria of fundamental truth. . . .

There is an essential deficiency in every speculation of this sort. It turns entirely upon an appeal to our ignorance. Its language is as follows: 'You cannot account for certain events from the known laws of the subjects to which they belong; therefore they are not deducible from those laws; therefore you must admit a new principle into the system for the express purpose of accounting for them.' But there cannot be a sounder maxim of reasoning, than that which points out to us the error of admitting into our hypotheses unnecessary principles, or referring the phenomena that occur, to remote and extraordinary sources, when they may with equal facility be referred to sources which obviously exist, and the results of which we daily observe. . . . If we consider the infinitely various causes by which the human mind is perceptibly modified, and the different principles, argument, imitation, inclination, early prejudice and imaginary interest, by which opinion is generated, we shall readily perceive, that nothing can be more difficult than to assign any opinion, existing among the human species, and at the same time incapable of being generated by any of these causes and principles.

A careful enquirer will be strongly inclined to suspect the soundness of opinions, which rest for their support on so ambiguous a foundation as that of innate impression. We cannot reasonably question the existence of facts; that is, we cannot deny the existence of our sensations, or the series in which they occur. We cannot deny the axioms of mathematics; for they exhibit nothing more than a consistent use of words, and affirm of some idea that it is itself and not something else. We can entertain little doubt of the validity of mathematical demonstrations, which appear to be irresistible conclusions deduced from identical propositions. We ascribe a certain value, sometimes greater and sometimes less, to considerations drawn from analogy. But what degree of weight shall we attribute to affirmations which pretend to rest upon none of these grounds? The most preposterous propositions, incapable of any rational defence, have in different ages and countries appealed to this inexplicable authority, and passed for infallible and innate. The enquirer that has no other object than truth, that refuses to be misled, and is determined to proceed only upon just and sufficient evidence, will find little reason to be satisfied with dogmas which rest upon no other foundation, than a pretended necessity impelling the human mind to yield its assent.

But there is a still more irresistible argument proving to us the absurdity of the supposition of innate principles. Every principle is a proposition: either it affirms, or it denies. Every proposition consists in the connection of at least two distinct ideas, which are affirmed to agree or disagree with each other. It is impossible that the proposition can be innate, unless the ideas to which it relates be also innate. A connection where there is nothing to be connected, a proposition where there is neither subject nor conclusion, is the most incoherent of all suppositions. But nothing can be more incontrovertible, than that we do not bring pre-established ideas into the world with us.

Let the innate principle be, that 'virtue is a rule to which we are obliged to conform.' Here are three principal and leading ideas, not to mention subordinate ones, which it is necessary to form, before we can so much as understand the proposition. What is virtue? Previously to our forming an idea corresponding to this general term, it seems necessary that we should have observed the several features by which virtue is distinguished, and the several subordinate articles of right conduct, that taken together, constitute that mass of practical judgements to which we give the denomination of virtue. These are so far from being innate, that the most impartial and laborious enquirers are not yet agreed respecting them. . . .

Who is there in the present state of scientifical improvement, that will believe that this vast chain of perceptions and notions, is something that we bring into the world with us, a mystical magazine, shut up in the human embryo, whose treasures are to be gradually unfolded as circumstances shall require? Who does not perceive, that they are regularly generated in the mind by a series of impressions, and digested and arranged by association and reflection?

But, if we are not endowed with innate principles of judgement, it has nevertheless been supposed by some persons, that we might have instincts to action, leading us to the performance of certain useful and necessary functions, independently of any previous reasoning as to the advantage of these functions. These instincts, like the innate principles of judgement we have already examined, are conceived to be original, a separate endowment annexed to our being, and not anything that irresistibly flows from the mere faculty of perception and thought, as acted upon by the circumstances, either of our animal frame, or of the external objects, by which we are affected. They are liable therefore to the same objection as that already urged against innate principles. The system by which they are attempted to be established, is a mere appeal to our ignorance, assuming that we are fully acquainted with all the possible operations of known powers, and imposing upon us an unknown power as indispensable to the accounting for certain phenomena. If we were wholly unable to solve these phenomena, it would yet behove us to be extremely cautious in affirming that known principles and causes are inadequate to their solution. If we are able upon strict and mature investigation to trace the greater part of them to their source, this necessarily adds force to the caution here recommended.

An unknown cause is exceptionable, in the first place, inasmuch as to multiply causes is contrary to the experienced operation of scientifical improvement. It is exceptionable, secondly, because its tendency is to break that train of antecedents and consequents, of which the history of the universe is composed. It introduces an action apparently extraneous, instead of imputing the nature of what follows, to the properties of that which preceded. It bars the progress of enquiry by introducing that which is occult, mysterious and incapable of further investigation. It allows nothing to the future advancement of human knowledge; but represents the limits of what is already known, as the limits of human understanding.

Let us review a few of the most common examples adduced in favour of human instincts, and examine how far they authorize the conclusion that is attempted to be drawn from them: and first, some of those actions which appear to rise in the most instantaneous and irresistible manner.

A certain irritation of the palm of the hand will produce that contraction of the fingers, which accompanies the action of grasping. This contraction will at first take place unaccompanied with design, the object will be grasped without any intention to retain it, and let go again without thought or observation. After a certain number of repetitions, the nature of the action will be perceived; it will be performed with a consciousness of its tendency; and even the hand stretched out upon the approach of any object that is desired. Present to the child, thus far instructed, a lighted candle. The sight of it will produce a pleasurable state of the organs of perception. He will probably stretch out his hand to the flame, and will have no apprehension of the pain of burning, till he has felt the sensation.

.   .   .   .

It has been said, that the desire of self-preservation is innate. I demand what is meant by this desire? Must we not understand by it, a preference of existence to non-existence? Do we prefer anything but because it is apprehended to be good? It follows, that we cannot prefer existence, previously to our experience of the motives for preference it possesses. Indeed the ideas of life and death are exceedingly complicated, and very tardy in their formation. A child desires pleasure and loaths pain, long before he can have any imagination respecting the ceasing to exist.

Again, it has been said, that self-love is innate. But there cannot be an error more easy of detection. By the love of self we understand the approbation of pleasure, and dislike of pain: but this is only the faculty of perception under another name. Who ever denied that man was a percipient being? Who ever dreamed that there was a particular instinct necessary to render him percipient?

Pity has sometimes been supposed an instance of innate principle; particularly as it seems to arise with greater facility in young persons, and persons of little refinement, than in others. But it was reasonable to expect, that threats and anger, circumstances that have been associated with our own sufferings, should excite painful feelings in us in the case of others, independently of any laboured analysis. The cries of distress, the appearance of agony or corporal infliction, irresistibly revive the memory of the pains accompanied by those symptoms in ourselves. Longer experience and observation enable us to separate the calamities of others and our own safety, the existence of pain in one subject and of pleasure or benefit in others, or in the same at a future period, more accurately than we could be expected to do previously to that experience.

If then it appear that the human mind is unattended either with innate principles or instincts, there are only two remaining circumstances that can be imagined to anticipate the effects of institution, and fix the human character independently of every species of education: these are, the qualities that may be produced in the human mind previously to the era of our birth, and the differences that may result from the different structure of the greater or subtler elements of the animal frame.

To objections derived from these sources the answer will be in both cases similar.

First, ideas are to the mind nearly what atoms are to the body. The whole mass is in a perpetual flux; nothing is stable and permanent; after the lapse of a given period not a single particle probably remains the same. Who knows not that in the course of a human life the character of the individual frequently undergoes two or three revolutions of its fundamental stamina? The turbulent man will frequently become contemplative, the generous be changed into selfish, and the frank and good-humoured into peevish and morose. . . . If it is thus in habits apparently the most rooted, who will be disposed to lay any extraordinary stress upon the impressions which an infant may have received in the womb of his mother?

.   .   .   .

It is in corporeal structure as in intellectual impressions. The first impressions of our infancy are so much upon the surface, that their effects scarcely survive the period of the impression itself. The mature man seldom retains the faintest recollection of the incidents of the two first years of his life. Is it to be supposed that that which has left no trace upon the memory, can be in an eminent degree powerful in its associated effects? Just so in the structure of the animal frame. What is born into the world is an unfinished sketch, without character or decisive feature impressed upon it. In the sequel there is a correspondence between the physiognomy and the intellectual and moral qualities of the mind. But is it not reasonable to suppose that this is produced, by the continual tendency of the mind to modify its material engine in a particular way? There is for the most part no essential difference between the child of the lord and of the porter. Provided he do not come into the world infected with any ruinous distemper, the child of the lord, if changed in the cradle, would scarcely find any greater difficulty than the other, in learning the trade of his foster father, and becoming a carrier of burdens. The muscles of those limbs which are most frequently called into play, are always observed to acquire peculiar flexibility or strength. It is not improbable, if it should be found that the capacity of the skull of a wise man is greater than that of a fool, that this enlargement should be produced by the incessantly repeated action of the intellectual faculties, especially if we recollect of how flexible materials the skulls of infants are composed, and at how early an age persons of eminent intellectual merit acquire some portion of their future characteristics.

In the meantime it would be ridiculous to question the real differences that exist between children at the period of their birth. Hercules and his brother, the robust infant whom scarcely any neglect can destroy, and the infant that is with difficulty reared, are undoubtedly from the moment of parturition very different beings. If each of them could receive an education precisely equal and eminently wise, the child labouring under original disadvantage would be benefited, but the child to whom circumstances had been most favourable in the outset, would always retain his priority. These considerations however do not appear materially to affect the doctrine of the present chapter; and that for the following reasons.

First, education never can be equal. The inequality of external circumstances in two beings whose situations most nearly resemble, is so great as to baffle all power of calculation. In the present state of mankind this is eminently the case. There is no fact more palpable, than that children of all sizes and forms indifferently become wise. It is not the man of great stature or vigorous make that outstrips his fellow in understanding. It is not the man who possesses all the external senses in the highest perfection. It is not the man whose health is most vigorous and invariable. Those moral causes that awaken the mind, that inspire sensibility, imagination and perseverance, are distributed without distinction to the tall or the dwarfish, the graceful or the deformed, the lynx-eyed or the blind. . . .

Secondly, it is sufficient to recollect the nature of moral causes to be satisfied that their efficiency is nearly unlimited. The essential differences that are to be found between individual and individual, originate in the opinions they form, and the circumstances by which they are controlled. It is impossible to believe that the same moral train would not make nearly the same man. . . . In fine, it is impression that makes the man, and, compared with the empire of impression, the mere differences of animal structure are inexpressibly unimportant and powerless.

. . . .

The result of these considerations is, that at the moment of birth man has really a certain character, and each man a character different from his fellows. The accidents which pass during the months of percipiency in the womb of the mother, produce a real effect. Various external accidents, unlimited as to the period of their commencement, modify in different ways the elements of the animal frame. Everything in the universe is linked and united together. No event, however minute and imperceptible, is barren of a train of consequences, however comparatively evanescent those consequences may in some instances be found. If there have been philosophers that have asserted otherwise, and taught that all minds from the period of birth were precisely alike, they have reflected discredit by such an incautious statement upon the truth they proposed to defend.

But, though the original differences of man and man be arithmetically speaking something, speaking in the way of a general and comprehensive estimate they may be said to be almost nothing. If the early impressions of our childhood may by a skilful observer be as it were obliterated almost as soon as made, how much less can the confused and unpronounced impressions of the womb, be expected to resist the multiplicity of ideas that successively contribute to wear out their traces? If the temper of the man appear in many instances to be totally changed, how can it be supposed that there is anything permanent and inflexible in the propensities of a new-born infant? and, if not in the character of the disposition, how much less in that of the understanding?

Speak the language of truth and reason to your child, and be under no apprehension for the result. Show him that what you recommend is valuable and desirable, and fear not but he will desire it. Convince his understanding, and you enlist all his powers animal and intellectual in your service. How long has the genius of education been disheartened and unnerved by the pretence that man is born all that it is possible for him to become? How long has the jargon imposed upon the world, which would persuade us that in instructing a man you do not add to, but unfold his stores? The miscarriages of education do not proceed from the boundedness of its powers, but from the mistakes with which it is accompanied. We often inspire disgust, where we mean to infuse desire. We are wrapped up in ourselves, and do not observe, as we ought, step by step the sensations that pass in the mind of our hearer. We mistake compulsion for persuasion, and delude ourselves into the belief that despotism is the road to the heart.

Education will proceed with a firm step and with genuine lustre, when those who conduct it shall know what a vast field it embraces; when they shall be aware, that the effect, the question whether the pupil shall be a man of perseverance and enterprise or a stupid and inanimate dolt, depends upon the powers of those under whose direction he is placed, and the skill with which those powers shall be applied. . . .

Apply these considerations to the subject of politics, and they will authorize us to infer, that the excellencies and defects of the human character, are not derived from causes beyond the reach of ingenuity to modify and correct. If we entertain false views and be involved in pernicious mistakes, this disadvantage is not the offspring of an irresistible destiny. . . . Show me in the clearest and most unambiguous manner that a certain mode of proceeding is most reasonable in itself or most conducive to my interest, and I shall infallibly pursue that mode, as long as the views you suggested to me continue present to my mind. The conduct of human beings in every situation is governed, by the judgements they make and the sensations that are communicated to them.

It has appeared that the characters of men are determined in all their most essential circumstances by education. By education in this place I would be understood to convey the most comprehensive sense that can

possibly be annexed to that word, including every incident that produces an idea in the mind, and can give birth to a train of reflections.
It may be of use for a clearer understanding of the subject we here
examine, to consider education under three heads; the education of
accident, or those impressions we receive independently of any design
on the part of the preceptor; education commonly so-called, or the
impressions which he intentionally communicates; and political education, or the modification our ideas receive from the form of government under which we live. In the course of this successive review we
shall be enabled in some degree to ascertain the respective influence
which is to be attributed to each.

It is not unusual to hear persons dwell with emphasis on the wide
difference of the results in two young persons who have been educated
together; and this has been produced as a decisive argument in favour
of the essential differences we are supposed to bring into the world with
us. But this could scarcely have happened but from extreme inattention
in the persons who have so argued. Innumerable ideas, or changes in
the state of the percipient being, probably occur in every moment of
time. How many of these enter into the plan of the preceptor? Two
children walk out together. One busies himself in plucking flowers or
running after butterflies, the other walks in the hand of their conductor.
Two men view a picture. They never see it from the same point of
view, and therefore strictly speaking never see the same picture. If they
sit down to hear a lecture or any piece of instruction, they never sit
down with the same degree of attention, seriousness or good humour.
The previous state of mind is different, and therefore the impression
received cannot be the same. It has been found in the history of several
eminent men, and probably would have been found much oftener,
had their juvenile adventures been more accurately recorded, that the
most trivial circumstance has sometimes furnished the original occasion
of awakening the ardour of their minds and determining the bent of
their studies.

It may however reasonably be suspected whether the education of
design be not, intrinsically considered, more powerful than the education of accident. If at any time it appear impotent, this is probably
owing to mistake in the project. The instructor continually fails in
wisdom of contrivance, or conciliation of manner, or both. It may
often happen, either from the pedantry of his habits, or the impatience
of his temper, that his recommendation shall operate rather as an
antidote than an attraction. . . . Children are a sort of raw material put

into our hands, a ductile and yielding substance, which, if we do not ultimately mould in conformity to our wishes, it is because we throw away the power committed to us, by the folly with which we are accustomed to exert it. . . .

It remains to be considered what share political institution and forms of government occupy in the education of every human being. Their degree of influence depends upon two essential circumstances.

First, it is nearly impossible to oppose the education of the preceptor, and the education we derive from the forms of government under which we live, to each other; and therefore, however powerful the former of these may be, absolutely considered, it can never enter the lists with the latter upon equal terms. Should any one talk to us of rescuing a young person from the sinister influence of a corrupt government by the power of education, it will be fair to ask, who is the preceptor by whom this task is to be effected? Is he born in the ordinary mode of generation, or does he descend among us from the skies? Has his character been in no degree modified, by that very influence he undertakes to counteract? It is beyond all controversy, that men who live in a state of equality, or that approaches equality, will be frank, ingenuous and intrepid in their carriage; while those who inhabit where a great disparity of ranks has prevailed, will be distinguished by coldness, irresoluteness, timidity and caution. Will the preceptor in question be altogether superior to these qualities? Which of us is there who utters his thoughts, in the fearless and explicit manner that true wisdom would prescribe? Who, that is sufficiently critical and severe, does not detect himself every hour in some act of falsehood or equivocation, that example and early habits have planted too deeply to be eradicated? But the question is not, what extraordinary persons can be found, who may shine illustrious exceptions to the prevailing degeneracy of their neighbours. As long as parents and teachers in general shall fall under the established rule, it is clear that politics and modes of government will educate and infect us all. They poison our minds, before we can resist, or so much as suspect their malignity. Like the barbarous directors of the Eastern seraglios, they deprive us of our virility, and fit us for their despicable employment from the cradle. So false is the opinion that has too generally prevailed, that politics is an affair with which ordinary men have little concern.

Secondly, supposing the preceptor had all the qualifications that can reasonably be imputed, let us recollect for a moment what are the influences with which he would have to struggle. Political institution, by the consequences with which it is pregnant, strongly suggests to every one who enters within its sphere, what is the path he should avoid, as well as what he should pursue. Under a government fundamentally erroneous, he will see intrepid virtue proscribed, and a servile and corrupt spirit uniformly encouraged. But morality itself is nothing but a calculation of consequences. What strange confusion will the spectacle of that knavery which is universally practised through all the existing classes of society, produce in the mind? The preceptor cannot go out of the world, or prevent the intercourse of his pupil with human beings of a character different from his own. Attempts of this kind are generally unhappy, stamped with the impression of artifice, intolerance and usurpation. From earliest infancy therefore there will be two principles contending for empire, the peculiar and elevated system of the preceptor, and the grovelling views of the great mass of mankind. These will generate confusion, uncertainty and irresolution. At no period of life will the effect correspond to what it would have been, if the community were virtuous and wise. But its effect, obscure and imperceptible for a time, may be expected to burst into explosion at the period of puberty. When the pupil first becomes master of his own actions, and chooses his avocations and his associates, he will necessarily be acquainted with many things of which before he had very slender notions. At this time the follies of the world wear their most alluring face. He can scarcely avoid imagining that he has hitherto laboured under some species of delusion. Delusion, when detected, causes him upon whom it was practised to be indignant and restive. The only chance which remains, is that, after a time, he should be recalled and awakened: and against this chance there are the progressive enticements of society; sensuality, ambition, sordid interest, false ridicule, and the incessant decay of that unblemished purity which attended him in his outset. The best that can be expected, is that he should return at last to sobriety and truth, with a mind debilitated and relaxed by repeated errors, and a moral constitution in which the seeds of degeneracy have been deeply and extensively sown.

CHAPTER V

THE VOLUNTARY ACTIONS OF MEN ORIGINATE IN THEIR OPINIONS

IF, by the reasons already given, we have removed the supposition of any original bias in the mind that is inaccessible to human skill, and shown that the defects to which we are now subject are not irrevocably entailed upon us, there is another question of no less importance to be decided, before the ground can appear to be sufficiently cleared for political melioration. There is a doctrine, the advocates of which have not been less numerous than those for innate principles and instincts, teaching 'that the conduct of human beings in many important particulars is not determined upon any grounds of reasoning and comparison, but by immediate and irresistible impression, in defiance of the conclusions and conviction of the understanding. Man is a compound being,' say the favourers of this hypothesis, 'made up of powers of reasoning and powers of sensation. These two principles are in perpetual hostility; and, as reason will in some cases subdue all the allurements of sense, so there are others in which the headlong impulses of sense will for ever defeat the tardy decisions of judgement. He that should attempt to regulate man entirely by his understanding, and supersede the irregular influences of material excitement; or that should imagine it practicable by any process and in any length of time to reduce the human species under the influence of general truth;[1] would show himself profoundly ignorant of some of the first laws of our nature.'

[1] Objections have been started to the use of the word truth in this absolute construction, as if it implied in the mind of the writer the notion of something having an independent and separate existence, whereas nothing can be more certain than that truth, that is, affirmative and negative propositions, has strictly no existence but in the mind of him who utters or hears it. But these objections seem to have been taken up too hastily. It cannot be denied, that there are some propositions which are believed for a time and afterwards refuted; and others, such as most of the theorems of mathematics, and many of those of natural philosophy, respecting which there is no probability that they ever will be refuted. Every subject of enquiry is susceptible of affirmation and negation; and those propositions concerning it, which describe the real relations of things, may in a certain sense, whether we be or be not aware that they do so, be said to be true. Taken in this sense, truth is immutable. He that speaks of its immutability, does nothing more than predict with greater or less probability, and say, 'This is what I believe, and what all reasonable beings, till they shall fall short of me in their degree of information, will continue to believe.'

This doctrine, which in many cases has passed so current as to be thought scarcely a topic for examination, is highly worthy of a minute analysis. If true, it no less than the doctrine of innate principles, opposes a bar to the efforts of philanthropy, and the improvement of social institutions. Certain it is, that our prospects of melioration depend upon the progress of enquiry and the general advancement of knowledge. If therefore there be points, and those important ones, in which, so to express myself, knowledge and the thinking principle in man cannot be brought into contact, if, however great be the improvement of his reason, he will not the less certainly in many cases act in a way irrational and absurd, this consideration must greatly overcloud the prospect of the moral reformer.

There is another consequence that will flow from the vulgarly received doctrine upon this subject. If man be, by the very constitution of his nature, the subject of opinion, and if truth and reason when properly displayed, give us a complete hold upon his choice, then the search of the political enquirer will be much simplified. Then we have only to discover what form of civil society is most conformable to reason, and we may rest assured that, as soon as men shall be persuaded from conviction to adopt that form, they will have acquired to themselves an invaluable benefit. But, if reason be frequently inadequate to its task, if there be an opposite principle in man resting upon its own ground, and maintaining a separate jurisdiction, the most rational principles of society may be rendered abortive, it may be necessary to call in mere sensible causes to encounter causes of the same nature, folly may be the fittest instrument to effect the purposes of wisdom, and vice to disseminate and establish the public benefit. In that case the salutary prejudices and useful delusions (as they have been called) of aristocracy, the glittering diadem, the magnificent canopy, the ribands, stars and titles of an illustrious rank, may at last be found the fittest instruments for guiding and alluring to his proper ends the savage, man.[1]

Such is the nature of the question to be examined, and such its connection with the enquiry concerning the influence of political institutions.

The more accurately to conceive the topic before us, it is necessary to observe that it relates to the voluntary actions of man.

The distinction between voluntary and involuntary action, if properly stated, is exceedingly simple. That action is involuntary, which takes

[1] V. xv.

place in us, either without foresight on our part, or contrary to the full bent of our inclinations. Thus, if a child or a person of mature age burst into tears in a manner unexpected or unforeseen by himself, or if he burst into tears, though his pride or any other principle make him exert every effort to restrain them, this action is involuntary. Voluntary action is, where the event is foreseen previously to its occurrence, and the hope or fear of that event forms the excitement,[1] or, as it is most frequently termed, the motive,[2] inducing us, if hope be the passion, to endeavour to forward, and, if fear, to endeavour to prevent it. It is this motion, in this manner generated, to which we annex the idea of voluntariness. Let it be observed that the word, action, is here used in the sense of natural philosophers, as descriptive of a change taking place in any part of the universe, without entering into the question whether that change be necessary or free.

Now let us consider what are the inferences that immediately result from the above simple and unquestionable explanation of voluntary action.

'Voluntary action is accompanied with foresight; the hope or fear of a certain event is its motive.' But foresight is not an affair of simple and immediate impulse: it implies a series of observations so extensive as to enable us from like antecedents to infer like consequents. Voluntary action is occasioned by the idea of consequences to result. Wine is set before me, and I fill my glass. I do this, either because I foresee that the flavour will be agreeable to my palate, or that its effect will be to produce gaiety and exhilaration, or that my drinking it will prove the kindness and good humour I feel towards the company with which I am engaged. If in any case my action in filling dwindle into mechanical or semi-mechanical, done with little or no adverting of the mind to its performance, it so far becomes an involuntary action. But, if every voluntary action be performed for the sake of its consequences, then in every voluntary action there is comparison and judgement. Every such action proceeds upon the apprehended truth of some proposition. The mind decides 'this is good' or 'desirable;' and immediately upon that decision, if accompanied with a persuasion that we are competent to

---

[1] [In the first two editions 'motive' is not defined as 'the hope or fear' of an event, but rather as the 'idea of certain consequences' to follow an event.]

[2] The term motive is applicable in all cases, where the regular operations of inanimate matter are superseded by the interference of intelligence. Whatever sensation or perception in the mind is capable of influencing this interference, is called motive. Motive therefore is applicable to the case of all actions originating in sensation or perception, whether voluntary or involuntary.

accomplish this good or desirable thing, the limbs proceed to their office. The mind decides 'this is better than something else;' either wine and cordials are before me, and I choose the wine rather than the cordials; or the wine only is presented or thought of, and I decide that to take the wine is better than to abstain from it. Thus it appears that in every voluntary action there is preference or choice, which indeed are synonymous terms.

This full elucidation of the nature of voluntary action enables us to proceed a step further. Hence it appears that the voluntary actions of men in all cases originate in their opinions. The actions of men, it will readily be admitted, originate in the state of their minds immediately previous to those actions. Actions therefore which are preceded by a judgement 'this is good,' or 'this is desirable,' originate in the state of judgement or opinion upon that subject. It may happen that the opinion may be exceedingly fugitive; it may have been preceded by aversion and followed by remorse; but it was unquestionably the opinion of the mind at the instant in which the action commenced.

. . . . .

From this view of the subject we shall easily be led to perceive, how little the fact of the variableness and inconstancy of human conduct, is incompatible with the principle here delivered, that the voluntary actions of men in all cases originate in their opinions. The persuasion that exists in the mind of the drunkard in committing his first act of intoxication, that in so doing he complies with the most cogent and irresistible reasons capable of being assigned upon the subject, may be exceedingly temporary; but it is the clear and unequivocal persuasion of his mind at the moment that he determines upon the action. The thoughts of the murderer will frequently be in a state of the most tempestuous fluctuation; he may make and unmake his diabolical purpose fifty times in an hour; his mind may be torn a thousand ways by terror and fury, malignity and remorse. But, whenever his resolution is formed, it is formed upon the suggestions of the rational faculty; and, when he ultimately works up his mind to the perpetration, he is then most strongly impressed with the superior recommendations of the conduct he pursues. One of the fallacies by which we are most frequently induced to a conduct which our habitual judgement dis-approves, is that our attention becomes so engrossed by a particular view of the subject, as wholly to forget, for the moment, those con-siderations which at other times were accustomed to determine our

opinion. In such cases it frequently happens, that the neglected consideration recurs the instant the hurry of action has subsided, and we
stand astonished at our own infatuation and folly.

This reasoning, however clear and irresistible it may appear, is yet
exposed to one very striking objection. 'According to the ideas here
delivered, men always proceed in their voluntary actions upon judgements extant to their understanding. Such judgements must be attended
with consciousness; and, were this hypothesis a sound one, nothing
could be more easy than for a man in all cases to assign the precise
reason that induced him to any particular action. The human mind
would then be a very simple machine, always aware of the grounds
upon which it proceeded, and self-deception would be impossible.
But this statement is completely in opposition to experience and history.
Ask a man the reason why he puts on his clothes, why he eats his dinner,
or performs any other ordinary action of his life. He immediately
hesitates, endeavours to recollect himself, and often assigns a reason the
most remote from what the true philosophy of motive would have
led us to expect. Nothing is more clear, than that the moving cause of
this action was not expressly present to his apprehension at the time
he performed it. Self-deception is so far from impossible, that it is one
of the most ordinary phenomena with which we are acquainted. Nothing
is more usual than for a man to impute his actions to honourable
motives, when it is nearly demonstrable that they flowed from some
corrupt and contemptible source. On the other hand many persons
suppose themselves to be worse, than an impartial spectator will find
any good reason to believe them. A penetrating observer will frequently be able to convince his neighbour that upon such an occasion
he was actuated by motives very different from what he imagined.
Philosophers to this hour dispute whether human beings in their most
virtuous exertions, are under the power of disinterested benevolence,
or merely of an enlightened self-interest. Here then we are presented,
in one or other of these sets of philosophers, with a striking instance of
men's acting from motives diametrically opposite to those which they
suppose to be the guides of their conduct. Self-examination is to a
proverb one of the most arduous of those tasks which true virtue
imposes. Are not these facts in express contradiction to the doctrine,
that the voluntary actions of men in all cases originate in the judgements of the understanding?'

Undoubtedly the facts which have been here enumerated appear to
be strictly true. To determine how far they affect the doctrine of the

present chapter, it is necessary to return to our analysis of the phenomena of the human mind. Hitherto we have considered the actions of
human beings only under two classes, voluntary and involuntary. In
strictness however there is a third class, which belongs to neither, yet
partakes of the nature of both.

We have already defined voluntary action to be that of which certain
consequences, foreseen, and considered either as objects of desire or
aversion, are the motive. Foresight and volition are inseparable. But
what is foreseen must, by the very terms, be present to the understanding. Every action therefore, so far as it is perfectly voluntary, flows
solely from the decision of the judgement. But the actions above
cited, such as relate to our garments and our food, are only imperfectly
voluntary.[1]

In respect of volition there appear to be two stages in the history of
the human mind. Foresight is the result of experience; therefore foresight, and by parity of reasoning volition, cannot enter into the earliest
actions of a human being. As soon however as the infant perceives the
connection between certain attitudes and gestures and the circumstance
of receiving suck, for example, he is brought to desire those preliminaries for the sake of that result. Here, so far as relates to volition and
the judgement of the understanding, the action is as simple as can well
be imagined. Yet, even in this instance, the motive may be said to be
complex. Habit, or custom, has its share. This habit is founded in
actions originally involuntary and mechanical, and modifies after various
methods such of our actions as are voluntary.

But there are habits of a second sort. In proportion as our experience
enlarges, the subjects of voluntary action become more numerous. In
this state of the human being, he soon comes to perceive a considerable similarity between situation and situation. In consequence he feels
inclined to abridge the process of deliberation, and to act today con-
formably to the determination of yesterday. Thus the understanding
fixes for itself resting places, is no longer a novice, and is not at the
trouble continually to go back and revise the original reasons which
determined it to a course of action. Thus the man acquires habits, from
which it is very difficult to wean him, and which he obeys without
being able to assign either to himself or others, any explicit reason for
his proceeding. This is the history of prepossession and prejudice.

---

[1] This distribution is in substance the same as that of [David] Hartley [1705–57]; but
is here introduced without any attention to adopt the peculiarities of his phraseology.
Observations on Man [1749], I. iii. 21.

Let us consider how much there is of voluntary, and how much of involuntary in this species of action. Let the instance be of a man going to church today. He has been accustomed, suppose, to a certain routine of this kind from his childhood. Most undoubtedly then, in performing this function today, his motive does not singly consist of inducements present to his understanding. His feelings are not of the same nature, as those of a man who should be persuaded by a train of reasoning, to perform that function for the first time in his life. His case is partly similar to that of a scholar who has gone through a course of geometry, and who now believes the truth of the propositions upon the testimony of his memory, though the proofs are by no means present to his understanding. Thus the person in question, is partly induced to go to church by reasons which once appeared sufficient to his understanding, and the effects of which remain, though the reasons are now forgotten, or at least are not continually recollected. He goes partly for the sake of decorum, character, and to secure the goodwill of his neighbours. A part of his inducement also perhaps is, that his parents accustomed him to go to church at first, from the mere force of authority, and that the omission of a habit to which we have been formed, is apt to sit awkwardly and uneasily upon the human mind. Thus it happens that a man who should scrupulously examine his own conduct in going to church, would find great difficulty in satisfying his mind as to the precise motive, or proportion contributed by different motives, which maintained his adherence to that practice.

It is probable however that, when he goes to church, he determines that this action is right, proper or expedient, referring for the reasons which prove this rectitude or expediency, to the complex impression which remains in his mind, from the inducements that at different times inclined him to that practice. It is still more reasonable to believe that, when he sets out, there is an express volition, foresight or apprehended motive inducing him to that particular action, and that he proceeds in such a direction, because he knows it leads to the church. Now, so much of this action as proceeds from actually existing foresight and apprehended motive, it is proper to call perfectly voluntary. So much as proceeds upon a motive, out of sight, and the operation of which depends upon habit, is imperfectly voluntary.

This sort of habit however must be admitted to retain something of the nature of voluntariness for two reasons. First, it proceeds upon judgement, or apprehended motives, though the reasons of that judgement be out of sight and forgotten; at the time the individual performed the first action of the kind, his proceeding was perfectly voluntary. Secondly, the custom of language authorizes us in denominating every action as in some degree voluntary, which a volition, foresight or apprehended motive in a contrary direction, might have prevented from taking place.

Perhaps no action of a man arrived at years of maturity is, in the sense above defined, perfectly voluntary; as there is no demonstration in the higher branches of the mathematics, which contains the whole of its proof within itself, and does not depend upon former propositions, the proofs of which are not present to the mind of the learner. The subtlety of the human mind in this respect is incredible. Many single actions, if carefully analysed and traced to their remotest source, would be found to be the complex result of different motives, to the amount perhaps of some hundreds.

In the meantime it is obvious to remark, that the perfection of the human character consists in approaching as nearly as possible to the perfectly voluntary state. We ought to be upon all occasions prepared to render a reason of our actions. We should remove ourselves to the furthest distance from the state of mere inanimate machines, acted upon by causes of which they have no understanding. We should be cautious of thinking it a sufficient reason for an action, that we are accustomed to perform it, and that we once thought it right. The human understanding has so powerful a tendency to improvement, that it is more than probable that, in many instances, the arguments which once appeared to us sufficient, would upon re-examination appear inadequate and futile. We should therefore subject them to perpetual revisal. In our speculative opinions and our practical principles we should never consider the book of enquiry as shut. We should accustom ourselves not to forget the reasons that produced our determination, but be ready upon all occasions clearly to announce and fully to enumerate them.

Having thus explained the nature of human actions, involuntary, imperfectly voluntary, and voluntary, let us consider how far this explanation affects the doctrine of the present chapter. Now it should seem that the great practical political principle remains as entire as ever. Still volition and foresight, in their strict and accurate construction, are inseparable. All the most important occasions of our lives, are capable of being subjected at pleasure to a decision, as nearly as possible, perfectly voluntary. Still it remains true that, when the understanding clearly perceives rectitude, propriety and eligibility to belong to a certain conduct, and so long as it has that perception, that conduct will infallibly be adopted. A perception of truth will inevitably be produced by a clear evidence brought home to the understanding, and the constancy of the perception will be proportioned to the apprehended value of the thing perceived. Reason therefore and conviction still appear to be the proper instrument, and the sufficient instrument for regulating the actions of mankind.

Having sufficiently established the principle, that in all cases of volition we act, not from impulse, but opinion, there is a further obstacle to be removed, before this reasoning can be usefully applied to the subject of political melioration. It may be objected, by a person who should admit the force of the above arguments, 'that little was gained by this exposition to the cause it was intended to promote. Whether or no the actions of men frequently arise, as some authors have asserted, from immediate impression, it cannot however be denied that the perturbations of sense frequently seduce the judgement, and that the ideas and temporary notions they produce, are too strong for any force that can be brought against them. But, what man is now in this respect, he will always to a certain degree remain. He will always have senses, and, in spite of all the attempts which can be made to mortify them, their pleasures will always be accompanied with irritation and allurement. Hence it appears, that all ideas of vast and extraordinary improvement in man are visionary, that he will always remain in some degree the dupe of illusion, and that reason, and absolute, impartial truth, can never hope to possess him entire.'

The first observation that suggests itself upon this statement is, that the points already established tend in some degree to set this new question in a clearer light. From them it may be inferred that the contending forces of reason and sense, in the power they exercise over our conduct, at least pass through the same medium, and assume the same form. It is opinion contending with opinion, and judgement with judgement; and this consideration is not unattended with encouragement. When we discourse of the comparative powers of appetite and reason, we speak of those actions, which have the consent of the mind, and partake of the nature of voluntary. The question neither is nor deserves to be, respecting cases where no choice is exerted, and no preference shown. Every man is aware, that the cases, into which volition enters either for a part or the whole, are sufficiently numerous, to decide upon all that is most important in the events of our life. It follows therefore that, in the contention of sense and reason, it cannot be improbable to hope that the opinion which is intrinsically the best founded, shall ultimately prevail.

But let us examine a little minutely these pleasures of sense, the attractions of which are supposed to be so irresistible. In reality they are in no way enabled to maintain their hold upon us, but by means of the adscititious ornaments with which they are assiduously connected. Reduce them to their true nakedness, and they would be generally despised. Where almost is the man, who would sit down with impatient eagerness to the most splendid feast, the most exquisite viands and highly flavoured wines, 'taste after taste upheld with kindliest change,'[1] if he must sit down alone, and it were not relieved and assisted by the more exalted charms of society, conversation and mutual benevolence? Strip the commerce of the sexes of all its attendant circumstances; and the effect would be similar. Tell a man that all women, so far as sense is concerned, are nearly alike. Bid him therefore take a partner without any attention to the symmetry of her person, her vivacity, the voluptuous softness of her temper, the affectionate kindness of her feelings, her imagination or her wit. You would probably instantly convince him that the commerce itself, which by superficial observers is put for the whole, is the least important branch of the complicated consideration to which it belongs. It is probable that he who should form himself with the greatest care upon a system of solitary sensualism, would come at last to a decision not very different from that which Epicurus is said to have adopted, in favour of fresh herbs and water from the spring.

'But let it be confessed that the pleasures of sense are unimportant and trivial. It is next to be asked, whether, trifling as they are, they may not nevertheless possess a delusive and treacherous power, by means of which they may often be enabled to overcome every opposition?'

The better to determine this question, let us suppose a man to be engaged in the progressive voluptuousness of the most sensual scene. Here, if ever, we may expect sensation to be triumphant. Passion is in this case in its full career. He impatiently shuts out every consideration that may disturb his enjoyment; moral views and dissuasives can no longer obtrude themselves into his mind; he resigns himself, without power of resistance, to his predominant idea. Alas, in this situation, nothing is so easy as to extinguish his sensuality! Tell him at this moment that his father is dead, that he has lost or gained a considerable sum of money, or even perhaps that his favourite horse is stolen from the

---

[1] Milton, *Paradise Lost*, Book V.

meadow, and his whole passion shall be instantly annihilated: So vast is the power which a mere proposition possesses over the mind of man. So conscious are we of the precariousness of the fascination of the senses that upon such occasions we provide against the slightest interruption. If our little finger ached, we might probably immediately bid adieu to the empire of this supposed almighty power. . . . The only means probably, by which any man ever succeeds in indulging the pleasures of sense, in contradiction to the habitual persuasion of his judgement, is by contriving to forget everything that can be offered against them. If, notwithstanding all his endeavours, the unwished for idea intrudes, the indulgence instantly becomes impossible. Is it to be supposed that that power of sensual allurement, which must be carefully kept alive, and which the slightest accident overthrows, can be invincible only to the artillery of reason, and that the most irresistible considerations of justice, interest and happiness will never be able habitually to control it?

To consider the subject in another point of view. It seems to be a strange absurdity, to hear men assert, that the attractions of sensual pleasure are irresistible, in contradiction to the multiplied experience of all ages and countries. Are all good stories of our nature false? Did no man ever resist temptation? On the contrary, have not all the considerations which have power over our hopes, our fears, or our weaknesses been, in competition with a firm and manly virtue, employed in vain? But what has been done, may be done again. What has been done by individuals, cannot be impossible, in a widely different state of society, to be done by the whole species.

The system we are here combating, of the irresistible power of sensual allurements, has been numerously supported, and a variety of arguments has been adduced in its behalf. Among other things it has been remarked, 'that, as the human mind has no innate and original principles, so all the information it has, is derived from sensation; and everything that passes within it, is either direct impression upon our external organs, or the substance of such impressions modified and refined through certain intellectual strainers and alembics. It is therefore reasonable to conclude, that the original substance should be most powerful in its properties, and the pleasures of external sense more genuine than any other pleasure. Every sensation is, by its very nature, accompanied with the idea of pleasure or pain in a vigorous or feeble degree. The only thing which can or ought to excite desire, is happiness or agreeable sensation. It is impossible that the hand can be stretched out to obtain anything, except so far as it is considered as desirable; and to be desirable is the same thing as to have a tendency to communicate pleasure. Thus, after all the complexities of philosophy, we are brought back to this simple and irresistible proposition, that man is an animal purely sensual. Hence it follows, that in all his transactions much must depend upon immediate impression, and little is to be attributed to the generalities of ratiocination.'

All the premises in the objection here stated are unquestionably true. Man is just such an animal as the objection describes. Everything within him that has a tendency to voluntary action, is an affair of external or internal sense, and has relation to pleasure or pain. But it does not follow from hence, that the pleasures of our external organs, are more exquisite than any other pleasures. It is by no means unexampled for the result of a combination of materials to be more excellent than the materials themselves. . . . In reality the pleasures of a savage, or, which is much the same thing, of a brute, are feeble indeed compared with those of the man of civilization and refinement. Our sensual pleasures, commonly so called, would be almost universally despised, had we not the art to combine them with the pleasures of intellect and cultivation. No man ever performed an act of exalted benevolence, without having sufficient reason to know, at least so long as the sensation was present to his mind, that all the gratifications of appetite were contemptible in the comparison. That which gives the last zest to our enjoyments, is the approbation of our own minds, the consciousness that the exertion we have made, was such as was called for by impartial justice and reason; and this consciousness will be clear and satisfying in proportion as our decision in that respect is unmixed with error. Our perceptions can never be so luminous and accurate in the belief of falsehood as of truth.

The great advantage possessed by the allurements of sense is, 'that the ideas suggested by them are definite and precise, while those which deal in generalities are apt to be faint and obscure. The difference is like that between things absent and present; of the recommendations possessed by the latter we have a more vivid perception, and seem to have a better assurance of the probability of their attainment. These circumstances must necessarily, in the comparison instituted by the mind in all similar cases, to a certain degree incline the balance towards that side. Add to which, that what is present forces itself upon our attention, while that which is absent, depends for its recurrence upon the capriciousness of memory.'

But these advantages are seen upon the very face of them to be of a precarious nature. If my ideas of virtue, benevolence and justice, or whatever it is that ought to restrain me from an improper leaning to the pleasures of sense, be now less definite and precise, they may be gradually and unlimitedly improved. If I do not now sufficiently perceive all the recommendations they possess, and their clear superiority over the allurements of sense, there is surely no natural impossibility in my being made to understand a distinct proposition, or in my being fully convinced by an unanswerable argument. As to recollection, that is certainly a faculty of the mind which is capable of improvement; and the point, of which I have been once intimately convinced and have had a lively and profound impression, will not easily be forgotten when the period of action shall arrive.

It has been said 'that a rainy day will frequently convert a man of valour into a coward.' If that should be the case, there is no presumption in affirming that his courage was produced by very slight and inadequate motives. How long would a sensation of this kind be able to hold out against the idea of the benefits to arise from his valour, safety to his family and children, defeat to an unjust and formidable assailant, and freedom and felicity to be secured to his country? In reality, the atmosphere, instead of considerably affecting the mass of mankind, affects in an eminent degree only a small part of that mass. The majority are either above or below it; are either too gross to feel strongly these minute variations, or too busy to attend to them. The case is to a considerable degree the same with the rest of our animal sensations. . . .

Pain is probably more formidable in its attacks upon us, and more exquisitely felt than any species of bodily pleasure. Yet all history affords us examples, where pain has been contemned and defied by the energies of intellectual resolution. Do we not read of Mutius Scaevola who suffered his hand to be destroyed by fire without betraying any symptom of emotion, and archbishop Cranmer who endured the same trial two hundred years ago in our own country? . . . When we read such stories, we recognize in them the genuine characteristics of man. Man is not a vegetable to be governed by sensations of heat and cold, dryness and moisture. He is a reasonable creature, capable of perceiving what is eligible and right, of fixing indelibly certain principles upon his mind, and adhering inflexibly to the resolutions he has made.

Let us attend for a moment to the general result of the preceding discussions. The tendency of the whole is, to ascertain an important principle in the science of the human mind. If the arguments here adduced be admitted to be valid, it necessarily follows, that whatever can be adequately brought home to the conviction of the understanding, may be depended upon as affording a secure hold upon the conduct. We are no longer at liberty to consider man as divided between two independent principles, or to imagine that his inclinations are in any case inaccessible through the medium of his reason. We find the thinking principle within us to be uniform and simple; in consequence of which we are entitled to conclude, that it is in every respect the proper subject of education and persuasion, and is susceptible of unlimited improvement. There is no conduct, in itself reasonable, which the refutation of error, and dissipating of uncertainty, will not make appear to be such. There is no conduct which can be shown to be reasonable, the reasons of which may not sooner or later be made impressive, irresistible, and matter of habitual recollection. Lastly, there is no conduct, the reasons of which are thus conclusive and thus communicated, which will not infallibly and uniformly be adopted by the man to whom they are communicated.

It may not be improper to attend a little to the light which may be derived from these speculations upon certain maxims, almost universally received, but which, as they convey no distinct ideas, may be productive of mischief, and can scarcely be productive of good.

The first of these is, that the passions ought to be purified, but not to be eradicated. Another, conveying nearly the same lesson, but in different words, is, that passion is not to be conquered by reason, but by bringing some other passion into contention with it.

The word passion is a term extremely vague in its signification. It is used principally in three senses. It either represents the ardour and vehemence of mind with which any object is pursued; or secondly, that temporary persuasion of excellence and desirableness, which accompanies any action performed by us contrary to our more customary and usual habits of thinking; or lastly, those external modes or necessities to which the whole human species is alike subject, such as hunger, the passion between the sexes, and others. In which of these senses is the word to be understood in the maxims above stated?

In the first sense, it has sufficiently appeared that none of our sensations, or, which is the same thing, none of our ideas, are unaccompanied with a consciousness of pleasure or pain; consequently all our volitions are attended with complacence or aversion. In this sense without doubt passion cannot be eradicated; but in this sense also passion is so far from being incompatible with reason, that it is inseparable from it. Virtue, sincerity, justice, and all those principles which are begotten and cherished in us by a due exercise of reason, will never be very strenuously espoused, till they are ardently loved; that is, till their value is clearly perceived and adequately understood. In this sense nothing is necessary, but to show us that a thing is truly good and worthy to be desired, in order to excite in us a passion for its attainment. If therefore this be the meaning of passion in the above proposition, it is true that passion ought not to be eradicated, but it is equally true that it cannot be eradicated: it is true, that the only way to conquer one passion is by the introduction of another; but it is equally true that, if we employ our rational faculties, we cannot fail of thus conquering our erroneous propensities. The maxims therefore are nugatory.

In the second sense, our passions are ambition, avarice, the love of power, the love of fame, envy, revenge, and innumerable others. Miserable indeed would be our condition, if we could only expel one bad passion by another of the same kind, and there was no way of rooting out delusion from the mind, but by substituting another delusion in its place. But it has been demonstrated at large that this is not the case. Truth is not less powerful, or less friendly to ardent exertion, than error, and needs not fear its encounter. Falsehood is not, as such a principle would suppose, the only element in which the human mind can exist, so that, if the space which the mind occupies be too much rarefied and cleared, its existence or health will be in some degree injured. On the contrary, we need not fear any sinister consequences, from the subversion of error, and introducing as much truth into the mind as we can possibly accumulate. All those notions by which we are accustomed to ascribe to anything a value which it does not really possess, should be eradicated without mercy; and truth, a sound and just estimate of things, which is not less favourable to zeal or activity, should be earnestly and incessantly cultivated.

In the third sense of the word passion, as it describes the result of those circumstances which are common to the whole species, such as hunger and the propensity to the intercourse of the sexes, it seems sufficiently reasonable to say that no attempt ought to be made to eradicate them. But this sentiment was hardly worth the formality of a maxim. So far as these propensities ought to be conquered or restrained, there is no reason why this should not be effected by the due exercise of the understanding. From these illustrations it is sufficiently apparent, that the care recommended to us not to extinguish or seek to extinguish our passions, is founded in a confused or mistaken view of the subject.

Another maxim not inferior in reputation to those above recited, is that of following nature. But the term nature here, is still more loose and unintelligible than the term passion was before. If it be meant that we ought to accommodate ourselves to hunger and the other appetites which are common to our species, this is probably true. But these appetites, some of them in particular, lead to excess, and the mischief with which they are pregnant is to be corrected, not by consulting our appetites, but our reason. If it be meant that we should follow instinct, it has been proved that we have no instincts. The advocates of this maxim are apt to consider whatever now exists among mankind as inherent and perpetual, and to conclude that this is to be maintained, not in proportion as it can be shown to be reasonable, but because it is natural. Thus it has been said, that man is naturally a religious animal, and for this reason, and not in proportion to our power of demonstrating the being of a God or the truth of Christianity, religion is to be maintained. Thus again it has been called natural, that men should form themselves into immense tribes or nations, and go to war with each other. Thus persons of narrow views and observation, regard everything as natural and right, that happens, however capriciously or for however short a time, to prevail in the society in which they live. The only things which can be said to compose the nature or constitution of man, are our external structure, which itself is capable of being modified with indefinite variety; the appetites and impressions growing out of that structure; and the capacity of combining ideas and inferring conclusions. The appetites common to the species we cannot wholly destroy: the faculty of reason it would be absurd systematically to counteract, since it is only by some sort of reasoning, bad or good, that we can so much as adopt any system. In this sense therefore no doubt we ought to follow nature, that is, to employ our understandings and increase our discernment. But, by conforming ourselves to the principles of our constitution in this respect, we most effectually exclude all following, or implicit assent. If we would fully comport ourselves in a manner correspondent to our properties and powers, we must bring everything to the standard of reason. Nothing must be admitted either as principle or precept, that will not support this trial. Nothing must be sustained, because it is ancient, because we have been accustomed to regard it as sacred, or because it has been unusual to bring its validity into question. Finally, if by following nature, be understood that we must fix our preference upon things that will conduce to human happiness, in this there is some truth. But the truth it contains, is extremely darkened by the phraseology in which it is couched. We must consider our external structure, so far as relates to the mere question of our preservation. As to the rest, whatever will make a reasonable nature happy will make us happy; and our preference ought to be bestowed upon that species of pleasure which has most independence and most animation.

The corollaries respecting political truth, deducible from the simple proposition, which seems clearly established by the reasonings of the present chapter, that the voluntary actions of men are in all instances conformable to the deductions of their understanding, are of the highest importance. Hence we may infer what are the hopes and prospects of human improvement. The doctrine which may be founded upon these principles, may perhaps best be expressed in the five following propositions: Sound reasoning and truth, when adequately communicated, must always be victorious over error: Sound reasoning and truth are capable of being so communicated: Truth is omnipotent: The vices and moral weakness of man are not invincible: Man is perfectible, or in other words susceptible of perpetual improvement.

These propositions will be found in part synonymous with each other. But the time of the enquirer will not be unprofitably spent, in copiously clearing up the foundations of moral and political system. It is extremely beneficial that truth should be viewed on all sides, and examined under different aspects. The propositions are even little more than so many different modes of stating the principal topic of this chapter. But, if they will not admit each of a distinct train of arguments in its support, it may not however be useless to bestow upon each a short illustration.

The first of these propositions is so evident, that it needs only be stated, in order to the being universally admitted. Is there anyone who can imagine that, when sound argument and sophistry are fairly brought into comparison, the victory can be doubtful? Sophistry may assume a plausible appearance, and contrive to a certain extent to bewilder the understanding. But it is one of the prerogatives of truth, to follow it in its mazes and strip it of disguise. Nor does any difficulty from this consideration, interfere with the establishment of the present proposition. We suppose truth not merely to be exhibited, but adequately communicated; that is in other words, distinctly apprehended by the person to whom it is addressed. In this case the victory is too sure to admit of being controverted by the most inveterate scepticism.

The second proposition is, that sound reasoning and truth are capable of being adequately communicated by one man to another. This proposition may be understood of such communication, either as it affects the individual, or the species. First of the individual.

In order to its due application in this point of view, opportunity for the communication must necessarily be supposed. The incapacity of human intellect at present, requires that this opportunity should be of long duration or repeated recurrence. We do not always know how to communicate all the evidence we are capable of communicating, in a single conversation, and much less in a single instant. But, if the communicator be sufficiently master of his subject, and if the truth be altogether on his side, he must ultimately succeed in his undertaking. We suppose him to have sufficient urbanity to conciliate the goodwill, and sufficient energy to engage the attention, of the party concerned. In that case, there is no prejudice, no blind reverence for established systems, no false fear of the inferences to be drawn, that can resist him. He will encounter these one after the other, and he will encounter them with success. Our prejudices, our undue reverence, and imaginary fears, flow out of some views the mind has been induced to entertain; they are founded in the belief of some propositions. But every one of these propositions is capable of being refuted. The champion we describe, proceeds from point to point; if in any his success have been doubtful, that he will retrace and put out of the reach of mistake; and it is evidently impossible that with such qualifications and such perseverance he should not ultimately accomplish his purpose.

Such is the appearance which this proposition assumes when examined in a loose and practical view. In strict consideration it will not admit of debate. Man is a rational being. If there be any man who is incapable of making inferences for himself, or of understanding, when stated in the most explicit terms, the inferences of another, him we consider as an abortive production, and not in strictness belonging to the human species. It is absurd therefore to say that sound reasoning and truth cannot be communicated by one man to another. Whenever in any case he fails, it is that he is not sufficiently laborious, patient and clear. We suppose of course the person who undertakes to communicate the truth, really to possess it, and be master of his subject; for it is scarcely worth an observation to say, that that which he has not himself, he cannot communicate to another.

If truth therefore can be brought home to the conviction of the individual, let us see how it stands with the public or the world. Now in the first place, it is extremely clear that, if no individual can resist the force of truth, it can only be necessary to apply this proposition from individual to individual, and we shall at length comprehend the whole. Thus the affirmation in its literal sense is completely established.

With respect to the chance of success, this will depend, first, upon the precluding all extraordinary convulsions of nature, and after this upon the activity and energy of those to whose hands the sacred cause of truth may be entrusted. It is apparent that, if justice be done to its merits, it includes in it the indestructible germ of ultimate victory. Every new convert that is made to its cause, if he be taught its excellence as well as its reality, is a fresh apostle to extend its illuminations through a wider sphere. In this respect it resembles the motion of a falling body, which increases its rapidity in proportion to the squares of the distances. Add to which, that, when a convert to truth has been adequately informed, it is barely possible that he should ever fail in his adherence; whereas error contains in it the principle of its own mortality. Thus the advocates of falsehood and mistake must continually diminish, and the well-informed adherents of truth incessantly multiply.

It has sometimes been affirmed that, whenever a question is ably brought forward for examination, the decision of the human species must ultimately be on the right side. But this proposition is to be understood with allowances. Civil policy, magnificent emoluments and sinister motives may upon many occasions, by distracting the attention, cause the worse reason to pass as if it were the better. . . . Perhaps it will be said that, though the effects of truth may be obscured for a time, they will break out in the sequel with double lustre. But this at least depends upon circumstances. No comet must come in the meantime, and sweep away the human species: no Attila must have it in his power once again to lead back the flood of barbarism to deluge the civilized world: and the disciples, or at least the books of the original champions must remain, or their discoveries and demonstrations must be nearly lost to the world.

The third of the propositions enumerated is, that truth is omnipotent. This proposition, which is convenient for its brevity, must be understood with limitations. It would be absurd to affirm that truth, unaccompanied by the evidence which proves it to be such, or when that evidence is partially and imperfectly stated, has any such property. But it has sufficiently appeared from the arguments already adduced, that truth, when adequately communicated, is, so far as relates to the conviction of the understanding, irresistible. There may indeed be propositions, which, though true in themselves, may be beyond the sphere of human knowledge, or respecting which human beings have not yet discovered sufficient arguments for their support. In that case, though true in themselves, they are not truths to us. The reasoning by which they are attempted to be established, is not sound reasoning. It may perhaps be found that the human mind is not capable of arriving at absolute certainty upon any subject of enquiry; and it must be admitted that human science is attended with all degrees of certainty, from the highest moral evidence to the slightest balance of probability. But human beings are capable of apprehending and weighing all these degrees; and to know the exact quantity of probability which I ought to ascribe to any proposition, may be said to be in one sense the possessing certain knowledge. It would further be absurd, if we regard truth in relation to its empire over our conduct, to suppose that it is not limited in its operations by the faculties of our frame. It may be compared to a connoisseur, who, however consummate be his talents, can extract from a given instrument only such tones as that instrument will afford. But, within these limits, the deduction which forms the principal substance of this chapter, proves to us, that whatever is brought home to the conviction of the understanding, so long as it is present to the mind, possesses an undisputed empire over the conduct. Nor will he who is sufficiently conversant with the science of intellect, be hasty in assigning the bounds of our capacity. There are some things which the structure of our bodies will render us for ever unable to effect; but in many cases the lines, which appear to prescribe a term to our efforts, will, like the mists that arise from a lake, retire further and further, the more closely we endeavour to approach them.

Fourthly, the vices and moral weakness of man are not invincible. This is the preceding proposition with a very slight variation in the statement. Vice and weakness are founded upon ignorance and error; but truth is more powerful than any champion that can be brought into the field against it; consequently truth has the faculty of expelling weakness and vice, and placing nobler and more beneficent principles in their stead.

Lastly, man is perfectible. This proposition needs some explanation.

By perfectible, it is not meant that he is capable of being brought to perfection. But the word seems sufficiently adapted to express the faculty of being continually made better and receiving perpetual improvement; and in this sense it is here to be understood. The term perfectible, thus explained, not only does not imply the capacity of being brought to perfection, but stands in express opposition to it. If we could arrive at perfection, there would be an end to our improvement. There is however one thing of great importance that it does imply: every perfection or excellence that human beings are competent to conceive, human beings, unless in cases that are palpably and unequivocally excluded by the structure of their frame, are competent to attain.

This is an inference which immediately follows from the omnipotence of truth. Every truth that is capable of being communicated, is capable of being brought home to the conviction of the mind. Every principle which can be brought home to the conviction of the mind, will infallibly produce a correspondent effect upon the conduct. If there were not something in the nature of man incompatible with absolute perfection, the doctrine of the omnipotence of truth would afford no small probability that he would one day reach it. Why is the perfection of man impossible?

The idea of absolute perfection is scarcely within the grasp of human understanding. If science were more familiarized to speculations of this sort, we should perhaps discover that the notion itself was pregnant with absurdity and contradiction.

It is not necessary in this argument to dwell upon the limited nature of the human faculties. We can neither be present to all places nor to all times. We cannot penetrate into the essences of things, or rather we have no sound and satisfactory knowledge of things external to ourselves, but merely of our own sensations. We cannot discover the causes of things, or ascertain that in the antecedent which connects it with the consequent, and discern nothing but their contiguity.[1] With what pretence can a being thus shut in on all sides lay claim to absolute perfection?

But, not to insist upon these considerations, there is one principle in the human mind, which must for ever exclude us from arriving at a close of our acquisitions, and confine us to perpetual progress. The human mind, so far as we are acquainted with it, is nothing else but a faculty of perception. All our knowledge, all our ideas, everything we possess as intelligent beings, comes from impression. All the minds that exist, set out from absolute ignorance. They received first one impression, and then a second. As the impressions became more numerous,

[1] IV. vii.

and were stored by the help of memory, and combined by the faculty of association, so the experience increased, and with the experience the knowledge, the wisdom, everything that distinguishes man from what we understand by a 'clod of the valley.' This seems to be a simple and incontrovertible history of intellectual being; and, if it be true, then as our accumulations have been incessant in the time that is gone, so as long as we continue to perceive, to remember or reflect, they must perpetually increase.

CHAPTER VI

OF THE INFLUENCE OF CLIMATE

Two points further are necessary to be illustrated, in order to render our view of man in his social capacity impartial and complete. There are certain physical causes which have commonly been supposed to oppose an immovable barrier to the political improvement of our species: climate, which is imagined to render the introduction of liberal principles upon this subject in some cases impossible: and luxury, which, in addition to this disqualification, precludes their revival even in countries where they had once most eminently flourished.

An answer to both these objections is included in what has been offered upon the subject of the voluntary actions of man. If truth, when properly displayed, be omnipotent, then neither climate nor luxury are invincible obstacles. But so much stress has been laid upon these topics, and they have been so eloquently enforced by poets and men like poets, that it seems necessary to bestow upon them a distinct examination.

'It is impossible,' say some, 'to establish a system of political liberty in certain warm and effeminate climates.' To enable us to judge of the reasonableness of this affirmation, let us consider what process would be necessary in order to introduce political liberty into any country.

The answer to this question is to be found in the answer to that other, whether freedom have any real and solid advantages over slavery? If it have, then our mode of proceeding respecting it, ought to be exactly parallel to that we should employ in recommending any other benefit. If I would persuade a man to accept a great estate, supposing that possession to be a real advantage; if I would induce him to select for his companion a beautiful and accomplished woman, or for his friend a wise, a brave and disinterested man; if I would persuade him to prefer ease to pain, and gratification to torture, what more is necessary, than that I should inform his understanding, and make him see these things in their true and genuine colours? Should I find it necessary to enquire first of what climate he was a native, and whether that were favourable to the possession of a great estate, a fine woman, or a generous friend?

The advantages of liberty over slavery are not less real, though unfortunately they have been made less palpable in their application to the welfare of communities at large, than the advantages to accrue in the cases above enumerated. Every man has a confused sense of the real state of the question; but he has been taught to believe that men would tear each other to pieces, if they had not priests to direct their consciences, lords to consult for their tranquillity, and kings to pilot them in safety through the dangers of the political ocean. But whether they be misled by these or other prejudices, whatever be the fancied terror that induces them quietly to submit to have their hands bound behind them, and the scourge vibrated over their heads, all these are questions of reason. Truth may be presented to them in such irresistible evidence, perhaps by such just degrees familiarized to their apprehension, as ultimately to conquer the most obstinate prepossessions. . . . It is the property of truth to spread; and, exclusively of any powerful counteraction, its advocates in each succeeding year will be somewhat more numerous than in that which went before. The causes, which suspend its progress, arise, not from climate, but from the watchful and intolerant jealousy of despotic sovereigns.—What is here stated is in fact little more than a branch of the principle which has been so generally recognized, 'that government is founded in opinion.'[1]

.   .   .   .

The result of these reasonings is of the utmost importance to him who speculates upon principles of government. There have been writers on this subject who, admitting, and even occasionally declaiming with enthusiasm upon the advantages of liberty and the equal claims of mankind to every social benefit, have yet concluded, 'that the corruptions of despotism, and the usurpations of aristocracy, were congenial to certain ages and divisions of the world, and under proper limitations entitled to our approbation.' But this hypothesis will be found unable to endure the test of serious reflection. There is no

---

[1] Hume, *Essays, Moral and Political*, I. iv.

state of mankind that renders them incapable of the exercise of reason. There is no period in which it is necessary to hold the human species in a condition of pupilage. If there were, it would seem but reasonable that their superintendents and guardians, as in the case of infants of another sort, should provide for the means of their subsistence without calling upon them for the exertions of their own understanding. Wherever men are competent to look the first duties of humanity in the face, and to provide for their defence against the invasions of hunger and the inclemencies of the sky, it can scarcely be thought that they are not equally capable of every other exertion that may be essential to their security and welfare.

The real enemies of liberty in any country are not the people, but those higher orders who find their imaginary profit in a contrary system. Infuse just views of society into a certain number of the liberally educated and reflecting members; give to the people guides and instructors; and the business is done. This however is not to be accomplished but in a gradual manner, as will more fully appear in the sequel. The error lies, not in tolerating the worst forms of government for a time, but in supposing a change impracticable, and not incessantly looking forward to its accomplishment.

CHAPTER VII

OF THE INFLUENCE OF LUXURY

THE second objection to the principles already established, is derived from the influence of luxury, and affirms, 'that nations, like individuals, are subject to the phenomena of youth and old age, and that, when a people by effeminacy and depravation of manners have sunk into decrepitude, it is not within the compass of human ability to restore them to vigour and innocence.'

This idea has been partly founded upon the romantic notions of pastoral life and the golden age. Innocence is not virtue. Virtue demands the active employment of an ardent mind in the promotion of the general good. No man can be eminently virtuous, who is not accustomed to an extensive range of reflection. He must see all the benefits to arise from a disinterested proceeding, and must understand the proper method of producing those benefits. Ignorance, the slothful habits and limited views of uncultivated life, have not in them more of true virtue, though they may be more harmless, than luxury, vanity and extravagance. Individuals of exquisite feeling, whose disgust has been excited by the hardened selfishness or the unblushing corruption which have prevailed in their own times, have recurred in imagination to the forests of Norway or the bleak and uncomfortable Highlands of Scotland in search of a purer race of mankind. This imagination has been the offspring of disappointment, not the dictate of reason and philosophy.

It may be true, that ignorance is nearer than prejudice to the reception of wisdom, and that the absence of virtue is a condition more auspicious, than the presence of its opposite. In this case it would have been juster to compare a nation sunk in luxury, to an individual with confirmed habits of wrong, than to an individual whom a debilitated constitution was bringing fast to the grave. But neither would that comparison have been fair and equitable.

.   .   .   .   .

. . . the power of reasonable and just ideas in changing the character of nations, is in one respect infinitely greater than any power which can be brought to bear upon a solitary individual. The case is not of that customary sort, where the force of theory alone is tried in curing any person of his errors; but is as if he should be placed in an entirely new situation. His habits are broken through, and his motives of action changed. Instead of being perpetually recalled to vicious practices by the recurrence of his former connections, the whole society receives an impulse, from the same cause that acts upon the individual. New ideas are suggested, and the languor and imbecility which might be incident to each, are counteracted by the spectacle of general enthusiasm and concert.

.   .   .   .

CHAPTER VIII

HUMAN INVENTIONS SUSCEPTIBLE OF
PERPETUAL IMPROVEMENT

BEFORE we proceed to the direct subject of the present enquiry, it may not be improper to resume the subject of human improvableness, and consider it in a somewhat greater detail. An opinion has been extensively entertained, 'that the differences of the human species in different ages and countries, particularly so far as relates to moral principles of conduct, are extremely insignificant and trifling; that we are deceived in this respect by distance and confounded by glare; but that in reality the virtues and vices of men, collectively taken, always have remained, and of consequence,' it is said, 'always will remain, nearly at the same point.'

The erroneousness of this opinion will perhaps be more completely exposed, by a summary recollection of the actual history of our species, than by the closest deductions of abstract reason. We will in this place simply remind the reader of the great changes which man has undergone as an intellectual being, entitling us to infer the probability of improvements not less essential, to be realized in future. The conclusion to be deduced from this delineation, that his moral improvements will in some degree keep pace with his intellectual, and his actions correspond with his opinions, must depend for its force upon the train of reasoning which has already been brought forward under that head.[1]

.   .   .   .

One of the acquisitions most evidently requisite as a preliminary to our present improvements, is that of language. But it is impossible to conceive an acquisition, that must have been in its origin more different from what at present it is found, or that less promised that copiousness and refinement it has since exhibited.

Its beginning was probably from those involuntary cries, which infants, for example, are found to utter in the earliest stages of their existence, and which, previously to the idea of exciting pity or procuring assistance, spontaneously arise from the operation of pain upon our animal frame. . . . But the distance is extreme from these simple modes of communication, which we possess in common with some of the inferior animals, to all the analysis and abstraction which languages require.

Abstraction indeed, though, as it is commonly understood, it be one of the sublimest operations of mind, is in some sort coeval with and inseparable from the existence of mind.[2] The next step to simple

[1] Ch. v.

[2] The question, whether or not the human mind is capable of forming abstract ideas, has been the subject of much profound and serious disquisition. It is certain that we have a general standard of some sort, in consequence of which, if an animal is presented to our view, we can in most cases decide that it is, or is not, a horse, a man, etc.; nor is it to be

perception is that of comparison, or the coupling together of two ideas and the perception of their resemblances and differences. Without comparison there can be no preference, and without preference no voluntary action: though it must be acknowledged, that this comparison is an operation which may be performed by the mind without adverting to its nature, and that neither the brute nor the savage has a consciousness of the several steps of the intellectual progress. Comparison immediately leads to imperfect abstraction. The sensation of today is classed, if similar, with the sensation of yesterday, and an inference is made respecting the conduct to be adopted. Without this degree of abstraction, the faint dawnings of language already described, could never have existed. Abstraction, which was necessary to the first existence of language, is again assisted in its operations by language. That generalization, which is implied in the very notion of a thinking being, being

imagined that we should be unable to form such judgements, even if we were denied the use of speech.

It is a curious fact, and on that account worthy to be mentioned in this place, that the human mind is perhaps incapable of entertaining any but general ideas. Take, for example, a wine-glass. If, after this glass is withdrawn, I present to you another from the same set, you will probably be unable to determine whether it is another or the same. It is with a like inattention that people in general view a flock of sheep. The shepherd only distinguishes the features of every one of his sheep from the features of every other. But it is impossible so to individualize our remarks, as to cause our idea to be truly particular, and not special. Thus there are memorable instances of one man so nearly resembling another, as to be able to pass himself upon the wife and all the relatives of this man, as if he were the same.

The opposition which has been so ingeniously maintained against the doctrine of abstract ideas, seems chiefly to have arisen from a habit of using the term idea, not, as Locke has done, for every conception that can exist in the mind, but as constantly descriptive of an image, or picture. The following view of the subject will perhaps serve in some degree to remove any ambiguity that might continue to rest upon it.

Ideas, considering that term as comprehending all perceptions, both primary, or of the senses, and secondary, or of the memory, may be divided into four classes: 1. perfect. The existence of these we have disproved. 2. imperfect, such as those which are produced in us by a near and careful inspection of any visible object. 3. imperfect, such as those produced by a slight and distant view. 4. imperfect, so as to have no resemblance to an image of any external object. The perception produced in us in slight and current discourse by the words, river, field, are of this nature; and have no more resemblance to the image of any visible object, than the perception ordinarily produced in us by the words, conquest, government, virtue.

The subject of this last class of ideas is very ingeniously treated by Burke, in his *Enquiry into the Sublime*, Part V [1756]. He has however committed one material error in the discussion, by representing these as instances of the employment of 'words without ideas'. If we recollect that brutes have similar abstractions, and a general conception, of the female of their own species, of man, of food, of the smart of a whip, etc. we shall probably admit that such perceptions (and in all events they are perceptions, or, according to the established language upon the subject, ideas) are not necessarily connected with the employment of words.

thus embodied and rendered a matter of sensible impression, makes the mind acquainted with its own powers, and creates a restless desire after further progress.

. . . .

A second invention, well calculated to impress us with a sense of the progressive nature of man, is that of alphabetical writing. Hieroglyphical or picture-writing appears at some time to have been universal, and the difficulty of conceiving the gradation from this to alphabetical is so great, as to have induced Hartley, one of the most acute philosophical writers, to have recourse to miraculous interposition as the only adequate solution. In reality no problem can be imagined more operose, than that of decomposing the sounds of words into four and twenty simple elements or letters, and again finding these elements in all other words. . . .

. . . .

Let us however suppose man to have gained the two first elements of knowledge, speaking and writing; let us trace him through all his subsequent improvements, through whatever constitutes the inequality between Newton and the ploughman, and indeed much more than this, since the most ignorant ploughman in civilized society is infinitely different from what he would have been, when stripped of all the benefits he has derived from literature and the arts. Let us survey the earth covered with the labours of man, houses, enclosures, harvests, manufactures, instruments, machines, together with all the wonders of painting, poetry, eloquence and philosophy.

. . . Is it possible for us to contemplate what [man] has already done, without being impressed with a strong presentiment of the improvements he has yet to accomplish? There is no science that is not capable of additions; there is no art that may not be carried to a still higher perfection. If this be true of all other sciences, why not of morals? If this be true of all others arts, why not of social institution? The very conception of this as possible, is in the highest degree encouraging. If we can still further demonstrate it to be a part of the natural and regular progress of mind, our confidence and our hopes will then be complete. This is the temper with which we ought to engage in the study of political truth. Let us look back, that we may profit by the experience of mankind; but let us not look back, as if the wisdom of our ancestors was such, as to leave no room for future improvement.

BOOK II

PRINCIPLES OF SOCIETY

CHAPTER I

INTRODUCTION

In the preceding book we have cleared the foundations for the remaining branches of enquiry, and shown what are the prospects it is reasonable to entertain as to future political improvement. The effects which are produced by positive institutions, have there been delineated, as well as the extent of the powers of man, considered in his social capacity. It is time that we proceed to those disquisitions which are more immediately the object of the present work.

Political enquiry may be distributed under two heads: first, what are the regulations which will conduce to the well-being of man in society; and, secondly, what is the authority which is competent to prescribe regulations.

The regulations to which the conduct of men living in society ought to be conformed, may be considered in two ways: first, those moral laws which are enjoined upon us by the dictates of enlightened reason; and, secondly, those principles a deviation from which the interest of the community may be supposed to render it proper to repress by sanctions and punishment.

Morality is that system of conduct which is determined by a consideration of the greatest general good: he is entitled to the highest moral approbation, whose conduct is, in the greatest number of instances, or in the most momentous instances, governed by views of benevolence, and made subservient to public utility. In like manner the only regulations which any political authority can be justly entitled to enforce, are such as are best adapted to public utility. Consequently, just political regulations are nothing more than a certain select part of moral law. The supreme power in a state ought not, in the strictest sense, to require anything of its members, that an understanding suffi-ciently enlightened would not prescribe without such interference.[1]

These considerations seem to lead to the detection of a mistake which has been very generally committed, by political writers of our own country. They have for the most part confined their researches to the question of What is a just political authority or the most eligible form of government, consigning to others the delineation of right principles of conduct and equitable regulations. But there appears to be something preposterous in this mode of proceeding. A well-constituted govern-ment is only the means for enforcing suitable regulations. One form of government is preferable to another in exact proportion to the security it affords, that nothing shall be done in the name of the community, which is not conducive to the welfare of the whole. The question therefore, What it is which is thus conducive, is upon every account entitled to the first place in our disquisitions.

One of the ill consequences which have resulted from this distorted view of the science of politics, is a notion very generally entertained, that a community, or society of men, has a right to lay down whatever rules it may think proper for its own observance. This will presently be proved to be an erroneous position.[2] It may be prudent in an individual to submit in some cases to the usurpation of a majority; it may be unavoidable in a community to proceed upon the imperfect and erroneous views they shall chance to entertain: but this is a mis-fortune entailed upon us by the nature of government, and not a matter of right.[3]

A second ill consequence that has arisen from this proceeding, is that, politics having been thus violently separated from morality, govern-ment itself has no longer been compared with its true criterion. Instead of enquiring what species of government was most conducive to the public welfare, an unprofitable disquisition has been instituted respecting the probable origin of government; and its different forms have been estimated, not by the consequences with which they were pregnant, but the source from which they sprung. Hence men have been prompted to look back to the folly of their ancestors, rather than forward to the benefits derivable from the improvements of human knowledge. Hence, in investigating their rights, they have recurred less to the great principles of morality, than to the records and charters of a barbarous age. As if men were not entitled to all the benefits of the social state, till they could prove their inheriting them from some bequest of their

[1] III. v.   [2] II. v.   [3] II. v.

distant progenitors. As if men were not as justifiable and meritorious, in planting liberty in a soil in which it had never existed, as in restoring it where it could be proved only to have suffered a temporary suspension.

The reasons here assigned, strongly tend to evince the necessity of establishing the genuine principles of society, before we enter upon the direct consideration of government. It may be proper in this place to state the fundamental distinction which exists between these topics of enquiry. Men associated at first for the sake of mutual assistance. They did not foresee that any restraint would be necessary, to regulate the conduct of individual members of the society, towards each other, or towards the whole. The necessity of restraint grew out of the errors and perverseness of a few. An acute writer has expressed this idea with peculiar felicity. 'Society and government,' says he, 'are different in themselves, and have different origins. Society is produced by our wants, and government by our wickedness. Society is in every state a blessing; government even in its best state but a necessary evil.'[1]

CHAPTER II

OF JUSTICE

FROM what has been said it appears, that the subject of our present enquiry is strictly speaking a department of the science of morals. Morality is the source from which its fundamental axioms must be drawn, and they will be made somewhat clearer in the present instance, if we assume the term justice as a general appellation for all moral duty.

That this appellation is sufficiently expressive of the subject will appear, if we examine mercy, gratitude, temperance, or any of those duties which, in looser speaking, are contradistinguished from justice. Why should I pardon this criminal, remunerate this favour, or abstain from this indulgence? If it partake of the nature of morality, it must be either right or wrong, just or unjust. It must tend to the benefit of the individual, either without trenching upon, or with actual advantage to the mass of individuals. Either way it benefits the whole, because individuals are parts of the whole. Therefore to do it is just, and to forbear it is unjust.—By justice I understand that impartial treatment of every man in matters that relate to his happiness, which is measured

---

[1] Thomas Paine, *Common Sense*, p. 1.

solely by a consideration of the properties of the receiver, and the capacity of him that bestows. Its principle therefore is, according to a well-known phrase, to be 'no respecter of persons.'

Considerable light will probably be thrown upon our investigation, if, quitting for the present the political view, we examine justice merely as it exists among individuals. Justice is a rule of conduct originating in the connection of one percipient being with another. A comprehensive maxim which has been laid down upon the subject is, 'that we should love our neighbour as ourselves.' But this maxim, though possessing considerable merit as a popular principle, is not modelled with the strictness of philosophical accuracy.

In a loose and general view I and my neighbour are both of us men; and of consequence entitled to equal attention. But, in reality, it is probable that one of us, is a being of more worth and importance than the other. A man is of more worth than a beast; because, being possessed of higher faculties, he is capable of a more refined and genuine happiness. In the same manner the illustrious archbishop of Cambray was of more worth than his valet, and there are few of us that would hesitate to pronounce, if his palace were in flames, and the life of only one of them could be preserved, which of the two ought to be preferred.

But there is another ground of preference, beside the private consideration of one of them being further removed from the state of a mere animal. We are not connected with one or two percipient beings, but with a society, a nation, and in some sense with the whole family of mankind. Of consequence that life ought to be preferred which will be most conducive to the general good. In saving the life of Fenelon,[1] suppose at the moment he conceived the project of his immortal *Telemachus*, I should have been promoting the benefit of thousands, who have been cured by the perusal of that work, of some error, vice and consequent unhappiness. Nay, my benefit would extend further than this; for every individual, thus cured, has become a better member of society, and has contributed in his turn to the happiness, information and improvement of others.

Suppose I had been myself the valet; I ought to have chosen to die, rather than Fenelon should have died. The life of Fenelon was really preferable to that of the valet. But understanding is the faculty that perceives the truth of this and similar propositions; and justice is the principle that regulates my conduct accordingly. It would have been

---

[1] [François de Salignac de la Mothe Fenelon, 1651–1715. *Telemachus* was published in 1699.]

just in the valet to have preferred the archbishop to himself. To have done otherwise would have been a breach of justice.[1]

Suppose the valet had been my brother, my father or my benefactor.[2] This would not alter the truth of the proposition. The life of Fenelon would still be more valuable than that of the valet; and justice, pure, unadulterated justice, would still have preferred that which was most valuable. Justice would have taught me to save the life of Fenelon at the expense of the other. What magic is there in the pronoun 'my,' that should justify us in overturning the decisions of impartial truth? My brother or my father may be a fool or a profligate, malicious, lying or dishonest. If they be, of what consequence is it that they are mine?

'But to my father I am indebted for existence; he supported me in the helplessness of infancy.' When he first subjected himself to the necessity of these cares, he was probably influenced by no particular motives of benevolence to his future offspring. Every voluntary benefit however entitles the bestower to some kindness and retribution. Why? Because a voluntary benefit is an evidence of benevolent intention, that is, in a certain degree, of virtue. It is the disposition of the mind, not the external action separately taken, that entitles to respect. But the merit of this disposition is equal, whether the benefit were conferred upon me or upon another. I and another man cannot both be right in preferring our respective benefactors, for my benefactor cannot be at the same time both better and worse than his neighbour. My benefactor ought to be esteemed, not because he bestowed a benefit upon me, but because he bestowed it upon a human being. His desert will be in exact proportion to the degree, in which that human being was worthy of the distinction conferred.

Thus every view of the subject brings us back to the consideration of my neighbour's moral worth, and his importance to the general weal, as the only standard to determine the treatment to which he is entitled. Gratitude therefore, if by gratitude we understand a sentiment of preference which I entertain towards another, upon the ground of my having been the subject of his benefits, is no part either of justice or virtue.[3]

[1] The question, how far impartial justice is a motive capable of operating upon the mind, will be found examined at length, IV. x.

[2] [Throughout this discussion Godwin used, in the first edition, 'mother', 'sister', and 'chambermaid' where now appear 'father', 'brother', and 'valet' respectively.]

[3] This argument is stated with great clearness, in an *Essay on the Nature of True Virtue* [1765], by Jonathan Edwards, author of a celebrated work on the Freedom of the Will.

It may be objected, 'that my relation, my companion, or my benefactor, will of course in many instances obtain an uncommon portion
of my regard: for, not being universally capable of discriminating the
comparative worth of different men, I shall inevitably judge most
favourably of him, of whose virtues I have received the most unquestionable proofs; and thus shall be compelled to prefer the man of
moral worth whom I know, to another who may possess, unknown
to me, an essential superiority.'

This compulsion however is founded only in the imperfection of
human nature. It may serve as an apology for my error, but can never
change error into truth. It will always remain contrary to the strict
and universal decisions of justice. The difficulty of conceiving this,
is owing merely to our confounding the disposition from which an
action is chosen, with the action itself. The disposition, that would
prefer virtue to vice, and a greater degree of virtue to a less, is undoubtedly a subject of approbation; the erroneous exercise of this
disposition, by which a wrong object is selected, if unavoidable, is to
be deplored, but can by no colouring and under no denomination be
converted into right.[1]

It may in the second place be objected, 'that a mutual commerce of
benefits tends to increase the mass of benevolent action, and that to
increase the mass of benevolent action is to contribute to the general
good.' Indeed! Is the general good promoted by falsehood, by treating
a man of one degree of worth, as if he had ten times that worth? or as
if he were in any degree different from what he really is? Would not
the most beneficial consequences result from a different plan; from my
constantly and carefully enquiring into the deserts of all those with
whom I am connected, and from their being sure, after a certain
allowance for the fallibility of human judgement, of being treated by
me exactly as they deserved? Who can describe the benefits that would
result from such a plan of conduct, if universally adopted?

It would perhaps tend to make the truth in this respect more
accurately understood, to consider that, whereas the received morality
teaches me to be grateful, whether in affection or in act, for benefits
conferred on myself, the reasonings here delivered, without removing
the tie upon me from personal benefits (except where benefit is conferred from an unworthy motive), multiply the obligation, and enjoin
me to be also grateful for benefits conferred upon others. My obligation
towards my benefactor, supposing his benefit to be justly conferred,

[1] Ch. iv.

is in no sort dissolved; nor can anything authorize me to supersede it, but the requisition of a superior duty. That which ties me to my benefactor, upon these principles, is the moral worth he has displayed; and it will frequently happen that I shall be obliged to yield him the preference, because, while other competitors may be of greater worth, the evidence I have of the worth of my benefactor is more complete.

There seems to be more truth, in the argument, derived chiefly from the prevailing modes of social existence, in favour of my providing, in ordinary cases, for my wife and children, my brothers and relations, before I provide for strangers, than in those which have just been examined. As long as the providing for individuals is conducted with its present irregularity and caprice, it seems as if there must be a certain distribution of the class needing superintendence and supply, among the class affording it; that each man may have his claim and resource. But this argument is to be admitted with great caution. It belongs only to ordinary cases; and cases of a higher order, or a more urgent necessity, will perpetually occur, in competition with which these will be altogether impotent. We must be severely scrupulous in measuring the quantity of supply; and, with respect to money in particular, should remember how little is yet understood of the true mode of employing it for the public benefit.

Nothing can be less exposed to reasonable exception than these principles. If there be such a thing as virtue, it must be placed in a conformity to truth, and not to error. It cannot be virtuous, that I should esteem a man, that is, consider him as possessed of estimable qualities, when in reality he is destitute of them. It surely cannot conduce to the benefit of mankind, that each man should have a different standard of moral judgement and preference, and that the standard of all should vary from that of reality. Those who teach this, impose the deepest disgrace upon virtue. They assert in other words, that, when men cease to be deceived, when the film is removed from their eyes, and they see things as they are, they will cease to be either good or happy. Upon the system opposite to theirs, the soundest criterion of virtue is, to put ourselves in the place of an impartial spectator, of an angelic nature, suppose, beholding us from an elevated station, and uninfluenced by our prejudices, conceiving what would be his estimate of the intrinsic circumstances of our neighbour, and acting accordingly.[1]

---

[1] [Later in life Godwin had more to say about the Fenelon case and its implications. See pp. 325 f.]

Having considered the persons with whom justice is conversant, let us next enquire into the degree in which we are obliged to consult the good of others. And here, upon the very same reasons, it will follow, that it is just I should do all the good in my power. Does a person in distress apply to me for relief? It is my duty to grant it, and I commit a breach of duty in refusing. If this principle be not of universal application, it is because, in conferring a benefit upon an individual, I may in some instances inflict an injury of superior magnitude upon myself or society. Now the same justice, that binds me to any individual of my fellow-men, binds me to the whole. If, while I confer a benefit upon one man, it appear, in striking an equitable balance, that I am injuring the whole, my action ceases to be right, and becomes absolutely wrong. But how much am I bound to do for the general weal, that is, for the benefit of the individuals of whom the whole is composed? Everything in my power. To the neglect of the means of my own existence? No; for I am myself a part of the whole. Beside, it will rarely happen that the project of doing for others everything in my power, will not demand for its execution the preservation of my own existence; or in other words, it will rarely happen that I cannot do more good in twenty years, than in one. If the extraordinary case should occur, in which I can promote the general good by my death more than by my life, justice requires that I should be content to die. In other cases, it will usually be incumbent on me, to maintain my body and mind in the utmost vigour, and in the best condition for service.[1]

Suppose, for example, that it is right for one man to possess a greater portion of property than another, whether as the fruit of his industry, or the inheritance of his ancestors. Justice obliges him to regard this property as a trust, and calls upon him maturely to consider in what manner it may be employed for the increase of liberty, knowledge and virtue. He has no right to dispose of a shilling of it at the suggestion of his caprice. So far from being entitled to well-earned applause, for having employed some scanty pittance in the service of philanthropy, he is in the eye of justice a delinquent, if he withhold any portion from that service. Could that portion have been better or more worthily employed? That it could, is implied in the very terms of the proposition. Then it was just it should have been so employed.—In the same manner as my property, I hold my person as a trust in behalf of man-

---

[1] [Godwin has here a footnote reference to the First Appendix to this chapter. The Appendix is entitled 'On Suicide'; it is similar to the argument in this paragraph and has been omitted.]

kind. I am bound to employ my talents, my understanding, my strength and my time, for the production of the greatest quantity of general good. Such are the declarations of justice, so great is the extent of my duty.

But justice is reciprocal. If it be just that I should confer a benefit, it is just that another man should receive it, and, if I withhold from him that to which he is entitled, he may justly complain. My neighbour is in want of ten pounds that I can spare. There is no law of political institution to reach this case, and transfer the property from me to him. But in a passive sense, unless it can be shown that the money can be more beneficently employed, his right is as complete, (though actively he have not the same right, or rather duty, to possess himself of it), as if he had my bond in his possession, or had supplied me with goods to the amount.[1]

To this it has sometimes been answered, 'that there is more than one person, who stands in need of the money I have to spare, and of consequence I must be at liberty to bestow it as I please.' By no means. If only one person offer himself to my knowledge or search, to me there is but one. Those others that I cannot find, belong to other rich men to assist (every man is in reality rich, who has more than his just occasions demand), and not to me. If more than one person offer, I am obliged to balance their claims, and conduct myself accordingly. It is scarcely possible that two men should have an exactly equal claim, or that I should be equally certain respecting the claim of the one as of the other.

It is therefore impossible for me to confer upon any man a favour; I can only do him right. Whatever deviates from the law of justice, though it should be in the too much done in favour of some individual or some part of the general whole, is so much subtracted from the general stock, so much of absolute injustice.

The reasonings here alleged, are sufficient, clearly to establish the competence of justice as a principle of deduction in all cases of moral enquiry. They are themselves rather of the nature of illustration and example, and, if error be imputable to them in particulars, this will not invalidate the general conclusion, the propriety of applying moral justice as a criterion in the investigation of political truth.

Society is nothing more than an aggregation of individuals. Its claims and duties must be the aggregate of their claims and duties, the one no more precarious and arbitrary than the other. What has the

[1] Ch. v.

society a right to require from me? The question is already answered: everything that it is my duty to do. Anything more? Certainly not. Can it change eternal truth, or subvert the nature of men and their actions? Can it make my duty consist in committing intemperance, in maltreating or assassinating my neighbour?—Again, what is it that the society is bound to do for its members? Everything that is requisite for their welfare. But the nature of their welfare is defined by the nature of mind. That will most contribute to it, which expands the understanding, supplies incitements to virtue, fills us with a generous consciousness of our independence, and carefully removes whatever can impede our exertions.

Should it be affirmed, 'that it is not in the power of any political system to secure to us these advantages,' the conclusion will not be less incontrovertible. It is bound to contribute everything it is able to these purposes. Suppose its influence in the utmost degree limited; there must be one method, approaching nearer than any other to the desired object, and that method ought to be universally adopted. There is one thing that political institutions can assuredly do, they can avoid positively counteracting the true interests of their subjects. But all capricious rules and arbitrary distinctions do positively counteract them. There is scarcely any modification of society but has in it some degree of moral tendency. So far as it produces neither mischief nor benefit, it is good for nothing. So far as it tends to the improvement of the community, it ought to be universally adopted.

CHAPTER III

OF THE EQUALITY OF MANKIND

THE principles of justice, as explained in the preceding chapter, proceed upon the assumption of the equality of mankind. This equality is either physical or moral. Physical equality may be considered, either as it relates to the strength of the body, or the faculties of the mind.

This part of the subject has been exposed to cavil and objection. It has been said, 'that the reverse of this equality is the result of our experience. Among the individuals of our species, we actually find that there are not two alike. One man is strong, and another weak. One man is wise, and another foolish. All that exists in the world of the inequality of conditions, is to be traced to this as their source. The strong man possesses power to subdue, and the weak stands in need of an ally to protect. The consequence is inevitable: the equality of conditions is a chimerical assumption, neither possible to be reduced into practice, nor desirable, if it could be so reduced.'

Upon this statement two observations are to be made. First, this inequality was in its origin infinitely less, than it is at present. In the uncultivated state of man, diseases, effeminacy and luxury were little known; and, of consequence, the strength of every one, much more nearly approached to the strength of his neighbour. In the uncultivated state of man, the understandings of all were limited, their wants, their ideas and their views nearly upon a level. It was to be expected that, in their first departure from this state, great irregularities would introduce themselves; and it is the object of subsequent wisdom and improvement to mitigate these irregularities.

Secondly, notwithstanding the encroachments that have been made upon the equality of mankind, a great and substantial equality remains. There is no such disparity among the human race, as to enable one man to hold several other men in subjection, except so far as they are willing to be subject. All government is founded in opinion. Men at present live under any particular form, because they conceive it their interest to do so. One part indeed of a community or empire, may be held in subjection by force; but this cannot be the personal force of their despot; it must be the force of another part of the community, who are of opinion that it is their interest to support his authority. Destroy this opinion, and the fabric which is built upon it falls to the ground. It follows therefore that all men are essentially independent.—So much for the physical equality.

The moral equality is still less open to reasonable exception. By moral equality I understand, the propriety of applying one unalterable rule of justice to every case that may arise. This cannot be questioned, but upon arguments that would subvert the very nature of virtue. 'Equality,' it has been affirmed, 'will always be an unintelligible fiction, so long as the capacities of men shall be unequal, and their pretended claims have neither guarantee nor sanction by which they can be enforced.'[1] But surely justice is sufficiently intelligible in its own nature, abstractedly from the consideration whether it be or be not reduced into practice. Justice has relation to beings endowed with perception, and capable of pleasure and pain. Now it immediately results from the nature of such beings, independently of any arbitrary constitution, that

---

[1] [Guillaume Thomas François] Raynal [1713–96], Révolution d'Amérique [1781], p. 34.

pleasure is agreeable and pain odious, pleasure to be desired and pain to be disapproved. It is therefore just and reasonable that such beings should contribute, so far as it lies in their power, to the pleasure and benefit of each other. Among pleasures, some are more exquisite, more unalloyed and less precarious than others. It is just that these should be preferred.

From these simple principles we may deduce the moral equality of mankind. We are partakers of a common nature, and the same causes that contribute to the benefit of one, will contribute to the benefit of another. Our senses and faculties are of the same denomination. Our pleasures and pains will therefore be alike. We are all of us endowed with reason, able to compare, to judge and to infer. The improvement therefore, which is to be desired for one, is to be desired for another. We shall be provident for ourselves, and useful to each other in proportion as we rise above the sphere of prejudice. The same independence, the same freedom from any such restraint, as should prevent us from giving the reins to our own understanding, or from uttering, upon all occasions, whatever we think to be true, will conduce to the improvement of all. There are certain opportunities and a certain situation most advantageous to every human being, and it is just that these should be communicated to all, as nearly as the general economy will permit.

There is indeed one species of moral inequality, parallel to the physical inequality that has been already described. The treatment to which men are entitled, is to be measured by their merits and their virtues. That country would not be the seat of wisdom and reason, where the benefactor of his species was regarded with no greater degree of complacence than their enemy. But in reality this distinction, so far from being adverse to equality in any tenable sense, is friendly to it, and is accordingly known by the appellation of equity, a term derived from the same origin. Though in some sense an exception, it tends to the same purpose to which the principle itself is indebted for its value. It is calculated to infuse into every bosom an emulation of excellence. The thing really to be desired, is the removing as much as possible arbitrary distinctions, and leaving to talents and virtue the field of exertion unimpaired. We should endeavour to afford to all the same opportunities and the same encouragement, and to render justice the common interest and choice.

It should be observed, that the object of this chapter, is barely to present a general outline of the principle of equality. The practical inferences that flow from it, must remain to be detailed under subsequent heads of enquiry.

CHAPTER IV

OF PERSONAL VIRTUE AND DUTY

THERE are two subjects, of the utmost importance to a just delineation of the principles of society, which are, on that account, entitled to a separate examination; the duties incumbent on men living in society, and the rights accruing to them. These are merely different modes of expressing the principle of justice, as it shall happen to be considered in its relation to the agent or the patient. Duty is the treatment I am bound to bestow upon others; right is the treatment I am entitled to expect from them. This will more fully appear in the sequel.

First, of personal virtue and duty.

Virtue, like every other term of general science, may be understood either absolutely, or as the qualification and attribute of a particular being: in other words, it is one thing to enquire whether an action is virtuous, and another to enquire whether a man is virtuous. The former of these questions is considerably simple; the latter is more complex, and will require an examination of several circumstances, before it can be satisfactorily determined.

In the first sense I would define virtue to be any action or actions of an intelligent being, proceeding from kind and benevolent intention, and having a tendency to contribute to general happiness. Thus defined, it distributes itself under two heads; and, in whatever instance either the tendency or the intention is wanting, the virtue is incomplete. An action, however pure may be the intention of the agent, the tendency of which is mischievous, or which shall merely be nugatory and useless in its character, is not a virtuous action. Were it otherwise, we should be obliged to concede the appellation of virtue to the most nefarious deeds of bigots, persecutors and religious assassins, and to the weakest observances of a deluded superstition. Still less does an action, the consequences of which shall be supposed to be in the highest degree beneficial, but which proceeds from a mean, corrupt and degrading motive, deserve the appellation of virtue. A virtuous action is that, of which both the motive and the tendency concur to excite our approbation.

Let us proceed from the consideration of the action to that of the agent. Before we can decide upon the degree in which any man is entitled to be denominated virtuous, we must compare his performance with his means. It is not enough, that his conduct is attended with an overbalance of good intention and beneficial results. If it appear that he has scarcely produced the tenth part of that benefit, either in magnitude or extent, which he was capable of producing, it is only in a very limited sense that he can be considered as a virtuous man.

What is it therefore, we are led to enquire, that constitutes the capacity of any man? Capacity is an idea produced in the mind by a contemplation of the assemblage of properties in any substance, and the uses to which a substance so circumstanced may be applied. Thus a given portion of metal, may be formed, at the pleasure of the manufacturer, into various implements, a knife, a razor, a sword, a dozen of coat buttons, etc. This is one stage of capacity. A second is, when it has already received the form of a knife, and, being dismissed by the manufacturer, falls into the hands of the person who intends it for his private use. By this person it may be devoted to purposes, beneficial, pernicious or idle.—To apply these considerations to the nature of a human being.

We are not here enquiring respecting the capacity of man absolutely speaking, but of an individual; the performer of a given action, or the person who has engaged in a certain series of conduct. In the same manner therefore as the knife may be applied to various purposes at the pleasure of its possessor, so an individual endowed with certain qualifications, may engage in various pursuits, according to the views that are presented to him, and the motives that actuate his mind.

Human capacity however, is a subject attended with greater ambiguity than the capacity of inanimate substances. Capacity assumes something as fixed, and enquires into the temporary application of these permanent qualities. But it is easier to define, with tolerable precision, the permanent qualities, of an individual knife, for example, than of an individual man. Everything in man may be said to be in a state of flux; he is a Proteus whom we know not how to detain. That of which I am capable, for instance, as to my conduct today, falls extremely short of that of which I am capable, as to my conduct in the two or three next ensuing years. For what I shall do today I am dependent upon my ignorance in some things, my want of practice in others, and the erroneous habits I may in any respect have contracted. But many of these disadvantages may be superseded, when the question is respecting what I shall produce in the two or three next years of my life. Nor is this all. Even my capacity of today, is in a great degree determinable by the motives that shall excite me. When a man is placed in circumstances of a very strong and impressive nature, he is frequently found to possess or instantaneously to acquire, capacities which neither he nor his neighbours previously suspected. We are obliged however in the decisions of morality to submit to these uncertainties. It is only after having formed the most accurate notions we are able respecting the capacity of a man, and comparing this capacity with his performance, that we can decide, with any degree of satisfaction, whether he is entitled to the appellation of virtuous.

There is another difficulty which adheres to this question. Is it the motive alone that we are entitled to take into consideration, when we decide upon the merits of the individual, or are we obliged, as in the case of virtue absolutely taken, to consider both the motives and the tendency of his conduct? The former of these has been frequently asserted. But the assertion is attended with serious difficulties.

First, vice as it is commonly understood, is, so far as regards the motive, purely negative. To virtue it is necessary, that it proceed from kind and benevolent intention; but malevolence, or a disposition to draw a direct gratification from the sufferings of others, is not necessary to vice. It is sufficient that the agent regards with neglect those benevolent considerations which are allied to general good. This mode of applying the terms of morality, seems to arise from the circumstance, that, in estimating the merits of others, we reasonably regard the actual benefit or mischief that is produced as the principal point; and consider the disposition that produces it, merely as it tends to insure to us a continuation of benefit or injury.

Secondly, actions in the highest degree injurious to the public, have often proceeded from motives uncommonly conscientious. The most determined political assassins, . . . seem to have been deeply penetrated with anxiety for the eternal welfare of mankind. For these objects they sacrificed their ease, and cheerfully exposed themselves to tortures and death. Benevolence probably had its part in lighting the fires of Smithfield, and pointing the daggers of Saint Bartholomew. The authors of the Gunpowder Treason were, in general, men remarkable for the sanctity of their lives, and the austerity of their manners.

The nature whether of religious imposture, or of persevering enterprise in general, seems scarcely to have been sufficiently developed by the professors of moral enquiry. Nothing is more difficult, than for a man to recommend with enthusiasm, that which he does not think intrinsically admirable. Nothing is more difficult, than for a man to engage in an arduous undertaking, that he does not persuade himself will in some way be extensively useful. When archbishop Becket set himself against the whole power of Henry the second, and bore every species of contumely with an unalterable spirit, we may easily discover the haughtiness of the priest, the insatiable ambition that delighted to set its foot upon the neck of kings, and the immeasurable vanity that snuffed with transport the incense of an adoring multitude; but we may see with equal evidence, that he regarded himself as the champion of the cause of God, and expected the crown of martyrdom in a future state.

Precipitate and superficial judges conclude, that he who imposes upon others, is in most cases aware of the delusion himself. But this seldom happens. Self-deception is of all things the most easy. Whoever ardently wishes to find a proposition true, may be expected insensibly to veer towards the opinion that suits his inclination. It cannot be wondered at, by him who considers the subtlety of the human mind,[1] that belief should scarcely ever rest upon the mere basis of evidence, and that arguments are always viewed through a delusive medium, magnifying them into Alps, or diminishing them to nothing.

In the same manner as the grounds of our opinions are complicated, so are the motives to our actions. It is probable that no wrong action is perpetrated from motives entirely pure. It is probable that conscientious assassins and persecutors, have some mixture of ambition or the love of fame, and some feelings of animosity and ill will. But the deception they put upon themselves may nevertheless be complete. They stand acquitted at the bar of their own examination; and their injurious conduct, if considered under the head of motive only, is probably as pure, as much of that conduct which falls with the best title under the denomination of virtue.

For, thirdly, those actions of men, which tend to increase the general happiness, and are founded in the purest motives, have some alloy in the causes from which they proceed. It has been seen, that the motives of each single action, in a man already arrived at maturity, are innumerable:[2] into this mixture it is scarcely to be supposed, that something improper, mean, and inconsistent with that impartial estimate of things which is the true foundation of virtue, will not insinuate itself. It seems reasonable to believe, that such actions, as are known

---

[1] I. v, p. 46.   [2] I. v, p. 46.

most admirably to have contributed to the benefit of mankind, have sprung from views, of all others the least adulterated. But it cannot be doubted that many actions, considerably useful, and to a great degree well-intended, have had as much alloy in their motive, as other actions which, springing from a benevolent disposition, have been extensively detrimental.

From all these considerations it appears, that, if we were to adjust the standard of virtue from intention alone, we should reverse all the received ideas respecting it, giving the palm to some of the greatest pests of mankind, at the expense of others who have been no contemptible benefactors. Intention no doubt is of the essence of virtue. But it will not do alone. In deciding the merits of others, we are bound, for the most part, to proceed in the same manner, as in deciding the merits of inanimate substances. The turning point is their utility. Intention is of no further value than as it leads to utility: it is the means, and not the end. We shall overturn therefore every principle of just reasoning, if we bestow our applause upon the most mischievous of mankind, merely because the mischief they produce arises from mistake; or if we regard them in any other light, than we would an engine of destruction and misery, that is constructed of very costly materials.

The reasonings of the early part of this chapter upon the subject of virtue, may equally be applied to elucidate the term duty. Duty is that mode of action on the part of the individual, which constitutes the best possible application of his capacity to the general benefit. The only distinction to be made, between what was there adduced upon the subject of personal virtue, and the observations which most aptly apply to the consideration of duty, consists in this: that, though a man should in some instances neglect the best application of his capacity, he may yet be entitled to the appellation of virtuous; but duty is uniform, and requires of us that best application in every situation that presents itself.

This way of considering the subject furnishes us with the solution of a question, which has been supposed to be attended with considerable difficulty. Is it my duty to comply with the dictates of my erroneous conscience? Was it the duty of Everard Digby to blow up king James and his parliament with gunpowder? Certainly not. Duty is the application of capacity to the real, not imaginary, benefit of mankind. It was his duty to entertain a sincere and ardent desire for the improvement and happiness of others. With this duty he probably complied. But it was not his duty to apply that desire to a purpose, dreadful, and pregnant with inexhaustible mischief. With the prejudices he entertained, perhaps it was impossible for him to do otherwise. But it would be absurd to say that it was his duty to labour under prejudice. Perhaps it will be found that no man can in any instance act otherwise than he does.[1] But this, if true, will not annihilate the meaning of the term duty. It has already been seen, that the idea of capacity and the best application of capacity, is equally intelligible of inanimate substances. Duty is a species under this generical term, and implies merely the best application of capacity in an intelligent being, whether that application originate in a self-moving power, or in the irresistible impulse of motives and considerations presented to the understanding. To talk of the duty of doing wrong, can answer no other purpose than to take away all precision and meaning from language.

CHAPTER V

OF RIGHTS

THE rights of man have, like many other political and moral questions, furnished a topic of eager and pertinacious dispute, more by a confused and inaccurate statement of the subject of enquiry, than by any considerable difficulty attached to the subject itself.

The real or supposed rights of man are of two kinds, active and passive; the right in certain cases to do as we list; and the right we possess to the forbearance or assistance of other men.

The first of these a just philosophy will probably induce us universally to explode.

There is no sphere in which a human being can be supposed to act, where one mode of proceeding will not, in every given instance, be more reasonable than any other mode. That mode the being is bound by every principle of justice to pursue.

Morality is nothing else but that system, which teaches us to contribute upon all occasions, to the extent of our power, to the well-being and happiness of every intellectual and sensitive existence. But there is no action of our lives, which does not in some way affect that happiness. Our property, our time, and our faculties, may all of them be made to contribute to this end. The periods, which cannot be spent in the active production of happiness, may be spent in preparation. There is not one

[1] IV. vii.

of our avocations or amusements, that does not, by its effects, render us more or less fit to contribute our quota to the general utility. If then every one of our actions fall within the province of morals, it follows that we have no rights in relation to the selecting them. No one will maintain, that we have a right to trespass upon the dictates of morality.

It has been observed by natural philosophers, that a single grain of sand more or less in the structure of the earth, would have produced an infinite variation in its history. If this be true in inanimate nature, it is much more so in morals. The encounter of two persons of opposite sexes, so as to lead to the relation of marriage, in many cases obviously depends upon the most trivial circumstances, any one of which being changed, the relation would not have taken place. Let the instance be the father and mother of Shakespeare. If they had not been connected, Shakespeare would never have been born. . . . The determination of mind, in consequence of which the child contracts some of his earliest propensities, which call out his curiosity, industry and ambition, or on the other hand leave him unobserving, indolent and phlegmatic, is produced by circumstances so minute and subtle, as in few instances to have been made the subject of history. The events which afterwards produce his choice of a profession or pursuit, are not less precarious. Every one of these incidents, when it occurred, grew out of a series of incidents that had previously taken place. Everything is connected in the universe. If any man asserted that, if Alexander had not bathed in the river Cydnus, Shakespeare would never have written, it would be impossible to prove that his assertion was untrue.

To the inference we are deducing from this statement of facts, it may be objected, 'that it is true that all events in the universe are connected, and that the most memorable revolutions may depend for their existence upon trivial causes; but it is impossible for us to discern the remote bearings and subtle influences of our own actions; and by what we cannot discern it can never be required of us to regulate our conduct.' This is no doubt true, but its force in the nature of an objection will be taken away, if we consider, first, that, though our ignorance will justify us in neglecting that which, had we been better informed, we should have seen to be most beneficial, it can scarcely be considered as conferring on us an absolute right to incur that neglect. Secondly, even under the limited powers of our discernment, it will seldom happen to a man eminently conscientious and benevolent, to see no appearance of superiority, near or remote, direct or indirect, in favour of one side of any alternative proposed to his choice, rather than the other. We are bound to regulate ourselves by the best judgement we can exert. Thirdly, if anything remain to the active rights of man after this deduction, and if he be at liberty to regulate his conduct in any instance, independently of the dictates of morality, it will be, first, an imperfect, not an absolute right, the offspring of ignorance and imbecility; and, secondly, it will relate only to such insignificant matters, if such there be, as, after the best exercise of human judgement, cannot be discerned to have the remotest relation to the happiness of mankind.

Few things have contributed more to undermine the energy and virtue of the human species, than the supposition that we have a right, as it has been phrased, to do what we will with our own. It is thus that the miser, who accumulates to no end that which diffused would have conduced to the welfare of thousands, that the luxurious man, who wallows in indulgence and sees numerous families around him pining in beggary, never fail to tell us of their rights, and to silence animadversion and quiet the censure of their own minds, by observing, 'that they came fairly into possession of their wealth, that they owe no debts, and that of consequence no man has authority to enquire into their private manner of disposing of that which appertains to them.' We have in reality nothing that is strictly speaking our own. We have nothing that has not a destination prescribed to it by the immutable voice of reason and justice; and respecting which, if we supersede that destination, we do not entail upon ourselves a certain portion of guilt.

As we have a duty obliging us to a certain conduct respecting our faculties and our possessions, so our neighbour has a duty respecting his admonitions and advice. He is guilty of an omission in this point, if he fail to employ every means in his power for the amendment of our errors, and to have recourse for that purpose, as he may see occasion, to the most unreserved animadversion upon our propensities and conduct. It is absurd to suppose that certain points are especially within my province, and therefore he may not afford me, invited or uninvited, his assistance in arriving at a right decision. He is bound to form the best judgement he is able, respecting every circumstance that falls under his observation; what he thinks, he is bound to declare to others; and, if to others, certainly not less to the party immediately concerned. The worst consequences, through every rank and department of life, have arisen, from men's supposing their personal affairs in any case to be so sacred, that every one, except themselves, was bound to be blind and dumb in relation to them.

The ground of this error has been a propensity, to which we are frequently subject, of concluding from the excess to the thing itself. Undoubtedly our neighbour is to be directed in his animadversions, not by a spirit of levity and impertinence, but by a calculation of the eventual utility. Undoubtedly there is one person who must, in almost all instances, be the real actor, and other persons may not, but with caution and sober reflection, occupy his time with their suggestions as to the conduct he ought to pursue. There is scarcely any tyranny more gross, than that of the man who should perpetually intrude upon us his crude and half-witted advices, or who, not observing when, in point of strength and clearness, he had done justice to his own conception, should imagine it to be his duty to repeat and press it upon us without end. Advice perhaps requires above all things, that it should be administered with simplicity, disinterestedness, kindness and moderation. . . .

. . . . .

It is scarcely necessary to add, that, if individuals have no rights, neither has society, which possesses nothing but what individuals have brought into a common stock. The absurdity of the common opinion, as applied to this subject, is still more glaring, if possible, than in the view in which we have already considered it. According to the usual sentiment, every club assembling for any civil purpose, every congregation of religionists assembling for the worship of God, has a right to establish any provisions or ceremonies, no matter how ridiculous or detestable, provided they do not interfere with the freedom of others. Reason lies prostrate at their feet; they have a right to trample upon and insult her as they please. It is in the same spirit we have been told, that every nation has a right to choose its form of government. An acute and original author was probably misled by the vulgar phraseology on this subject, when he asserted, that, 'at a time when neither the people of France nor the national assembly were troubling themselves about the affairs of England or the English parliament, Mr. Burke's conduct was unpardonable in commencing an unprovoked attack upon them.'[1]

It is, no doubt, the inevitable result of human imperfection, that men and societies of men should model their conduct by the best judgement they are able to form, whether that judgement be sound or erroneous. But, as it has been before shown that it cannot be their duty to do

[1] Thomas Paine, *Rights of Man*, p. 1.

anything detrimental to the general happiness,[1] so it appears with equal evidence that they cannot have a right to do so. There cannot be a more absurd proposition, than that which affirms the right of doing wrong. A mistake of this sort, has been attended with the most pernicious consequences in public and political affairs. It cannot be too strongly inculcated, that societies and communities of men are in no case empowered to establish absurdity and injustice; that the voice of the people is not, as has sometimes been ridiculously asserted, 'the voice of truth and of God;' and that universal consent cannot convert wrong into right. The most insignificant individual ought to hold himself free to animadvert upon the decisions of the most august assembly; and other men are bound in justice to listen to him, in proportion to the soundness of his reasons, and the strength of his remarks, and not for any accessory advantages he may derive from rank or exterior importance. The most crowded forum, or the most venerable senate, cannot make one proposition to be a rule of justice, that was not substantially so, previously to their decision. They can only interpret and announce that law, which derives its real validity from a higher and less mutable authority. If we submit to their decisions in cases where we are not convinced of their rectitude, this submission is an affair of prudence only; a reasonable man will lament the emergence, while he yields to the necessity. If a congregation of men agree universally to cut off their right hand, to shut their ears upon free enquiry, or to affirm two and two upon a particular occasion to be sixteen, in all these cases they are wrong, and ought unequivocally to be censured for usurping an authority that does not belong to them. They ought to be told, 'Gentlemen, you are not, as in the intoxication of power you have been led to imagine, omnipotent; there is an authority greater than yours, to which you are bound assiduously to conform yourselves.' No man, if he were alone in the world, would have a right to make himself impotent or miserable.

So much for the active rights of man, which, if there be any cogency in the preceding arguments, are all of them superseded and rendered null by the superior claims of justice. His passive rights, when freed from the ambiguity that has arisen from the improper mixture and confounding of these two heads, will probably be found liable to little controversy.[2]

---

[1] Ch. iv, p.83 f.

[2] [In the first edition Godwin rejected all rights on the grounds hitherto considered. The discussion of passive rights appears first in the second edition.]

In the first place he is said to have a right to life and personal liberty. This proposition, if admitted, must be admitted with great limitation. He has no right to his life, when his duty calls him to resign it. Other men are bound (it would be improper in strictness of speech, upon the ground of the preceding explanations, to say they have a right) to deprive him of life or liberty, if that should appear in any case to be indispensably necessary to prevent a greater evil. The passive rights of man will be best understood from the following elucidation.

Every man has a certain sphere of discretion, which he has a right to expect shall not be infringed by his neighbours. This right flows from the very nature of man. First, all men are fallible: no man can be justified in setting up his judgement as a standard for others. We have no infallible judge of controversies; each man in his own apprehension is right in his decisions; and we can find no satisfactory mode of adjusting their jarring pretensions. If every one be desirous of imposing his sense upon others, it will at last come to be a controversy, not of reason, but of force. Secondly, even if we had an infallible criterion, nothing would be gained, unless it were by all men recognized as such. If I were secured against the possibility of mistake, mischief and not good would accrue, from imposing my infallible truths upon my neighbour, and requiring his submission independently of any conviction I could produce in his understanding. Man is a being who can never be an object of just approbation, any further than he is independent. He must consult his own reason, draw his own conclusions, and conscientiously conform himself to his ideas of propriety. Without this, he will be neither active, nor considerate, nor resolute, nor generous.

For these two reasons it is necessary, that every man should stand by himself, and rest upon his own understanding. For that purpose each must have his sphere of discretion. No man must encroach upon my province, nor I upon his. He may advise me, moderately and without pertinaciousness, but he must not expect to dictate to me. He may censure me freely and without reserve; but he should remember that I am to act by my deliberation and not his. He may exercise a republican boldness in judging, but he must not be peremptory and imperious in prescribing. Force may never be resorted to, but in the most extraordinary and imperious emergency. I ought to exercise my talents for the benefit of others; but that exercise must be the fruit of my own conviction; no man must attempt to press me into the service. I ought to appropriate such part of the fruits of the earth, as by any accident comes into my possession, and is not necessary to my benefit, to the use of others; but they must obtain it from me by argument and expostulation, not by violence. It is in this principle, that what is commonly called the right of property is founded. Whatever then comes into my possession, without violence to any other man, or to the institutions of society, is my property. This property, it appears by the principles already laid down, I have no right to dispose of at my caprice; every shilling of it is appropriated by the laws of morality; but no man can be justified, in ordinary cases at least, in forcibly extorting it from me. When the laws of morality shall be clearly understood, their excellence universally apprehended, and themselves seen to be coincident with each man's private advantage, the idea of property in this sense will remain, but no man will have the least desire, for purposes of ostentation or luxury, to possess more than his neighbours.

A second branch of the passive rights of man, consists in the right each man possesses to the assistance of his neighbour. This will be fully elucidated hereafter.[1]

CHAPTER VI

OF THE RIGHT OF PRIVATE JUDGEMENT

I T has appeared, that the most essential of those rights which constitute the peculiar sphere appropriate to each individual, and the right upon which every other depends as its basis, is the right of private judgement. It will therefore be of use to say something distinctly on this head.

To a rational being there can be but one rule of conduct, justice, and one mode of ascertaining that rule, the exercise of his understanding.

If in any instance I am made the mechanical instrument of absolute violence, in that instance I fall under a pure state of external slavery. If on the other hand, not being under the influence of absolute compulsion, I am wholly prompted by something that is frequently called by that name, and act from the hope of reward or the fear of punishment, the subjection I suffer is doubtless less aggravated, but the effect upon my moral habits may be in a still higher degree injurious.

In the meantime, with respect to the conduct I should observe upon such occasions, a distinction is to be made. Justice, as it was defined in a preceding chapter, is coincident with utility. I am myself a part of

[1] Book VIII.

the great whole, and my happiness is a part of that complex view of things by which justice is regulated. The hope of reward therefore, and the fear of punishment, however wrong in themselves, and inimical to the improvement of the mind, are motives which, so long as they are resorted to in society, must and ought to have some influence with my mind.

There are two descriptions of tendency that may belong to any action, the tendency which it possesses by the necessary and unalterable laws of existence, and the tendency which results from the arbitrary interference of some intelligent being. The nature of happiness and misery, pleasure and pain, is independent of positive institution. It is immutably true, that whatever tends to procure a balance of the former is to be desired, and whatever tends to procure a balance of the latter is to be rejected. In like manner there are certain features and principles inseparable from such a being as man; there are causes which, in their operation upon him, are in their own nature generative of pleasure, and some of a pleasure more excellent than others. Every action has a result which may be said to be peculiarly its own, and which will always follow upon it, unless so far as it may happen to be superseded by the operation of other and extrinsical causes.

The tendency of positive institution is of two sorts, to furnish an additional motive to the practice of virtue or right; and to inform the understanding, as to what actions are right, and what actions are wrong. Much cannot be said in commendation of either of these tendencies.

First, positive institution may furnish an additional motive to the practice of virtue. I have an opportunity of essentially contributing to the advantage of twenty individuals; they will be benefited, and no other persons will sustain a material injury. I ought to embrace this opportunity. Here let us suppose positive institution to interfere, and to annex some great personal reward to the discharge of my duty. This immediately changes the nature of the action. Before, I preferred it for its intrinsic excellence. Now, so far as the positive institution operates, I prefer it, because some person has arbitrarily annexed to it a great weight of self-interest. But virtue, considered as the quality of an intelligent being, depends upon the disposition with which the action is accompanied. Under a positive institution then, this very action, which is intrinsically virtuous, may, so far as relates to the agent, become vicious. The vicious man would before have neglected the advantage of these twenty individuals, because he would not bring a certain inconvenience or trouble upon himself. The same man, with the same disposition, will now promote their advantage, because his own welfare is concerned in it. Twenty, other things equal, is twenty times better than one. He that is not governed by the moral arithmetic of the case, or who acts from a disposition directly at war with that arithmetic, is unjust.[1] In other words, moral improvement will be forwarded, in proportion as we are exposed to no other influence, than that of the tendency which belongs to an action by the necessary and unalterable laws of existence. This is probably the meaning of the otherwise vague and obscure principle, 'that we should do good, regardless of the consequences'; and by that other, 'that we may not do evil, from the prospect of good to result from it.' The case would have been rendered still more glaring, if, instead of the welfare of twenty, we had supposed the welfare of millions to have been concerned. In reality, whether the disparity be great or small, the inference must be the same.

Secondly, positive institution may inform the understanding, as to what actions are right, and what actions are wrong. Here it may be of advantage to us to reflect upon the terms understanding and information. Understanding, particularly as it is concerned with moral subjects, is the percipient of truth. This is its proper sphere. Information, so far as it is genuine, is a portion detached from the great body of truth. You inform me, 'that Euclid asserts the three angles of a plane triangle to be equal to two right angles.' Still I am unacquainted with the truth of this proposition. 'But Euclid has demonstrated it. His demonstration has existed for two thousand years, and, during that term, has proved satisfactory to every man by whom it has been understood.' I am nevertheless uninformed. The knowledge of truth, lies in the perceived agreement or disagreement of the terms of a proposition. So long as I am unacquainted with the middle term by means of which they may be compared, so long as they are incommensurate to my understanding, you may have furnished me with a principle from which I may reason truly to further consequences; but, as to the principle itself, I may strictly be said to know nothing.

Every proposition has an intrinsic evidence of its own. Every consequence has premises from which it flows; and upon them, and not upon anything else, its validity depends. If you could work a miracle to prove, 'that the three angles of a triangle were equal to two right angles,' I should still know, that the proposition had been either true or false previously to the exhibition of the miracle; and that there was no necessary connection between any one of its terms and the miracle

[1] IV. x.

exhibited. The miracle would take off my attention from the true question, to a question altogether different, that of authority. By the authority adduced I might be prevailed on to yield an irregular assent to the proposition; but I could not properly be said to perceive its truth.

But this is not all. If it were, it might perhaps be regarded as a refinement foreign to the concerns of human life. Positive institutions do not content themselves with requiring my assent to certain propositions, in consideration of the testimony by which they are enforced. This would amount to no more, than advice flowing from a respectable quarter, which, after all, I might reject, if it did not accord with the mature judgement of my own understanding. But in the very nature of these institutions there is included a sanction, a motive either of punishment or reward, to induce me to obedience.

It is commonly said, 'that positive institutions ought to leave me free in matters of conscience, but may properly interfere with my conduct in civil concerns.' But this distinction seems to have been very lightly taken up. What sort of moralist must he be, whose conscience is silent as to what passes in his intercourse with other men? Such a distinction proceeds upon the supposition, 'that it is of great consequence whether I bow to the east or the west; whether I call the object of my worship Jehovah or Allah; whether I pay a priest in a surplice or a black coat. These are points in which an honest man ought to be rigid and inflexible. But as to those other, whether he shall be a tyrant, a slave or a free citizen; whether he shall bind himself with multiplied oaths impossible to be performed, or be a rigid observer of truth; whether he shall swear allegiance to a king *de jure* or a king *de facto*, to the best or the worst of all possible governments; respecting these points he may safely commit his conscience to the keeping of the civil magistrate.' In reality, by as many instances as I act contrary to the unbiased dictate of my own judgement, by so much I abdicate the most valuable part of the character of man.

I am satisfied at present, that a certain conduct, suppose it be a rigid attention to the confidence of private conversation, is incumbent on me. You tell me, 'there are certain cases of such peculiar emergency as to supersede this rule.' Perhaps I think there are not. If I admit your proposition, a wide field of enquiry is opened, respecting what cases do or do not deserve to be considered as exceptions. It is little likely that we should agree respecting all these cases. How then does the law treat me, for my conscientious discharge of what I conceive to be my

I

duty? Because I will not turn informer (which, it may be, I think an infamous character) against my most valued friend, the law accuses me of misprision of treason, felony, or murder, and perhaps hangs me. I believe a certain individual to be a confirmed villain and a most dangerous member of society, and feel it to be my duty to warn others, perhaps the public, against the effect of his vices. Because I publish what I know to be true, the law convicts me of libel, *scandalum magnatum*, and crimes of I know not what complicated denomination.

If the evil stopped here, it would be well. If I only suffered a certain calamity, suppose death, I could endure it. Death has hitherto been the common lot of men, and I expect, at some time or other, to submit to it. Human society must, sooner or later, be deprived of its individual members, whether they be valuable, or whether they be inconsiderable. But the punishment acts, not only retrospectively upon me, but prospectively upon my contemporaries and countrymen. My neighbour entertains the same opinion respecting the conduct he ought to hold, as I did. The executioner of public justice however interposes with a powerful argument, to convince him that he has mistaken the path of abstract rectitude.

What sort of converts will be produced by this unfeeling logic? 'I have deeply reflected,' suppose, 'upon the nature of virtue, and am convinced that a certain proceeding is incumbent on me. But the hangman, supported by an act of parliament, assures me I am mistaken.' If I yield my opinion to his *dictum*, my action becomes modified, and my character also. An influence like this, is inconsistent with all generous magnanimity of spirit, all ardent impartiality in the discovery of truth, and all inflexible perseverance in its assertion. Countries, exposed to the perpetual interference of decrees, instead of arguments, exhibit within their boundaries the mere phantoms of men. We can never judge from an observation of their inhabitants, what men would be, if they knew of no appeal from the tribunal of conscience, and if, whatever they thought, they dared to speak, and dared to act.

At present there will perhaps occur to the majority of readers, but few instances of laws, which may be supposed to interfere with the conscientious discharge of duty. A considerable number will occur in the course of the present enquiry. More would readily offer themselves to a patient research. Men are so successfully reduced to a common standard by the operation of positive law, that, in most countries, they are capable of little more than, like parrots, repeating what others have said. This uniformity is capable of being produced in two ways, by energy of mind and indefatigableness of enquiry, enabling a considerable number to penetrate with equal success into the recesses of truth; and by pusillanimity to temper, and a frigid indifference to right and wrong, produced by the penalties which are suspended over such as shall disinterestedly enquire, and communicate and act upon the result of their enquiries. It is easy to perceive which of these, is the cause of the uniformity that prevails in the present instance.

One thing more in enforcement of this important consideration. 'I have done something,' suppose, 'which though wrong in itself, I believe to be right; or I have done something which I usually admit to be wrong; but my conviction upon the subject is not so clear and forcible, as to prevent my yielding to a powerful temptation.' There can be no doubt, that the proper way of conveying to my understanding a truth of which I am ignorant, or of impressing upon me a firmer persuasion of a truth with which I am acquainted, is by an appeal to my reason. Even an angry expostulation with me upon my conduct, will but excite similar passions in me, and cloud, instead of illuminate, my understanding. There is certainly a way of expressing truth, with such benevolence as to command attention, and such evidence as to enforce conviction in all cases whatever.

Punishment inevitably excites in the sufferer, and ought to excite, a sense of injustice. Let its purpose be, to convince me of the truth of a position, which I at present believe to be false. It is not, abstractedly considered, of the nature of an argument, and therefore it cannot begin with producing conviction. Punishment is a comparatively specious name; but is in reality nothing more than force put upon one being, by another who happens to be stronger. But strength apparently does not constitute justice. The case of punishment, in the view in which we now consider it, is the case of you and me differing in opinion, and your telling me that you must be right, since you have a more brawny arm, or have applied your mind more to the acquiring skill in your weapons than I have.

But let us suppose, 'that I am convinced of my error, but that my conviction is superficial and fluctuating, and the object you propose is to render it durable and profound.' Ought it to be thus durable and profound? There are no doubt arguments and reasons calculated to render it so. Is the subject in reality problematical, and do you wish by the weight of your blows, to make up for the deficiency of your logic? This can never be defended. An appeal to force must appear to both parties, in proportion to the soundness of their understanding, to be a confession of imbecility. He that has recourse to it, would have no occasion for this expedient, if he were sufficiently acquainted with the powers of that truth it is his office to communicate. If there be any man who, in suffering punishment, is not conscious of injury, he must have had his mind previously debased by slavery, and his sense of moral right and wrong blunted by a series of oppressions.

If there be any truth more unquestionable than the rest, it is, that every man is bound to the exertion of his faculties in the discovery of right, and to the carrying into effect all the right with which he is acquainted. It may be granted, that an infallible standard, if it could be discovered, would be considerably beneficial. But this infallible standard itself would be of little use in human affairs, unless it had the property of reasoning as well as deciding, of enlightening the mind as well as constraining the body. If a man be in some cases obliged to prefer his own judgement, he is in all cases obliged to consult that judgement, before he can determine whether the matter in question be of the sort provided for or no. So that from this reasoning it ultimately appears, that the conviction of a man's individual understanding, is the only legitimate principle, imposing on him the duty of adopting any species of conduct.

Such are the genuine principles of human society. Such would be the unconstrained condition of its members, in a state, where every individual within the society, and every neighbour without, was capable of listening with sobriety to the dictates of reason. We shall not fail to be impressed with considerable regret, if, when we descend to the present mixed characters of mankind, we find ourselves obliged in any degree to depart from so simple and grand a principle. The universal exercise of private judgement is a doctrine so unspeakably beautiful, that the true politician will certainly feel infinite reluctance in admitting the idea of interfering with it. A principal object in the subsequent stages of enquiry, will be to discuss the emergency of the cases, that may be thought to demand this interference.

BOOK III

PRINCIPLES OF GOVERNMENT

CHAPTER I

SYSTEMS OF POLITICAL WRITERS

HAVING in the preceding book attempted a general delineation of the principles of rational society, it is proper that we, in the next place, proceed to the topic of government.

It has hitherto been the persuasion of communities of men in all ages and countries, that there are occasions, in which it becomes necessary, to supersede private judgement, for the sake of public good, and to control the acts of the individual, by an act to be performed in the name of the whole.

Previously to our deciding upon this question, it will be of advantage to enquire into the nature of government, and the manner in which this control may be exercised, with the smallest degree of violence and usurpation in regard to the individual. This point being determined, will assist us finally to ascertain, both the quantity of evil which government in its best form involves, and the urgency of the case which has been supposed to demand its interference.

There can be little ground to question the necessity, and consequently the justice, of force to be, in some cases, interposed between individual and individual. Violence is so prompt a mode of deciding differences of opinion and contentions of passion, that there will infallibly be some persons who will resort to this mode. How is their violence to be repressed, or prevented from being accompanied occasionally with the most tragical effects? Violence must necessarily be preceded by an opinion of the mind dictating that violence; and, as he who first has resort to force instead of argument, is unquestionably erroneous, the best and most desirable mode of correcting him, is by convincing him of his error. But the urgency of the case, when, for example, a dagger is pointed to my own breast or that of another, may be such as not to afford time for expostulation. Hence the propriety and duty of defence.

Is not defence equally necessary, on the part of a community, against a foreign enemy, or the contumacy of its own members? This is perhaps the most forcible view, in which the argument in favour of the institution of government has yet been placed. But, waving this question for the present, the enquiry now proposed is, if action on the part of the community should in any instance be found requisite, in what manner is it proper or just that the force, acting in behalf of the community, should be organized?

There are three hypotheses that have been principally maintained upon this subject. First, the system of force, according to which it is affirmed, 'that, inasmuch as it is necessary that the great mass of mankind should be held under the subjection of compulsory restraint, there can be no other criterion of that restraint, than the power of the individuals who lay claim to its exercise, the foundation of which power exists, in the unequal degrees in which corporal strength, and intellectual sagacity, are distributed among mankind.'

There is a second class of reasoners, who deduce the origin of all government from divine right, and affirm, 'that, as men derived their existence from an infinite creator at first, so are they still subject to his providential care, and of consequence owe allegiance to their civil governors, as to a power which he has thought fit to set over them.'

The third system is that which has been most usually maintained by the friends of equality and justice; the system, according to which the individuals of any society, are supposed to have entered into a contract with their governors or with each other, and which founds the authority of government in the consent of the governed.

The two first of these hypotheses may easily be dismissed. That of force appears to proceed upon the total negation of abstract and immutable justice, affirming every government to be right, that is possessed of power sufficient to enforce its decrees. It puts a violent termination upon all political science; and is calculated for nothing further, than to persuade men, to sit down quietly under their present disadvantages, whatever they may be, and not exert themselves to discover a remedy for the evils they suffer. The second hypothesis is of an equivocal nature. It either coincides with the first, and affirms all existing power to be alike of divine derivation; or it must remain totally useless, till a criterion can be found, to distinguish those governments which are approved by God, from those which cannot lay claim to that sanction. The criterion of patriarchal descent will be of no avail, till the true claimant and rightful heir can be discovered. If we make utility and justice the test of God's approbation, this hypothesis will be liable to little objection; but then on the other hand little will be gained by it, since those who have not introduced divine right into the argument, will yet readily grant, that a government which can be shown to be agreeable to utility and justice, is a rightful government.

The third hypothesis demands a more careful examination. If any error have insinuated itself into the support of truth, it becomes of particular consequence to detect it. Nothing can be of more importance, than to separate prejudice and mistake on the one hand, from reason and demonstration on the other. Wherever they have been confounded, the cause of truth must necessarily be the sufferer. That cause, so far from being injured by a dissolution of the unnatural alliance, may be expected to derive from that dissolution a superior degree of prosperity and lustre.

CHAPTER II

OF THE SOCIAL CONTRACT

UPON the first statement of the system of a social contract various difficulties present themselves. Who are the parties to this contract? For whom did they consent, for themselves only or for others? For how long a time is this contract to be considered as binding? If the consent of every individual be necessary, in what manner is that consent to be given? Is it to be tacit, or declared in express terms?

Little will be gained for the cause of equality and justice, if our ancestors, at the first institution of government, had a right indeed of choosing the system of regulations under which they thought proper to live, but at the same time could barter away the understandings and independence of all that came after them, to the latest posterity. But, if the contract must be renewed in each successive generation, what periods must be fixed on for that purpose? And if I be obliged to submit to the established government till my turn comes to assent to it, upon what principle is that obligation founded? Surely not upon the contract into which my father entered before I was born?

Secondly, what is the nature of the consent, in consequence of which I am to be reckoned a party to the frame of any political constitution?

It is usually said, 'that acquiescence is sufficient; and that this acquiescence is to be inferred from my living quietly under the protection of the laws.' But if this be true, an end is as effectually put to all political science, all discrimination of better and worse, as by any system invented by the most slavish sycophant. Upon this hypothesis every government that is quietly submitted to, is a lawful government, whether it be the usurpation of Cromwell, or the tyranny of Caligula.[1] Acquiescence is frequently nothing more, than a choice on the part of the individual, of what he deems the least evil. In many cases it is not so much as this, since the peasant and the artisan, who form the bulk of a nation, however dissatisfied with the government of their country, seldom have it in their power to transport themselves to another. It is also to be observed upon the system of acquiescence, that it is in little agreement with the established opinions and practices of mankind. Thus what has been called the law of nations, lays least stress upon the allegiance of a foreigner settling among us, though his acquiescence is certainly most complete; while natives removing into an uninhabited region are claimed by the mother country, and removing into a neighbouring territory are punished by municipal law, if they take arms against the country in which they were born. But surely acquiescence can scarcely be construed into consent, while the individuals concerned, are wholly unapprised of the authority intended to be rested upon it.[2]

Locke, the great champion of the doctrine of an original contract, has been aware of this difficulty, and therefore observes, that 'a tacit consent indeed obliges a man to obey the laws of any government, as long as he has any possessions, or enjoyment of any part of the dominions of that government; but nothing can make a man a member of the commonwealth, but his actually entering into it by positive engagement, and express promise and compact.'[3] A singular distinction! implying upon the face of it, that an acquiescence, such as has just been described, is sufficient to render a man amenable to the penal regulations of society; but that his own consent is necessary to entitle him to the privileges of a citizen.

A third objection to the social contract will suggest itself, as soon as we attempt to ascertain the extent of the obligation, even supposing it to have been entered into in the most solemn manner by every member of the community. Allowing that I am called upon, at the period of

---

[1] [Gaius Caesar, Emperor of Rome, A.D. 37–41.]   [2] Hume, II. xii.
[3] *Two Treatises of Government*, III. viii. 119, 122.

my coming of age for example, to declare my assent or dissent to any system of opinions or any code of practical institutes; for how long a period does this declaration bind me? Am I precluded from better information for the whole course of my life? And, if not for my whole life, why for a year, a week or even an hour? If my deliberate judgement, or my real sentiment, be of no avail in the case, in what sense can it be affirmed that all lawful government is founded in consent?

But the question of time is not the only difficulty. If you demand my assent to any proposition, it is necessary that the proposition should be stated simply and clearly. So numerous are the varieties of human understanding, in all cases where its independence and integrity are sufficiently preserved, that there is little chance of any two men coming to a precise agreement, about ten successive propositions that are in their own nature open to debate. What then can be more absurd, than to present to me the laws of England in fifty volumes folio, and call upon me to give an honest and uninfluenced vote upon their contents?

But the social contract, considered as the foundation of civil government, requires of me more than this. I am not only obliged to consent to all the laws that are actually upon record, but to all the laws that shall hereafter be made. It was under this view of the subject that Rousseau, in tracing the consequences of the social contract, was led to assert, that 'the great body of the people, in whom the sovereign authority resides, can neither delegate nor resign it. The essence of that authority,' he adds, 'is the general will; and will cannot be represented. It must either be the same or another; there is no alternative. The deputies of the people cannot be its representatives; they are merely its attorneys. The laws which the community does not ratify in person, are no laws, are nullities.'[1]

The difficulty here stated, has been endeavoured to be provided against by some late advocates for liberty, in the way of addresses of adhesion; addresses, originating in the various districts and departments of a nation, and without which no regulation of constitutional importance is to be deemed valid. But this is a very superficial remedy. The addressers of course have seldom any other alternative, than that above alluded to, of indiscriminate admission or rejection. There is an infinite difference between the first deliberation, and the subsequent exercise of a negative. The former is a real power, the latter is seldom more than the shadow of a power. Not to add, that addresses are a most precarious and equivocal mode of collecting the sense of a nation. They are usually

[1] *Du Contrat Social*, III. xv.

voted in a tumultuous and summary manner; they are carried along by the tide of party; and the signatures annexed to them are obtained by indirect and accidental methods, while multitudes of bystanders, unless upon some extraordinary occasion, remain ignorant of or indifferent to the transaction.

Lastly, if government be founded in the consent of the people, it can have no power over any individual by whom that consent is refused. If a tacit consent be not sufficient, still less can I be deemed to have consented to a measure upon which I put an express negative. This immediately follows from the observations of Rousseau. If the people, or the individuals of whom the people is constituted, cannot delegate their authority to a representative; neither can any individual delegate his authority to a majority, in an assembly of which he is himself a member. That must surely be a singular species of consent, the external indications of which are often to be found, in an unremitting opposition in the first instance, and compulsory subjection in the second.

CHAPTER III

OF PROMISES

THE whole principle of an original contract, rests upon the obligation under which we are conceived to be placed, to observe our promises. The reasoning upon which it is founded, is, 'that we have promised obedience to government, and therefore are bound to obey.' The doctrine of a social contract would never have been thought worth the formality of an argument, had it not been presumed to be one of our first and paramount obligations, to perform our engagements. It may be proper therefore to enquire into the nature of this obligation.

And here the first observation that offers itself, upon the principle of the doctrines already delivered,[1] is, that promises and compacts are in no sense the foundation of morality.

The foundation of morality is justice. The principle of virtue is an irresistible deduction from the wants of one man, and the ability of another to relieve them. It is not because I have promised, that I am bound to do that for my neighbour, which will be beneficial to him, and not injurious to me. This is an obligation which arises out of no compact, direct or understood; and would still remain, though it were

[1] II. ii, etc.

impossible that I should experience a return, either from him or any other human being. It is not on account of any promise or previous engagement, that I am bound to tell my neighbour the truth. Undoubtedly one of the reasons why I should do so, is, because the obvious use of the faculty of speech is to inform, and not to mislead. But it is an absurd account of this motive, to say, that my having recourse to the faculty of speech, amounts to a tacit engagement that I will use it for its genuine purposes. The true ground of confidence between man and man, is the knowledge we have of the motives by which the human mind is influenced; our perception, that the motives to deceive can but rarely occur, while the motives to veracity will govern the stream of human actions.

This position will be made still more incontrovertible, if we bestow a moment's attention upon the question, Why should we observe our promises? The only rational answer that can be made is, because it tends to the welfare of intelligent beings. But this answer is equally cogent, if applied to any other branch of morality. It is therefore absurd to rest the foundation of morality thus circuitously upon promises, when it may with equal propriety be rested upon that from which promises themselves derive their obligation.[1]

Again; when I enter into an engagement, I engage for that which is in its own nature conducive to human happiness, or which is not so. Can my engagement always render that which before was injurious agreeable to, and that which was beneficial the opposite of duty? Previously to my entering into a promise, there is something which I ought to promise, and something which I ought not. Previously to my entering into a promise, all modes of action were not indifferent. Nay, the very opposite of this is true. Every conceivable mode of action, has its appropriate tendency, and shade of tendency, to benefit, or to mischief, and consequently its appropriate claim to be performed or avoided. Thus clearly does it appear that promises and compacts are not the foundation of morality.

Secondly, I observe, that promises are, absolutely considered, an evil, and stand in opposition to the genuine and wholesome exercise of an intellectual nature.

Justice has already appeared to be the sum of moral and political duty. But the measure of justice, is the useful or injurious characters of the men with whom I am concerned; the criterion of justice, is the influence my conduct will have upon the stock of general good. Hence

---

[1] Hume, II. xii.

it inevitably follows, that the motives by which duty requires me to govern my actions, must be such as are of general application.

What is it then to which the obligation of a promise applies? What I have promised, is what I ought to have performed, if no promise had intervened, or it is not. It is conducive, or not conducive, to the generating of human happiness. If it be the former, then promise comes in merely as an additional inducement, in favour of that which, in the eye of morality, was already of indispensable obligation. It teaches me to do something from a precarious and temporary motive, which ought to be done for its intrinsic recommendations. If therefore right motives and a pure intention are constituent parts of virtue, promises are clearly at variance with virtue.

But promises will not always come in reinforcement of that which was duty before the promise was made. When it is otherwise, there is obviously a contention, between what would have been obligatory, if no promise had intervened, and what the promise which has been given, has a tendency to render obligatory.

Nor can it with much cogency be alleged in this argument, that promises may at least assume an empire over things indifferent. There is nothing which is truly indifferent. All things in the universe are connected together.[1] It is true, that many of these links in human affairs, are too subtle to be traced by our grosser optics. But we should observe as many of them as we are able. He that is easily satisfied as to the morality of his conduct, will suppose that questions of duty are of rare occurrence, and perhaps lament that there is so little within his sphere to perform. But he that is anxiously alive to the inspirations of virtue, will scarcely find an hour in which he cannot, by act or preparation, contribute to the general weal. If then every shilling of our property, and every faculty of our mind, have received their destination from the principles of unalterable justice, promises have scarcely an atom of ground upon which they can properly and legitimately be called to decide.

There is another consideration of great weight in this case. Our faculties and our possessions are the means by which we are enabled to benefit others. Our time is the theatre in which only these means can unfold themselves. There is nothing the right disposal of which is more sacred. In order to the employing our faculties and our possessions in the way most conducive to the general good, we are bound to acquire all the information which our opportunities enable us to acquire. Now

[1] II. v, p. 85.

one of the principal means of information, is time. We must therefore devote to that object all the time our situation will allow. But we
abridge, and that in the most essential point, the time of gaining information, if we bind ourselves today, to the conduct we will observe
two months hence. He who thus anticipates upon the stores of knowledge, is certainly not less improvident, than he who lives by antici-
pating the stores of fortune.

An active and conscientious man will continually add to his materials
of judgement. Nor is it enough to say, that every man ought to regard
his judgement as immature, and look forward with impatience to the
moment which shall detect his present oversights. Beside this, it will
always happen, that, however mature the faculties of any individual
may deserve to be considered, he will be perpetually acquiring new
information as to that respecting which his conduct is to be decided at
some future period. Let the case be of an indentured servant. Why
should I, unless there be something in the circumstances obliging me to
submit to this disadvantage, engage to allow him to reside for a term of
years under my roof, and to employ towards him a uniform mode of
treatment, whatever his character may prove in the sequel? Why should
he engage to live with and serve me however tyrannical, cruel or
absurd may be my carriage towards him? We shall both of us hereafter know more of each other, and of the benefits or inconveniences
attendant on our connection. Why preclude ourselves from the use of
this knowledge? Such a situation will inevitably generate a perpetual
struggle, between the independent dictates of reason, and the conduct
which the particular compact into which we have entered, may be
supposed to prescribe.

It follows from what has been here adduced, that promises, in the
same sense as has already been observed of government, are an evil,
though, it may be, in some cases a necessary evil.—To remove the
obscurity which might otherwise accompany this mode of expression,
it is perhaps proper to advert to the sense in which the word evil is
here used.

Evil may be either general or individual: an event may either be
productive of evil in its direct and immediate operation, or in a just
balance and comprehensive estimate of all the effects with which it is
pregnant. In whichsoever of these senses the word is understood, the
evil is not imaginary, but real.

Evil is a term, which differs from pain, only as it has a more comprehensive meaning. It may be defined to signify, whatever is painful

itself, or is connected with pain, as an antecedent is connected with its consequent. Thus explained, it appears that a thing not immediately painful may be evil, but in a somewhat improper and imperfect sense. It bears the name of evil not upon its own account. Nothing is evil in the fullest sense but pain.

To this it may be added that pain is always an evil. Pleasure and pain, happiness and misery, constitute the whole ultimate subject of moral enquiry. There is nothing desirable, but the obtaining of the one, and the avoiding of the other. All the researches of human imagination cannot add a single article to this summary of good. Hence it follows that, wherever pain exists, there is evil. Were it otherwise, there would be no such thing as evil. If pain in one individual be not an evil, then it would not be an evil for pain to be felt by every individual that exists, and for ever. The universe is no more than a collection of individuals.

To illustrate this by an obvious example. The amputation of a leg is an evil of considerable magnitude. The pain attendant on the operation is exquisite. The cure is slow and tormenting. When cured, the man who has suffered the amputation, is precluded for ever, from a variety, both of agreeable amusements, and useful occupations. Suppose him to suffer this operation from pure wantonness, and we shall then see its calamity in the most striking light. Suppose, on the other hand, the operation to be the only alternative for stopping a mortification, and it becomes relatively good. But it does not, upon this account, cease to be an absolute evil. The painful sensation, at least to a considerable degree, remains; and the abridgement of his pleasures and utility for the rest of his life, is in no respect altered.

The case of promises is considerably similar to this. So far as they have any effect, they depose us, as to the particular to which they relate, from the use of our own understanding; they call off our attention from the direct tendencies of our conduct, and fix it upon a merely local and precarious consideration. There may be cases in which they are necessary and ought to be employed: but we should never suffer ourselves, by their temporary utility to be induced to forget their intrinsic nature, and the demerits which adhere to them independently of any peculiar concurrence of circumstances.

Thirdly, it may be added to the preceding observations, that promises are by no means of so frequent necessity as has been often imagined.

It may be asked, 'How, without the intervention of promises, can the affairs of the world be carried on?' To this it will be a sufficient answer in the majority of instances, to say, that they will be best carried on by rational and intelligent beings acting as if they were rational and intelligent. Why should it be supposed that affairs would not for the most part go on sufficiently well, though my neighbour could no further depend upon my assistance, than it appeared reasonable to grant it? This will, upon many occasions, be a sufficient dependence, if I be honest; nor will he, if he be honest, desire anything further.

But it will be alleged, 'Human pursuits are often of a continued tenor, made up of a series of actions, each of which is adopted, not for its own sake, but for the sake of some conclusion in which it terminates. Many of these depend for their success upon co-operation and concert. It is therefore necessary that I should have some clear and specific reason to depend upon the fidelity of my coadjutor, that so I may not be in danger, when I have for a length of time persisted in my exertions, of being frustrated by some change that his sentiments have undergone in the interval.' To this it may be replied, that such a pledge of fidelity is less frequently necessary than is ordinarily imagined. Were it to be superseded in a variety of cases, men would be taught to have more regard to their own exertions, and less to the assistance of others, which caprice may refuse, or justice oblige them to withhold. They would acquire such merit, as should oblige every honest man, if needful, to hasten to their succour; and engage in such pursuits, as, not depending upon the momentary caprice of individuals, rested for their success upon the less precarious nature of general circumstances.

Having specified the various limitations that exist as to the utility of promises, it remains for us to discuss their form and obligation in the cases where they may be conceived to be necessary.

Promises are of two kinds, perfect and imperfect. A perfect promise is where the declaration of intention is made by me, for the express purpose of serving as a ground of expectation to my neighbour respecting my future conduct. An imperfect promise is where it actually thus serves as a ground of expectation, though that was not my purpose when I made the declaration. Imperfect promises are of two classes: I may have reason, or I may have no reason, to know, when I make the declaration, that it will be acted upon by my neighbour, though not assuming the specific form of an engagement.

As to imperfect promises it may be observed, that they are wholly unavoidable. No man can always refrain from declaring his intention as to his future conduct. Nay, it should seem that, in many cases, if a man enquire of me the state of my mind in this respect, duty obliges me to inform him of this as I would of any other fact. Were it otherwise, a perpetual coldness and reserve would pervade all human intercourse. But the improvement of mankind rests upon nothing so essentially, as upon the habitual practice of candour, frankness and sincerity.

Perfect promises will also in various instances occur. I have occasion for an interview with a particular person tomorrow. I inform him of my intention of being upon a certain spot at a given hour of the day. It is convenient to him to go to the same place at the same time, for the purpose of meeting me. In this case, it is impossible to prevent the mutual declaration of intention, from serving as a sort of pledge of the performance. Qualifying expressions will make little alteration: the ordinary circumstances which qualify engagements, will in most cases be understood, whether they are stated or no. Appointments of this sort, so far from deserving to be uniformly avoided, ought in many cases to be sought, that there may be as little waste of time or exertion on either side, as the nature of the situation will admit.

To proceed from the manner in which engagements are made, to the obligation that results from them. This obligation is of different degrees according to the nature of the case; but it is impossible to deny that it may be of the most serious import. We have already seen that each man is entitled to his sphere of discretion, which another may not, unless under the most imperious circumstances, infringe.[1] But I infringe it as substantially, by leading him into a certain species of conduct through the means of delusive expectations, as by any system of usurpation it is possible to employ. A person promises me, I will suppose, five hundred pounds for a certain commodity, a book it may be, which I am to manufacture. I am obliged to spend several months in the production. Surely, after this, he can rarely be justified in disappointing me, and saying, I have found a better object upon which to employ my money. . . .

The case here is of the same nature as of any other species of property. Property is sacred: there is but one way in which duty requires the possessor to dispose of it, but I may not forcibly interfere, and dispose of it in the best way in his stead. This is the ordinary law of property, as derived from the principles of universal morality.[2] But there are cases that supersede this law. The principle that attributes to every man the disposal of his property, as well as that distributes to every man his sphere of discretion, derives its force in both instances, from the consideration, that a greater sum of happiness will result from its

[1] II. v.   [2] Book VIII.

observance than its infringement. Wherever therefore the contrary to this is clearly the case, there the force of the principle is suspended. What shall prevent me from taking by force from my neighbour's store, if the alternative be that I must otherwise perish with hunger? What shall prevent me from supplying the distress of my neighbour, from property that, strictly speaking, is not my own, if the emergency be terrible, and will not admit of delay? Nothing; unless it be the punishment that is reserved for such conduct in some instances; since it is no more fitting that I should bring upon myself calamity and death, than that I should suffer them to fall upon another.

The vesting of property in any individual admits of different degrees of fullness, and, in proportion to that fullness, will be the mischief resulting from its violation. If then it appear that, even when the vesting amounts to the fullness of regular possession, there are cases in which it ought to be violated, the different degrees that fall short of this, will admit of still greater modification. It is in vain that the whole multitude of moralists assures us, that the sum I owe to another man, is as little to be infringed upon, as the wealth of which he is in possession. Every one feels the fallacy of this maxim. The sum I owe to another, may in many cases be paid, at my pleasure, either today or tomorrow, either this week or next. The means of payment, particularly with a man of slender resources, must necessarily be fluctuating, and he must employ his discretion, as to the proportion between his necessary and his gratuitous disbursements. When he ultimately fails of payment, the mischief he produces is real, but is not so great, at least in ordinary cases, as that which attends upon robbery. In fine, it is a law resulting from the necessity of nature, that he who has any species of property in trust, for however short a time, must have a discretion, sometimes less and sometimes greater, as to the disposal of it.

To return once more to the main principle in this gradation. The property, most completely sanctioned by all the general rules that can be devised, is yet not inviolable. The imperious principle of self-preservation may authorize me to violate it. A great and eminent balance of good to the public may authorize its violation; and upon this ground we see proprietors occasionally compelled to part with their possessions, under every mode of government in the world. As a general maxim it may be admitted, that force is a legitimate means of prevention, where the alternative is complete, and the employment of force will not produce a greater evil, or subvert the general tranquillity. But, if direct force be in certain cases justifiable, indirect force, or the employment of the means placed in my hands without an anxious enquiry respecting the subordinate regulations of property, where the benefit to be produced is clear, is still more justifiable. Upon this ground, it may be my duty to relieve, upon some occasions, the wretchedness of my neighbour, without having first balanced the debtor and creditor side of my accounts, or when I know that balance to be against me. Upon this ground, every promise is considered as given under a reserve for unforeseen and imperious circumstances, whether that reserve be specifically stated or no. Upon the same ground an appointment for an interview is considered as subject to a similar reserve; though the time of my neighbour, which I dissipate upon that supposition, is as real a property as his wealth, is a part of that sphere over which every man is entitled to the exercise of his separate discretion. It is impossible that human society can subsist, without frequent encroachments of one man upon his neighbour: we sufficiently discharge our duty, if we habitually recollect that each man has his province, and endeavour to regulate our conduct accordingly.

These principles are calculated to set in a clearer light than they have often been exhibited, the cases that authorize the violation of promises. Compact is not the foundation of morality; on the contrary, it is an expedient to which we are sometimes obliged to have resort, but the introduction of which must always be regarded by an enlightened observer with jealousy. It ought never to be called forth but in cases of the clearest necessity. It is not the principle upon which our common happiness reposes; it is only one of the means for securing that happiness. The adherence to promises therefore, as well as their employment in the first instance, must be decided by the general criterion, and maintained only so far as, upon a comprehensive view, it shall be found productive of a balance of happiness.

There is further an important distinction to be made, between a promise given without an intention to perform it, and a promise which information, afterwards acquired, persuades me to violate. The first can scarcely in any instance take place, without fixing a stain upon the promiser, and exhibiting him, to say the least, as a man greatly deficient in delicacy of moral discrimination. The case of the second is incomparably different. Every engagement into which I have entered, an adherence to which I shall afterwards find to be a material obstacle to my utility . . . ought to be violated: nor can there be any limitation upon this maxim, except where the violation will greatly encroach upon the province and jurisdiction of my neighbour.

Let us apply these remarks upon the nature of promises, to the doctrine of a social contract. It is not through the medium of any supposed promise or engagement, that we are induced to believe, that the conduct of our neighbour will not be ridiculously inconsistent or wantonly malicious. If he protest in the most solemn way against being concluded by any such promise, at the same time that he conducts himself in a rational and sober manner, he will not find us less disposed to confide in him. We depend as readily upon a foreigner, that he will not break the laws, and expose himself to their penalties (for this has been supposed to be one of the principal branches of the social contract), as we do upon our countryman. If we do not depend equally upon the Arabs who inhabit the plains of Asia, it is not because we impute to them a deficiency in their social contract, but because we are ignorant of their principles of conduct, or know that those principles do not afford us a sufficient security, as to the particulars of our intercourse with them. Tell a man what will be the solid and substantial effects of his proceeding, how it will affect his neighbours, and what influence it will have upon his own happiness, and you speak to the unalienable feelings of the human mind. But tell him that, putting these things for the present out of our consideration, it is sufficient that he has promised a certain conduct, or that, if he have not expressly promised it, he has promised it by implication, or that, if he have not promised it, his ancestors a few generations back promised it for him; and you speak of a motive that scarcely finds a sympathetic chord in one human breast, and that few will so much as understand.

. . . .

There is another principle concerned in this subject, and that is sincerity: I may not evade the laws of the society by any dishonourable subterfuge or contemptible duplicity. But the obligation of sincerity, like all the other great principles of morality, is not founded in promises, but in the indefeasible benefit annexed to its observance. Add to which, the sincerity I am bound to practise towards the magistrate, particularly in a case where his requisition shall be unjust, is not different in its principle, and is certainly of no higher obligation, than the sincerity I am bound to practise towards a private individual.

Let us however suppose that the assertion of an implied contract in every community is true, or let us take the case where an actual engagement has been entered into by the members of the society. This appears from what has been already delivered, to be of that class of promises which are of slightest obligation. In the notion of a social contract little is made over, little expectation is excited, and therefore little mischief is included in its breach. What we most expect and require in a member of the same community, is the qualities of a man, and the conduct that ought to be observed indifferently by a native or a stranger. Where a promise or an oath is imposed upon me superfluously, as is always the case with promises of allegiance; or where I am compelled to make it by the operation of a penalty; the treatment I suffer is atrociously unjust, and of consequence the breach of such a promise is peculiarly susceptible of apology. A promise of allegiance is a declaration that I approve the actual constitution of things, and, so far as it is binding, an engagement that I will continue to support that constitution. But I shall support it, for as long a time, and in as great a degree, as I approve of it, without needing the intervention of a promise. It will be my duty not to undertake its destruction by precipitate and unpromising means, for a much more cogent reason than can be deduced from any promise I have made. An engagement for anything further than this, is both immoral and absurd: it is an engagement to a nonentity, a constitution; a promise that I will abstain from doing that which I believe to be beneficial to my fellow citizens.

CHAPTER IV

OF POLITICAL AUTHORITY

HAVING rejected the hypotheses that have most generally been advanced as to the rational basis of a political authority, let us enquire whether we may not arrive at the same object, by a simple investigation of the obvious reason of the case, without refinement of system or fiction of process.

Government then being first supposed necessary for the welfare of mankind, the most important principle that can be imagined relative to its structure, seems to be this; that, as government is a transaction in the name and for the benefit of the whole, every member of the community ought to have some share in the selection of its measures. The arguments in support of this proposition are various.

First, it has already appeared that there is no satisfactory criterion, marking out any man, or set of men, to preside over the rest.

Secondly, all men are partakers of the common faculty, reason; and may be supposed to have some communication with the common instructor, truth. It would be wrong in an affair of such momentous concern, that any chance for additional wisdom should be rejected; nor can we tell, in many cases, till after the experiment, how eminent any individual may be found, in the business of guiding and deliberating for his fellows.

Thirdly, government is a contrivance instituted for the security of individuals; and it seems both reasonable, that each man should have a share in providing for his own security; and probable, that partiality and cabal will by this means be most effectually excluded.

Lastly, to give each man a voice in the public concerns comes nearest to that fundamental purpose of which we should never lose sight, the uncontrolled exercise of private judgement. Each man will thus be inspired with a consciousness of his own importance, and the slavish feelings that shrink up the soul in the presence of an imagined superior, will be unknown.

Admitting then the propriety of each man having a share in directing the affairs of the whole in the first instance, it seems necessary that he should concur in electing a house of representatives, if he be the member of a large state; or, even in a small one, that he should assist in the appointment of officers and administrators;[1] which implies, first, a delegation of authority to these officers, and, secondly, a tacit consent, or rather an admission of the necessity, that the questions to be debated should abide the decision of a majority.

But to this system of delegation the same objections may be urged, that were cited from Rousseau under the head of a social contract. It may be alleged that, 'if it be the business of every man to exercise his own judgement, he can in no instance surrender this function into the hands of another.'

To this objection it may be answered, first, that the parallel is by no means complete, between an individual's exercise of his judgement in a case that is truly his own, and his exercise of his judgement in an article where the province of a government is already admitted. If there be something contrary to the simplest ideas of justice in such a delegation, this is an evil inseparable from political government. The true and only adequate apology of government is necessity; the office of common deliberation is solely, to supply the most eligible means of meeting that necessity.

Secondly, the delegation we are here considering, is not, as the word

[1] We shall be led, in a subsequent branch of this enquiry, to investigate how far either of these measures is inseparable from the maintenance of social order. V. xxiv.

in its most obvious sense may seem to imply, the act of one man committing to another, a function which, strictly speaking, it became him to exercise for himself. Delegation, in every instance in which it can be reconciled with justice, proposes for its object the general good. The individuals to whom the delegation is made, are either more likely, from talents or leisure, to perform the function in the most eligible manner, or there is at least some public interest requiring that it should be performed by one or a few persons, rather than by every individual for himself. This is the case, whether in that first and simplest of all political delegations, the prerogative of a majority, or in the election of a house of representatives, or in the appointment of public officers. Now all contest, as to the person who shall exercise a certain function and the propriety of resigning it, is frivolous, the moment it is decided how and by whom it can most advantageously be exercised. It is of no consequence that I am the parent of a child, when it has once been ascertained that the child will live with greater benefit under the superintendence of a stranger.

Lastly, it is a mistake to imagine that the propriety of restraining me, when my conduct is injurious, rises out of any delegation of mine. The justice of employing force upon certain emergencies, was at least equally cogent before the existence of society.[1] Force ought never to be resorted to but in cases of absolute necessity; and, when such cases occur, it is the duty of every man to defend himself from violation. There is therefore no delegation necessary on the part of the offender; but the community, in the censure it exercises over him, puts itself in the place of the injured party.

From what is here stated, we may be enabled to form the clearest and most unexceptionable idea of the nature of government. Every man, as was formerly observed,[2] has a sphere of discretion; that sphere is limited by the co-ordinate sphere of his neighbour. The maintenance of this limitation, the office of taking care that no man exceeds his sphere, is the first business of government. Its powers, in this respect, are a combination of the powers of individuals to control the excesses of each other. Hence is derived to the individuals of the community, a second and indirect province, of providing, by themselves or their representatives, that this control is not exercised in a despotical manner, or carried to an undue excess.

It may perhaps be imagined by some persons, that the doctrine here delivered, of the justice of proceeding in common concerns by a com-

<hr />

[1] Ch. i, p. 97.   [2] IIX. v.

mon deliberation, is nearly coincident with that which affirms a lawful government to derive its authority from a social contract. Let us consider what is the true difference between them: and this seems principally to lie in the following particular.

The principle of a social contract, is an engagement, to which a man is bound by honour, fidelity or consistency to adhere. According to the principle here laid down, he is bound to nothing. He joins in the common deliberation, because he foresees that some authority will be exercised, and because this is the best chance that offers itself, for approximating the exercise of that authority, to the dictates of his own understanding. But, when the deliberation is over, he finds himself as much disengaged as ever. If he conform to the mandate of authority, it is either because he individually approves it, or from a principle of prudence, because he foresees that a greater mass of evil will result from his disobedience, than of good. He obeys the freest and best constituted authority, upon the same principle that would lead him, in most instances, to yield obedience to a despotism; only with this difference, that, if the act of authority be erroneous, he finds it less probable that it will be corrected in the first instance, than in the second, since it proceeds from the erroneous judgement of a whole people.—But all this will appear with additional evidence, when we come to treat of the subject of obedience.

Too much stress has undoubtedly been laid upon the idea, as of a grand and magnificent spectacle, of a nation deciding for itself upon some great public principle, and of the highest magistracy yielding its claims when the general voice has pronounced. The value of the whole must at last depend upon the quality of their decision. Truth cannot be made more true by the number of its votaries. Nor is the spectacle much less interesting, of a solitary individual, bearing his undaunted testimony in favour of justice, though opposed by misguided millions. Within certain limits however the beauty of the exhibition may be acknowledged. That a nation should exercise undiminished its function of common deliberation, is a step gained, and a step that inevitably leads to an improvement of the character of individuals. That men should agree in the assertion of truth, is no unpleasing evidence of their virtue. Lastly, that an individual, however great may be his imaginary elevation, should be obliged to yield his personal pretensions to the sense of the community, at least bears the appearance of a practical confirmation of the great principle, that all private considerations must yield to the general good.

CHAPTER V

OF LEGISLATION

HAVING thus far investigated the nature of political functions, it seems necessary that some explanation should be given upon the subject of legislation. 'Who is it that has authority to make laws? What are the characteristics of that man or body of men, in whom the tremendous faculty is vested, of prescribing to the rest of the community, what they are to perform, and what to avoid?'

The answer to these questions is exceedingly simple: Legislation, as it has been usually understood, is not an affair of human competence. Immutable reason is the true legislator, and her decrees it behoves us to investigate. The functions of society extend, not to the making, but the interpreting of law; it cannot decree, it can only declare that, which the nature of things has already decreed, and the propriety of which irresistibly flows from the circumstances of the case.

Montesquieu says that, 'in a free state, every man will be his own legislator.'[1] This is not true, in matters the most purely individual, unless in the limited sense already explained. It is the office of conscience to determine, 'not like an Asiatic cadi, according to the ebbs and flows of his own passions, but like a British judge, who makes no new law, but faithfully declares that law which he finds already written.'[2] The same distinction is to be made upon the subject of political authority. All government is, strictly speaking, executive. It has appeared to be necessary, with respect to men as we at present find them, that force should sometimes be employed in repressing injustice; and for the same reasons, that this force should, as far as possible, be vested in the community. To the public support of justice therefore the authority of the community extends. But no sooner does it wander in the smallest degree from the line of justice, than its proper authority is at an end; it may be submitted to by its subjects from necessity; from necessity it may be exercised, as an individual complies with his ill-informed conscience in default of an enlightened one; but it ought never to be confounded with the lessons of real duty, or the decisions of impartial truth.

[1] *Esprit des Loix*, XI. vi.
[2] [Laurence] Sterne [1713–68], *Sermons* [1751], 'Of a Good Conscience.'

CHAPTER VI

OF OBEDIENCE

THE two great questions upon which the theory of government depends, are: Upon what foundation can political authority with the greatest propriety rest? and, What are the considerations which bind us to political obedience? Having entered at length into the first of these questions, it is time that we should proceed to the examination of the second.

One of the most popular theories, relative to the foundation of political authority, we have seen to be that of an original contract, affirming, that the criterion of political justice is to be found, in the conventions and rules which have been adjusted by the community at large. In pursuance of this original position, the same theorists have necessarily gone on and affirmed, that the true source of obligation to political obedience was to be found in the same principle, and that, in obeying a government regularly constituted, we did nothing more than perform our engagements.

The reasonings in support of this hypothesis are obvious. 'Suppose a number of persons living in any neighbourhood, should perceive that great common benefit would accrue from building a bridge, sinking a canal, or making a highway. The simplest mode for them to adopt, is, to consult together, and raise the money necessary for effecting this desirable purpose, by each man assessing himself according to his ability, and contributing his quota to a common fund. Now it is plain that, in this case, each pays his assessment (supposing the payment to be voluntary) in consideration of the previous agreement; his contribution would be of no avail, however desirable was the object to be effected, had he not reason to depend upon the rest of the neighbourhood, that they would pay theirs. But government,' say the advocates of an original contract, 'when regularly constituted, is precisely such a provision, as the one here stated for building a bridge, or making a road: it is a consultation and settlement among the different members of a community, as to the regulations most conducive to the benefit of the whole. It is upon this principle that taxes are paid, and that the force of the community is drawn out in such proportions, as are necessary to repress the external or internal disturbers of its tranquillity. The ground therefore upon which each man contributes his share of effort or property, is, that he may perform his contract, and discharge that for which he has engaged as a member of the community.'

The refutation of this hypothesis has been anticipated in the preceding chapters.—Government can with no propriety be compared to the construction of a bridge or a canal, a matter of mere convenience and refinement. It is supposed to be of the most irresistible necessity; it is indisputably an affair of hardship and restraint. It constitutes other men the arbitrators of my actions, and the ultimate disposers of my destiny.—Almost every member of every community that has existed on the face of the earth, might reasonably say, 'I know of no such contract as you describe; I never entered into any such engagement; I never promised to obey; it must therefore be an iniquitous imposition to call upon me to do something, under pretence of a promise I never made.'—The reason a man lives under any particular government is partly necessity; he cannot easily avoid living under some government, and it is often scarcely in his power to abandon the country in which he was born: it is also partly a choice of evils; no man can be said, in this case, to enjoy that freedom which is essential to the forming a contract, unless it could be shown that he had a power of instituting, somewhere, a government adapted to his own conceptions.—Government in reality, as has abundantly appeared, is a question of force, and not of consent. It is desirable, that a government should be made as agreeable as possible to the ideas and inclinations of its subjects; and that they should be consulted, as extensively as may be, respecting its construction and regulations. But, at last, the best constituted government that can be formed, particularly for a large community, will contain many provisions that, far from having obtained the consent of all its members, encounter even in their outset a strenuous, though ineffectual, opposition.—From the whole of these reasonings it appears, that, in those measures which have the concurrence of my judgement, I may reasonably be expected to co-operate with willingness and zeal; but, for the rest, my only justifiable ground of obedience is, that I will not disturb the repose of the community, or that I do not perceive the question to be of sufficient magnitude to authorize me in incurring the penalty.

To understand the subject of obedience with sufficient accuracy, it is necessary that we should attend to the various shades of meaning of which the word is susceptible.

Every voluntary action is an act of obedience; in performing it, we comply with some view, and are guided by some incitement or motive.

The purest kind of obedience is, where an action flows from the independent conviction of our private judgement, where we are directed, not by the precarious and mutable interference of another, but by a recollection of the intrinsic and indefeasible tendency of the action to be performed.[1] In this case the object of obedience, is the dictate of the understanding: the action may, or may not, be such as my neighbours or the community will approve, but this approbation does not constitute its direct motive.

The kind of obedience, which stands next to this in its degree of voluntariness, arises in the following manner. Every man is capable of comparing himself with his fellow. Every man will find, that there are some points, in which he is the equal or perhaps the superior of other men, but that there are certainly some points, in which other men are superior to him. The superiority in question in the present instance, is superiority of intellect or information. It may happen, that the point in which another man surpasses me, is a point of some importance to my welfare or convenience. I want, for example, to build a house, or to sink a well. It may happen that I have not leisure or means to acquire the science necessary for this purpose. Upon that supposition I am not to be blamed, if I employ a builder for the first, or a mechanic for the second; nor shall I be liable to blame, if I work in person under his direction. This sort of obedience is distinguished by the appellation of confidence; and to justify, in a moral view, the reposing of confidence, the only thing necessary is, that it should be fitter and more beneficial, all things considered, that the function to be performed should be performed by another person, than that it should be performed by me.

The third and last kind of obedience necessary to be averted to upon the present occasion, is, where I do that which is not prescribed to me by my private judgement, merely on account of the mischievous consequences that I foresee will be annexed to my omission, by the arbitrary interference of some voluntary being.

The most important observation that arises upon the statement of this scale of obedience, is, that obedience in the second degree, ought to be guarded with as much jealousy, and kept by the person yielding obedience within as narrow limits, as possible. The last sort of obedience will frequently be necessary. Voluntary beings constitute a large portion of the universe; we shall often have occasion to foresee their arbitrary determinations and conduct, nor can knowledge, as such, in any instance fail to be a desirable acquisition; our conduct therefore

[1] II. vi.

must and ought to be modified by their interferences. Morality, as has already been frequently observed, consists entirely in an estimate of consequences; he is the truly virtuous man, who produces the greatest portion of benefit his situation will admit. The most exalted morality indeed, that in which the heart reposes with the most unmingled satisfaction, relates to the inherent and indefeasible tendencies of actions. But we shall be by no means excusable, if we overlook, in our system of conduct, the arbitrary awards of other men. Nothing can be more certain, than that an action, suppose of inferior moment or utility, which for its own sake might be right to be performed, it may become my duty to neglect, if I know that by performing it I shall incur the penalty of death.

The mischiefs attendant on the frequent recurrence of this species of obedience, and the grounds upon which its interference is to be guarded against, as extensively as circumstances will admit, have already been stated.[1] Yet obedience flowing from the consideration of a penalty, is less a source of degradation and depravity, than a habit of obedience founded in confidence. The man who yields it, may reserve, in its most essential sense, his independence. He may be informed in judgement, and resolved in purpose, as to every moral and social obligation. He may suffer his understanding neither to be seduced nor confounded; he may observe, in its fullest extent, the mistake and pre-possession of his neighbour, to which he thus finds it necessary to accommodate himself. It seems possible, that he who thus pities the folly, while he complies with the necessity, may still, even under this discipline, grow in discrimination and sagacity.

The greatest mischief that can arise in the progress of obedience, is, where it shall lead us, in any degree, to depart from the independence of our understanding, a departure which general and unlimited confidence necessarily includes. In this view, the best advice that could be given to a person in a state of subjection, is, 'Comply, where the necessity of the case demands it; but criticize while you comply. Obey the unjust mandates of your governors; for this prudence and a consideration of the common safety may require; but treat them with no false lenity, regard them with no indulgence. Obey; this may be right; but beware of reverence. Reverence nothing but wisdom and skill: government may be vested in the fittest persons; then they are entitled to reverence, because they are wise, and not because they are governors: and it may be vested in the worst. Obedience will occasionally be right

---

[1] II. vi.

in both cases: you may run south, to avoid a wild beast advancing in that direction, though you want to go north. But be upon your guard against confounding things, so totally unconnected with each other, as a purely political obedience, and respect. Government is nothing but regulated force; force is its appropriate claim upon your attention. It is the business of individuals to persuade; the tendency of concentrated strength, is only to give consistency and permanence to an influence more compendious than persuasion.'

All this will be made somewhat clearer, if we reflect on the proper correlative of obedience, authority: and here let us recur to the three sorts of obedience above specified.

The first kind of authority then, is the authority of reason, what is really such, or is only conceived to be such. The terms, both authority and obedience, are less frequently employed in this sense than in either of the following.

The second species of authority, is that which depends for its validity upon the confidence of him with whom it prevails, and is where, not having myself acquired such information as to enable me to form a judicious opinion, I yield a greater or less degree of deference to the known sentiment and decision of another. This seems to be the strictest and most precise meaning of the word authority; as obedience, in its most refined sense, denotes that compliance which is the offspring of respect.

Authority in the last of the three senses alluded to, is where a man, in issuing his precept, does not deliver that which may be neglected with impunity; but his requisition is attended with a sanction, and the violation of it will be followed with a penalty. This is the species of authority which properly connects itself with the idea of government. It is a violation of political justice, to confound the authority which depends upon force, with the authority which arises from reverence and esteem; the modification of my conduct which might be due in the case of a wild beast, with the modification which is due to superior wisdom. These two kinds of authority may happen to vest in the same person; but they are altogether distinct and independent of each other.

The consequence which has flowed from confounding them, has been, a greater debasement of the human character, than could easily have followed upon direct and unqualified slavery. The principle of confidence, and the limitations with which it ought to be attended, are capable of an easy and convincing explication. I am bound, to the fullest extent that is consistent with my opportunities and situation, to exercise my understanding. Man is the ornament of the universe, only in proportion as he consults his judgement. Whatever I submit to from the irresistible impulse of necessity, is not mine, and debases me only as it tends gradually to shackle the intrepidity of my character. With respect to some men therefore it may be innoxious. But, where I make the voluntary surrender of my understanding, and commit my conscience to another man's keeping, the consequence is clear. I then become the most mischievous and pernicious of animals. I annihilate my individuality as a man, and dispose of my force as an animal to him among my neighbours, who shall happen to excel in imposture and artifice, and to be least under restraint from the scruples of integrity and justice. I put an end, as to my own share, to that happy collision of understandings, upon which the hopes of human improvement depend. I can have no genuine fortitude, for fortitude is the offspring of conviction. I can have no conscious integrity, for I do not understand my own principles, and have never brought them to the test of examination. I am the ready tool of injustice, cruelty and profligacy; and, if at any time I am not employed in their purposes, it is the result of accident, not of my own precaution and honesty.

The understanding must first be consulted, and then, no doubt, confidence will come in for its share of jurisdiction. The considerations, which will have influence in the mind of an impartial enquirer, to enforce, or to give an air of doubtfulness to, his opinions, are numerous. Among these, he will not refuse attention to the state of opinion in the present or any preceding generation of men. In the meantime it will rarely happen, that the authority of other men's judgement in cases of general enquiry, will be of great weight. Either men of equal talents and integrity have embraced both sides; or their prejudice, and deficiency as to the materials of judging, have been such, as extremely to weaken their testimony. Add to this, that the only ground of opinion, strictly so called, is the intrinsic evidence of the opinion itself; upon that our judgement must be formed; and the decision of others can have no effect, but that of increasing or diminishing our doubt of the rectitude of our own perceptions. The direct province of confidence, is to supply, in the best way the case will admit, the defect of our knowledge; but it can never, strictly speaking, furnish knowledge itself. Its proper use belongs rather to the circumstance, of actions immediately to be determined on, than to matters of speculation and principle. Thus, I ought not perhaps to refuse weight to the advice of some men, even when the reasons by which they enforce their advice are conceived by me to be problematical: and thus, I am bound, as before stated, to trust another, in the moment of emergency, in the art he has studied, rather than myself by whom that study was never undertaken. Except when the nature of my situation calls upon me to act, I shall do more wisely in refraining from any decision, in questions where I am not assisted to decide by information that is properly my own.

One of the lessons most assiduously inculcated upon mankind in all ages and countries, is that of reverence to our superiors. If by this maxim be intended our superiors in wisdom, it may be admitted, but with some qualification. But, if it imply our superiors in station only, nothing can be more contrary to reason and justice. Is it not enough that they have usurped certain advantages over us to which they can show no equitable claim; and must we also humble our courage, and renounce our independence, in their presence? Why reverence a man because he happens to be born to certain privileges; or because a concurrence of circumstances (for wisdom, as we have already seen, gives a claim to respect utterly distinct from power) has procured him a share in the legislative or executive government of our country? Let him content himself with the obedience which is the result of force; for to that only is he entitled.

Reverence to our superiors in wisdom is to be admitted, but with considerable limitations. I am bound, as has already appeared, to repose certain functions, such as that of building my house, or educating my child, in the hands of him by whom those functions will most properly be discharged. It may be right, that I should act under the person to whom I have thus given my suffrage, in cases where I have reason to be persuaded of his skill, and cannot be expected to acquire the necessary skill myself. But in those cases of general justice which are equally within the province of every human understanding, I am a deserter from the requisitions of duty, if I do not assiduously exert my faculties, or if I be found to act contrary to the conclusions they would dictate, from deference to the opinions of another.—The reverence we are here considering is a reverence prompting us to some kind of obedience; there is another kind, terminating in esteem only, that, so far from deserving to be confined within these strict limitations, we are bound to extend to every man who is the possessor of estimable qualities.

The reverence which is due from a child to his parent, or rather to his senior in age and experience, falls under the same rules as have already been delivered. Wherever I have good reason to believe, that another person knows better than myself what is proper to be done, there I ought to conform to his direction. But the advantage which he possesses, must be obvious, otherwise I shall not be justified in my proceeding. If I take into the account every chance for advantage, I shall never act upon the result of my own reflections. The mind of one man is essentially distinct from the mind of another. If each do not preserve his individuality, the judgement of all will be feeble, and the progress of our common understanding inexpressibly retarded. Hence it follows, that the deference of a child becomes vicious, whenever he has reason to doubt that the parent possesses essential information, of which he is deprived. Nothing can be more necessary for the general benefit, than that we should divest ourselves, as soon as the proper period arrives, of the shackles of infancy; that human life should not be one eternal childhood; but that men should judge for themselves, unfettered by the prejudices of education, or the institutions of their country.

To a government therefore, that talked to us of deference to political authority, and honour to be rendered to our superiors, our answer should be: 'It is yours, to shackle the body, and restrain our external actions; that is a restraint we understand. Announce your penalties; and we will make our election of submission or suffering. But do not seek to enslave our minds. Exhibit your force in its plainest form, for that is your province; but seek not to inveigle and mislead us. Obedience and external submission is all you are entitled to claim; you can have no right to extort our deference, and command us not to see, and disapprove of, your errors.' In the meantime it should be observed, that it is by no means a necessary consequence, that we should disapprove of all the measures of government; but there must be disapprobation, wherever there is a question of strict political obedience.

A corollary which flows from these principles is deserving of our attention. Confidence is in all cases the offspring of ignorance. It must therefore continually decline, in relation, as was above stated, to 'those cases of general justice which are equally within the province of every human understanding,'[1] in proportion as wisdom and virtue shall increase. But the questions that belong to the department of government, are questions of general justice. The conduct of an enlightened and virtuous man, can only be conformable to the regulations of government, so far as those regulations are accidentally coincident with his private judgement, or as he acts with prudent and judicious submission to the necessity of the case. He will not act from confidence; for he has him-

[1] p. 123.

self examined, as it was his duty to do, the merits of the action: and he has not failed to detect the imposture, that would persuade us there is a mystery in government, which uninitiated mortals must not presume to penetrate. Now it is sufficiently known that the empire of government is built in opinion;[1] nor is it enough for this purpose, that we refuse to contribute to overturn it by violence, the opinion must go to the extent of prompting us to actual support. No government can subsist in a nation, the individuals of which shall merely abstain from tumultuous resistance, while in their genuine sentiments they censure and despise its institution. In other words, government cannot proceed but upon confidence, as confidence on the other hand cannot exist without ignorance. The true supporters of government are the weak and uninformed, and not the wise. In proportion as weakness and ignorance shall diminish, the basis of government will also decay. This however is an event which ought not to be contemplated with alarm. A catastrophe of this description, would be the true euthanasia of government. If the annihilation of blind confidence and implicit opinion can at any time be effected, there will necessarily succeed in their place, an unforced concurrence of all in prompting the general welfare. But, whatever may be the event in this respect, and the future history of political societies,[2] we shall do well to remember this characteristic of government, and apply it as the universal touchstone of the institution itself. As in the commencement of the present Book we found government indebted for its existence to the errors and perverseness of a few, so it now appears, that it can no otherwise be perpetuated, than by the infantine and uninstructed confidence of the many. It may be to a certain degree doubtful, whether the human species will ever be emancipated from their present subjection and pupillage, but let it not be forgotten that this is their condition. The recollection will be salutary to individuals, and may ultimately be productive of benefit to all.

CHAPTER VII

OF FORMS OF GOVERNMENT

THERE is one other topic relative to general principles of government, which it seems fitting and useful to examine in this place. 'Is there a scheme of political institution, which, as coming nearest to perfection,

---

[1] I. vi, p. 61; II. iii, p. 77.   [2] V. xxii and xxiv.

ought to be prescribed to all nations; or, on the other hand, are different forms of government best adapted to the condition of different nations, each worthy to be commended in its peculiar place, but none proper to be transplanted to another soil?'

The latter part of this alternative is the creed which has ordinarily prevailed; but it is attended with obvious objections.

If one form of government makes one nation happy, why should it not equally contribute to the felicity of another?

The points in which human beings resemble, are infinitely more considerable than those in which they differ. We have the same senses; and the impressions on those senses which afflict me, may ordinarily be expected to be sources of anguish to you. It is true that men differ in their habits and tastes. But these are accidental varieties. There is but one perfection to man; one thing most honourable; one thing that, to a well-organized and healthful mind, will produce the most exquisite pleasure. All else is deviation and error; a disease, to be cured, not to be encouraged. Sensual pleasure on the one hand, or intellectual on the other, is, absolutely speaking, the highest and most desirable. . . .

If then it appears, that the means which are beneficial to one man, ought, in the most important instances, to be deemed most desirable for others, the same principle which applies to all other sources of moral influence, will also apply to government. Every political system must have a certain influence, upon the moral state of the nation among whom it exists. Some are more favourable, or less inimical, to the general interest, than others. That form of society, which is most conducive to improvement, to the exalted and permanent pleasure of man, the sound politician would wish to see universally realized.

Such is the true theory of this subject, taken in its most absolute form; but there are circumstances that qualify the universality of these principles.

The best gift that can be communicated to man, is valuable only so far as it is esteemed. It is in vain that you heap upon me benefits, that I neither understand nor desire. The faculty of understanding is an essential part of every human being, and cannot with impunity be overlooked, in any attempt to alter or meliorate his condition. Government, in particular, is founded in opinion; nor can any attempt to govern men, otherwise than in conformity to their own conceptions, be expected to prove salutary. A project therefore to introduce abruptly any species of political institution, merely from a view to its absolute excellence, and without taking into account the state of the public mind, must be absurd and injurious. The best mode of political society, will, no doubt, be considered by the enlightened friend of his species, as the ultimate object of his speculations and efforts. But he will be on his guard against precipitate measures. The only mode for its secure and auspicious establishment, is through the medium of a general preference in its favour.

The consequence which flows from this view of the subject, is, in a certain degree, favourable to the ideas which were stated in the beginning of the chapter, as constituting the more general and prevailing opinion.

'Different forms of government, are best adapted to the condition of different nations.' Yet there is one form, in itself considered, better than any other form. Every other mode of society, except that which conduces to the best and most pleasurable state of the human species, is at most only an object of toleration. It must of necessity be ill in various respects; it must entail mischiefs; it must foster unsocial and immoral prejudices. Yet upon the whole, it may be, like some excrescences and defects in the human frame, it cannot immediately be removed without introducing something worse. In the machine of human society all the wheels must move together. He that should violently attempt to raise any one part into a condition more exalted than the rest, or force it to start away from its fellows, would be the enemy, and not the benefactor, of his contemporaries.

It follows however, from the principles already detailed, that the interests of the human species require a gradual, but uninterrupted change. He who should make these principles the regulators of his conduct, would not rashly insist upon the instant abolition of all existing abuses. But he would not nourish them with false praise. He would show no indulgence to their enormities. He would tell all the truth he could discover, in relation to the genuine interests of mankind. Truth, delivered in a spirit of universal kindness, with no narrow resentments or angry invective, can scarcely be dangerous, or fail, so far as relates to its own operation, to communicate a similar spirit to the hearer. Truth, however unreserved be the mode of its enunciation, will be sufficiently gradual in its progress. It will be fully comprehended, only by slow degrees, by its most assiduous votaries; and the degrees will be still more temperate, by which it will pervade so considerable a portion of the community, as to render them mature for a change of their common institutions.

Again: if conviction of the understanding be the compass which is to direct our proceedings in the general affairs, we shall have many reforms, but no revolutions.[1] As it is only in a gradual manner that the public can be instructed, a violent explosion in the community, is by no means the most likely to happen, as the result of instruction. Revolutions are the produce of passion, not of sober and tranquil reason. There must be an obstinate resistance to improvement on the one side, to engender a furious determination of realizing a system at a stroke on the other. The reformers must have suffered from incessant counteraction, till, inflamed by the treachery and art of their opponents, they are wrought up to the desperate state of imagining that all must be secured in the first favourable crisis, as the only alternative for its being ever secured. It would seem therefore, that the demand of the effectual ally of the public happiness, upon those who enjoy the privileges of the state, would be, 'Do not give us too soon; do not give us too much; but act under the incessant influence of a disposition to give us something.'

Government, under whatever point of view we examine this topic, is unfortunately pregnant with motives to censure and complaint. Incessant change, everlasting innovation, seem to be dictated by the true interests of mankind. But government is the perpetual enemy of change. What was admirably observed of a particular system of government,[2] is in a great degree true of all: They 'lay their hand on the spring there is in society, and put a stop to its motion.' Their tendency is to perpetuate abuse. Whatever was once thought right and useful, they undertake to entail to the latest posterity. They reverse the genuine propensities of man, and, instead of suffering us to proceed, teach us to look backward for perfection. They prompt us to seek the public welfare, not in alteration and improvement, but in a timid reverence for the decisions of our ancestors, as if it were the nature of the human mind, always to degenerate, and never to advance.

Man is in a state of perpetual mutation. He must grow either better or worse, either correct his habits or confirm them. The government under which we are placed, must either increase our passions and prejudices by fanning the flame, or, by gradually discouraging, tend to extirpate them. In reality, it is impossible to conceive a government that shall have the latter tendency. By its very nature positive institution has a tendency to suspend the elasticity and progress of mind. Every scheme for embodying imperfection must be injurious. That which is today a considerable melioration, will at some future period, if preserved

---

[1] IV. ii.

[2] The Spartan: [John] Logan [1748–88], *Philosophy of History* [1781], p. 69.

unaltered, appear a defect and disease in the body politic. It is earnestly to be desired, that each man should be wise enough to govern himself, without the intervention of any compulsory restraint; and, since government, even in its best state, is an evil, the object principally to be aimed at is, that we should have as little of it, as the general peace of human society will permit.

BOOK IV

OF THE OPERATION OF OPINION
IN SOCIETIES AND INDIVIDUALS

CHAPTER I

OF RESISTANCE

[GODWIN begins this book by summarizing the subjects that he has already treated. He then observes that various miscellaneous topics, which are of considerable importance, remain to be examined, and he proposes to deal with some of these in the current book. These topics, he continues, 'are of different classes, and in a certain degree detached from each other; but may perhaps without impropriety be ranged under two branches: the mode in which the speculative opinions of individuals are to be rendered effectual for the melioration of society; and the mode in which opinion is found to operate in modifying the conduct of individuals'. The first topic to be considered is the right of forceful resistance to political authority.]

. . . 'A nation, ' it has commonly been said, 'has a right to shake off any authority that is usurped over it.' This is a proposition that has generally passed without question, and certainly no proposition can appear more plausible. But, if we examine it minutely, we shall find that it is attended with equivocal circumstances. What do we mean by a nation? Is the whole people concerned in this resistance, or only a part? If the whole be prepared to resist, the whole is persuaded of the injustice of the usurpation. What sort of usurpation is that, which can be exercised by one or a few persons, over a whole nation, universally disapproving of it? Government is founded in opinion.[1] Bad government deceives us first, before it fastens itself upon us like an incubus, oppressing all our efforts. A nation in general must have learned to respect a king and a house of lords, before a king and a house of lords can exercise any authority over them. If a man or a set of men, un-

[1] I. vi, p. 61 ; II, iii, p. 77.

sanctioned by any previous prejudice in their favour, pretend to exercise sovereignty in a country, they will become objects of derision, rather than of serious resistance. Destroy the existing prejudice in favour of any of our present institutions, and they will fall into similar disuse and contempt.

It has sometimes been supposed, 'that an army, foreign or domestic, may be sufficient to hold a people in subjection, completely against their inclination.' . . . A weak, superstitious or ignorant people may be held in the chains of foreign power; but the school of moral and political independence, sends forth pupils of a very different character. In the encounter with their penetration and discernment, tyranny will feel itself powerless and transitory. In a word, either the people are unenlightened and unprepared for a state of freedom, and then the struggle and the consequences of the struggle will be truly perilous; or the progress of political knowledge among them is decisive, and then every one will see how futile and short-lived will be the attempt to hold them in subjection, by means of garrisons and a foreign force. The party attached to liberty is, upon that supposition, the numerous one; they are the persons of true energy, and who have an object worthy of their zeal. Their oppressors, few in number, and degraded to the rank of lifeless machines, wander with no certain destination or prospect, over the vast surface, and are objects of pity, rather than serious alarm. . . . Men would not be inclined pertinaciously to object to a short delay, if they recollected the advantages and the certainty of success with which it is pregnant.—Meanwhile these reasonings turn upon the probability, that the purposes of liberty will be full as effectually answered, without the introduction of force: there can be little doubt of the justifiableness, of a whole nation having recourse to arms, if a case can be made out, in which it shall be impossible for them to prevent the introduction of slavery in any other way.

The same reasonings, with little variation, will apply to the case of an unquestionable majority of a nation, as to that of the whole. The majority of a nation is irresistible; it as little needs to have recourse to violence; there is as little reason to expect that any usurper will be so mad as to contend with it. If ever it appear to be otherwise, it is because, in one of two ways, we deceive ourselves with the term majority. First, nothing is more obvious, than the danger incident to a man of a sanguine temper, of over-estimating the strength of his party. . . .

A second deception that lurks under the word majority, lies, not in the question of number, but of quality and degree of illumination. A majority, we say perhaps, is dissatisfied with the present state of things, and wishes for such a specific alteration. Alas, it is to be feared, that the greater part of this majority are often mere parrots, who have been taught a lesson, of the subject of which they understand little or nothing. . . . It would probably be easy to show, that what they profess to desire, is little better than what they hate. What they hate, is not the general depravation of the human character; and what they desire, is not its improvement. It is an insult upon human understanding, when we speak of persons in this state of infantine ignorance, to say that the majority of the nation is on the side of political renovation. . . .

There is an obvious remedy to each of the deceptions here enumerated: Time. Is it doubtful whether the reformers be a real majority of the inhabitants of any country? Is it doubtful whether the majority truly understand the object of their professed wishes, and therefore whether they be ripe for its reception, and competent to its assertion? Wait but a little while, and the doubt will probably be solved, in the manner that the warmest friend of human happiness and improvement would desire. If the system of independence and equality be the truth, it may be expected hourly to gain converts. The more it is discussed, the more will it be understood, and its value cherished and felt. If the state of the majority be doubtful, a very few years, perhaps a shorter time, will tend to place it beyond the reach of controversy. The great cause of humanity, which is now pleading in the face of the universe, has but two enemies; those friends of antiquity, and those friends of innovation, who, impatient of suspense, are inclined violently to interrupt the calm, the incessant, the rapid and auspicious progress which thought and reflection appear to be making in the world. Happy would it be for mankind, if those persons who interest themselves most zealously in these great questions, would confine their exertions, to the diffusing, in every possible mode, a spirit of enquiry, and the embracing every opportunity of increasing the stock, and generalizing the communication, of political knowledge!

A third situation, which may be conceived to exist in a country, where political reform has been made a topic of considerable attention, is that, where neither the whole, nor the majority, of the nation, is desirous of the reform in question, . . . In this case nothing can be more indefensible, than a project for introducing by violence that state of society, which our judgements may happen to approve. In the first place, no persons are ripe for the participation of a benefit, the advantage of which they do not understand. No people are competent to enjoy a state of freedom, who are not already imbued with a love of freedom. The most dreadful tragedies will infallibly result, from an attempt to goad mankind prematurely into a position, however abstractedly excellent, for which they are in no degree prepared. Secondly, to endeavour to impose our sentiments by force, is the most detestable species of persecution. Others are as much entitled to deem themselves in the right as we are. The most sacred of all privileges, is that, by which each man has a certain sphere, relative to the government of his own actions, and the exercise of his discretion, not liable to be trenched upon by the intemperate zeal or dictatorial temper of his neighbour.[1] To dragoon men into the adoption of what we think right, is an intolerable tyranny. It leads to unlimited disorder and injustice. Every man thinks himself in the right; and, if such a proceeding were universally introduced, the destiny of mankind would be no longer a question of argument, but of strength, presumption or intrigue.

. . . It seems most accurate to say, that any number of persons, who are able to establish and maintain a system of mutual regulation for themselves conformable to their own opinions, without imposing a system of regulation upon a considerable number of others inconsistent with the opinion of these others, have a right, or, more properly speaking, a duty obliging them, to adopt that measure. That any man, or body of men, should impose their sense upon persons of a different opinion, is, absolutely speaking, wrong, and in all cases deeply to be regretted: but this evil it is perhaps in some degree necessary to incur, for the sake of a preponderating good. All government includes in it this evil, as one of its fundamental characteristics.

There is one circumstance, of much importance to be attended to in this disquisition. Superficial thinkers lay great stress upon the external situation of men, and little upon their internal sentiments. Persevering enquiry will probably lead to a mode of thinking the reverse of this. To be free is a circumstance of little value, if we could suppose men in a state of external freedom, without the magnanimity, energy and firmness, that constitute almost all that is valuable in a state of freedom. On the other hand, if a man have these qualities, there is little left for him to desire. He cannot be degraded; he cannot readily become either useless or unhappy. He smiles at the impotence of despotism; he fills up his existence with serene enjoyment and industrious benevolence. Civil liberty is chiefly desirable, as a means to procure and perpetuate this temper of mind. They therefore begin at the wrong end, who make

[1] II. v and vi.

haste to overturn and confound the usurped powers of the world. Make men wise, and by that very operation you make them free. Civil liberty follows as a consequence of this; no usurped power can stand against the artillery of opinion. Everything then is in order, and succeeds at its appointed time. How unfortunate is it, that men are so eager to strike, and have so little constancy to reason!

It is probable, that this question of resistance would never have admitted of so long a controversy, if the advocates of the system of liberty promulgated in the last century, had not, unobserved to themselves, introduced a confusion into the question. Resistance may be employed, either to repel the injuries committed against the nation generally, or such as, in their immediate application, relate to the individual. To the first of these the preceding reasonings principally apply. The injuries to a nation depend for their nature, for the most part, upon their permanency, and therefore admit of the utmost sobriety and deliberation as to the mode in which they are to be remedied. Individuals may be injured or destroyed by a specific act of tyranny, but nations cannot; the principal mischief to the nation lies in the presage contained in the single act, of the injustice that is to continue to be exercised. Resistance, by the very meaning of the term, as it is used in political enquiry, signifies a species of conduct that is to be adopted, in relation to an established authority: but an old grievance, seems obviously to lead, as its counterpart, to a gradual and temperate remedy.

The consideration which, by being confounded with this, has served to mislead certain enquirers, is that of what is commonly known by the name of self-defence, or, more properly, the duty obliging each individual to repel, as far as lies in his power, any violent attack made either upon himself or another. This, by the terms of the question, is a circumstance that does not admit of delay; the benefit of the remedy entirely depends upon the time of the application. The principle in this case is of easy development. Force is an expedient, the use of which is much to be deplored. It is contrary to the nature of intellect, which cannot be improved but by conviction and persuasion. It corrupts the man that employs it, and the man upon whom it is employed. But it seems that there are certain cases, so urgent, as to oblige us to have recourse to this injurious expedient: in other words, there are cases, where the mischief to accrue from not violently counteracting the perverseness of the individual, is greater, than the mischief which the violence necessarily draws along with it. Hence it appears, that the ground justifying resistance, in every case where it can be justified, is that of the good, likely to result from such interference, being greater than the good to result from omitting it.

There are probably cases, where, as in a murder for example about to be committed on a useful and valuable member of society, the chance of preventing it, by any other means than instantaneous resistance, is so small, as by no means to vindicate us in incurring the danger of so mischievous a catastrophe. But will this justify us, in the case of an individual oppressed by the authority of a community? Let us suppose, that there is a country, in which some of its best citizens are selected as objects of vengeance, by an alarmed and jealous tyranny. It cannot reasonably be doubted, that every man, a condemned felon or murderer, is to be commended, for quietly withdrawing himself from the execution of the law; much more such persons as have now been described. But ought those well-affected citizens that are still at large, to rise in behalf of their brethren under persecution? Every man that is disposed to enter into such a project, and who is anxious about the moral rectitude of his conduct, must rest its justification upon one of the two grounds above stated: either the immediate purpose of his rising is the melioration of public institutions, or it is to be estimated with reference to the meritoriousness of the individuals in question. The first of these has been sufficiently discussed; we will suppose therefore that he confines himself to the last. Here, as has been already observed, the whole, as a moral question, will turn upon the comparative benefit or mischief to result from the resistance to be employed. The disparity is great indeed, between the resistance ordinarily suggested by the term self-defence, and the resistance which must expect to encounter in its progress the civil power of the country. In the first, the question is of a moment; if you succeed in the instant of your exertion, you may expect the applause, rather than the prosecution, of executive authority. But, in the latter, the end will scarcely be accomplished, but by the overthrow of the government itself. Let the lives of the individuals in supposition be as valuable as you please, the value will necessarily be swallowed up, in the greater questions that occur in the sequel. Those questions therefore are the proper topics of attention; and we shall be to blame, if we suffer ourselves to be led unawares, into a conduct, the direct tendency of which is the production of one sort of event, while all we intended was the production of another. The value of individuals ought not to be forgotten; there are men whose safety should be cherished by us with anxious attention; but it is difficult to imagine a case, in which, for their sake, the lives of thousands, and the fate of millions, should be committed to risk.

CHAPTER II

OF REVOLUTIONS

T HE question of resistance is closely connected with that of revolutions. It may be proper therefore, before we dismiss this part of the subject, to enter into some disquisition, respecting the nature and effects of that species of event which is commonly known by this appellation, and the sentiments which a good citizen should entertain concerning it.

. . . .

Revolution is instigated by a horror against tyranny, yet its own tyranny is not without peculiar aggravations. There is no period more at war with the existence of liberty. The unrestrained communication of opinions has always been subjected to mischievous counteraction, but upon such occasions it is trebly fettered. At other times men are not so much alarmed for its effects. But in a moment of revolution, when everything is in crisis, the influence even of a word is dreaded, and the consequent slavery is complete. Where was there a revolution, in which a strong vindication of what it was intended to abolish, was permitted, or indeed almost any species of writing or argument, that was not, for the most part, in harmony with the opinions which happened to prevail? An attempt to scrutinize men's thoughts, and punish their opinions, is of all kinds of despotism the most odious; yet this attempt is peculiarly characteristic of a period of revolution.

The advocates of revolution usually remark, 'that there is no way to rid ourselves of our oppressors, and prevent new ones from starting up in their room, but by inflicting on them some severe and memorable retribution.' Upon this statement it is particularly to be observed, that there will be oppressors, as long as there are individuals inclined, either from perverseness, or rooted and obstinate prejudice, to take party with the oppressor. We have therefore to terrify, not only the man of crooked ambition, but all those who would support him, either from a corrupt motive, or a well-intended error. Thus, we propose to make men free; and the method we adopt, is to influence them, more rigorously than ever, by the fear of punishment. We say that government has usurped too much, and we organize a government, tenfold more encroaching in its principles, and terrible in its proceedings. Is slavery the best project that can be devised, for making men free? Is a display of terror the readiest mode, for rendering them fearless, independent and enterprising?

During a period of revolution, enquiry, and all those patient speculations to which mankind are indebted for their greatest improvements, are suspended. Such speculations demand a period of security and permanence; they can scarcely be pursued, when men cannot foresee what shall happen tomorrow, and the most astonishing vicissitudes are affairs of perpetual recurrence. Such speculations demand leisure, and a tranquil and dispassionate temper; they can scarcely be pursued, when all the passions of man are afloat, and we are hourly under the strongest impressions, of fear and hope, apprehension and desire, dejection and triumph. . . .

. . . Revolutions are a struggle between two parties, each persuaded of the justice of its cause, a struggle, not decided by compromise or patient expostulation, but by force only. Such a decision can scarcely be expected to put an end to the mutual animosity and variance.

Perhaps no important revolution was ever bloodless. It may be useful in this place, to recollect in what the mischief of shedding blood consists. The abuses which at present exist in political society are so enormous, the oppressions which are exercised so intolerable, the ignorance and vice they entail so dreadful, that possibly a dispassionate enquirer might decide that, if their annihilation could be purchased, by an instant sweeping of every human being now arrived at years of maturity, from the face of the earth, the purchase would not be too dear. It is not because human life is of so considerable value, that we ought to recoil from the shedding of blood. Alas! the men that now exist, are for the most part poor and scanty in their portion of enjoyment, and their dignity is no more than a name. Death is in itself among the slightest of human evils. An earthquake, which should swallow up a hundred thousand individuals at once, would chiefly be to be regretted for the anguish it entailed upon survivors; in a fair estimate of those it destroyed, it would often be comparatively a trivial event. The laws of nature which produce it, are a fit subject of investigation; but their effects, contrasted with many other events, are scarcely a topic of regret. The case is altogether different, when man falls by the hand of his neighbour. Here a thousand ill passions are generated. The perpetrators, and the witnesses of murders, become obdurate, unrelenting and inhuman. Those who sustain the loss of relations or friends by a catastrophe of this sort, are filled with indignation and revenge. Distrust is propagated from man to man, and the dearest ties of human society are dissolved. It is impossible to devise a temper, more inauspicious to the cultivation of justice, and the diffusion of benevolence.

To the remark, that revolutions can scarcely be unaccompanied with the shedding of blood, it may be added that they are necessarily crude and premature. Politics is a science. The general features of the nature of man are capable of being understood, and a mode may be delineated which, in itself considered, is best adapted to the condition of man in society. If this mode ought not, everywhere, and instantly, to be sought to be reduced into practice, the modifications that are to be given it in conformity to the variation of circumstances, and the degrees in which it is to be realized, are also a **topic** of scientifical disquisition. Now it is clearly the nature of science to be progressive in its advances. . . . Political knowledge is, no doubt, in its infancy; and, as it is an affair of life and action, will, in proportion as it gathers vigour, manifest a more uniform and less precarious influence upon the concerns of human society. . . .

The only method according to which social improvements can be carried on, with sufficient prospect of an auspicious event, is, when the improvement of our institutions advances, in a just proportion to the illumination of the public understanding. There is a condition of political society best adapted to every different stage of individual improvement. The more nearly this condition is successively realized, the more advantageously will the general interest be consulted. There is a sort of provision in the nature of the human mind for this species of progress. Imperfect institutions, as has already been shown,[1] cannot long support themselves, when they are generally disapproved of, and their effects truly understood. There is a period, at which they may be expected to decline and expire, almost without an effort. . . .

Under this view of the subject then it appears, that revolutions, instead of being truly beneficial to mankind, answer no other purpose, than that of marring the salutary and uninterrupted progress, which might be expected to attend upon political truth and social improvement. They disturb the harmony of intellectual nature. They propose to give us something, for which we are not prepared, and which we cannot effectually use. They suspend the wholesome advancement of science, and confound the process of nature and reason.

. . . . .

[1] I. vi.

There is one general observation which ought to be made, before the subject is dismissed. It has perhaps sufficiently appeared, from the preceding discussion, that revolutions are necessarily attended with many circumstances worthy of our disapprobation, and that they are by no means essential to the political improvement of mankind. Yet, after all, it ought not to be forgotten, that, though the connection be not essential or requisite, revolutions and violence have too often been coeval with important changes of the social system. What has so often happened in time past, is not unlikely occasionally to happen in future. The duty therefore of the true politician, is to postpone revolution, if he cannot entirely prevent it. It is reasonable to believe that, the later it occurs, and the more generally ideas of political good and evil are previously understood, the shorter, and the less deplorable, will be the mischiefs attendant on revolution. The friend of human happiness, will endeavour to prevent violence; but it would be the mark of a weak and valetudinarian temper, to turn away our eyes from human affairs in disgust, and refuse to contribute our labours and attention to the general weal, because perhaps, at last, violence may forcibly intrude itself. It is our duty, to make a proper advantage of circumstances as they arise, and not to withdraw ourselves, because everything is not conducted according to our ideas of propriety. The men who grow angry with corruption, and impatient at injustice, and through those sentiments favour the abettors of revolution, have an obvious apology to palliate their error; theirs is the excess of a virtuous feeling. At the same time, however amiable may be the source of their error, the error itself is probably fraught with consequences pernicious to mankind.

CHAPTER III

OF POLITICAL ASSOCIATIONS

A QUESTION suggests itself under this branch of enquiry, respecting the propriety of associations among the people at large, for the purpose of operating a change in their political institutions.

.   .   .   .

One of the most obvious features of political association, is its tendency to make a part stand for the whole. A number of persons, sometimes greater and sometimes less, combine together. The tendency of their combination, often avowed, but always unavoidable, is to give to their opinion a weight and operation, which the opinion of un-connected individuals cannot have. A greater number, some from the urgency of their private affairs, some from a temper averse to scenes of concourse and contention, and others from a conscientious dis-approbation of the measures pursued, withhold themselves from such combinations. The acrimonious, the intemperate, and the artful, will generally be found among the most forward in matters of this kind. The prudent, the sober, the sceptical, and the contemplative, those who have no resentments to gratify, and no selfish purposes to promote, will be overborne and lost in the progress. What justification can be advanced, for a few persons who thus, from mere impetuosity and incontinence of temper, occupy a post, the very principle of which is, the passing them for something greater and more important in the community than they are? Is the business of reform likely to be well and judiciously conducted in such hands? Add to this, that associations in favour of one set of political tenets, are likely to engender counter-associations in favour of another. Thus we should probably be involved in all the mischiefs of resistance, and all the uproar of revolution.

. . . . .

If we would arrive at truth, each man must be taught to enquire and think for himself. If a hundred men spontaneously engage the whole energy of their faculties upon the solution of a given question, the chance of success will be greater, than if only ten men are so employed. By the same reason, the chance will also be increased, in proportion as the intellectual operations of these men are individual, and their conclusions are suggested by the reason of the thing, uninfluenced by the force either of compulsion or sympathy. But, in political associa-tions, the object of each man, is to identify his creed with that of his neighbour. We learn the Shibboleth of a party. We dare not leave our minds at large in the field of enquiry, lest we should arrive at some tenet disrelished by our party. We have no temptation to enquire. Party has a more powerful tendency, than perhaps any other circumstance in human affairs, to render the mind quiescent and stationary. Instead of making each man an individual, which the interest of the whole requires, it resolves all understandings into one common mass, and subtracts from each the varieties, that could alone distinguish him from a brute machine. Having learned the creed of our party, we have no longer any employment for those faculties, which might lead us to detect its errors. . . . In fine, from these considerations it appears, that associations, instead of promoting the growth and diffusion of truth, tend only to check its accumulation, and render its operation, as far as possible, unnatural and mischievous.

.   .   .   .

But, though association, in the received sense of that term, must be granted to be an instrument of very dangerous nature, unreserved communication, especially among persons who are already awakened to the pursuit of truth, is of no less unquestionable advantage. There is at present in the world a cold reserve, that keeps man at a distance from man. There is an art, in the practice of which individuals communicate for ever, without any one telling his neighbour what estimate he forms of his attainments and character, how they ought to be employed, and how to be improved. There is a sort of domestic tactics, the object of which is to elude curiosity, and keep up the tenor of conversation, without the disclosure either of our feelings or opinions. The friend of justice will have no object more deeply at heart, than the annihilation of this duplicity. . . . Among the topics to which he will be anxious to awaken attention, politics will occupy a principal share.

Books have by their very nature but a limited operation; though, on account of their permanence, their methodical disquisition, and their easiness of access, they are entitled to the foremost place. The number of those who almost wholly abstain from reading, is exceedingly great. Books, to those by whom they are read, have a sort of constitutional coldness. We review the arguments of an 'insolent innovator' with sullenness, and are unwilling to expand our minds to take in their force. . . . But conversation accustoms us to hear a variety of sentiments, obliges us to exercise patience and attention, and gives freedom and elasticity to our disquisitions. . . .

It follows, that the promoting the best interests of mankind, eminently depends upon the freedom of social communication. . . .

.   .   .   .

CHAPTER IV

OF TYRANNICIDE

A QUESTION, connected with the mode of effecting political melioration, and which has been eagerly discussed among political reasoners, is that of tyrannicide. . . .

.   .   .   .

. . . The tyrant has . . . no particular sanctity annexed to his person, and may be killed with as little scruple as any other man, when the object is that of repelling personal assault. In all other cases, the extirpation of the offender by a self-appointed authority, does not appear to be the appropriate mode of counteracting injustice.

For, . . . either the nation, whose tyrant you would destroy, is ripe for the assertion and maintenance of its liberty, or it is not. If it be, the tyrant ought to be deposed with every appearance of publicity. Nothing can be more improper, than for an affair, interesting to the general weal, to be conducted as if it were an act of darkness and shame. . . .

If, on the other hand, the nation be not ripe for a state of freedom, the man who assumes to himself the right of interposing violence, may indeed show the fervour of his conception, and gain a certain notoriety; but he will not fail to be the author of new calamities to his country. The consequences of tyrannicide are well known. If the attempt prove abortive, it renders the tyrant ten times more bloody, ferocious and cruel than before. If it succeed, and the tyranny be restored, it produces the same effect upon his successors. In the climate of despotism some solitary virtues may spring up. But, in the midst of plots and conspiracies, there is neither truth, nor confidence, nor love, nor humanity.

.   .   .   .

CHAPTER V

OF THE CULTIVATION OF TRUTH

THAT we may adequately understand the power and operation of opinion in meliorating the institutions of society, it is requisite that we should consider the value and energy of truth. There is no topic more fundamental to the principles of political science, or to the reasonings of this work. It is from this point that we may most perspicuously trace the opposite tenets, of the advocates of privilege and aristocracy on the one hand, and the friends of equality, and one universal measure of justice, on the other. The partisans of both, at least the more enlightened and honourable partisans, acknowledge one common object, the welfare of the whole, of the community and mankind. But the adherents of the old systems of government affirm, 'that the imbecility of the human mind, is such as to make it unadvisable, that man should be trusted with himself; that his genuine condition is that of perpetual pupillage; that he is regulated by passions and partial views, and cannot be governed by pure reason and truth; that it is the business of a wise man not to subvert, either in himself or others, delusions which are useful, and prejudices which are salutary; and that he is the worst enemy of his species, who attempts, in whatever mode, to introduce a form of society, where no advantage is taken to restrain us from vices by illusion, from which we cannot be restrained by reason.' Every man who adheres, in whole, or in part, to the tenets here enumerated, will perhaps, in proportion as he follows them into their genuine consequences, be a partisan of aristocracy.

Tenets the opposite of these, constitute the great outline of the present work. If there be any truth in the reasonings hitherto adduced, we are entitled to conclude that morality, the science of human happiness, the principle which binds the individual to the species, and the inducements which are calculated to persuade us to model our conduct, in the way most conducive to the advantage of all, does not rest upon imposture and delusion, but upon grounds, that discovery will never undermine, and wisdom never refute. We do not need therefore to be led to that which is fitting and reasonable, by deceitful allurements. We have no cause to fear, that the man, who shall see furthest, and judge with the most perfect penetration, will be less estimable and useful, or will find fewer charms in another's happiness and virtue, than if he were under the dominion of error. If the conduct I am required to observe be reasonable, there is no plainer or more forcible mode of persuading me to adopt it, than to exhibit it in its true colours, and show me the benefits that will really accrue from it. As long as these benefits are present to my mind, I shall have a desire, an ardour for performing the action which leads to them, to the full as great as the occasion will justify; and, if the occasion be of real magnitude, my ardour will be more genuine, and better endure the test of experiment, than it can, when combined with narrow views or visionary credulity. Truth and falsehood cannot subsist together: he that sees the merits of a case in all clearness, cannot in that instance be the dupe either of prejudice or superstition. Nor is there any reason to believe, that sound conviction will be less permanent in its influence, than sophistry and error.[1]

The value of truth will be still further illustrated, if we consider it in detail, and enquire into its effects, either abstractedly, under which form it bears the appellation of science and knowledge; or practically,

[1] I. v; V. xv.

as it relates to the incidents and commerce of ordinary life, where it is known by the denomination of sincerity.

Abstractedly considered, it conduces to the happiness and virtue of the individual, as well as to the improvement of our social institutions.

In the discovery and knowledge of truth seems to be comprised, for the most part, all that an impartial and reflecting mind is accustomed to admire. No one is ignorant of the pleasures of knowledge. In human life there must be a distribution of time, and a variety of occupations. Now there is perhaps no occupation so much at our command, no pleasure of the means of which we are so little likely to be deprived, as that which is intellectual. Sublime and expansive ideas produce delicious emotions. The acquisition of truth, the perception of the regularity with which proposition flows out of proposition, and one step of science leads to another, has never failed to reward the man who engaged in this species of employment. Knowledge contributes two ways to our happiness: first by the new sources of enjoyment which it opens upon us, and next by furnishing us with a clue in the selection of all other pleasures. No well-informed man can seriously doubt of the advantages with respect to happiness, of a capacious and improved intellect, over the limited conceptions of a brute. Virtuous sentiments are another source of personal pleasure, and that of a more exquisite kind than intellectual improvements. But virtue itself depends for its value upon the energies of intellect. If the beings we are capable of benefiting, were susceptible of nothing more than brutes are, we should have little pleasure in benefiting them, or in contemplating their happiness. But man has so many enjoyments, is capable of so high a degree of perfection, of exhibiting, socially considered, so admirable a spectacle, and of himself so truly estimating and favouring the spectacle, that, when we are engaged in promoting his benefit, we are indeed engaged in a sublime and ravishing employment. This is the case, whether our exertions are directed to the advantage of the species, or the individual. We rejoice when we save an ordinary man from destruction, more than when we save a brute, because we recollect how much more he can feel, and how much more he can do. The same principle produces a still higher degree of congratulation, in proportion as the man we save is more highly accomplished in talents and virtues.

Secondly, truth conduces to our improvement in virtue. Virtue, in its purest and most liberal sense, supposes an extensive survey of causes and their consequences, that, having struck a just balance between the benefits and injuries that adhere to human affairs, we may adopt the proceeding which leads to the greatest practicable advantage. Virtue, like every other endowment of man, admits of degrees. He therefore must be confessed to be most virtuous, who chooses with the soundest judgement the greatest and most universal overbalance of pleasure. But, in order to choose the greatest and most excellent pleasures, he must be intimately acquainted with the nature of man, its general features and its varieties. In order to forward the object he has chosen, he must have considered the different instruments for impressing mind, and the modes of applying them, and must know the properest moment for bringing them into action. In whatever light we consider virtue, whether we place it in the act or the disposition, its degree must be intimately connected with the degree of knowledge. No man can so much as love virtue sufficiently, who has not an acute and lively perception of its beauty, and its tendency to produce the most solid and permanent happiness. What comparison can be made, between the virtue of Socrates, and that of a Hottentot or a Siberian? A humorous example how universally this truth has been perceived, may be taken from Tertullian, who, as a father of the church, was obliged to maintain the hollowness and insignificance of pagan virtues, and accordingly assures us, 'that the most ignorant peasant under the Christian dispensation, possesses more real knowledge than the wisest of the ancient philosophers.'[1]

We shall be more fully aware of the connection between virtue and knowledge, if we consider that the highest employment of virtue is to propagate itself. Virtue alone deserves to be considered as leading to true happiness, the happiness which is most solid and durable. Sensual pleasures are momentary; they fill a very short portion of our time with enjoyment, and leave long intervals of painful vacuity. They charm principally by their novelty; by repetition they first abate of their poignancy, and at last become little less than wearisome. It is perhaps partly to be ascribed to the high estimation in which sensual pleasures are held, that old age is so early and regular in its ravages. Our taste for these pleasures necessarily declines; with our taste our activity; and with our activity gradually crumble away the cheerfulness, the energy, and the lives, of those whose dependence was placed upon these resources. Even knowledge, and the enlargement of intellect, are poor, when unmixed with sentiments of benevolence and sympathy. Emotions are scarcely ever thrilling and electrical, without something of social feeling. When the mind expands in works of taste and imagination,

[1] *Apologia*, Ch. xlvi. See this subject further pursued in the Appendix.

it will usually be found that there is something moral in the cause which gives birth to this expansion; and science and abstraction will soon become cold, unless they derive new attractions from ideas of society. In proportion therefore to the virtue of the individual, will be the permanence of his cheerfulness, and the exquisiteness of his emotions. Add to which, benevolence is a resource which is never exhausted; but on the contrary, the more habitual are our patriotism and philanthropy, the more will they become invigorating and ardent.

It is also impossible that any situation can occur in which virtue cannot find room to expatiate. In society there is continual opportunity for its active employment. I cannot have intercourse with a human being, who may not be the better for that intercourse. If he be already just and virtuous, these qualities are improved by communication. If he be imperfect and erroneous, there must always be some prejudice I may contribute to destroy, some motive to delineate, some error to remove. If I be prejudiced and imperfect myself, it cannot however happen that my prejudices and imperfections shall be exactly coincident with his. I may therefore inform him of the truths that I know, and, even by the collision of prejudices, truth is elicited. . . .

All these reasonings are calculated to persuade us that the most precious boon we can bestow upon others is virtue, and that the highest employment of virtue is to propagate itself. But, as virtue is inseparably connected with knowledge in my own mind, so by knowledge only can it be imparted to others. How can the virtue we have just been contemplating be produced, but by infusing comprehensive views, and communicating energetic truths? Now that man alone is qualified to infuse these views, and communicate these truths, who is himself pervaded with them.

Let us suppose for a moment virtuous dispositions existing without knowledge or outrunning knowledge, the last of which is certainly possible; and we shall presently find how little such virtue is worthy to be propagated. The most generous views will, in such cases, frequently lead to the most nefarious actions. A Cranmer will be incited to the burning of heretics, and a Digby contrive the Gunpowder Treason. But, to leave these extreme instances: in all cases where mistaken virtue leads to cruel and tyrannical actions, the mind will be rendered discontented and morose by the actions it perpetrates. Truth, immortal and ever present truth, is so powerful, that, in spite of all his prejudices, the upright man will suspect himself, when he resolves upon an action that is at war with the plainest principles of morality. He will become melancholy, dissatisfied and anxious. His firmness will degenerate into obstinacy, and his justice into inexorable severity. The further he pursues his system, the more erroneous will he become. The further he pursues it, the less will he be satisfied with it. As truth is an endless source of tranquillity and delight, error will be a prolific fountain of new mistakes and discontent.

As to the third point, which is most essential to the enquiry in which we are engaged, the tendency of truth to the improvement of our political institutions, there can be little room for scepticism or controversy. If politics be a science, investigation must be the means of unfolding it. If men resemble each other in more numerous and essential particulars than those in which they differ, if the best purposes that can be accomplished respecting them, be to make them free, virtuous and wise, there must be one best method of advancing these common purposes, one best mode of social existence deducible from the principles of their nature. If truth be one, there must be one code of truths on the subject of our reciprocal duties. Nor is investigation only the best mode of ascertaining the principles of political justice and happiness; it is also the best mode of introducing and establishing them. Discussion is the path that leads to discovery and demonstration. Motives ferment in the minds of great bodies of men, till their modes of society experience a variation, not less memorable than the variation of their sentiments. The more familiar the mind becomes with the ideas of which these motives consist, and the propositions that express them, the more irresistibly is it propelled to a general system of proceeding in correspondence with them.

APPENDIX

OF THE CONNECTION BETWEEN
UNDERSTANDING AND VIRTUE

A PROPOSITION which, however evident in itself, seems never to have been considered with the attention it deserves, is that which affirms the connection between understanding and virtue. Can an honest ploughman be as virtuous as Cato? Is a man of weak intellects and narrow education, as capable of moral excellence, as the sublimest genius or the mind most stored with information and science?

To determine these questions it is necessary we should recollect the nature of virtue. Considered as a personal quality, it consists in the disposition of the mind, and may be defined a desire to promote the happiness of intelligent beings in general, the quantity of virtue being as the quantity of desire. Now desire is wholly inseparable from preference, or a perception of the excellence, real or supposed, of any object. I say real or supposed, for an object totally destitute of real and intrinsic excellence, may become an object of desire on account of the imaginary excellence that is ascribed to it. Nor is this the only mistake to which human intellect is liable. We may desire an object of absolute excellence, not for its real and genuine recommendations, but for some fictitious attractions we may impute to it. This is always in some degree the case, when a beneficial action is performed from an ill motive.

How far is this mistake compatible with real virtue? If I desire the happiness of intelligent beings, without a strong and vivid perception of what it is in which their happiness consists, can this desire be admitted for virtuous? Nothing seems more inconsistent with our ideas of virtue. A virtuous preference, is the preference of an object, for the sake of certain qualities which really belong to it. To attribute virtue to any other species of preference, would be nearly the same, as to suppose that an accidental effect of my conduct, which was out of my view at the time of adopting it, might entitle me to the appellation of virtuous.

Hence it appears, first, that virtue consists in a desire of the happiness of the species: and, secondly, that that desire only can be eminently virtuous, which flows from a distinct perception of the value, and consequently of the nature, of the thing desired. But how extensive must be the capacity that comprehends the full value and the real ingredients of true happiness? It must begin with a collective idea of the human species. It must discriminate, among the different causes that produce a pleasurable state of mind, that which produces the most exquisite and durable pleasure. Eminent virtue requires that I should have a grand view of the tendency, of knowledge to produce happiness, and of just political institution to favour the progress of knowledge. It demands that I should perceive in what manner social intercourse may be made conducive to virtue and felicity, and imagine the unspeakable advantages that may arise from a coincidence and succession of generous efforts. These things are necessary, not merely for the purpose of enabling me to employ my virtuous disposition in the best manner, but also of giving to that disposition a just animation and vigour. God, according to the ideas usually conceived of that being, is more benevolent than man, because he has a constant and clear perception of the nature of that end which his providence pursues.

A further proof, that a powerful understanding is inseparable from eminent virtue, will suggest itself, if we recollect, that earnest desire, in matters that fall within the compass of human exertion, never fails in some degree to generate capacity.

This proposition has been beautifully illustrated by the poets, when they have represented the passion of love, as immediately leading, in the breast of the lover, to the attainment of many arduous accomplishments. It unlocks his tongue, and enables him to plead the cause of his passion with insinuating eloquence. . . .

.   .   .   .

Let the object be, for a person, uninstructed in the rudiments of drawing, to make a copy of some celebrated statue. At first, we will suppose, his attempt shall be mean and unsuccessful. If his desire be feeble, he will be deterred by the miscarriage of this essay. If his desire be ardent and invincible, he will return to the attack. He will derive instruction from his failure. . . . He will correct his mistakes, derive encouragement from a partial success, and new incentives from miscarriage itself.

The case is similar in virtue as in science. If I have conceived an earnest desire of being the benefactor of my species, I shall, no doubt, find out a channel in which for my desire to operate, and shall be quick-sighted in discovering the defects, or comparative littleness, of the plan I may have chosen. But the choice of an excellent plan for the accomplishment of an important purpose, and the exertion of a mind perpetually watchful to remove its defects, imply considerable understanding. The further I am engaged in the pursuit of this plan, the more will my capacity increase. If my mind flag and be discouraged in the pursuit, it will not be merely want of understanding, but want of desire. My desire and my virtue will be less, than those of the man, who goes on with unremitted constancy in the same career.

Thus far we have only been considering how impossible it is that eminent virtue should exist in a weak understanding; and it is surprising that such a proposition should ever have been contested. It is a curious question to examine, how far the converse of this proposition is true, and in what degree eminent talents are compatible with the absence of virtue.

From the arguments already adduced, it appears that virtuous desire is wholly inseparable from a strong and vivid perception of the nature and value of the object of virtue. Hence it seems most natural to conclude, that, though understanding, or strong percipient power, is the indispensable prerequisite of virtue, yet it is necessary that this power should be exercised upon this object, in order to its producing the desired effect. Thus it is in art. Without genius no man ever was a poet; but it is necessary that general capacity should have been directed to this particular channel, for poetical excellence to be the result.

There is however some difference between the two cases. Poetry is the business of a few, virtue and vice are the affair of all men. . . . It must be granted that, where every other circumstance is equal, that man will be most virtuous, whose understanding has been most actively employed in the study of virtue. But morality has been, in a certain degree, an object of attention to all men. No person ever failed, more or less, to apply the standard of just and unjust to his own actions and those of others; and this has, of course, been generally done with most ingenuity by men of the greatest capacity.

It must further be remembered, that a vicious conduct is always the result of narrow views. A man of powerful capacity, and extensive observation, is least likely to commit the mistake, either of seeing himself as the only object of importance in the universe, or of conceiving that his own advantage may best be promoted by trampling on that of others. . . .

.   .   .   .   .

. . . men of talents, even when they are erroneous, are not destitute of virtue, . . . there is a fullness of guilt of which they are incapable. There is no ingredient that so essentially contributes to a virtuous character, as a sense of justice. Philanthropy, as contradistinguished to justice, is rather an unreflecting feeling, than a rational principle. It leads to an absurd indulgence, which is frequently more injurious, than beneficial, even to the individual it proposes to favour. It leads to a blind partiality, inflicting calamity, without remorse, upon many perhaps, in order to promote the imagined interest of a few. But justice measures by one unalterable standard the claims of all, weighs their opposite pretensions, and seeks to diffuse happiness, because happiness is the fit and proper condition of a conscious being. Wherever therefore a strong sense of justice exists, it is common and reasonable to say, that in that mind exists considerable virtue, though the individual, from an unfortunate concurrence of circumstances, may, with all his great qualities, be the instrument of a very small portion of benefit. Can great intellectual power exist, without a strong sense of justice?

.   .   .   .

CHAPTER VI

OF SINCERITY

IT was further proposed to consider the value of truth in a practical view, as it relates to the incidents and commerce of ordinary life, under which form it is known by the denomination of sincerity.

The powerful recommendations attendant upon sincerity are obvious. It is intimately connected with the general dissemination of innocence, energy, intellectual improvement, and philanthropy.

.   .   .   .

An impartial distribution of commendation and blame to the actions of men, would be a most powerful incentive to virtue. But this distribution, at present, scarcely in any instance exists. One man is satirized with bitterness, and the misconduct of another is treated with inordinate lenity. . . . The basest hypocrite passes through life with applause; and the purest character is loaded with unmerited aspersions. The benefactors of mankind, are frequently the objects of their bitterest hatred, and most unrelenting ingratitude. What encouragement then is afforded to virtue? Those who are smitten with the love of distinction, will rather seek it in external splendour, and unmeaning luxury, than in moral attainments. While those who are led to benevolent pursuits by the purest motives, yet languish under the privation of that honour and esteem, which would give new firmness to rectitude, and ardour to benevolence.

A genuine and unalterable sincerity would not fail to reverse the scene.[1] Every idle or malignant tale now produces its effect, because men are unaccustomed to exercise their judgement upon the probabilities of human action, or to possess the materials of judgement. But then the rash assertions of one individual, would be corrected by the maturer information of his neighbour. Exercised in discrimination, we should be little likely to be misled. The truth would be known, the whole truth, and the unvarnished truth. This would be a trial, that the most

[1] VI. vi.

stubborn obliquity would be found unable to withstand. If a just and impartial character were awarded to all human actions, vice would be universally deserted, and virtue everywhere practised. Sincerity therefore, once introduced into the manners of mankind, would necessarily bring every other virtue in its train.

.   .   .   .

What is it that, at this day, enables a thousand errors to keep their station in the world; priestcraft, tests, bribery, war, cabal, and whatever else excites the disapprobation of the honest and enlightened mind? Cowardice; the timid reserve which makes men shrink from telling what they know; and the insidious policy that annexes persecution and punishment, to an unrestrained and spirited discussion of the true interests of society. Men either refrain from the publication of unpalatable opinions, because they are unwilling to make a sacrifice of their worldly prospects; or they publish them in a frigid and enigmatical spirit, stripped of their true character, and incapable of their genuine operation. If every man today would tell all the truth he knew, it is impossible to predict how short would be the reign of usurpation and folly.

. . . At present, men meet together with the temper, less of friends, than enemies. Every man eyes his neighbour, as if he expected to receive from him a secret wound. . . . In youth, it may be, he accommodates himself with a pliant spirit to the manners of the world; and, while he loses no jot of his gaiety, learns from it no other lessons, than those of selfishness and cheerful indifference. Observant of the game that goes forward around him, he becomes skilful in his turn to elude the curiosity of others, and smiles inwardly at the false scent he prompts them to follow. Dead to the emotions of a disinterested sympathy, he can calmly consider men as the mere neutral instruments of his enjoyments. He can preserve himself in a true equipoise between love and hatred. . . .

How would the whole of this be reversed by the practice of sincerity? We could not be indifferent, to men whose custom it was to tell us the truth. Hatred would perish, from a failure in its principal ingredient, the duplicity and impenetrableness of human actions. No man could acquire a distant and unsympathetic temper. Reserve, deceitfulness, and an artful exhibition of ourselves, take from the human form its soul, and leave us the unanimated semblance of what man might have been; of what he would have been, were not every impulse of the mind thus stunted and destroyed. If our emotions were not checked, we should be truly friends with each other. Our character would expand: the luxury of indulging our feelings, and the exercise of uttering them, would raise us to the stature of men. . . .

. . . . .

. . . Sincerity may be considered as of three degrees. First, a man may conceive that he sufficiently preserves his veracity, if he never utter anything that cannot be explained into a consistency with truth. . . . Or, secondly, it may happen that his delicacy shall not stop here, and he may resolve, not only to utter nothing that is literally untrue, but also nothing which he knows or believes will be understood by the hearer in a sense that is untrue. . . . The third and highest degree of sincerity, consists in the most perfect frankness, discards every species of concealment or reserve, and, as Cicero expresses it, 'utters nothing that is false, and withholds nothing that is true.'

The two first of these, by no means answer the genuine purposes of sincerity. . . .

. . . the only species of sincerity which can in any degree prove satisfactory to the enlightened moralist and politician, is that where the frankness is perfect, and every degree of reserve is discarded.

Nor is there any danger that such a character should degenerate into ruggedness and brutality. Sincerity, upon the principles on which it is here recommended, is practised from a consciousness of its utility, and from sentiments of philanthropy. It will communicate frankness to the voice, fervour to the gesture, and kindness to the heart. Even in expostulation and censure, friendliness of intention and mildness of proceeding, may be eminently conspicuous. There should be no mixture of disdain and superiority. The interest of him who is corrected, not the triumph of the corrector, should be the principle of action. True sincerity will be attended with that equality which is the only sure foundation of love, and that love which gives the best finishing and lustre to a sentiment of equality.

APPENDIX, No. I

ILLUSTRATIONS OF SINCERITY

THERE is an important enquiry which cannot fail to suggest itself in this place. 'Universal sincerity has been shown to be pregnant with unspeakable advantages. The enlightened friend of the human species, cannot fail anxiously to anticipate the time, when each man shall speak truth with his neighbour. But what conduct does it behove us to observe in the interval? Are we to practise an unreserved and uniform sincerity, while the world about us acts upon so different a plan? If sincerity should ever become characteristic of the community in which we live, our neighbour will then be prepared to hear the truth, and to make use of the communication in a way that shall be manly, generous and just. But, at present, we shall be liable to waken the resentment of some, and to subject to a trial beyond its strength the fortitude of others. By a direct and ill-timed truth we may not only incur the forfeiture of our worldly prospects, but of our usefulness, and sometimes of our lives.'

·   ·   ·   ·

The duty of sincerity is one of those general principles, which reflection and experience have enjoined upon us, as conducive to the happiness of mankind. Let us enquire then into the nature and origin of general principles. Engaged, as men are, in perpetual intercourse with their neighbours, and constantly liable to be called upon without the smallest previous notice, in cases where the interest of their fellows is deeply involved, it is not possible for them, upon all occasions, to deduce, through a chain of reasoning, the judgement which should be followed. Hence the necessity of resting places for the mind, of deductions, already stored in the memory, and prepared for application as circumstances may demand. We find this necessity equally urgent upon us in matters of science and abstraction, as in conduct and morals. Theory has also a further use. It serves as a perpetual exercise and aliment to the understanding, and renders us competent and vigorous to judge in every situation that can occur. Nothing can be more idle and shallow, than the competition which some men have set up, between theory and practice. It is true that we can never predict, from theory alone, the success of any given experiment. It is true that no theory, accurately speaking, can possibly be practical. It is the business of theory, to collect the circumstances of a certain set of cases, and arrange them. It would cease to be theory, if it did not leave out many circumstances; it collects such as are general, and leaves out such as are particular. In practice however, those circumstances inevitably arise, which are necessarily omitted in the general process: they cause the phenomenon, in various ways, to include features which were not in the prediction, and to be diversified in those that were. Yet theory is of the highest use; and those who decry it, may even be proved not to understand themselves. They do not mean that men should always act in a particular case, without illustration from any other case, for that would be to deprive us of all understanding. The moment we begin to compare cases, and infer, we begin to theorize; no two things in the universe were ever perfectly alike. The genuine exercise of man therefore, is to theorize, for this is, in other words, to sharpen and improve his intellect; but not to become the slave of theory, or at any time to forget that it is, by its very nature, precluded from comprehending the whole of what claims our attention.

To apply this to the case of morals. General principles of morality are so far valuable, as they truly delineate the means of utility, pleasure, or happiness. But every action of any human being, has its appropriate result; and, the more closely it is examined, the more truly will that result appear. General rules and theories are not infallible. It would be preposterous to suppose that, in order to judge fairly, and conduct myself properly, I ought only to look at a thing from a certain distance, and not consider it minutely. On the contrary, I ought, as far as lies in my power, to examine everything upon its own grounds, and decide concerning it upon its own merits. To rest in general rules, is sometimes a necessity which our imperfection imposes upon us, and sometimes the refuge of our indolence; but the true dignity of human reason is, as much as we are able, to go beyond them, to have our faculties in act upon every occasion that occurs, and to conduct ourselves accordingly.

. . . .

To return to the particular case of sincerity. Sincerity and plain dealing, are obviously, in the majority of human actions, the best policy, if we consider only the interest of the individual, and extend our calculation of that interest only over a very short period. No man will be wild enough to assert, even in this limited sense, that it is seldomer our policy to speak truth, than to lie. Sincerity and plain dealing, are eminently conducive to the interest of mankind at large, because they afford ground for that confidence and reasonable expectation, which are essential both to wisdom and virtue. Yet it may with propriety be asked, 'Whether cases do not exist of peculiar emergency, where the general principle of sincerity and speaking the truth, ought to be superseded?'

[Godwin concludes, after considerable debate, that there are cases in which one ought not to tell the truth: when, for example, I find myself 'with a drunken bigot in a corner, who should require of me an assent to his creed with a pistol at my breast.' Furthermore,] if there be cases where I ought not to scruple to violate the truth, inasmuch as the alternative consists in my certain destruction, it is at least as much incumbent on me, when the life of my neighbour is at stake. Indeed, the moment any exception is admitted to the general principle of unreserved sincerity, it becomes obviously impossible to fix the nature of all the exceptions. The rule respecting them must be, that, wherever a great and manifest evil arises from disclosing the truth, and that evil appears to be greater than the evil, to arise from violating, in this instance, the general barrier of human confidence and virtue, there the obligation of sincerity is suspended.

Nor is it a valid objection to say, 'that, by such a rule, we are making every man a judge in his own case.' In the courts of morality it cannot be otherwise; a pure and just system of thinking, admits not of the existence of any infallible judge to whom we can appeal. It might indeed be further objected, 'that, by this rule, men will be called upon to judge in the moment of passion and partiality, instead of being referred to the past decisions of their cooler reason.' But this also is an inconvenience inseparable from human affairs. We must and ought to keep ourselves open, to the last moment, to the influence of such considerations as may appear worthy to influence us. To teach men that they must not trust their own understandings, is not the best scheme for rendering them virtuous and consistent. On the contrary, to inure them to consult their understanding, is the way to render it worthy of becoming their director and guide.

. . . .

CHAPTER VII

OF FREE WILL AND NECESSITY

THUS we have engaged in the discussion of various topics, respecting the mode in which improvement may most successfully be introduced into the institutions of society. We have seen, under the heads of resistance, revolution, associations and tyrannicide, that nothing is more to be deprecated than violence and a headlong zeal, that everything may be trusted to the tranquil and wholesome progress of knowledge, and that the office of the enlightened friend of political justice, for the most part, consists in this only, a vigilant and perpetual endeavour to assist the progress. We have traced the effects which are to be produced, by the cultivation of truth, and the practice of sincerity. It remains to turn our attention to the other branch of the subject proposed to be investigated in the present book; the mode in which, from the structure of the human mind, opinion is found to operate in modifying the conduct of individuals.

Some progress was made in the examination of this point, in an earlier division of the present work.[1] An attentive enquirer will readily perceive, that no investigation can be more material, to such as would engage in a careful development of the principles of political justice. It cannot therefore be unproductive of benefit, that we should here trace into their remoter ramifications, the principles which were then delivered; as well as turn our attention to certain other considerations connected with the same topic, which we have not hitherto had occasion to discuss. Of the many controversies which have been excited relative to the operation of opinion, none are of more importance, than the question respecting free will and necessity, and the question respecting self-love and benevolence. These will occupy a principal portion of the enquiry.[2]

We will first endeavour to establish the proposition, that all the actions of men are necessary. It was impossible that this principle should not, in an indirect manner, be frequently anticipated in the preceding parts of this work. But it will be found strongly entitled to a separate consideration. The doctrine of moral necessity, includes in it consequences of the highest moment, and leads to a more bold and comprehensive view of man in society, than can possibly be entertained by him who has embraced the opposite opinion.

To the right understanding of any arguments that may be adduced under this head, it is requisite that we should have a clear idea of the meaning of the term, necessity. He who affirms that all actions are necessary, means that the man, who is acquainted with all the circumstances under which a living or intelligent being is placed upon any given occasion, is qualified to predict the conduct he will hold, with as much certainty, as he can predict any of the phenomena of inanimate nature. Upon this question the advocate of liberty in the philosophical sense, must join issue. He must, if he mean anything, deny this certainty of

---

[1] I. v.

[2] The reader, who is indisposed to abstruse speculations, will find the other members of the treatise sufficiently connected, without an express reference to this and the three following chapters of the present book.

conjunction between moral antecedents and consequents. Where all is constant and invariable, and the events that arise, uniformly correspond to the circumstances in which they originate, there can be no liberty.

It is generally acknowledged that, in the events of the material universe, everything is subjected to this necessity. The tendency of investigation and enquiry, relatively to this topic of human science, has been, more effectually to exclude the appearance of irregularity, as our improvements extended. Let us recollect what is the species of evidence that has satisfied philosophers upon this point. Their only solid ground of reasoning, has been from experience. The argument which has induced mankind, to conceive of the universe as governed by certain laws, has been, an observed similarity in the succession of events. If, when we had once remarked two events succeeding each other, we had never had occasion to see that individual succession repeated; if we saw innumerable events in perpetual progression, without any apparent order, so that all our observation would not enable us, when we beheld one, to pronounce that another, of such a particular class, might be expected to follow; we should never have formed the conception of necessity, or have had an idea corresponding to that of laws and system.

Hence it follows that all that, strictly speaking, we know of the material universe, is this uniformity of events. When we see the sun constantly rise in the morning, and set at night, and have had occasion to observe this phenomenon invariably taking place through the whole period of our existence, we cannot avoid receiving this as a law of the universe, and a ground for future expectation. But we never see any principle or virtue by which one event is conjoined to, or made the antecedent of, another.

Let us take some familiar illustrations of this truth. Can it be imagined that any man, by the inspection and analysis of gunpowder, would have been enabled, previously to experience, to predict its explosion? Would he, previously to experience, have been enabled to predict, that one piece of marble, having a flat and polished surface, might with facility be protruded along another in a horizontal, but would, with considerable pertinacity, resist separation in a perpendicular direction? The simplest phenomena, of the most hourly occurrence, were originally placed at an equal distance from human sagacity.

There is a certain degree of obscurity, incident to this subject, arising from the following circumstance. All human knowledge is the result of perception. We know nothing of any substance, a supposed material body, for example, but by experience. If it were unconjoined, and bore no relation, to the phenomena of any other substance, it would be no subject of human intelligence. We collect a number of these concurrences, and, having, by their perceived uniformity, reduced them into classes, form a general idea annexed to that part of the subject which stands as the antecedent. It must be admitted, that a definition of any substance, that is, anything that deserves to be called knowledge respecting it, will enable us to predict some of its future probable consequences, and that for this plain reason, that definition is prediction under another name. But, though, when we have gained the idea of impenetrability as a general phenomenon of matter, we can predict some of the variations to which it leads, there are others which we cannot predict: or, in other words, we know none of these variations but such as we have actually remarked, added to an expectation that similar events will arise under similar circumstances, proportioned to the constancy with which they have been observed to take place in our past experience. Finding, as we do by repeated experiments, that material substances have the property of resistance, and that one substance in a state of rest, when struck upon by another, passes into a state of motion, we are still in want of more particular observation, to enable us to predict the specific varieties, that will follow from this collision, in each of the bodies. Enquire of a man who knows nothing more of matter than its general property of impenetrability, what will be the result of one ball of matter impinging upon another, and you will soon find how little this general property can inform him of the particular laws of motion. We suppose him to know that motion will follow in to the second ball. But what quantity of motion will be communicated? What result will follow upon the collision, in the impelling ball? Will it continue to move in the same direction? Will it recoil in the opposite direction? Will it fly off obliquely; or will it subside into a state of rest? All these events will be found equally probable, by him whom a series of observations upon the past, has not instructed as to what he is to expect from the future.

From these remarks we may sufficiently collect what is the species of knowledge we possess respecting the laws of the material universe. No experiments we are able to make, no reasonings we are able to deduce, can ever instruct us in the principle of causation, or show us for what reason it is that one event has, in every instance in which it has been known to occur, been the precursor of another event of a given description. Yet this observation does not, in the slightest degree, invalidate our inference from one event to another, or affect the operations of moral prudence and expectation. The nature of the human mind is such, as to oblige us, after having seen two events perpetually conjoined, to pass, as soon as one of them occurs, to the recollection of the other: and, in cases where this transition never misleads us, but the ideal succession is always found to be an exact copy of the future event, it is impossible that this species of foresight should not be converted into a general foundation of inference and reasoning. We cannot take a single step upon this subject, which does not partake of the species of operation we denominate abstraction. Till we have been led to consider the rising of the sun tomorrow, as an incident of the same species as its rising today, we cannot deduce from it similar consequences. It is the business of science to carry this task of generalization to its furthest extent, and to reduce the diversified events of the universe to a small number of original principles.

Let us proceed to apply these reasonings concerning matter, to the illustration of the theory of mind. Is it possible in this latter theory, as in the former subject, to discover any general principles? Can intellect be made a topic of science? Are we able to reduce the multiplied phenomena of mind to any certain standard of reasoning? If the affirmative of these questions be conceded, the inevitable consequence appears to be, that mind, as well as matter, exhibits a constant conjunction of events, and furnishes all the ground that any subject will afford, for an opinion of necessity. It is of no importance that we cannot see the ground of that necessity, or imagine how sensations, pleasurable or painful, when presented to the mind of a percipient being, are able to generate volition and animal motion; for, if there be any truth in the above statement, we are equally incapable of perceiving a ground of connection between any two events in the material universe, the common and received opinion, that we do perceive such ground of connection, being, in reality, nothing more than a vulgar prejudice.

That mind is a topic of science, may be argued from all those branches of literature and enquiry which have mind for their subject. What species of amusement or instruction would history afford, if there were no ground of inference from moral antecedents to their consequents, if certain temptations and inducements did not, in all ages and climates, introduce a certain series of actions, if we were unable to trace a method and unity of system in men's tempers, propensities and transactions? The amusement would be inferior to that which we derive from the perusal of a chronological table, where events have no order but that of time; since, however the chronologist may neglect to mark the regularity of conjunction between successive transactions, the mind of the reader is busied in supplying that regularity from memory or imagination: but the very idea of such regularity would never have suggested itself, if we had never found the source of that idea in experience. The instruction arising from the perusal of history would be absolutely none; since instruction implies, in its very nature, the classing and generalizing of objects. But, upon the supposition on which we are arguing, all objects would be irregular and disjunct, without the possibility of affording any grounds of reasoning or principles of science.

The idea correspondent to the term character, inevitably includes in it the assumption of necessity and system. The character of any man, is the result of a long series of impressions, communicated to his mind and modifying it in a certain manner, so as to enable us, a number of these modifications and impressions being given, to predict his conduct. Hence arise his temper and habits, respecting which we reasonably conclude, that they will not be abruptly superseded and reversed; and that, if ever they be reversed, it will not be accidentally, but in consequence of some strong reason persuading, or some extraordinary event modifying his mind. If there were not this original and essential conjunction between motives and actions, and, which forms one particular branch of this principle, between men's past and future actions, there could be no such thing as character, or as a ground of inference, enabling us to predict what men would be, from what they have been.

From the same idea of regularity and conjunction, arise all the schemes of policy, in consequence of which men propose to themselves, by a certain plan of conduct to prevail upon others to become the tools and instruments of their purposes. All the arts of courtship and flattery, of playing upon men's hopes and fears, proceed upon the supposition, that mind is subject to certain laws, and that, provided we be skilful and assiduous enough in applying the motive, the action will inevitably follow.

Lastly, the idea of moral discipline proceeds entirely upon this principle. If I carefully persuade, exhort, and exhibit motives to another, it is because I believe that motives have a tendency to influence his conduct. If I reward or punish him, either with a view to his own improvement, or as an example to others, it is because I have been led to believe that rewards and punishments are calculated to affect the dispositions and practices of mankind.

There is but one conceivable objection, against the inference from these premises to the necessity of human actions. It may be alleged, that 'though there is a real coherence between motives and actions, yet this coherence may not amount to a certainty, and, of consequence, the mind still retains an inherent activity, by which it can at pleasure supersede and dissolve it. Thus for example, when I address argument and persuasion to my neighbour, to induce him to adopt a certain species of conduct, I do it not with a certain expectation of success, and am not utterly disappointed if my efforts fail of their object. I make a reserve for a certain faculty of liberty he is supposed to possess, which may at last counteract the best digested projects.'

But in this objection there is nothing peculiar to the case of mind. It is just so in matter. I see a part only of the premises, and therefore can pronounce only with uncertainty upon the conclusion. A philosophical experiment, which has succeeded a hundred times, may altogether fail in the next trial. But what does the philosopher conclude from this? Not that there is a liberty of choice in his retort and his materials, by which they baffle the best-informed expectations. Not that the established order of antecedents and consequents is imperfect, and that part of the consequent happens without an antecedent. But that there was some other antecedent concerned, to which at the time he failed to advert, but which a fresh investigation will probably lay open to him. When the science of the material universe was in its infancy, men were sufficiently prompt to refer events to accident and chance; but the further they have extended their enquiries and observation, the more reason they have found to conclude, that everything takes place according to necessary and universal laws.

The case is exactly parallel with respect to mind. The politician and the philosopher, however they may speculatively entertain the opinion of free will, never think of introducing it into their scheme of accounting for events. If an incident turn out otherwise than they expected, they take it for granted, that there was some unobserved bias, some habit of thinking, some prejudice of education, some singular association of ideas, that disappointed their prediction; and, if they be of an active and enterprising temper, they return, like the natural philosopher, to search out the secret spring of this unlooked for event.

The reflections into which we have entered upon the laws of the universe, not only afford a simple and impressive argument in favour of the doctrine of necessity, but suggest a very obvious reason why the doctrine opposite to this, has been, in a certain degree, the general opinion of mankind. It has appeared that the idea of uniform conjunction between events of any sort, is the lesson of experience, and the vulgar never arrive at the universal application of this principle even to the phenomena of the material universe. In the easiest and most familiar instances, such as the impinging of one ball of matter upon another and its consequences, they willingly admit the interference of chance and irregularity. In this instance however, as both the impulse and its consequences are subjects of observation to the senses, they readily imagine, that they perceive the absolute principle which causes motion to be communicated from the first ball to the second. Now the very same prejudice and precipitate conclusion, which induce them to believe that they discover the principle of motion in objects of sense, act in an opposite direction with respect to such objects as cannot be subjected to the examination of sense. The power by which a sensation, pleasurable or painful, when presented to the mind of a percipient being, produces volition and animal motion, no one can imagine that he sees; and therefore they readily conclude that there is no uniformity of conjunction in these events.

But, if the vulgar will universally be found to be the advocates of free will, they are not less strongly, however inconsistently, impressed with the belief of the doctrine of necessity. It is a well-known and a just observation, that, were it not for the existence of general laws, to which the events of the material universe always conform, man could never have been either a reasoning or a moral being. The most considerable actions of our lives are directed by foresight. It is because he foresees the regular succession of the seasons, that the farmer sows his field, and, after the expiration of a certain term, expects a crop. There would be no kindness in my administering food to the hungry, and no injustice in my thrusting a drawn sword against the bosom of my friend, if it were not the established quality of food to nourish, and of a sword to wound.

But the regularity of events in the material universe, will not of itself afford a sufficient foundation of morality and prudence. The voluntary conduct of our neighbours, enters for a share, into almost all those calculations upon which our plans and determinations are founded. If voluntary conduct, as well as material impulse, were not subjected to general laws, and a legitimate topic of prediction and foresight, the certainty of events in the material universe would be productive of little benefit. But, in reality, the mind passes from one of these topics of speculation to the other, without accurately distributing them into classes, or imagining that there is any difference in the certainty with which they are attended. Hence it appears that the most uninstructed peasant or artisan is practically a necessarian. The farmer calculates as securely upon the inclination of mankind to buy his corn when it is brought into the market, as upon the tendency of the seasons to ripen it. The labourer no more suspects that his employer will alter his mind, and not pay him his daily wages, than he suspects that his tools will refuse to perform those functions today, in which they were yesterday employed with success.[1]

Another argument in favour of the doctrine of necessity, not less clear and irresistible than that from the uniformity of conjunction of antecedents and consequents, will arise from a reference to the nature of voluntary action. The motions of the animal system distribute themselves into two great classes, voluntary and involuntary. 'Voluntary action,' as we formerly observed,[2] 'is, where the event is foreseen, previously to its occurrence, and the hope or fear of that event, forms the excitement, prompting our effort to forward or retard it.'

Here then the advocates of intellectual liberty have a clear dilemma proposed to their choice. They must ascribe this freedom, this imperfect conjunction of antecedents and consequents, either to our voluntary or our involuntary actions. They have already made their determination. They are aware that to ascribe freedom to that which is involuntary, even if the assumption could be maintained, would be altogether foreign to the great subjects of moral, theological or political enquiry. Man would not be in any degree more an agent or an accountable being, though it could be proved that all his involuntary motions sprung up in a fortuitous and capricious manner.

But, on the other hand, to ascribe freedom to our voluntary actions, is an express contradiction in terms. No motion is voluntary, any further than it is accompanied with intention and design, and has for its proper antecedent, the apprehension of an end to be accomplished. So far as it flows, in any degree, from another source, it is involuntary. The newborn infant foresees nothing, therefore all his motions are involuntary. A person arrived at maturity, takes an extensive survey of the consequences of his actions, therefore he is eminently a voluntary and rational being. If any part of my conduct be destitute of all foresight of the events to result, who is there that ascribes to it depravity and vice? Xerxes acted just as soberly as such a reasoner, when he caused his attendants to inflict a thousand lashes on the waves of the Hellespont.

The truth of the doctrine of necessity will be still more evident, if we consider the absurdity of the opposite hypothesis. One of its

---

[1] The reader will find the substance of the above arguments in a more diffusive form, in Hume's *Enquiry Concerning Human Understanding*, being the third part of his essays.
[2] I. v, p. 41.

principal ingredients is self-determination. Liberty, in an imperfect and popular sense, is ascribed to the motions of the animal system, when they result from the foresight and deliberation of the intellect, and not from external compulsion. It is in this sense that the word is commonly used in moral and political reasoning. Philosophical reasoners therefore, who have desired to vindicate the property of freedom, not only to our external motions, but to the acts of the mind, have been obliged to repeat this process. Our external actions are then said to be free, when they truly result from the determination of the mind. If our volitions, or internal acts, be also free, they must in like manner result from the determination of the mind, or in other words, 'the mind in adopting them' must be 'self-determined.' Now nothing can be more evident, than that that in which the mind exercises its freedom, must be an act of the mind. Liberty therefore, according to this hypothesis, consists in this, that every choice we make, has been chosen by us, and every act of the mind, been preceded and produced by an act of the mind. This is so true, that, in reality, the ultimate act is not styled free, from any quality of its own, but because the mind, in adopting it, was self-determined, that is, because it was preceded by another act. The ultimate act resulted completely from the determination that was its precursor. It was itself necessary; and, if we would look for freedom, it must be to that preceding act. But, in that preceding act also, if the mind were free, it was self-determined, that is, this volition was chosen by a preceding volition, and, by the same reasoning, this also by another antecedent to itself. All the acts, except the first, were necessary, and followed each other, as inevitably as the links of a chain do, when the first link is drawn forward. But then neither was this first act free, unless the mind in adopting it were self-determined, that is, unless this act were chosen by a preceding act. Trace back the chain as far as you please, every act at which you arrive is necessary. That act, which gives the character of freedom to the whole, can never be discovered; and, if it could, in its own nature includes a contradiction.

Another idea which belongs to the hypothesis of free will, is, that the mind is not necessarily inclined this way or that, by the motives which are presented to it, by the clearness or obscurity with which they are apprehended, or by the temper and character which preceding habits may have generated; but that, by its inherent activity, it is equally capable of proceeding either way, and passes to its determination from a previous state of absolute indifference. Now what sort of activity is that, which is equally inclined to all kinds of actions? Let us suppose a particle of matter endowed with an inherent propensity to motion. This propensity must either be to move in one particular direction, and then it must for ever move in that direction, unless counteracted by some external impression; or it must have an equal tendency to all directions, and then the result must be a state of perpetual rest.

The absurdity of this consequence is so evident, that the advocates of intellectual liberty have endeavoured to destroy its force, by means of a distinction. 'Motive,' it has been said, 'is indeed the occasion, the *sine qua non* of volition, but it has no inherent power to compel volition. Its influence depends upon the free and unconstrained surrender of the mind. Between opposite motives and considerations, the mind can choose as it pleases, and, by its determination, can convert the motive which is weak and insufficient in the comparison, into the strongest.' But this hypothesis will be found exceedingly inadequate to the purpose for which it is produced. Not to repeat what has been already alleged to prove, that inherent power of production in an antecedent, is, in all cases, a mere fiction of the mind, it may easily be shown, that motives must either have a fixed and certain relation to their consequents, or they can have none.

For, first it must be remembered, that the ground or reason of any event, of whatever nature it be, must be contained among the circumstances which precede that event. The mind is supposed to be in a state of previous indifference, and therefore cannot be, in itself considered, the source of the particular choice that is made. There is a motive on one side and a motive on the other: and between these lie the true ground and reason of preference. But, wherever there is a tendency to preference, there may be degrees of tendency. If the degrees be equal, preference cannot follow: it is equivalent to the putting equal weights into the opposite scales of a balance. If one of them have a greater tendency to preference than the other, that which has the greatest tendency, must ultimately prevail. When two things are balanced against each other, so much amount may be conceived to be struck off from each side, as exists in the smaller sum, and the overplus that belongs to the greater, is all that truly enters into the consideration.

Add to this, secondly, that, if motive have not a necessary influence, it is altogether superfluous. The mind cannot first choose to be influenced by a motive, and afterwards submit to its operation: for in that case the preference would belong wholly to this previous volition. The determination would in reality be complete in the first instance; and the motive, which came in afterwards, might be the pretext, but could not be the true source of the proceeding.[1]

Lastly, it may be observed upon the hypothesis of free will, that the whole system is built upon a distinction where there is no difference, to wit, a distinction between the intellectual and active powers of the mind. A mysterious philosophy taught men to suppose, that, when an object was already felt to be desirable, there was need of some distinct power to put the body in motion. But reason finds no ground for this supposition; nor is it possible to conceive (in the case of an intellectual faculty placed in an aptly organized body, where preference exists, together with a sentiment, the dictate of experience, of our power to obtain the object preferred) of anything beyond this, that can contribute to render a certain motion of the animal frame the necessary result. We need only attend to the obvious meaning of the terms, in order to perceive that the will is merely, as it has been happily termed, 'the last act of the understanding',[2] 'one of the different cases of the association of ideas'.[3] What indeed is preference, but a feeling of something that really inheres, or is supposed to inhere, in the objects themselves? It is the comparison, true or erroneous, which the mind makes, respecting such things as are brought into competition with each other. This is indeed the same principle as was established upon a former occasion, when we undertook to prove that the voluntary actions of men originate in their opinions.[4] But, if this fact had been sufficiently attended to, the freedom of the will would never have been gravely maintained by philosophical writers; since no man ever imagined, that we were free to feel or not to feel an impression made upon our organs, and to believe or not to believe a proposition demonstrated to our understanding.

It must be unnecessary to add anything further on this head, unless it be a momentary recollection of the sort of benefit that freedom of the will would confer upon us, supposing it possible. Man being, as we have here found him to be, a creature, whose actions flow from the simplest principle, and who is governed by the apprehensions of his understanding, nothing further is requisite but the improvement of his reasoning faculty, to make him virtuous and happy. But did he possess a faculty independent of the understanding, and capable of resisting from mere caprice the most powerful arguments, the best education and the most

---

[1] The argument from the impossibility of free will is treated with great force of reasoning in Jonathan Edwards's Enquiry into the Freedom of the Will [1754].

[2] [Samuel] Clarke [1675–1729].   [3] [David] Hartley [1705–57].

[4] I. v.

sedulous instruction might be of no use to him. This freedom we shall easily perceive to be his bane and his curse; and the only hope of lasting benefit to the species, would be, by drawing closer the connection between the external motions and the understanding, wholly to extirpate it. The virtuous man, in proportion to his improvement, will be under the constant influence of fixed and invariable principles; and such a being as we conceive God to be, can never in any one instance have exercised this liberty, that is, can never have acted in a foolish and tyrannical manner. Freedom of the will is absurdly represented as necessary to render the mind susceptible of moral principles; but in reality, so far as we act with liberty, so far as we are independent of motives, our conduct is as independent of morality as it is of reason, nor is it possible that we should deserve either praise or blame for a proceeding thus capricious and indisciplinable.

CHAPTER VIII

INFERENCES FROM THE DOCTRINE OF NECESSITY

CONSIDERING then the doctrine of moral necessity as sufficiently established, let us proceed to the consequences that are to be deduced from it. This view of things presents us with an idea of the universe, as of a body of events in systematical arrangement, nothing in the boundless progress of things interrupting this system, or breaking in upon the experienced succession of antecedents and consequents. In the life of every human being there is a chain of events, generated in the lapse of ages which preceded his birth, and going on in regular procession through the whole period of his existence, in consequence of which it was impossible for him to act in any instance otherwise than he has acted.

The contrary of this having been the conception of the mass of mankind in all ages, and the ideas of contingency and accident having perpetually obtruded themselves, the established language of morality has been universally tinctured with this error. It will therefore be of no trivial importance, to enquire, how much of this language is founded in the truth of things, and how much of what is expressed by it, is purely imaginary. Accuracy of language is the indispensable prerequisite of sound knowledge; and, without attention to that subject, we can never ascertain the extent and importance of the consequences of necessity.

First then it appears, that, in the emphatical and refined sense in which the word has sometimes been used, there is no such thing as action. Man is in no case, strictly speaking, the beginner of any event or series of events that takes place in the universe, but only the vehicle through which certain antecedents operate, which antecedents, if he were supposed not to exist, would cease to have that operation. Action however, in its more simple and obvious sense, is sufficiently real, and exists equally both in mind and in matter. When a ball upon a billiard-board is struck by the mace, and afterwards impinges upon a second ball, the ball which was first in motion, is said to act upon the second, though the results are in the strictest conformity to the impression received, and the motion it communicates is precisely determined by the circumstances of the case. Exactly similar to this, upon the reasonings already delivered, are the actions of the human mind. Mind is a real principle, an indispensable link in the great chain of the universe; but not, as has sometimes been supposed, a principle of that paramount description, as to supersede all necessities, and be itself subject to no laws and methods of operation.

Is this view of things incompatible with the existence of virtue?

If by virtue we understand, the operation of an intelligent being in the exercise of an optional power, so that, under the same precise circumstances, it might or might not have taken place, undoubtedly it will annihilate it.

But the doctrine of necessity does not overturn the nature of things. Happiness and misery, wisdom and error will still be distinct from each other, and there will still be a correspondence between them. Wherever there is that which may be the means of pleasure or pain to a sensitive being, there is ground for preference and desire, or on the contrary for neglect and aversion. Benevolence and wisdom will be objects worthy to be desired, selfishness and error worthy to be disliked. If therefore by virtue we mean, that principle which asserts the preference of the former over the latter, its reality will remain undiminished by the doctrine of necessity.

Virtue, if we would reason accurately, should perhaps be considered by us, in the first instance, objectively, rather than as modifying any particular beings.[1] Virtuous conduct, is conduct proposing to itself a

[1] II. iv.

certain end; by its tendency to answer that end, its value and purity are to be tried. Its purpose is the production of happiness, and the aptitude or inaptitude of particular beings in this respect, will decide their importance in the scale of existence. This aptitude is usually termed capacity or power. Now power, in the sense of the hypothesis of liberty, is altogether chimerical. But power, in the sense in which it is sometimes affirmed of inanimate substances, is equally true of those which are animate. A candlestick has the power or capacity of retaining a candle in a perpendicular direction. A knife has a capacity of cutting. In the same manner a human being has a capacity of walking: though it may be no more true of him, than of the inanimate substance, that he has an option to exercise or not to exercise that capacity. Again, there are different degrees as well as different classes of capacity. One knife is better adapted for the purposes of cutting than another.

There are two considerations relative to any particular being, that generate approbation, and this whether the being be possessed of consciousness or no. These considerations are, capacity, and the application of capacity. We approve of a sharp knife rather than a blunt one, because its capacity is greater. We approve of its being employed in carving food, rather than in maiming men or other animals, because that application of its capacity is preferable. But all approbation or preference is relative to utility or general good. A knife is as capable as a man, of being employed in purposes of utility; and the one is no more free than the other as to its employment. The mode in which a knife is made subservient to these purposes, is by material impulse. The mode in which a man is made subservient, is by inducement and persuasion. But both are equally the affair of necessity. The man differs from the knife, as the iron candlestick differs from the brass one; he has one more way of being acted upon. This additional way in man, is motive; in the candlestick, is magnetism.

Virtue is a term which has been appropriated to describe the effects produced by men, under the influence of motives, in promoting the general good: it describes the application of sentient and human capacity, and not the application of capacity in inanimate substances. The word, thus explained, is to be considered as rather similar to grammatical distinction, than to real and philosophical difference. Thus, in Latin, *bonus* is *good* as affirmed of a man, *bona* is *good* as affirmed of a woman. In the same manner we can as easily conceive of the capacity of an inanimate, as of an animate, substance being applied to the general good; and as accurately describe the best possible application of the one, as of the other. The end, that upon which the application depends for its value, is the same in both instances. But we call the latter virtue and duty, and not the former. These words may, in a popular sense, be considered as either masculine or feminine, but never neuter. The existence of virtue therefore, if by this term we mean the real and essential difference between virtue and vice, the importance of a virtuous character, and the approbation that is due to it, is not annihilated by the doctrine of necessity, but rather illustrated and confirmed.

But, if the doctrine of necessity do not annihilate virtue, it tends to introduce a great change into our ideas respecting it. According to this doctrine it will be absurd for a man to say, 'I will exert myself,' 'I will take care to remember,' or even 'I will do this.' All these expressions imply as if man were, or could be, something else than what motives make him. Man is in reality a passive, and not an active being. In another sense however he is sufficiently capable of exertion. The operations of his mind may be laborious, like those of the wheel of a heavy machine in ascending a hill, may even tend to wear out the substance of the shell in which it acts, without in the smallest degree impeaching its passive character. If we were constantly aware of this, our minds would not glow less ardently with the love of truth, justice, happiness and mankind. We should have a firmness and simplicity in our conduct, not wasting itself in fruitless struggles and regrets, not hurried along with infantine impatience, but seeing actions with their consequences, and calmly and unreservedly giving up to the influence of those comprehensive views which this doctrine inspires.

As to our conduct towards others, in instances where we were concerned to improve and meliorate their minds, we should address our representations and remonstrances to them with double confidence. The believer in free will, can expostulate, with or correct, his pupil, with faint and uncertain hopes, conscious that the clearest exhibition of truth is impotent, when brought into contest with the unhearing and indisciplinable faculty of will; or in reality, if he were consistent, secure that it could produce no effect. The necessarian on the contrary employs real antecedents, and has a right to expect real effects.

But, though he would represent, he would not exhort, for this is a term without a meaning. He would suggest motives to the mind, but he would not call upon it to comply, as if it had a power to comply, or not to comply. His office would consist of two parts, the exhibition of motives to the pursuit of a certain end, and the delineation of the easiest and most effectual way of attaining that end.

There is no better scheme, for enabling us to perceive, how far any idea that has been connected with the hypothesis of liberty, has a real foundation, than to translate the usual mode of expressing it, into the language of necessity. Suppose the idea of exhortation, so translated, to stand thus: 'To enable any arguments I may suggest to you, to make a suitable impression, it is necessary that they should be fairly considered. I proceed therefore to evince to you the importance of attention, knowing, that, if I can make this importance sufficiently manifest, attention will inevitably follow.' I should surely be far better employed, in enforcing directly the truth I am desirous to impress, than in having recourse to this circuitous mode, of treating attention as if it were a separate faculty. Attention will, in reality, always be proportionate to our apprehension of the importance of the subject proposed.

At first sight it may appear as if, the moment I was satisfied that exertion on my part was no better than a fiction, and that I was the passive instrument of causes exterior to myself, I should become indifferent to the objects which had hitherto interested me the most deeply, and lose all that inflexible perseverance, which seems inseparable from great undertakings. But this cannot be the true state of the case. The more I resign myself to the influence of truth, the clearer will be my perception of it. The less I am interrupted by questions of liberty and caprice, of attention and indolence, the more uniform will be my constancy. Nothing could be more unreasonable, than that the sentiment of necessity should produce in me a spirit of neutrality and indifference. The more certain is the conjunction between antecedents and consequents, the more cheerfulness should I feel in yielding to painful and laborious employments.

It is common for men impressed with the opinion of free will, to entertain resentment, indignation, and anger, against those who fall into the commission of vice. How much of these feelings is just, and how much erroneous? The difference between virtue and vice, will equally remain upon the opposite hypothesis. Vice therefore must be an object of rejection, and virtue of preference; the one must be approved, and the other disapproved. But our disapprobation of vice, will be of the same nature, as our disapprobation of an infectious distemper.

One of the reasons why we are accustomed to regard the murderer with more acute feelings of displeasure, than the knife he employs, is that we find a more dangerous property, and greater cause for apprehension, in the one than in the other. The knife is only accidentally an object of terror, but against the murderer we can never be enough upon our guard. In the same manner we regard the middle of a busy street with less complacency, as a place for walking, than the side; and the ridge of a house with more aversion than either. Independently therefore of the idea of freedom, mankind in general will find in the enormously vicious a sufficient motive of apprehension and displeasure. With the addition of that idea, it is no wonder that they should be prompted to sentiments of the most intemperate abhorrence.

These sentiments obviously lead, to the examination of the prevailing conceptions on the subject of punishment. The doctrine of necessity, would teach us to class punishment in the list of the means we possess of influencing the human mind, and may induce us to enquire into its utility, as an instrument for reforming error. The more the human mind can be shown to be under the influence of motive, the more certain it is that punishment will produce a great and unequivocal effect. But the doctrine of necessity will teach us to look upon punishment with no complacence, and at all times to prefer the most direct means of encountering error, the development of truth. Whenever punishment is employed under this system, it will be employed, not for any intrinsic recommendation it possesses, but only as it shall appear to conduce to general utility.

On the contrary it is usually imagined, that, independently of the supposed utility of punishment, there is proper desert in the criminal, a certain fitness in the nature of things that renders pain the suitable concomitant of vice. It is therefore frequently said, that it is not enough that a murderer should be transported to a desert island, where there should be no danger that his malignant propensities should ever again have opportunity to act; but that it is also right the indignation of mankind against him, should express itself, in the infliction of some actual ignominy and pain. On the contrary, under the system of necessity, the terms, guilt, crime, desert and accountableness, in the abstract and general sense in which they have sometimes been applied, have no place.

Correlative to the feelings of resentment, indignation and anger against the offences of others, are those of repentance, contrition and sorrow for our own. As long as we admit of an essential difference between virtue and vice, no doubt all erroneous conduct, whether of ourselves or others, will be regarded with disapprobation. But it will in both cases be considered, under the system of necessity, as a link in the great chain of events, which could not have been otherwise than it is. We shall therefore no more be disposed to repent of our own faults, than of the faults of others. It will be proper to view them both, as actions injurious to the public good, and the repetition of which is to be deprecated. Amidst our present imperfections, it will perhaps be useful to recollect what is the error by which we are most easily seduced. But, in proportion as our views extend, we shall find motives sufficient to the practice of virtue, without a partial retrospect to ourselves, or a recollection of our own propensities and habits.

In the ideas annexed to the words resentment and repentance, there is some mixture of true judgement and a sound conception of the nature of things. There is perhaps still more justice, in the notions conveyed by praise and blame, though these also have been vitiated and distorted by the hypothesis of liberty. When I speak of a beautiful landscape or an agreeable sensation, I employ the language of panegyric. I employ it still more emphatically, when I speak of a good action; because I am conscious, that the panegyric to which it is entitled, has a tendency to procure a repetition of such actions. So far as praise implies nothing more than this, it perfectly accords with the severest philosophy. So far as it implies, that the man could have abstained from the virtuous action I applaud, it belongs only to the delusive system of liberty.

A further consequence of the doctrine of necessity, is its tendency to make us survey all events with a tranquil and placid temper, and approve and disapprove without impeachment to our self-possession. It is true, that events may be contingent, as to any knowledge we possess respecting them, however certain they are in themselves. Thus the advocate of liberty, knows that his relation was either lost or saved in the great storm that happened two months ago; he regards this event as past and certain, and yet he does not fail to be anxious about it. But it is not less true, that anxiety and perturbation for the most part include in them, an imperfect sense of contingency, and a feeling as if our efforts could make some alteration in the event. When the person recollects with clearness that the event is over, his mind grows composed; but presently he feels as if it were in the power of God or man to alter it, and his agitation is renewed. To this may be further added the impatience of curiosity; but philosophy and reason have an evident tendency to prevent useless curiosity from disturbing our peace. He therefore who regards all things past, present, and to come, as links of an indissoluble chain, will, as often as he recollects this comprehensive view, find himself assisted to surmount the tumult of passion; and be enabled to reflect upon the moral concerns of mankind with the same clearness of perception, the same firmness of judgement, and the same constancy of temper, as we are accustomed to do upon the truths of geometry.

This however must be expected to be no more than a temporary exertion. A sound philosophy may afford us intervals of entire tranquillity. It will communicate a portion of this tranquillity to the whole of our character. But the essence of the human mind will still remain. Man is the creature of habit; and it is impossible for him to lose those things which afforded him a series of pleasurable sensations, without finding his thoughts in some degree unhinged, and being obliged, under the pressure of considerable disadvantages, to seek, in paths untried, and in new associations, a substitute for the benefits of which he has been deprived.

It would be of infinite importance to the cause of science and virtue, to express ourselves upon all occasions in the language of necessity. The contrary language is perpetually intruding, and it is difficult to speak two sentences, upon any topic connected with human action, without it. The expressions of both hypotheses are mixed in inextricable confusion, just as the belief of both hypotheses, however incompatible, will be found to exist in all uninstructed minds. The reformation of which I speak, will probably be found exceedingly practicable in itself; though, such is the subtlety of error, that we should, at first, find several revisals and much laborious study necessary, before it could be perfectly weeded out. This must be the author's apology, for not having attempted in the present work, what he recommends to others.[1]

CHAPTER IX

OF THE MECHANISM OF THE HUMAN MIND

THE doctrine of necessity being admitted, it follows that the theory of the human mind is properly, like the theory of every other series of events with which we are acquainted, a system of mechanism; understanding by mechanism nothing more, than a regular succession of phenomena, without any uncertainty of event, so that every consequent requires a specific antecedent, and could be no otherwise in any respect than as the antecedent determined it to be.

But there are two sorts of mechanism capable of being applied to the solution of this case, one which has for its medium only matter and motion, the other which has for its medium thought. . . .

.   .   .   .

[1] [Cf. pp. 336–340.]

There are various reasons calculated to persuade us that this last hypothesis is the most probable. . . .

[One] reason [is] the constancy with which thought, in innumerable instances, accompanies the functions of this mechanism. Now this constancy of conjunction, has been shown to be the only ground we have, in any imaginable subject, for proceeding from antecedent to consequent, and expecting, when we see one given event, that another event of a given sort will succeed it.[1] We cannot therefore reject the principle which supposes thought to be a real medium in the mechanism of man, but upon grounds that would vitiate our reasonings in every topic of human enquiry.

.   .   .   .

It being then sufficiently clear that . . . thought is the medium through which the motions of the animal system are generally carried on, let us proceed to consider what is the nature of those thoughts by which the limbs and organs of our body are set in motion. . . .

First, thought may be the source of animal motion, without partaking, in any degree, of volition, or design. It is certain that there is a great variety of motions in the animal system, which are, in every view of the subject, involuntary.[2] Such, for example, are the cries of an infant, when it is first impressed with the sensation of pain. In the first motions of the animal system, nothing of any sort could possibly be foreseen, and therefore nothing of any sort could be intended. Yet these motions have sensation or thought for their constant concomitant; and therefore all the arguments which have been already alleged, remain in full force, to prove that thought is the medium of their production.

.   .   .   .

Secondly, thought may be the source of animal motion, and at the same time be unattended with consciousness. . . . . . By the consciousness which accompanies any thought, there seems to be something implied distinct from the thought itself. Consciousness is a sort of supplementary reflection, by which the mind not only has the thought, but adverts to its own situation, and observes that it has it. Consciousness therefore, however nice the distinction, seems to be a second thought.

In order to ascertain whether every thought be attended with consciousness, it may be proper to consider whether the mind can ever have more than one thought at any one time. Now this seems altogether

[1] Ch. vii.   [2] I. v.

contrary to the very nature of mind. . . . In comparing two objects, we frequently endeavour, as it were, to draw them together in the mind, but we seem obliged to pass successively from the one to the other.

But, though it be intuitively true, that we can . . . have but one thought, at one time, . . . there is a collateral consideration, . . . that may be adduced in support of this proposition. It is at present generally admitted, by all accurate reasoners upon the nature of the human mind, that its whole internal history may be traced to one single principle, association. There are but two ways in which a thought can be excited in the mind, first, by external impression, secondly, by the property, which one thought existing in the mind, is found to have, of introducing a second thought through the means of some link of connection between them. This being premised, let us suppose a given mind to have two ideas at the same time. There can be no reason why either of these ideas should prove ungenerative, or why the two ideas they are best fitted to bring after them, should not co-exist, as well as their predecessors. Let the same process be repeated indefinitely. We have then two trains of thinking exactly contemporary in the same mind. Very curious questions will here arise. Have they any communication? Do they flow separately, or occasionally cross and interrupt each other? Can any reason be given, why one of them should not relate to the doctrine of fluxions, and the other to the drama? in other words, why the same man should not, at the same time, be both Newton and Shakespeare? Why may not one of these co-existing trains be of a joyful, and the other of a sorrowful tenor? There is no absurdity that may not be supported upon the assumption of this principle. In fact we have no other conception of identity, as it relates to the human mind, than that of a single idea, supersedable by external impression, or regularly leading on, by means of various connections, to an indefinite train of ideas in uninterrupted succession.

.   .   .   .

Consciousness, as it has been above defined, appears to be one of the departments of memory. Now the nature of memory, so far as it relates to the subject of which we are treating, is obvious. An infinite number of thoughts passed through my mind in the last five minutes of my existence. How many of them am I now able to recollect? How many of them shall I recollect tomorrow? One impression after another is perpetually effacing from this intellectual register. Some of them may with great attention and effort be revived; others obtrude themselves uncalled for; and a third sort are perhaps out of the reach of any power of thought to reproduce, as having never left their traces behind them for a moment. If the memory be capable of so many variations and degrees of intensity, may there not be some cases with which it never connects itself? If the succession of thoughts be so inexpressibly rapid, may they not pass over some topics with so delicate a touch, as to elude the supplement of consciousness?

It seems to be consciousness, rather than the succession of ideas, that measures time to the mind. The succession of ideas is, in all cases, exceedingly rapid, and it is by no means clear that it can be accelerated. . . . Yet time seems, to our apprehension, to flow, now with a precipitated, and now with a tardy course. The indolent man reclines for hours in the shade; and, though his mind be perpetually at work, the silent progress of time is unobserved. But, when acute pain, or uneasy expectation, obliges consciousness to recur with unusual force, the time appears insupportably long. Indeed it is a contradiction in terms to suppose that the succession of thoughts, where there is nothing that perceptibly links them together, where they totally elude the memory and instantly vanish, can be a measure of time to the mind. That there is such a state of mind, in some cases assuming a permanent form, has been so much the general opinion of mankind, that it has obtained a name, and is called reverie. It is probable from what has been said, that thoughts of reverie, understanding by that appellation thoughts untransmitted to the memory, perpetually take their turn with our more express and digested thoughts, even in the most active scenes of our life.

Lastly, thought may be the source of animal motion, and yet there may be no need of a distinct thought producing each individual motion. . . . In uttering a cry for example, the number of muscles and articulations of the body concerned in this operation is very great; shall we say that the infant has a distinct thought for each of these articulations?

.   .   .   .

The consequences, which seem deducible from this theory of mind, are sufficiently memorable. By shewing the extreme subtlety and simplicity of thought, it removes many of the difficulties, that might otherwise rest upon its finer and more evanescent operations. If thought, in order to be the source of animal motion, need not have, either the nature of volition, or the concomitant of consciousness, and if a single thought may become a complex source, and produce a variety of motions, it will then become exceedingly difficult to trace its operations, or to discover any circumstances in a particular instance of animal motion, which can sufficiently indicate that thought was not the principle of its production, ... Hence therefore it appears, that all those motions, which are observed to exist in substances having perception, and which are not to be discovered in substances of any other species, may reasonably be suspected to have thought, ... for their source.

There are various classes of motion which will fall under this definition, ... An example of one of these classes, suggests itself, in the phenomenon of walking. An attentive observer will perceive various symptoms, calculated to persuade him, that every step he takes, during the longest journey, is the production of thought. Walking is, in all cases, originally a voluntary motion. In a child, when he learns to walk, in a rope-dancers when he begins to practise that particular exercise, the distinct determination of mind, preceding each step, is sufficiently perceptible. ... But it is not unreasonable to believe, that a species of motion which began in express design, may, though it ceases to be the subject of conscious attention, owe its continuance to a continued series of thoughts flowing in that direction, and that, if life were taken away, material impulse would not carry on the exercise for a moment. ...

Another class of motions of a still subtler nature, are the regular motions of the animal economy, such as the circulation of the blood, and the pulsation of the heart. Are thought and perception the medium of these motions? We have the same argument here as in the former instances, conjunction of event. When thought begins, these motions also begin; and, when it ceases, they are at an end. They are therefore either the cause or effect of percipiency, or mind; but we shall be inclined to embrace the latter side of this dilemma, when we recollect, that we are probably acquainted with many instances in which thought is the immediate cause of motions, which scarcely yield in subtlety to these; but that, as to the origin of the faculty of thought, we are wholly uninformed. ...

. . . .

CHAPTER X

OF SELF-LOVE AND BENEVOLENCE

THE subject of the mechanism of the human mind, is the obvious counterpart of that which we are now to examine. Under the former of these topics we have entered, with considerable minuteness, into the nature of our involuntary actions; the decision of the latter will, in a great degree, depend upon an accurate conception of such as are voluntary. The question of self-love and benevolence, is a question relative to the feelings and ideas by which we ought to be governed, in our intercourse with our fellow-men, or, in other words, in our moral conduct. But it is universally admitted, that there can be no moral conduct, that we can be neither virtuous nor vicious, except in instances where our actions flow from intention, and are directed by foresight, or where they might have been so directed; and this is the definition of voluntary actions.[1] The question therefore of self-love and benevolence, is a question of voluntary action.

. . . . .

Voluntary action cannot exist but as the result of experience. Neither desire nor aversion can have place, till we have had a consciousness of agreeable and disagreeable sensations. Voluntary action implies desire, and the idea of certain means to be employed for the attainment of the thing desired.

The things first desired by every thinking being, will be agreeable sensation, and the means of agreeable sensation. If he foresee anything that is not apprehended to be pleasure or pain, or the means of pleasure or pain, this will excite no desire, and lead to no voluntary action.

A disposition to promote the benefit of another, my child, my friend, my relation, or my fellow-being, is one of the passions; understanding by the term passion, a permanent and habitual tendency towards a certain course of action. It is of the same general nature, as avarice, or the love of fame. The good of my neighbour could not, in the first instance, have been chosen, but as the means of agreeable sensation. His cries, or the spectacle of his distress importune me, and I am irresistibly impelled to adopt means to remove this importunity. The child perceives, in his own case, that menaces or soothing tend to stop his cries, and he is induced to employ, in a similar instance, that mode of the two which seems most within his reach. He thinks little of the sufferings endured, and is only uneasy at the impression made upon his organs. To this motive, he speedily adds the idea of esteem and gratitude, which are to be purchased by his beneficence. Thus the good of our neighbour, like the possession of money, is originally pursued for the sake of its advantage to ourselves.

But it is the nature of the passions, speedily to convert what at first were means, into ends. The avaricious man forgets the utility of money

[1] I. v, pp. 40 f., 46.

which first incited him to pursue it, fixes his passion upon the money itself, and counts his gold, without having in his mind any idea but that of seeing and handling it. Something of this sort happens very early in the history of every passion. The moment we become attached to a particular source of pleasure, beyond any idea we have of the rank it holds in the catalogue of sources, it must be admitted that it is loved for its own sake. The man who pursues wealth or fame with any degree of ardour, soon comes to concentre his attention in the wealth or the fame, without carrying his mind beyond, or thinking of anything that is to result from them.

This is merely one case of the phenomena of habit.[1] All indulgence of the senses, is originally chosen, for the sake of the pleasure that accrues. But the quantity of accruing pleasure or pain, is continually changing. This however is seldom adverted to; and when it is, the power of habit is frequently too strong to be thus subdued. The propensity to do again what we have been accustomed to do, recurs, when the motive that should restrain us has escaped from our thoughts. Thus the drunkard and the lecher continue to pursue the same course of action, long after the pains have outweighed the pleasures, and even after they confess and know this to be the real state of the case. . . .

If this be the case in the passion of avarice or the love of fame, it must also be true in the instance of beneficence, that, after having habituated ourselves to promote the happiness of our child, our family, our country or our species, we are at length brought to approve and desire their happiness without retrospect to ourselves. It happens in this instance, as in the former, that we are occasionally actuated by the most perfect disinterestedness, and willingly submit to tortures and death, rather than see injury committed upon the object of our affections.

Thus far there is a parallel nature in avarice and benevolence. But ultimately there is a wide difference between them. When once we have entered into so auspicious a path as that of disinterestedness, reflection confirms our choice, in a sense in which it never can confirm any of the factitious passions we have named. We find by observation, that we are surrounded by beings of the same nature with ourselves. They have the same senses, are susceptible of the same pleasures and pains, capable of being raised to the same excellence, and employed in the same usefulness.[2] We are able in imagination to go out of ourselves, and become impartial spectators of the system of which we are a part. We can then make an estimate of our intrinsic and absolute value; and detect the imposition

[1] I. v, p. 44.   [2] II. iii, p. 78.

of that self-regard, which would represent our own interest as of as much value as that of all the world beside. The delusion being thus sapped, we can, from time to time at least, fall back in idea into our proper post, and cultivate those views and affections which must be most familiar to the most perfect intelligence.

.   .   .   .

The hypothesis of disinterestedness would never have had so many adversaries, if the complexity of human motives had been sufficiently considered. To illustrate this, let it be recollected that every voluntary action has in it a mixture of involuntary.[1] In the sense in which we have used the word motive in an early part of this work,[2] it is equally descriptive of the cause of action in both cases. Motive may therefore be distinguished, according to its different relations, into direct and indirect; understanding by the direct, that which is present to the mind of the agent at the time of his determination, and which belongs to every voluntary action, and to so much of every action as is voluntary; and by the indirect, that which operates without being adverted to by the mind, whether in the case of actions originally involuntary, or that have become so, in whole, or in part, by the force of habit. Thus explained, it is incontrovertibly evident that the direct motive to many of our actions is purely disinterested. We are capable of self-oblivion, as well as of sacrifice. All that is strictly voluntary, in the beneficence of a man habitually generous and kind, commences from this point: if other considerations intervene in the sequel, they are indebted for their intervention to the disinterested motive. But, at the same time that this truth is clearly established, it is not less true, first, that the indirect and original motive, that which laid the foundation of all our habits, is the love of agreeable sensation.[3] Secondly, it is also to be admitted, that there is probably something personal directly and perceptibly mixing itself with such of our beneficent actions as are of a sensible duration. We are so accustomed to fix our attention upon agreeable sensation, that we can scarcely fail to recollect, at every interval, the gratitude we shall excite, or the approbation we shall secure, the pleasure that will result to ourselves from our neighbour's well-being, the joys of self-applause, or the uneasiness that attends upon ungratified desire. Yet, after every deduction that can be made, the disinterested and direct motive, the profit and advantage of our neighbour, seems to occupy the principal place. This is at least the first, often the only, thing in the view of the mind, at the

[1] I. v, p. 46.   [2] p. 41.   [3] [Cf. pp. 333–336.]

time the action is chosen. It is this from which, by way of eminence, it derives the character of voluntary action.

. . . . .

There is one further remark, which, . . . ought not to be omitted. If self-love be the only principle of action, there can be no such thing as virtue. Benevolent intention is essential to virtue.[1] Virtue, where it exists in any eminence, is a species of conduct, modelled upon a true estimate of the different reasons inviting us to preference. He, that makes a false estimate, and prefers a trivial and partial good to an important and comprehensive one, is vicious. Virtue requires a certain disposition and view of the mind, and does not belong to the good which may accidentally and unintentionally result from our proceeding. The creditor that, from pure hardness of disposition, should cast a man into prison who, unknown to him, was upon the point of committing some atrocious and sanguinary action, would be not virtuous but vicious. The mischief to result from the project of his debtor, was no part of his motive; he thought only of gratifying his inordinate passion. . . .

. . . . .

What are the inferences that ought to be made from this doctrine with respect to political institution? Certainly not that the interest of the individual, ought to be made incompatible with the part he is expected to take in the interest of the whole. This is neither desirable, nor even possible. But that social institution needs not despair of seeing men influenced by other and better motives. The true politician is bound to recollect, that the perfection of mind consists in disinterestedness. He should regard it as the ultimate object of his exertions, to induce men to estimate themselves at their just value, and neither to grant to themselves, nor claim from others, a higher consideration than they deserve. Above all, he should be careful not to add vigour to the selfish passions. He should gradually wean men from contemplating their own benefit in all that they do, and induce them to view with complacence the advantage that is to result to others. Great mischief, in this respect, has probably been done by those moralists, who think only of stimulating men to good deeds by considerations of frigid prudence and mercenary self-interest, and never apply themselves to excite one generous and magnanimous sentiment of our natures. This has been too much the case with the teachers of religion, even those of them who are most eager in their hostility to religious enthusiasm.

[1] II. iv.

The last perfection of the sentiment here vindicated, consists in that state of mind, which bids us rejoice as fully in the good that is done by others, as if it were done by ourselves. The man who shall have attained to this improvement, will be actuated neither by interest nor ambition, the love of honour, nor the love of fame. He has a duty indeed obliging him to seek the good of the whole; but that good is his only object. If that good be effected by another hand, he feels no disappointment. All men are his fellow labourers, but he is the rival of no man. Like Pedaretus in ancient story, he is ready to exclaim: 'I also have endeavoured to deserve; but there are three hundred citizens in Sparta better than myself, and I rejoice.'

CHAPTER XI

OF GOOD AND EVIL

THERE is no disquisition more essential either in morality or politics, than that which shall tend to give us clear and distinct ideas of good and evil, what it is we should desire, and what we should deprecate. . . .

The nature of good and evil, which is one of the plainest subjects upon which the human mind can be engaged, has been obscured by two sets of men: those who, from an eagerness to refine and exalt beyond measure the nature of virtue, have elevated it into something impossible and unmeaning: and those who, spurning the narrow limits of science and human understanding, have turned system builders, and fabricated a universe after their own peculiar fancy. We shall see, as we proceed, what has been the operation of these two errors. In the meantime it may be most safe, to examine the subject in its genuine simplicity, uninfluenced by the preconceptions of party.

Good is a general name, including pleasure, and the means by which pleasure is procured. Evil is a general name, including pain, and the means by which pain is produced. Of the two things included in these general names, the first is cardinal and substantive, the second has no intrinsic recommendations, but depends for its value on the other. Pleasure therefore is to be termed an absolute good; the means of pleasure are only relatively good. The same observation may be stated of pain.[1]

We inhabit a world where sensations do not come detached, but where everything is linked and connected together. Of consequence,

[1] III. iii, pp. 105 f.

among things absolutely good there may be two classes. There are some things that are good and only good, pleasures that do not draw after them mischief, anguish and remorse. There may be other pleasures that are attended in the sequel with an overbalance of pain, and which, though absolutely good, are relatively evil. There may also be pains which, taken together with their consequences, are salutary. But this does not alter the original proposition: where there is a mixture of evil, all is not good; just as, where there is a mixture of pain, all is not pleasure.

Let us see how this statement affects the theory and practice of virtue.

First, we are hereby enabled to detect their mistake, who denied that 'pleasure was the supreme good.' The error of the Epicurean philosophers seems to have been, not in affirming that 'pleasure was the supreme good,' for this cannot be refuted; but in confining that pleasure which is the proper scope of human actions, to the pleasure of the individual who acts, and not admitting that the pleasure of others was an object which, for its own sake, could, and ought to be pursued.[1]

That 'pleasure is the supreme good,' cannot be denied by him who is sufficiently attentive to the meaning of words. That which will give pleasure neither to ourselves nor others, and from which the fruits of joy can be reaped, in no stage, and at no period, is necessarily good for nothing.

The opposers of the Epicurean maxim, were terrified by a consequence which they hastily concluded might be built upon it. If pleasure were the only thing that is worthy to be desired, they thought that every man might reasonably be justified in 'walking in the sight of his own eyes,' and there would be no longer any rule of human conduct. Each man might say, 'Pleasure is the proper object of my pursuit; I best know what pleases me; and therefore, however opposite is the plan of my conduct to your conceptions, it is unreasonable and unjust for you to interfere with me.'

An inference the opposite of this, might, with more propriety, have been drawn from the maxim upon which we are descanting. Is 'pleasure the only good?' Then have we the most cogent reason for studying pleasure, and reducing it to a science, and not for leaving every man to pursue his own particular taste, which is nothing more than the result of his education, and of the circumstances in which he happens to have been placed, and which by other lessons and circumstances may be corrected.

[1] Ch. x.

No man is entitled to complain of my sober and dispassionate ex-postulations respecting the species of pleasure he thinks proper to pursue, because no man stands alone, and can pursue his private conceptions of pleasure, without affecting, beneficially or injuriously, the persons immediately connected with him, and, through them, the rest of the world. Even if he have persuaded himself that it is his business to pursue his own pleasure, and that he is not bound to attend ultimately to the pleasure of others, yet it may easily be shown that it is, generally speaking, the interest of each individual, that all should form their plan of personal pleasure with a spirit of deference and accommodation to the pleasure of each other.

But putting the circumstance of the action and reaction of men in society out of the question, still there will be a science of pleasure, and it will be idle and erroneous to consider each man separately, and leave each to find his source of pleasure suitable to his particular humour. We have a common nature, and that common nature ought to be consulted. There is one thing, or series of things, that constitutes the true perfection of man.[1]

In the discussions that took place a few years ago, in the English parliament and nation, respecting the slave-trade, the sentiment we are here combating, was used as a topic of argument, by some of those persons who, from certain deplorable prejudices, were able to prevail upon themselves to appear as advocates for this trade. 'The slaves in the West Indies,' they said, 'are contented with their situation, they are not conscious of the evils against which you exclaim; why then should you endeavour to alter their condition?'

The true answer to this question, even granting them their fact, would be: 'It is not very material to a man of a liberal and enlarged mind, whether they are contented or no. Are they contented? I am not contented for them. I see in them beings of certain capacities, equal to certain pursuits and enjoyments. It is of no consequence in the question, that they do not see this, that they do not know their own interests and happiness. . . . Abridged as they are of independence and enjoyment, they have neither the apprehension nor spirit of men. I cannot bear to see human nature thus degraded. It is my duty, if I can, to make them a thousand times happier, than they are, or have any conception of being.'

It is not difficult to form a scale of happiness. Suppose it to be something like the following.

The first class shall be such as we may perhaps sometimes find, among

[1] II. iii, p. 78; III. vii, p. 126.

the labouring inhabitants of the civilized states of Europe. We will conceive a man, working with his hands every day to obtain his subsistence. He rises early to his labour, and leaves off every night weary and exhausted. He takes a tranquil or a boisterous refreshment, and spends the hours of darkness in uninterrupted slumber. He does not quarrel with his wife, oftener than persons of his class regularly do; and his cares are few, as he has scarcely known the pressure of absolute want. He never repines, but when he witnesses luxuries he cannot partake, and that sensation is transient; and he knows no diseases but those which rise from perpetual labour. The range of his ideas is scanty; and the general train of his sensations, comes as near, as the nature of human existence will admit, to the region of indifference. This man is in a certain sense happy. He is happier than a stone.

Our next instance shall be taken from among the men of rank, fortune and dissipation. We will suppose the individual in question to have an advantageous person and a sound constitution. He enjoys all the luxuries of the palate, the choicest viands, and the best-flavoured wines. He takes his pleasures discreetly, so as not, in the pursuit of pleasure, to lose the power of feeling it. He shoots, he hunts. He frequents all public places. He sits up late in scenes of gay resort. He rises late. He has just time to ride and dress, before he goes into company again. With a happy flow of spirits and a perpetual variety of amusements, he is almost a stranger to *ennui*. But he is a model of ignorance. He never reads, and knows nothing beyond the topic of the day. He can scarcely conceive the meaning of the sublime or pathetic; and he rarely thinks of anything beyond himself. This man is happier than the peasant. He is happier, by all the pleasures of the palate, and all the gratifications of neatness, elegance and splendour, in himself, and the objects around him. Every day he is alive, inventing some new amusement, or enjoying it. He tastes the pleasures of liberty; he is familiar with the gratifications of pride: while the peasant strides through life, with something of the contemptible insensibility of an oyster.

The man of taste and liberal accomplishments, is more advantageously circumstanced than he whom we have last described. We will suppose him to possess as many of the gratifications of expense as he desires. But, in addition to these, like the mere man of fortune in comparison with the peasant, he acquires new senses, and a new range of enjoyment. The beauties of nature are all his own. He admires the overhanging cliff, the wide-extended prospect, the vast expanse of the ocean, the foliage of the woods, the sloping lawn and the waving grass. He knows the pleasures of solitude, when man holds commerce alone with the tranquil solemnity of nature. He has traced the structure of the universe; the substances which compose the globe we inhabit, and are the materials of human industry; and the laws which hold the planets in their course amidst the trackless fields of space. He studies; and has experienced the pleasures which result from conscious perspicacity and discovered truth. He enters, with a true relish, into the sublime and pathetic. He partakes in all the grandeur and enthusiasm of poetry. He is perhaps himself a poet. He is conscious that he has not lived in vain, and that he shall be recollected with pleasure, and extolled with ardour, by generations yet unborn. In this person, compared with the two preceding classes, we acknowledge something of the features of man. They were only a better sort of brutes; but he has sensations and transports of which they have no conception.

But there is a rank of man, more fitted to excite our emulation than this, the man of benevolence. Study is cold, if it be not enlivened with the idea of the happiness to arise to mankind from the cultivation and improvement of sciences.[1] The sublime and pathetic are barren, unless it be the sublime of true virtue, and the pathos of true sympathy. The pleasures of the mere man of taste and refinement, 'play round the head, but come not to the heart.' There is no true joy, but in the spectacle and contemplation of happiness. There is no delightful melancholy, but in pitying distress. The man who has once performed an act of exalted generosity, knows that there is no sensation of corporeal or intellectual taste to be compared with this. The man who has sought to benefit nations, rises above the mechanical ideas of barter and exchange. He asks no gratitude. To see that they are benefited, or to believe that they will be so, is its own reward. He ascends to the highest of human pleasures, the pleasures of disinterestedness. He enjoys all the good that mankind possess, and all the good that he perceives to be in reserve for them. No man so truly promotes his own interest, as he that forgets it. No man reaps so copious a harvest of pleasure, as he who thinks only of the pleasures of other men.

The inference from this survey of human life, is, that he who is fully persuaded that pleasure is the only good, ought by no means to leave every man to enjoy his peculiar pleasure according to his own peculiar humour. Seeing the great disparity there is between different conditions of human life, he ought constantly to endeavour to raise each class, and every individual of each class, to a class above it. This is the true

[1] Ch. v, pp. 145 f.

equalization of mankind. Not to pull down those who are exalted, and reduce all to a naked and savage equality. But to raise those who are abased; to communicate to every man all genuine pleasures, to elevate every man to all true wisdom, and to make all men participators of a liberal and comprehensive benevolence. This is the path in which the reformers of mankind ought to travel. This is the prize they should pursue. Do you tell me, 'that human society can never arrive at this improvement?' I do not stay to dispute that point with you. We can come nearer it than we are. We can come nearer and nearer yet. This will not be the first time that persons, engaged in the indefatigable pursuit of some accomplishment, have arrived at an excellence that surpassed their most sanguine expectations.

The result of this part of the subject is, that those persons have been grossly mistaken, who taught that virtue was to be pursued for its own sake, and represented pleasure and pain as trivial matters and unworthy consideration. Virtue is upon no other account valuable, than as it is the instrument of the most exquisite pleasure.—Be it observed, that it is one thing to say that pain is not an evil, which is absurd, and another thing to say that temporary pains and pleasures are to be despised, when the enduring of the one is necessary, and the declining the other unavoidable in the pursuit of excellent and permanent pleasure, which is a most fundamental precept of wisdom and morality.

Let us proceed to a second point announced by us in the outset, the consideration of how the subject of good and evil has been darkened by certain fabulists and system builders. The system alluded to under this head, is that of the optimists, who teach, 'that everything in the universe, is for the best; and that, if anything had happened otherwise than it has happened, the result would have been, a diminution of the degree of happiness and good.'

That we may escape the error into which these persons have been led, by the daringness of their genius, and their mode of estimating things in the gross, and not in detail, we must be contented to follow experience, and not to outrun it.

It has already appeared that there is in the universe absolute evil: and, if pain be evil (and it has been proved to be the only absolute evil), it cannot be denied that, in the part of the universe with which we are acquainted, it exists in considerable profusion. It has also appeared, that there is a portion of absolute evil, which is relatively good, and which therefore, the preceding circumstances being assumed, was desirable. Such, for example, is the amputation of a gangrened limb.

Whether or no those preceding circumstances were, universally, and in a comprehensive sense, good, which rendered the introduction of the absolute evil in question necessary, is, to say the least, a very doubtful point. But, if there be some presumption in the negative even in the smallest instance, this presumption against universal good is incalculably increased, when we recollect all the vice, disorder and misery, that exist in the world.

Let us consider what portion there is of truth, that has been mixed with the doctrine of optimism. This is the same thing as to enquire by means of what plausibilities it gained footing in the world. The answer to these questions lies in two circumstances.

First, there is a degree of improvement real and visible in the world. This is particularly manifest, in the history of the civilized part of mankind, during the three last centuries.... And, as improvements have long continued to be incessant, so there is no chance but they will go on. The most penetrating philosophy cannot prescribe limits to them, nor the most ardent imagination adequately fill up the prospect.

Secondly, the doctrine of necessity teaches us, that all things in the universe are connected together. Nothing could have happened otherwise than it has happened. Do we congratulate ourselves upon the rising genius of freedom? Do we view with pride the improvements of mankind, and contrast with wonder, man in the state in which he once was, naked, ignorant and brutal, with man as we now sometimes behold him, enriched with boundless stores of science, and penetrated with sentiments of the purest philanthropy? These things could not have existed in their present form, without having been prepared by all the preceding events. Everything the most seemingly insignificant, the most loathsome, or the most retrograde, was indissolubly bound to all that we most admire in the prospect before us....

There are three considerations which limit that idea of optimism, which some men have been inclined to deduce from the above circumstances.

First, it applies only to that part of the universe with which we are acquainted. That deduction, whatever it is, which is authorized by the above circumstances, depends upon their junction. The general tendency to improvement, would be an insufficient apology for untoward events, if everything were not connected; and the connection of all events, would have no just tendency to reconcile us to the scene, were it not for the visible improvement. But has improvement been the constant characteristic of the universe? The human species seems to be but, as it were, of yesterday. Will it continue for ever? The globe we inhabit bears strong marks of convulsion, such as the teachers of religion, and the professors of natural philosophy, agree to predict, will one day destroy the inhabitants of the earth. Vicissitude therefore, rather than unbounded progress, appears to be the characteristic of nature.

Secondly, the quantity of good deducible from these circumstances, instead of meriting the name of optimism, is, in one respect, directly contrasted with it. Nothing is positively best. So far from it, that the considerations here alleged, are calculated to prove, that everything is valuable, for this reason among others, that it leads to something better than itself.

Lastly, the points here affirmed, are by no means calculated to bear out the conclusion, that, if something else had happened, in the place of what did actually happen in any given instance, it might not have been a fortunate event. We are taught, by the doctrine of necessity, that nothing else could possibly happen under the circumstances; not that, if something else had been possible, it would not have been attended with more desirable consequences. . . .

It may be worthy of remark, that the support the system of optimism derives from the doctrine of necessity, is of a very equivocal nature. The doctrine of necessity teaches, that each event is the only thing, under the circumstances, that could happen; it would, of consequence, be as proper, upon this system, to say that everything that happens, is the worst, as that it is the best, that could possibly happen.

It was observed in the commencement of this discussion upon the subject of optimism, that, though there is some pain, or absolute evil, which, relatively taken, must be admitted to be attended with an overbalance of good, yet it is a matter of great delicacy and difficulty, in most instances, to decide in favour of pain, which, whatever be its relative value, is certainly a negative quantity to be deducted in the sum total of happiness. There is perhaps some impropriety in the phrase, thus applied, of relative good. Pain, under the most favourable circumstances, must be admitted to be absolutely, though not relatively, an evil. In every instance of this kind we are reduced to a choice of evils: consequently, whichever way we determine our election, it is still evil that we choose.

Taking these considerations along with us, the rashness of the optimist will appear particularly glaring, while we recollect the vast portion of pain and calamity that is to be found in the world. Let us not amuse ourselves with a pompous and delusive survey of the whole, but let us examine parts severally and individually. All nature swarms with life.

This may, in one view, afford an idea of an extensive theatre of pleasure. But unfortunately every animal preys upon his fellow. Every animal, however minute, has a curious and subtle structure, rendering him susceptible, as it should seem, of piercing anguish. We cannot move our foot, without becoming the means of destruction. The wounds inflicted are of a hundred kinds. These petty animals are capable of palpitating for days in the agonies of death. It may be said, with little licence of phraseology, that all nature suffers. There is no day nor hour, in which, in some regions of the many-peopled globe, thousands of men, and millions of animals, are not tortured, to the utmost extent that organized life will afford. Let us turn our attention to our own species. Let us survey the poor; oppressed, hungry, naked, denied all the gratifications of life, and all that nourishes the mind. They are either tormented with the injustice, or chilled into lethargy. Let us view man, writhing under the pangs of disease, or the fiercer tortures that are stored up for him by his brethren. Who is there that will look on, and say, 'All this is well; there is no evil in the world?' . . . The evil does not consist merely in the pain endured. It is the injustice that inflicts it, that gives it its sharpest sting. Malignity, an unfeeling disposition, vengeance and cruelty, are inmates of every climate. As these are felt by the sufferer with peculiar acuteness, so they propagate themselves. Severity begets severity, and hatred engenders hate.[1] The whole history of the human species, taken in one point of view, appears a vast abortion. Man seems adapted for wisdom and fortitude and benevolence. But he has always, through a vast majority of countries, been the victim of ignorance and supersition. . . .

A sound philosophy will teach us to contemplate this scene without madness. Instructed in its lessons, we shall remember that, though there is much of evil, there is also much of good in the world, much pleasure, as well as much pain. We shall not even pronounce that some small portion of this evil is not relatively not an evil. Above all, we shall be cheered with the thought of brighter prospects and happier times. But the optimist must be particularly rash, who takes upon him to affirm of all this mass of evil without exception, that it is relatively not evil, and that nothing could have happened otherwise than it has happened, without the total being worse than it is.

· · · ·

[1] Ch. ii, p. 137.

BOOK V

OF LEGISLATIVE AND EXECUTIVE POWER

CHAPTER I

INTRODUCTION

I N the preceding divisions of this work the ground has been sufficiently cleared, to enable us to proceed, with considerable explicitness and satisfaction, to the practical detail: in other words, to attempt the tracing out that application of the laws of general justice, which may best conduce to the gradual improvement of mankind.

It has appeared, that an enquiry concerning the principles and conduct of social intercourse, is the most important topic, upon which the mind of man can be exercised;[1] that, upon these principles, well or ill conceived, and the manner in which they are administered, the vices and virtues of individuals depend;[2] that political institution, to be good, must have constant relation to the rules of immutable justice;[3] and that those rules, uniform in their nature, are equally applicable to the whole human race.[4]

The different topics of political institution cannot perhaps be more perspicuously distributed, than under the four following heads: provisions for general administration;[5] provisions for the intellectual and moral improvement of individuals;[6] provisions for the administration of criminal justice;[7] and provisions for the regulation of property.[8] Under each of these heads it will be our business, in proportion as we adhere to the great and comprehensive principles already established, rather to clear away abuses, than to recommend further and more precise regulations, rather to simplify, than to complicate. Above all we should not forget, that government is, abstractedly taken, an evil, an usurpation upon the private judgement and individual conscience of

---

[1] Book I.   [2] Book I.   [3] II. ii.
[4] I. vi and vii; III. vii.   [5] [Book V.]   [6] [Book VI.]
[7] [Book VII.]   [8] [Book VIII.]

mankind;[1] and that, however we may be obliged to admit it as a necessary evil for the present, it behoves us, as the friends of reason and the human species, to admit as little of it as possible, and carefully to observe, whether, in consequence of the gradual illumination of the human mind, that little may not hereafter be diminished.

And first we are to consider the different provisions that may be made for general administration; including, under the phrase general administration, all that shall be found necessary, of what has usually been denominated, legislative and executive power. Legislation has already appeared to be a term not applicable to human society.[2] Men cannot do more than declare and interpret law; nor can there be an authority so paramount, as to have the prerogative of making that to be law, which abstract and immutable justice had not made to be law previously to that interposition. But it might, notwithstanding this, be found necessary, that there should be an authority empowered to declare those general principles, by which the equity of the community will be regulated, in particular cases upon which it may be compelled to decide. The question concerning the reality and extent of this necessity, it is proper to reserve for after-consideration.[3] Executive power consists of two very distinct parts: general deliberations relative to particular emergencies, which, so far as practicability is concerned, may be exercised either by one individual or a body of individuals, such as peace and war, taxation,[4] and the selection of proper periods for convoking deliberative assemblies: and particular functions, such as those of financial detail, or minute superintendence, which cannot be exercised unless by one or a small number of persons.

In reviewing these several branches of authority, and considering the persons to whom they may be most properly confided, we cannot perhaps do better, than adopt the ordinary distribution of forms of government, into monarchy, aristocracy and democracy. Under each of these heads we may enquire into the merits of their respective principles, first absolutely, and upon the hypothesis of their standing singly for the whole administration; and secondly, in a limited view, upon the supposition of their constituting one branch only of the system of government. It is usually alike incident to them all, to confide the minuter branches of executive detail to inferior agents.

---

[1] Book II.   [2] III. v.   [3] VII. viii.

[4] I state the article of taxation as a branch of executive government, since it is not, like law or the declaration of law, a promulgating of some general principle, but is a temporary regulation for some particular emergency.

One thing more it is necessary to premise. The merits of each of the three heads I have enumerated, are to be considered negatively. The corporate duties of mankind, are the result of their irregularities and follies in their individual capacity. If they had no imperfection, or if men were so constituted, as to be sufficiently, and sufficiently early, corrected by persuasion alone, society would cease from its functions. Of consequence, of the three forms of government, and their compositions, that is the best, which shall least impede the activity and application of our intellectual powers. It was in the recollection of this truth that I have preferred the term political institution to that of government, the former appearing to be sufficiently expressive of that relative form, whatever it be, into which individuals would fall, when there was no need of force to direct them into their proper channel, and were no refractory members to correct.

CHAPTER IV

OF A VIRTUOUS DESPOTISM

THERE is a principle, frequently maintained upon this subject,[1] which is entitled to impartial consideration. It is granted, by those who espouse it, 'that absolute monarchy, from the imperfection of those by whom it is administered, is, for the most part, productive of evil;' but they assert, 'that it is the best and most desirable of all forms under a good and virtuous prince. It is exposed,' say they, 'to the fate of all excellent natures, and, from the best thing, frequently, if corrupted, becomes the worst.'...

Now, whatever dispositions any man may possess in favour of the welfare of others, two things are necessary to give them validity; discernment and power. I can promote the welfare of a few persons, because I can be sufficiently informed of their circumstances. I can promote the welfare of many in certain general articles, because, for this purpose, it is only necessary, that I should be informed of the nature of the human mind as such, not of the personal situation of the individuals concerned. But for one man to undertake to administer the affairs of millions, to supply, not general principles and perspicuous reasoning, but particular application, and measures adapted to the necessities of the moment, is of all undertakings the most extravagant and absurd.

[1] See *Tom Jones*, XII. xii.

The most simple and obvious system of practical administration, is for each man to be the arbiter of his own concerns. If the imperfection, the narrow views, and the mistakes of human beings, render this, in certain cases, inexpedient and impracticable, the next resource is to call in the opinion of his peers, persons who, from their vicinity, may be presumed to have some general knowledge of the case, and who have leisure and means minutely to investigate the merits of the question. It cannot reasonably be doubted, that the same expedient which is resorted to in our civil and criminal concerns, would, by plain and uninstructed mortals, be adopted in the assessment of taxes, in the deliberations of commerce, and in every other article in which their common interests were involved, only generalizing the deliberative assembly, or panel, in proportion to the generality of the question to be decided.

Monarchy, instead of referring every question to the persons concerned or their neighbours, refers it to a single individual, placed at the greatest distance possible from the ordinary members of the society. Instead of distributing the causes to be judged, into as many parcels as convenience would admit, for the sake of providing leisure and opportunities of examination, it draws them to a single centre, and renders enquiry and examination impossible. A despot, however virtuously disposed, is obliged to act in the dark, to derive his knowledge from other men's information, and to execute his decisions by other men's instrumentality. Monarchy seems to be a species of government proscribed by the nature of man; and those persons, who furnished their despot with integrity and virtue, forgot to add omniscience and omnipotence, qualities not less necessary to fit him for the office they had provided.

. . . . .

Another position, not less generally asserted than the desirableness of a virtuous despotism, is, 'that republicanism is a species of government practicable only in a small state, while monarchy is best fitted to embrace the concerns of a vast and flourishing empire.' The reverse of this, so far at least as relates to monarchy appears, at first sight to be the truth. The competence of any government cannot be measured by a purer standard, than the extent and accuracy of its information. In this respect monarchy, appears in all cases, to be wretchedly deficient; but, if it can ever be admitted, it must surely be in those narrow and limited instances, where an individual can, with least absurdity, be supposed to be acquainted with the affairs and interests of the whole.[1]

[1] Paine's 'Letter to the Republicans' [1792—usually known as 'Essay to Aid New Republicans'].

CHAPTER VI

OF SUBJECTS

LET us proceed to consider the moral effects, which the institution of monarchical government is calculated to produce, upon the inhabitants of the countries in which it flourishes. And here it must be laid down as a first principle, that monarchy is founded in imposture. It is false, that kings are entitled to the eminence they obtain. They possess no intrinsic superiority over their subjects. The line of distinction that is drawn, is the offspring of pretence, an indirect means employed for effecting certain purposes, and not the language of truth. It tramples upon the genuine nature of things, and depends for its support upon this argument, 'that, were it not for impositions of a similar nature, mankind would be miserable.'

Secondly, it is false that kings can discharge the functions of royalty. They pretend to superintend the affairs of millions, and they are necessarily unacquainted with these affairs. The senses of kings are constructed like those of other men: they can neither see nor hear what is transacted in their absence. They pretend to administer the affairs of millions, and they possess no such supernatural powers, as should enable them to act at a distance. They are nothing of what they would persuade us to believe them. The king is often ignorant of that, of which half the inhabitants of his dominions are informed. His prerogatives are administered by others, and the lowest clerk in office, is frequently, to this and that individual, more effectually the sovereign, than the king himself. He is wholly unacquainted with what is solemnly transacted in his name.

To conduct this imposture with success, it is necessary to bring over to its party our eyes and our ears. Accordingly kings are always exhibited, with all the splendour of ornament, attendance and equipage. They live amidst a sumptuousness of expense; and this, not merely to gratify their appetites, but as a necessary instrument of policy. The most fatal opinion that could lay hold upon the minds of their subjects, is that kings are but men. Accordingly, they are carefully withdrawn from the profaneness of vulgar inspection; and, when they are shown to the public, it is with every artifice that may dazzle our sense, and mislead our judgement.

The imposture does not stop with our eyes, but addresses itself to our ears. Hence the inflated style of regal formality. The name of the king everywhere obtrudes itself upon us. It would seem as if everything in the country, the lands, the houses, the furniture, and the inhabitants, were his property. Our estates, are the king's dominions. Our bodies and minds, are his subjects. Our representatives, are his parliament. Our courts of law, are his deputies. All magistrates, throughout the realm, are the king's officers. His name occupies the foremost place in all statutes and decrees. He is the prosecutor of every criminal. He is 'Our Sovereign Lord the King.' Were it possible that he should die, 'the fountain of our blood, the means by which we live,' would be gone: every political function would be suspended. It is therefore one of the fundamental principles of monarchical government, that 'the king cannot die.' Our moral principles accommodate themselves to our veracity: and, accordingly, the sum of our political duties (the most important of all duties), is loyalty; to be true and faithful to the king; to honour a man whom, it may be, we ought to despise; and to obey; that is, to convert our shame into our pride, and to be ostentatious of the surrender of our own understandings. The morality of adults in this situation, is copied from the basest part of the morality sometimes taught to children; and the perfection of virtue is placed, in blind compliance, and unconditional submission.

What must be the effects of this machine upon the moral principles of mankind? Undoubtedly we cannot trifle with the principles of morality and truth, with impunity. However gravely the imposture may be carried on, it is impossible but that the real state of the case should be strongly suspected. Man in a state of society, if undebauched by falsehoods like these, which confound the nature of right and wrong, is not ignorant of what it is in which merit consists. He knows that one man is not superior to another, except so far as he is wiser or better. Accordingly these are the distinctions to which he aspires for himself. These are the qualities he honours and applauds in another, and which therefore the feelings of each man instigate his neighbours to acquire. But what a revolution is introduced among these original and undebauched sentiments, by the arbitrary distinctions which monarchy engenders? We still retain in our minds the standard of merit: but it daily grows more feeble and powerless; we are persuaded to think that it is of no real use in the transactions of the world, and presently lay it aside as Utopian and visionary.

Nor is this the whole of the injurious consequences produced, by the hyperbolical pretensions of monarchy. There is a simplicity in truth that refuses alliance with this impudent mysticism. No man is entirely ignorant of the nature of man. He will not indeed be incredulous to a degree of energy and rectitude, that may exceed the standard of his pre-conceived ideas. But for one man to pretend to think and act for a nation of his fellows, is so preposterous, as to set credibility at defiance. Is he persuaded that the imposition is salutary? He willingly assumes the right of introducing similar falsehoods into his private affairs. He becomes convinced, that veneration for truth, is to be classed among our errors and prejudices, and that, so far from being, as it pretends to be, in all cases salutary, it would lead, if ingenuously practised, to the destruction of mankind.

. . . .

Let us suppose an individual who by severe labour earns a scanty sub-sistence, to become, by accident or curiosity, a spectator of the pomp of a royal progress. Is it possible that he should not mentally apostrophize this elevated mortal, and ask, 'What has made thee to differ from me?' If no such sentiment pass through his mind, it is a proof that the corrupt institutions of society have already divested him of all sense of justice. The more simple and direct is his character, the more certainly will these sentiments occur. What answer shall we return to his enquiry? That the well-being of society, requires men to be treated otherwise than according to their intrinsic merit? Whether he be satisfied with this answer or no, will he not aspire to possess that (which in this instance is wealth), to which the policy of mankind has annexed such high dis-tinction? Is it not indispensable, that, before he believes in the recti-tude of this institution, his original feelings of right and wrong should be wholly reversed? If it be indispensable, then let the advocate of the monarchical system ingenuously declare, that, according to that system, the interest of society, in the first instance, requires the subversion of all principles of moral truth and justice.

. . . .

. . . one of the most essential ingredients in a virtuous character, is undaunted firmness; and nothing can more powerfully tend to destroy this principle than the spirit of a monarchical government. The first lesson of virtue is, Fear no man; the first lesson of such a constitution is, Fear the king. The true interest of man, requires the annihilation of factitious and imaginary distinctions; it is inseparable from monarchy to support and render them more palpable than ever. He that cannot speak to the proudest despot, with a consciousness that he is a man speaking to a man, and a determination to yield him no superiority to which his inherent qualifications do not entitle him, is wholly incapable of an illustrious virtue. How many such men are bred within the pale of monarchy? How long would monarchy maintain its ground in a nation of such men? Surely it would be wisdom in society, instead of conjuring up a thousand phantoms to seduce us into error, instead of surrounding us with a thousand fears to deprive us of energy, to remove every obstacle to our progress, and smooth the path of improvement.

·   ·   ·   ·

CHAPTER XI

MORAL EFFECTS OF ARISTOCRACY

THE features of aristocratical institution are principally two; privilege, and an aggravated monopoly of wealth. The first of these is the essence of aristocracy; the second, that without which aristocracy can rarely be supported. They are both of them in direct opposition to all sound morality, and all generous independence of character.

Inequality of wealth is perhaps the necessary result of the institution of property, in any state of progress at which the human mind has yet arrived; and cannot, till the character of the human species is essentially altered, be superseded, but by a despotic and positive interference, more injurious to the common welfare, than the inequality it attempted to remove. Inequality of wealth involves with it inequality of inheritance.

But the mischief of aristocracy is, that it inexpressibly aggravates and embitters an evil, which, in its mildest form, is deeply to be deplored. The first sentiment of an uncorrupted mind, when it enters upon the theatre of human life, is, Remove from me and my fellows all arbitrary hindrances; let us start fair; render all the advantages and honours of social institution accessible to every man, in proportion to his talents and exertions.

Is it true, as has often been pretended, that generous and exalted qualities are hereditary in particular lines of descent? They do not want the alliance of positive institution, to secure to them their proper ascendancy, and enable them to command the respect of mankind. Is it false? Let it share the fate of exposure and detection with other impostures. If I conceived of a young person that he was destined, from his earliest infancy, to be a sublime poet, or a profound philosopher, should I conceive that the readiest road to the encouraging and fostering his talents, was, from the moment of his birth, to put a star upon his breast, to salute him with titles of honour, and to bestow upon him, independently of all exertion, those advantages which exertion usually proposes to itself as its ultimate object of pursuit? No; I should send him to the school of man, and oblige him to converse with his fellows upon terms of equality.

Privilege is a regulation, rendering a few men, and those only, by the accident of their birth, eligible to certain situations. It kills all liberal ambition in the rest of mankind, by opposing to it an apparently insurmountable bar. It diminishes it in the favoured class itself, by showing them the principal qualification as indefeasibly theirs. Privilege entitles a favoured few to engross to themselves gratifications, which the system of the universe left at large to all her sons; it puts into the hands of these few, the means of oppression against the rest of their species; it fills them with vainglory, and affords them every incitement to insolence and a lofty disregard to the feelings and interests of others.

. . . .

Of all the principles of justice, there is none so material to the moral rectitude of mankind, as that no man can be distinguished but by his personal merit. When a man has proved himself a benefactor to the public, when he has already, by laudable perseverance, cultivated in himself talents, which need only encouragement and public favour to bring them to maturity, let that man be honoured. In a state of society where fictitious distinctions are unknown, it is impossible he should not be honoured. But that a man should be looked up to with servility and awe, because the king has bestowed on him a spurious name, or decorated him with a riband; that another should revel in luxury, because his ancestor three centuries ago bled in the quarrel of Lancaster or York; do we imagine that these iniquities can be practised without injury?

. . . .

CHAPTER XIV

GENERAL FEATURES OF DEMOCRACY

DEMOCRACY is a system of government, according to which every member of society is considered as a man, and nothing more. So far as positive regulation is concerned, if indeed that can, with any propriety, be termed regulation, which is the mere recognition of the simplest of all moral principles, every man is regarded as equal. Talents and wealth, wherever they exist, will not fail to obtain a certain degree of influence, without requiring positive institution to second their operation.

But there are certain disadvantages, that may seem the necessary result of democratical equality. In political society, it is reasonable to suppose, that the wise will be outnumbered by the unwise; and it will be inferred, 'that the welfare of the whole, will therefore be at the mercy of ignorance and folly.' It is true that the ignorant, will generally be sufficiently willing to listen to the judicious, 'but their very ignorance will incapacitate them from discerning the merit of their guides. The turbulent and crafty demagogue, will often possess greater advantages for inveigling their judgement, than the man who, with purer intentions, may possess a less brilliant talent. Add to this, that the demagogue has a never failing resource, in the ruling imperfection of human nature, that of preferring the specious present, to the substantial future. This is what is usually termed, playing upon the passions of mankind. Politics have hitherto presented an enigma, that all the wit of man has been insufficient to solve. Is it to be supposed, that the uninstructed multitude, should always be able to resist the artful sophistry, and captivating eloquence, that may be employed to perplex the subject with still further obscurity? Will it not often happen, that the schemes proposed by the ambitious disturber, will possess a meretricious attraction, which the severe and sober project of the discerning statesman shall be unable to compensate?

.   .   .   .

'A further ill consequence flows out of this circumstance. The multitude, conscious of their weakness in this respect, will, in proportion to their love of liberty and equality, be perpetually suspicious and uneasy. Has any man displayed uncommon virtues, or rendered eminent services to his country? He will presently be charged with secretly aiming at the tyranny. Various circumstances will come in aid of this accusation; the general love of novelty, envy of superior merit, and the incapacity of the multitude to understand the motives and character of those who excel them. . . . Thus will all that is liberal and refined, whatever the human mind in its highest state of improvement is able to conceive, be often overpowered by the turbulence of unbridled passion, and the rude dictates of savage folly.'

If this picture must be inevitably realized wherever democratical principles are established, the state of human nature would be peculiarly unfortunate. No form of government can be devised which does not partake of monarchy, aristocracy or democracy. We have taken a copious survey of the two former, and it would seem impossible that greater or more inveterate mischiefs can be inflicted on mankind, than those which are inflicted by them. No portrait of injustice, degradation and vice can be exhibited, that can surpass the fair and inevitable inferences from the principle upon which they are built. If then democracy can, by any arguments, be brought down to a level with such monstrous institutions as these, in which there is neither integrity nor reason, our prospects of the future happiness of mankind, will indeed be deplorable.

But this is impossible. Supposing that we should even be obliged to take democracy with all the disadvantages that were ever annexed to it, and that no remedy could be discovered for any of its defects, it would still be preferable to the exclusive system of other forms. . . .

In the estimate that is usually made of democracy, one of the sources of our erroneous judgement, lies in our taking mankind such as monarchy and aristocracy have made them, and thence judging how fit they are to manage for themselves. Monarchy and aristocracy would be no evils, if their tendency were not to undermine the virtues and the understandings of their subjects. The thing most necessary, is to remove all those restraints which prevent the human mind from attaining its genuine strength. Implicit faith, blind submission to authority, timid fear, a distrust of our powers, an inattention to our own importance and the good purposes we are able to effect, these are the chief obstacles to human improvement. Democracy restores to man a consciousness of his value, teaches him, by the removal of authority and oppression, to listen only to the suggestions of reason, gives him confidence to treat all other men with frankness and simplicity, and induces him to regard them no longer, as enemies against whom to be upon his guard, but as brethren whom it becomes him to assist. The citizen of a democratical state, when he looks upon the oppression and injustice that prevail in the countries around him, cannot but entertain an inexpressible esteem for the advantages he enjoys, and the most unalterable determination to preserve them. The influence of democracy upon the sentiments of its members, is altogether of the negative sort, but its consequences are inestimable. Nothing can be more unreasonable, than to argue, from men as we now find them, to men as they may hereafter be made. . . .

The road to the improvement of mankind, is in the utmost degree simple, to speak and act the truth. . . . To express ourselves to all men with honesty and unreserve, and to administer justice without partiality, are principles which, when once thoroughly adopted, are in the highest degree prolific. They enlighten the understanding, give decision to the judgement, and strip misrepresentation of its speciousness. . . . Nothing can be more worthy to be depended on, than the omnipotence of truth, or, in other words, than the connection between the judgement and the outward behaviour.[1] The contest between truth and falsehood is of itself too unequal, for the former to stand in need of support from any political ally. The more it is discovered, especially that part of it which relates to man in society, the more simple and self-evident will it appear; and it will be found impossible, any otherwise to account for its having been so long concealed, than from the pernicious influence of positive institution.

There is another obvious consideration, that has frequently been alleged to account for the imperfection of ancient democracies, which is worthy of our attention, though it be not so important as the argument which has just been stated. The ancients were unaccustomed to the idea of deputed or representative assemblies; and it is reasonable to suppose, that affairs might often be transacted, with the utmost order, in such assemblies, which might be productive of much tumult and confusion, if submitted to the personal discussion of the citizens at large.[2] By this happy expedient, we secure many of the pretended benefits of aristo-cracy, as well as the real benefits of democracy. The discussion of national affairs, is brought before persons of superior education and wisdom: we may conceive them, not only the appointed medium of the senti-ments of their constituents, but authorized, upon certain occasions, to act on their part, in the same manner as an unlearned parent delegates his authority over his child to a preceptor of greater accomplishments than himself. This idea, within proper limits, might probably be entitled to approbation, provided the elector had the wisdom not to recede from the exercise of his own understanding in political concerns, exerted his censorial power over his representative, and were accustomed, if the representative were unable, after the fullest explanation, to bring him over to his opinion, to transfer his deputation to another.

The true value of the system of representation, seems to be as follows. Large promiscuous assemblies, such as the assemblies of the people in Athens and Rome, must perhaps always be somewhat tumultuous, and

---

[1] I. v.

[2] The general grounds of this institution have been stated, III. iv. The exceptions which limit its value, will be seen in the twenty-third chapter of the present book.

liable to many of the vices of democracy enumerated in the commencement of this chapter. A representative assembly, deputed on the part of the multitude, will escape many of their defects. But representative government is necessarily imperfect. It is, as was formerly observed,[1] a point to be regretted, in the abstract notion of civil society, that a majority should overbear a minority, and that the minority, after having opposed and remonstrated, should be obliged practically to submit, to that which was the subject of their remonstrance. But this evil, inseparable from political government, is aggravated by representation, which removes the power of making regulations, one step further from the people whose lot it is to obey them. Representation therefore, though a remedy, or rather a palliative, for certain evils, is not a remedy so excellent or complete, as should authorize us to rest in it, as the highest improvement of which the social order is capable.[2]

Such are the general features of democratical government: but this is a subject of too much importance to be dismissed, without the fullest examination of everything that may enable us to decide upon its merits. We will proceed to consider the further objections that have been alleged against it.

CHAPTER XV

OF POLITICAL IMPOSTURE

ALL the arguments that have been employed to prove the insufficiency of democracy, grow out of this one root, the supposed necessity of deception and prejudice for restraining the turbulence of human passions. Without the assumption of this principle the argument could not be sustained for a moment. The direct and decisive answer would be, 'Are kings and lords intrinsically wiser and better than their humbler neighbours? Can there be any solid ground of distinction, except what is founded in personal merit? Are not men, really and strictly considered, equal, except so far as what is personal and inalienable, establishes a difference?' To these questions there can be but one reply, 'Such is the order of reason and absolute truth, but artificial distinctions are necessary for the happiness of mankind. Without deception and prejudice the turbulence of human passions cannot be restrained.' Let us then

---

[1] III. ii.   [2] See this subject pursued in Chs. xxiii and xxiv.

examine the merits of this theory; and these will be best illustrated by an instance.

[Godwin examines and criticizes the doctrine of eternal punishment in the passage omitted here. He then proceeds to the 'second instance' of Rousseau.]

.   .   .   .

It is affirmed by Rousseau, in his treatise of the Social Contract, 'that no legislator could ever establish a grand political system, without having recourse to religious imposture. To render a people, who are yet to receive the impressions of political wisdom, susceptible of the evidence of that wisdom, would be to convert the effect of civilization into the cause. The legislator being deprived of assistance from the two grand operative causes among men, reasoning and force, is obliged to have recourse to an authority of a different sort, which may draw without compulsion, and persuade without elucidation.'[1]

These are the dreams of a fertile conception, busy in the erection of imaginary systems. To a wary and sceptical mind, that project would seem to promise little substantial benefit, which set out from so erroneous a principle. To terrify or seduce men into the reception of a system, the reasonableness of which they were unable to perceive, is surely a very questionable method for rendering them sober, judicious, reasonable and happy.

... It is indeed scarcely possible to persuade a society of men to adopt any system, without convincing them that it is their wisdom to adopt it.

---

[1] *Du Contrat Social*, II. vii. Having frequently quoted Rousseau in the course of this work, it may be allowable to say one word of his general merits, as a moral and political writer. He has been subjected to continual ridicule, for the extravagance of the proposition with which he began his literary career; that the savage state, was the genuine and proper condition of man. It was however by a very slight mistake, that he missed the opposite opinion which it is the business of the present enquiry to establish. He only substituted, as the topic of his eulogium, the period that preceded government and laws, instead of the period that may possibly follow upon their abolition. ... He was the first to teach, that the imperfections of government, were the only perennial source of the vices of mankind; and this principle was adopted from him by Helvetius and others. But he saw further than this, that government, however reformed, was little capable of affording solid benefit to mankind, which they did not. This principle has since (probably without being suggested by the writings of Rousseau) been expressed with great perspicuity and energy, but not developed, by Thomas Paine, in the first page of his *Common Sense*.

Rousseau, notwithstanding his great genius, was full of weakness and prejudice. His *Emile* deserves perhaps, upon the whole, to be regarded as one of the principal reservoirs of philosophical truth, as yet existing in the world; though with a perpetual mixture of absurdity and mistake. In his writings expressly political, *Du Contrat Social* and *Considérations sur la Pologne*, the superiority of his genius seems to desert him. ...

It is difficult to conceive a company of such miserable dupes, as to receive a code, without any imagination that it is salutary or wise or just, but upon this single recommendation that it is delivered to them from the Gods. The only reasonable, and infinitely the most efficacious method of changing the established customs of any people, is by creating in them a general opinion of their erroneousness and insufficiency.

But, if it be indeed impracticable to persuade men into the adoption of any system, without employing as our principal argument, the intrinsic rectitude of that system, what is the argument which he would desire to use, who had most at heart the welfare and improvement of the persons concerned? Would he begin by teaching them to reason well, or to reason ill? by unnerving their mind with prejudice, or new stringing it with truth? How many arts, and how noxious to those towards whom we employ them, are necessary, if we would successfully deceive? We must not only leave their reason in indolence at first, but endeavour to supersede its exertion in any future instance. If men be, for the present, kept right by prejudice, what will become of them hereafter, if, by any future penetration, or any accidental discovery, this prejudice shall be annihilated? Detection is not always the fruit of systematical improvement, but may be effected by some solitary exertion of the faculty, or some luminous and irresistible argument, while everything else remains as it was. If we would first deceive, and then maintain our deception unimpaired, we shall need penal statutes, and licensers of the press, and hired ministers of falsehood and imposture. Admirable modes these for the propagation of wisdom and virtue!

There is another case, similar to that stated by Rousseau, upon which much stress has been laid by political writers. 'Obedience,' say they, 'must either be courted or compelled. We must either make a judicious use of the prejudices and the ignorance of mankind, or be contented to have no hold upon them but their fears, and to maintain social order entirely by the severity of punishment. To dispense us from this painful necessity, authority ought carefully to be invested with a sort of magic persuasion. Citizens should serve their country, not with a frigid submission that scrupulously weighs its duties, but with an enthusiasm that places its honour in its loyalty. For this reason, our governors and superiors must not be spoken of with levity. They must be considered, independently of their individual character, as deriving a sacredness from their office. They must be accompanied with splendour and veneration. Advantage must be taken of the imperfection of mankind. We ought to gain over their judgements through the medium of their

senses, and not leave the conclusions to be drawn, to the uncertain process of immature reason.'[1]

This is still the same argument under another form. It takes for
granted, that a true observation of things, is inadequate to teach us our
duty; and, of consequence, recommends an equivocal engine, which
may, with equal ease, be employed in the service of justice and injustice,
but would surely appear somewhat more in its place in the service of the
latter. It is injustice that stands most in need of superstition and mystery,
and will most frequently be a gainer by the imposition. This hypothesis
proceeds upon an assumption, which young men sometimes impute to
their parents and preceptors. It says, 'Mankind must be kept in ignorance:
if they know vice, they will love it too well; if they perceive the charms
of error, they will never return to the simplicity of truth.' And, strange
as it may appear, this barefaced and unplausible argument, has been the
foundation of a very popular and generally received hypothesis. It has
taught politicians to believe, that a people, once sunk into decrepitude,
as it has been termed, could never afterwards be endued with purity and
vigour.[2]

There are two modes, according to which the minds of human beings
may be influenced, by him who is desirous to conduct them. The
first of these, is a strong and commanding picture, taking hold of the
imagination, and surprising the judgement; the second, a distinct and
unanswerable statement of reasons, which, the oftener they are reflected
upon, and the more they are sifted, will be found by so much the more
cogent.

One of the tritest and most general, as well as most self-evident,
maxims in the science of the human mind, is, that the former of these is
only adapted to a temporary purpose, while the latter alone is adequate
to a purpose that is durable. How comes it then that, in the business of
politics and government, the purposes of which are evidently not temporary, the fallacious mode of proceeding should have been so generally
and so eagerly resorted to?

This may be accounted for from two considerations: first the diffi-
dence, and secondly, the vanity and self-applause, of legislators and
statesmen. It is an arduous task, always to assign reasons to those, whose
conduct we would direct; it is by no means easy, to answer objections

---

[1] This argument is the great commonplace of Mr. Burke's *Reflections on the Revolution
in France* [1790], and of a multitude of other works, ancient and modern, upon the subject
of government.
[2] I. vii.

and remove difficulties. It requires patience; it demands profound science and severe meditation. This is the reason why, in the instance already alluded to, parents and preceptors find a refuge for their indolence, while by false pretences they cheat the young into compliance, in preference to showing them, as far as they may be capable of understanding it, the true face of things. Statesmen secretly distrust their own powers, and therefore substitute quackery in the room of principle.

But, beside the recommendations that quackery derives from indolence and ignorance, it is also calculated to gratify the vanity of him that employs it. He that would reason with another, and honestly explain to him the motives of the action he recommends, descends to a footing of equality. But he who undertakes to delude us, and fashion us to his purpose by a specious appearance, has a feeling that he is our master. Though his task is neither so difficult nor so honourable as that of the ingenuous dealer, he regards it as more flattering. At every turn he admires his own dexterity; he triumphs in the success of his artifices, and delights to remark how completely mankind are his dupes.

.   .   .   .   .

The system of political imposture divides men into two classes, one of which is to think and reason for the whole, and the other to take the conclusions of their superiors on trust. This distinction is not founded in the nature of things; there is no such inherent difference between man and man, as it thinks proper to suppose. Nor is it less injurious, than it is unfounded. The two classes which it creates, must be more and less than man. It is too much to expect of the former, while we consign to them an unnatural monopoly, that they should rigidly consult for the good of the whole. It is an iniquitous requisition upon the latter, that they should never employ their understandings, or penetrate into the essences of things, but always rest in a deceitful appearance. It is iniquitous, to deprive them of that chance for additional wisdom, which would result, from a greater number of minds being employed in the enquiry, and from the disinterested and impartial spirit that might be expected to accompany it.

.   .   .   .   .

It may not be uninstructive to consider what sort of discourse must be held, or book written, by him who should make himself the champion of political imposture. . . .

The argument of such a system must, when attentively examined, be the most untenable that can be imagined. It undertakes to prove that we must not be governed by reason. To prove! How prove? Necessarily, from the resources of reason. What can be more contradictory? If I must not trust the conclusions of reason relative to the intrinsic value of things, why trust to your reasons in favour of the benefit of being deceived? You cut up your own argument by the roots. If I must reject the dictates of reason in one point, there can be no possible cause why I should adopt them in another. Moral reasons and inducements, as we have repeatedly shown, consist singly in this, an estimate of consequences. What can supersede this estimate? Not an opposite estimate; for, by the nature of morality, the purpose, in the first instance, is, to take into account all the consequences. Not something else, for a consideration of consequences is the only thing, with which morality and practical wisdom are directly concerned. The moment I dismiss the information of my own eyes and my own understanding, there is, in all justice, an end to persuasion, expostulation or conviction. There is no pretence, by which I can disallow the authority of inference and deduction in one instance, that will not justify a similar proceeding in every other. He that, in any case, designedly surrenders the use of his own understanding, is condemned to remain forever at the beck of contingence and caprice, and is even bound in consistency, no more to frame his course by the results of demonstration, than by the wildest dreams of delirium and insanity.

CHAPTER XVI

OF THE CAUSES OF WAR

EXCLUSIVELY of those objections which have been urged against the democratical system, as it relates to the internal management of affairs, there are others, upon which considerable stress has been laid, in relation to the transactions of a state with foreign powers, to war and peace, and to treaties of alliance and commerce.

There is indeed an eminent difference, with respect to these, between the democratical system and all others. It is perhaps impossible to show, that a single war ever did, or could have taken place, in the history of mankind, that did not in some way originate with those two great political monopolies, monarchy and aristocracy. This might have formed an additional article, in the catalogue of the evils to which they have given birth, little inferior to any of those we have enumerated. But nothing could be more idle, than to overcharge a subject, the evidence of which is irresistible.

What could be the source of misunderstanding between states, where no man, or body of men, found encouragement to the accumulation of privileges to himself, at the expense of the rest? Why should they pursue additional wealth or territory? These would lose their value, the moment they became the property of all. No man can cultivate more than a certain portion of land. Money is representative, and not real wealth. If every man in the society possessed a double portion of money, bread, and every other commodity, would sell at double their present price, and the relative situation of each individual, would be just what it had been before. War and conquest cannot be beneficial to the community. Their tendency is to elevate a few at the expense of the rest; and consequently they will never be undertaken, but where the many are the instruments of the few. But this cannot happen in a democracy, till the democracy shall become such only in name. If expedients can be devised for maintaining this species of government in its purity, or if there be anything, in the nature of wisdom and intellectual improvement, which has a tendency daily to make truth more prevalent over falsehood, the principle of offensive war will be extirpated. But this principle enters into the very essence of monarchy and aristocracy.

It is not meant here to be insinuated, that democracy has not repeatedly been a source of war. It was eminently so among the ancient Romans; the aristocracy found in it an obvious expedient for diverting the attention and encroachments of the people. It may be expected to be so, wherever the form of government is complicated, and the nation at large is enabled to become formidable to a band of usurpers. But war will be foreign to the character of any people, in proportion as their democracy becomes simple and unalloyed.

Meanwhile, though the principle of offensive war be incompatible with the genius of democracy, a democratical state may be placed in the neighbourhood of states whose government is less equal, and therefore it will be proper to enquire into the supposed disadvantages which the democratical state may sustain in the contest. The only species of war in which it can consistently be engaged, will be that the object of which is to repel wanton invasion. Such invasions will be little likely frequently to occur. For what purpose should a corrupt state attack a country, that has no feature in common with itself upon which to build a misunderstanding, and that presents, in the very nature of its government, a pledge of its inoffensiveness and neutrality? . . .

One of the most essential principles of political justice is diametrically the reverse of that, which imposters, as well as patriots, have too frequently agreed to recommend. Their perpetual exhortation has been, 'Love your country. Sink the personal existence of individuals in the existence of the community. Make little account of the particular men of whom the society consists, but aim at the general wealth, prosperity and glory. Purify your mind from the gross ideas of sense, and elevate it to the single contemplation of that abstract individual, of which particular men are so many detached members, valuable only for the place they fill.'[1]

The lessons of reason on this head are different from these. 'Society is an ideal existence, and not, on its own account, entitled to the smallest regard. The wealth, prosperity and glory of the whole are unintelligible chimeras. Set no value on anything, but in proportion as you are convinced of its tendency to make individual men happy and virtuous. Benefit, by every practicable mode, man wherever he exists; but be not deceived by the specious idea of affording services to a body of men, for which no individual man is the better. Society was instituted, not for the sake of glory, not to furnish splendid materials for the page of history, but for the benefit of its members. The love of our country, as the term has usually been understood, has too often been found to be one of those specious illusions, which are employed by imposters, for the purpose of rendering the multitude the blind instruments of their crooked designs.'

In the meantime, the maxims which are here controverted, have had by so much the more success in the world, as they bear some resemblance to the purest sentiments of virtue. Virtue is nothing else but kind and sympathetic feelings reduced into principle. Undisciplined feeling would induce me, now to interest myself exclusively for one man, and now for another, to be eagerly solicitous for those who are present to me, and to forget the absent. Feeling ripened into virtue, embraces the interests of the whole human race, and constantly proposes to itself the production of the greatest quantity of happiness. But, while it anxiously adjusts the balance of interests, and yields to no case, however urgent, to the prejudice of the whole, it keeps aloof from the unmeaning rant of romance, and uniformly recollects that happiness, in order to be real, must necessarily be individual.

The love of our country, has often been found to be a deceitful principle, as its direct tendency, is to set the interests of one division of mankind in opposition to another, and to establish a preference, built

[1] *Du Contrat Social*, etc. etc. etc.

upon accidental relations, and not upon reason. Much of what has been understood by the appellation, is excellent, but perhaps nothing that can be brought within the strict interpretation of the phrase. A wise and well-informed man will not fail to be the votary of liberty and justice. He will be ready to exert himself in their defence, wherever they exist. It cannot be a matter of indifference to him, when his own liberty and that of other men whose merits and capacities he has the best opportunity of being acquainted, are involved in the event of the struggle to be made. But his attachment will be to the cause, as the cause of man, and not to the country. Wherever there are individuals, who understand the value of political justice, and are prepared to assert it, that is his country. Wherever he can most contribute to the diffusion of these principles and the real happiness of mankind, that is his country. Nor does he desire, for any country, any other benefit than justice.

.   .   .   .

Because individuals were liable to error, and suffered their apprehensions of justice to be perverted by a bias in favour of themselves, government was instituted. Because nations were susceptible of a similar weakness, and could find no sufficient umpire to whom to appeal, war was introduced. Men were induced deliberately to seek each other's lives, and to adjudge the controversies between them, not according to the dictates of reason and justice, but as either should prove most successful in devastation and murder. This was no doubt in the first instance the extremity of exasperation and rage. But it has since been converted into a trade. One part of the nation pays another part, to murder and be murdered in their stead; and the most trivial causes, a supposed insult, or a sally of youthful ambition, have sufficed to deluge provinces with blood.

.   .   .   .

Accurately considered, there can probably be but two causes of war that can maintain any plausible claim to justice; and one of them, is among those which the logic of sovereigns, and the law of nations, as it has been termed, have been thought to proscribe: these are the defence of our own liberty, and of the liberty of others. The well-known objection to the latter of these cases, is, 'that one nation ought not to interfere in the internal transactions of another.' But certainly every people is fit for the possession of any immunity, as soon as they understand the nature of that immunity, and desire to possess it; and it is probable that this condition may be sufficiently realized, in cases, where, from the subtlety of intrigue, and the tyrannical jealousy of neighbouring kingdoms, they may be rendered incapable of effectually asserting their rights. This principle is capable of being abused by men of ambition and intrigue; but, accurately considered, the very same argument that should induce me to exert myself for the liberties of my own country, is equally cogent, so far as my opportunities and ability extend, with respect to the liberties of any other country. But what is my duty in this case, is the duty of all; and the exertion must be collective, where collective exertion only can be effectual.

CHAPTER XX

OF DEMOCRACY AS CONNECTED WITH THE TRANSACTIONS OF WAR

HAVING thus endeavoured to reduce the question of war to its true principles, it is time that we should recur to the maxim delivered at our entrance upon this subject, that individuals are everything, and society, abstracted from the individuals of which it is composed, nothing. An immediate consequence of this maxim is, that the internal affairs of the society are entitled to our principal attention, and the external are matters of inferior and subordinate consideration. The internal affairs are subjects of perpetual and hourly concern, the external are periodical and precarious only. That every man should be impressed with the consciousness of his independence, and rescued from the influence of extreme want and artificial desires, are purposes the most interesting that can suggest themselves to the human mind; but the life of man might pass, in a state uncorrupted by ideal passions, without its tranquillity being so much as once disturbed by foreign invasions. The influence that a certain number of millions, born under the same climate with ourselves, and known by the common appellation of English or French, shall possess over the administrative councils of their neighbour millions, is a circumstance of much too airy and distant consideration, to deserve to be made a principal object in the institutions of any people. The best influence we can exert, is that of a sage and upright example.

If therefore it should appear that, of these two articles, internal and external affairs, one must, in some degree, be sacrificed to the other, and that a democracy will, in certain respects, be less fitted for the affairs of war than some other species of government, good sense will not hesitate in the alternative. We shall have sufficient reason to be satisfied, if, together with the benefits of justice and virtue at home, we have no reason to despair of our safety from abroad. A confidence in this article will seldom deceive us, if our countrymen, however little trained to formal rules, and the uniformity of mechanism, have studied the profession of man, understand his attributes and his nature, and have their necks unbroken to the yoke of blind credulity and abject submission. Such men, inured, as we are now supposing them, to a rational state of society, will be full of calm confidence and penetrating activity, and these qualities will stand them in stead of a thousand lessons in the school of military mechanism. If democracy can be proved adequate to wars of defence, and other governments be better fitted for wars of a different sort, this would be an argument, not of its imperfection, but its merit.

.   .   .   .   .

CHAPTER XXII

OF THE FUTURE HISTORY OF POLITICAL SOCIETIES

THUS we have endeavoured to unfold and establish certain general principles, upon the subject of legislative and executive power. But there is one interesting topic that remains to be discussed. How much of either of these powers does the public benefit require us to maintain?

We have already seen,[1] that the only legitimate object of political institution, is the advantage of individuals. All that cannot be brought home to them, national wealth, prosperity and glory, can be advantageous only to those self-interested impostors, who, from the earliest accounts of time, have confounded the understandings of mankind, the more securely to sink them in debasement and misery.

The desire to gain a more extensive territory, to conquer or to hold in awe our neighbouring states, to surpass them in arts or arms, is a desire founded in prejudice and error. . . . the rivalship of nations is a creature of the imagination. If riches be our object, riches can only be created by commerce; and the greater is our neighbour's capacity to buy, the greater will be our opportunity to sell. The prosperity of all is the interest of all.

The more accurately we understand our own advantage, the less shall

[1] Ch. xvi, p. 212.

we be disposed to disturb the peace of our neighbour. The same principle is applicable to him in return. It becomes us therefore to desire that he may be wise. But wisdom is the growth of equality and independence, not of injury and oppression. If oppression had been the school of wisdom, the improvement of mankind would have been inestimable, for they have been in that school for many thousand years. We ought therefore to desire that our neighbour should be independent. We ought to desire that he should be free; for wars do not originate in the unbiased propensities of nations, but in the cabals of government and the propensities that governments inspire into the people at large.[1] . . .

Where nations are not brought into avowed hostility, all jealousy between them is an unintelligible chimera. I reside upon a certain spot, because that residence is most conducive to my happiness or usefulness. I am interested in the political justice and virtue of my species, because they are men, that is, creatures eminently capable of justice and virtue; and I have perhaps additional reason to interest myself for those who live under the same government as myself, because I am better qualified to understand their claims, and more capable of exerting myself in their behalf. But I can certainly have no interest in the infliction of pain upon others, unless so far as they are expressly engaged in acts of injustice. The object of sound policy and morality is to draw men nearer to each other, not to separate them; to unite their interests, not to oppose them.

. . . . .

. . . The appearance which mankind, in a future state of improvement, may be expected to assume, is a policy that, in different countries, will wear a similar form, because we have all the same faculties and the same wants; but a policy, the independent branches of which will extend their authority over a small territory, because neighbours are best informed of each other's concerns, and are perfectly equal to their adjustment. No recommendation can be imagined of an extensive, rather than a limited territory, except that of external security.

Whatever evils are included in the abstract idea of government, they are all of them extremely aggravated by the extensiveness of its juris-diction, and softened under circumstances of an opposite nature. . . .

. . . . .

Ambition and tumult, are evils that arise out of government, in an indirect manner, in consequence of the habits, which government intro-duces, of concert and combination extending themselves over multitudes

[1] Ch. xvi.

of men. There are other evils inseparable from its existence. The object of government, is the suppression of such violence, as well external as internal, as might destroy, or bring into jeopardy, the well-being of the community or its members; and the means it employs, are constraint and violence of a more regulated kind. For this purpose the concentration of individual forces becomes necessary, and the method in which this concentration is usually obtained, is also constraint. . . . Constraint, employed against delinquents, or persons to whom delinquency is imputed, is by no means without its mischiefs. Constraint, employed by the majority of a society, against the minority, who may differ from them upon some question of public good, is calculated, at first sight at least, to excite a still greater disapprobation.

Both these exertions may indeed appear to rest upon the same principle. Vice is unquestionably no more, in the first instance, than error of judgement, and nothing can justify an attempt to correct it by force, but the extreme necessity of the case.[1] The minority, if erroneous, fall under precisely the same general description, though their error may not be of equal magnitude. But the necessity of the case can seldom be equally impressive. If the idea of secession, for example, were somewhat more familiarized to the conceptions of mankind, it could seldom happen, that the secession of the minority from difference of opinion, could in any degree compare, in mischievous tendency, with the hostility of a criminal, offending against the most obvious principles of social justice. . . .

Government can have no more than two legitimate purposes, the suppression of injustice against individuals within the community, and the common defence against external invasion. The first of these purposes, which alone can have an uninterrupted claim upon us, is sufficiently answered, by an association, of such an extent, as to afford room for the institution of a jury, to decide upon the offences of individuals within the community, and upon the questions and controversies, respecting property, which may chance to arise. It might be easy indeed for an offender, to escape from the limits of so petty a jurisdiction; and it might seem necessary, at first, that the neighbouring parishes,[2] or jurisdictions, should be governed in a similar manner, or at least should be willing, whatever was their form of government, to co-operate with us, in the

---

[1] II. vi; IV. viii.

[2] The word parish, is here used, without regard to its origin, and merely in consideration of its being a word, descriptive of a certain small portion of territory, whether in population or extent, which custom has rendered familiar to us.

removal or reformation of an offender, whose present habits were alike injurious to us and to them. But there will be no need of any express compact, and still less of any common centre of authority, for this purpose. General justice, and mutual interest, are found more capable of binding men, than signatures and seals. In the meantime, all necessity for causing the punishment of the crime to pursue the criminal, would soon, at least, cease, if it ever existed. The motives to offence would become rare: its aggravations few: and rigour superfluous. The principal object of punishment, is restraint upon a dangerous member of the community; and the end of this restraint would be answered, by the general inspection, that is exercised by the members of a limited circle, over the conduct of each other, and by the gravity and good sense that would characterize the censures of men, from whom all mystery and empiricism were banished. No individual would be hardy enough in the cause of vice, to defy the general consent of sober judgement that would surround him. It would carry despair to his mind, or, which is better, it would carry conviction. He would be obliged, by a force not less irresistible than whips and chains, to reform his conduct.

In this sketch is contained the rude outline of political government. Controversies between parish and parish, would be, in an eminent degree, unreasonable, since, if any question arose, about limits, for example, the obvious principles of convenience could scarcely fail to teach us, to what district any portion of land should belong. No association of men, so long as they adhered to the principles of reason, could possibly have an interest in extending their territory. If we would produce attachment in our associates, we can adopt no surer method, than that of practising the dictates of equity and moderation; and, if this failed in any instance, it could only fail with him who, to whatever society he belonged, would prove an unworthy member. The duty of any society to punish offenders, is not dependent, upon the hypothetical consent of the offender to be punished, but upon the duty of necessary defence.

But however irrational might be the controversy of parish with parish in such a state of society, it would not be the less possible. For such extraordinary emergencies therefore, provision ought to be made. These emergencies are similar in their nature, to those of foreign invasion. They can only be provided against by the concert of several districts, declaring and, if needful, enforcing the dictates of justice.

One of the most obvious remarks that suggests itself, upon these two cases, of hostility between district and district, and of foreign invasion which the interest of all calls upon them jointly to repel, is, that it is their nature to be only of occasional recurrence, and that therefore the provisions to be made respecting them, need not be, in the strictest sense, of perpetual operation. In other words, the permanence of a national assembly, . . . cannot be necessary in a period of tranquillity, and may perhaps be pernicious. That we may form a more accurate judgement of this, let us recollect some of the principal features that enter into the constitution of a national assembly.

CHAPTER XXIII

OF NATIONAL ASSEMBLIES

IN the first place, the existence of a national assembly, introduces the evils of a fictitious unanimity. The public, guided by such an assembly, must act with concert, or the assembly is a nugatory excrescence. But it is impossible that this unanimity can really exist. The individuals who constitute a nation, cannot take into consideration a variety of important questions, without forming different sentiments respecting them. In reality, all questions that are brought before such an assembly, are decided by a majority of votes, and the minority, after having exposed, with all the power of eloquence, and force of reasoning, of which they are capable, the injustice and folly of the measures adopted, are obliged, in a certain sense, to assist in carrying them into execution. Nothing can more directly contribute to the depravation of the human understanding and character. . . . He that contributes his personal exertions, or his property, to the support of a cause which he believes to be unjust, will quickly lose that accurate discrimination, and nice sensibility of moral rectitude, which are the principal ornaments of reason.

. . . . .

. . . the debates of a national assembly are distorted from their reasonable tenor, by the necessity of their being uniformly terminated by a vote. Debate and discussion are, in their own nature, highly conducive to intellectual improvement; but they lose this salutary character, the moment they are subjected to this unfortunate condition. What can be more unreasonable, than to demand, that argument, the usual quality of which is gradually and imperceptibly to enlighten the mind, should declare its effect in the close of a single conversation? No sooner does this circumstance occur, than the whole scene changes its character. The orator no longer enquires after permanent conviction, but transitory effect. He seeks rather to take advantage of our prejudices, than to enlighten our judgement. That which might otherwise have been a scene of patient and beneficent enquiry, is changed into wrangling, tumult and precipitation.

.   .   .   .

The whole is then wound up, with that flagrant insult upon all reason and justice, the deciding upon truth by the casting up of numbers. Thus everything, that we have been accustomed to esteem most sacred, is determined, at best, by the weakest heads in the assembly, but, as it not less frequently happens, through the influence of the most corrupt and dishonourable intentions.

.   .   .   .

. . . national assemblies, or, in other words, assemblies instituted for the joint purpose of adjusting the differences between district and district, and of consulting respecting the best mode of repelling foreign invasion, however necessary to be had recourse to upon certain occasions, ought to be employed as sparingly as the nature of the case will admit. They should either never be elected but upon extraordinary emergencies, . . . or else sit periodically, one day for example in a year, with a power of continuing their sessions within a certain limit, to hear the complaints and representations of their constituents. The former of these modes is greatly to be preferred. . . . election itself is of a nature not to be employed, but when the occasion demands it. . . .

It will scarcely be denied, that the objections which have been most loudly reiterated against democracy, become null in an application to the form of government which has now been delineated. Here we shall with difficulty find an opening for tumult, for the tyranny of a multitude drunk with unlimited power, for political ambition on the part of the few, or restless jealousy and precaution on the part of the many. Here the demagogue would discover no suitable occasion, for rendering the multitude the blind instrument of his purposes. Men, in such a state of society, might be expected to understand their happiness, and to cherish it. The true reason why the mass of mankind has so often been made the dupe of knaves, has been the mysterious and complicated nature of the social system. Once annihilate the quackery of government, and the most home-bred understanding might be strong enough to detect the artifices, of the state juggler that would mislead him.

CHAPTER XXIV

OF THE DISSOLUTION OF GOVERNMENT

I T remains for us to consider, what is the degree of authority necessary to be vested, in such a modified species of national assembly as we have admitted into our system. Are they to issue their commands to the different members of the confederacy? Or is it sufficient, that they should invite them to co-operate for the common advantage, and, by arguments and addresses, convince them of the reasonableness of the measures they propose? The former of these might at first be necessary. The latter would afterwards become sufficient.[1] . . . An appeal, by the assembly, to the several districts, would not fail to unite the approbation of reasonable men, unless it contained in it something so evidently questionable, as to make it perhaps desirable that it should prove abortive.

This remark leads us one step further. Why should not the same distinction between commands and invitations, which we have just made in the case of national assemblies, be applied to the particular assemblies or juries of the several districts? At first, we will suppose, that some degree of authority and violence would be necessary. But this necessity does not appear to arise out of the nature of man, but out of the institutions by which he has been corrupted. Man is not originally vicious. He would not refuse to listen to, or to be convinced by, the expostulations that are addressed to him, had he not been accustomed to regard them as hypocritical, and to conceive that, while his neighbour, his parent, and his political governor, pretended to be actuated by a pure regard to his interest or pleasure, they were, in reality, at the expense of his, promoting their own. Such are the fatal effects of mysteriousness and complexity. Simplify the social system, in the manner which every motive, but those of usurpation and ambition, powerfully recommends; render the plain dictates of justice level to every capacity; remove the necessity of implicit faith; and we may expect the whole species to become reasonable and virtuous. It might then be sufficient for juries

---

[1] Such is the idea of the author of *Gulliver's Travels* (Part IV), a man who appears to have had a more profound insight into the true principles of political justice, than any preceding or contemporary author. It was unfortunate, that a work of such inestimable wisdom failed, at the period of its publication, from the mere playfulness of its form, in communicating adequate instruction to mankind. Posterity only will be able to estimate it as it deserves.

to recommend a certain mode of adjusting controversies, without assuming the prerogative of dictating that adjustment. It might then be sufficient for them to invite offenders to forsake their errors. If their expostulations proved, in a few instances, ineffectual, the evils arising out of this circumstance, would be of less importance, than those which proceed from the perpetual violation of the exercise of private judgement. But, in reality, no evils would arise: for, where the empire of reason was so universally acknowledged, the offender would either readily yield to the expostulations of authority; or, if he resisted, though suffering no personal molestation, he would feel so uneasy, under the unequivocal disapprobation, and observant eye, of public judgement, as willingly to remove to a society more congenial to his errors.

The reader has probably anticipated the ultimate conclusion from these remarks. If juries might at length cease to decide, and be contented to invite, if force might gradually be withdrawn and reason trusted alone, shall we not one day find, that juries themselves, and every other species of public institution, may be laid aside as unnecessary? Will not the reasonings of one wise man, be as effectual as those of twelve? Will not the competence of one individual to instruct his neighbours, be a matter of sufficient notoriety, without the formality of an election? Will there be many vices to correct, and much obstinacy to conquer? This is one of the most memorable stages of human improvement. With what delight must every well-informed friend of mankind look forward, to the auspicious period, the dissolution of political government, of that brute engine, which has been the only perennial cause of the vices of mankind, and which, as has abundantly appeared in the progress of the present work, has mischiefs of various sorts incorporated with its substance, and no otherwise removable than by its utter annihilation!

BOOK VI

OF OPINION CONSIDERED AS A SUBJECT OF POLITICAL INSTITUTION

─────

CHAPTER I

GENERAL EFFECTS OF THE POLITICAL SUPERINTENDENCE OF OPINION

. . . It is now more evident, than it was in any former period, that government, instead of being an object of secondary consideration, has been the principal vehicle of extensive and permanent evil to mankind. It was unavoidable therefore to say, 'since government can produce so much positive mischief, surely it can do some positive good.'

But these views, however specious and agreeable they may in the first instance appear, are liable to very serious question. If we would not be seduced by visionary good, we ought here, more than ever, to recollect the fundamental principles laid down and illustrated in this work, 'that government is, in all cases, an evil,' and 'that it ought to be introduced as sparingly as possible.' Man is a species of being, whose excellence depends upon his individuality; and who can be neither great nor wise, but in proportion as he is independent.

But, if we would shut up government within the narrowest practicable limits, we must beware how we let it loose in the field of opinion. Opinion is the castle, or rather the temple, of human nature; and, if it be polluted, there is no longer anything sacred or venerable in sublunary existence.

In treating of the subject of political obedience,[1] we settled, perhaps with some degree of clearness, the line of demarcation, between the contending claims of the individual, and of the community. We found, that the species of obedience which sufficiently discharged the claims of the community, was that which is paid to force, and not which is built

[1] III. vi.

upon a sentiment of deference; and that this species of obedience was, beyond all others, least a source of degeneracy in him that paid it. But, upon this hypothesis, whatever exterior compliance is yielded, opinion remains inviolate.

Here then we perceive, in what manner the purposes of government may be answered, and the independence of the individual suffer the smallest degree of injury. We are shown, how government, which is, in all cases, an evil, may most effectually be limited as to the noxiousness of its influence.

But, if this line be overstepped, if opinion be rendered a topic of political superintendence, we are immediately involved in a slavery, to which no imagination of man can set a termination. . . .

.   .   .   .

. . . Has society . . . any particular advantage, in its corporate capacity, for illuminating the understanding? Can it convey, into its addresses and expostulations, a compound or sublimate of the wisdom of all its members, superior in quality to the individual wisdom of any? If so, why have not societies of men written treatises of morality, of the philosophy of nature, or the philosophy of mind? Why have all the great steps of human improvement been the work of individuals?

If then society, considered as an agent, have no particular advantage for enlightening the understanding, the real difference, between the *dicta* of society, and the *dicta* of individuals, must be looked for in the article of authority. But authority is, by the very nature of the case, inadequate to the task it assumes to perform. Man is the creature of habit and judgement; and the empire of the former of these, though not perhaps more absolute, is at least more conspicuous. The most efficacious instrument I can possess for changing a man's habits, is to change his judgements. Even this instrument will seldom produce a sudden, though, when brought into full operation, it is perhaps sure of producing a gradual revolution. But this mere authority can never do. Where it does most in changing the characters of men, it only changes them into base and despicable slaves. Contending against the habits of an entire society, it can do nothing. It excites only contempt of its frivolous endeavours. If laws were a sufficient means for the reformation of error and vice, it is not to be believed but that the world, long ere this, would have become the seat of every virtue. Nothing can be more easy, than to command men, to be just and good, to love their neighbours, to practise universal sincerity, to be content with a little, and to resist the enticements of avarice and ambition. But, when we have done, will the actions of men be altered by our precepts? These commands have been issued for thousands of years; and, if it had been decreed that every man should be hanged that violated them, it is vehemently to be suspected that this would not have secured their influence.

.   .   .   .

We shall be still more completely aware of the pernicious tendency of positive institutions, if we proceed explicitly to contrast the nature of mind, and the nature of government. One of the most unquestionable characteristics of the human mind, has appeared to be, its progressive nature. Now, on the other hand, it is the express tendency of positive institution, to retain that with which it is conversant, for ever in the same state. Is then the perfectibility of understanding an attribute of trivial importance? Can we recollect, with coldness and indifference, the advantages with which this quality seems pregnant to the latest posterity? And how are these advantages to be secured? By incessant industry, by a curiosity never to be disheartened or fatigued, by a spirit of enquiry to which a philanthropic mind will allow no pause. The circumstance most indispensably necessary, is that we should never stand still, that everything most interesting to the general welfare, wholly delivered from restraint, should be in a state of change, moderate and as it were imperceptible, but continual. Is there anything that can look with a more malignant aspect upon the general welfare, than an institution tending to give permanence to certain systems and opinions? Such institutions are two ways pernicious; first, which is most material, because they render the future advances of mind inexpressibly tedious and operose; secondly, because, by violently confining the stream of reflection, and holding it for a time in an unnatural state, they compel it at last to rush forward with impetuosity, and thus occasion calamities, which, were it free from restraint, would be found extremely foreign to its nature. If the interference of positive institution had been out of the question, would the progress of intellect, in past ages, have been so slow, as to have struck the majority of ingenuous observers with despair? . . .

The just conclusion from the above reasonings, is nothing more than a confirmation, with some difference in the mode of application, of the fundamental principle, that government is little capable of affording benefit of the first importance to mankind. It is calculated to induce us to lament, not the apathy and indifference, but the inauspicious activity of government. It incites us to look for the moral improvement of the species, not in the multiplying of regulations, but in their repeal. It teaches us, that truth and virtue, like commerce, will then flourish most, when least subjected to the mistaken guardianship of authority and laws. This maxim will rise upon us in its importance, in proportion as we connect it with the numerous departments of political justice to which it will be found to have relation. As fast as it shall be adopted into the practice of mankind, it may be expected to deliver us from a weight, intolerable to mind, and, in the highest degree, hostile to the progress of truth.

CHAPTER II

OF RELIGIOUS ESTABLISHMENTS

ONE of the most striking instances of the injurious effects of the political patronage of opinion, as it at present exists in the world, is to be found in the system of religious conformity. . . .

First, the system of religious conformity, is a system of blind submission. In every country, possessing a religious establishment, the state, from a benevolent care, it may be, for the manners and opinions of its subjects, publicly excites a numerous class of men to the study of morality and virtue. What institution, we might obviously be led to enquire, can be more favourable to public happiness? . . . But, unfortunately, these very men are fettered in the outset, by having a code of propositions put into their hands, in a conformity to which all their enquiries must terminate. The direct tendency of science, is to increase from age to age, and to proceed, from the slenderest beginnings, to the most admirable conclusions. But care is taken, in the present case, to anticipate these conclusions, and to bind men, by promises and penalties, not to improve upon the science of their ancestors. The plan is designed indeed to guard against degeneracy and decline; but it makes no provision for advance. It is founded in the most sovereign ignorance of the nature of mind, which never fails to do either the one or the other.

Secondly, the tendency of a code of religious conformity, is to make men hypocrites. . . .

It would perhaps be regarded as incredible, if it rested upon the evidence of history alone, that a whole body of men, set apart as the instructors of mankind, weaned, as they are expected to be, from temporal ambition, and maintained upon the supposition that the existence of human virtue and divine truth depends on their exertions, should, with one consent, employ themselves in a casuistry, the object of which, is to prove the propriety of a man's declaring his assent to what he does not believe. These men either credit their own subterfuges, or they do not. If they do not, what can be expected from men so unprincipled and profligate? . . . If they do yield this credit, what must be their portion of moral sensibility and discernment? Can we believe that men shall enter upon their profession, with so notorious a perversion of reason and truth, and that no consequences will flow from it, to infect their general character? Rather, can we fail to compare their unnatural and unfortunate state, with the wisdom and virtue which the same industry and exertion might unquestionably have produced, if they had been left to their genuine operation? . . .

Such are the effects that a code of religious conformity produces upon the clergy; let us consider the effects that are produced upon their countrymen. They are bid to look for instruction and morality, to a denomination of men, formal, embarrassed and hypocritical, in whom the main spring of intellect is unbent and incapable of action. If the people be not blinded with religious zeal, they will discover and despise the imperfections of their spiritual guides. If they be so blinded, they will not the less transplant into their own characters, the imbecile and unworthy spirit they are not able to detect. . . . The most malicious enemy of mankind, could not have invented a scheme, more destructive of their true happiness, than that of hiring, at the expense of the state, a body of men, whose business it should seem to be, to dupe their contemporaries into the practice of virtue.

.   .   .   .   .

These arguments do not apply to any particular articles and creeds, but to the notion of ecclesiastical establishments in general. Wherever the state sets apart a certain revenue for the support of religion, it will infallibly be given to the adherents of some particular opinions, and will operate, in the manner of prizes, to induce men to embrace and profess those opinions. Undoubtedly, if I think it right to have a spiritual instructor, to guide me in my researches, and, at stated intervals, publicly to remind me of my duty, I ought to be at liberty to take the proper steps to supply myself in this respect. A priest, who thus derives his mission from the unbiased judgement of his parishioners, will stand a chance to possess, beforehand, and independently of corrupt influence, the requisites they demand. But why should I be compelled to contribute to the support of an institution, whether I approve of it or no? If public worship be conformable to reason, reason without doubt will prove adequate to its vindication and support. If it be from God, it is profanation to imagine that it stands in need of the alliance of the state. It must be, in an eminent degree, artificial and exotic, if it be incapable of preserving itself in existence, otherwise than by the inauspicious interference of political institution.

CHAPTER IV

OF TESTS

.   .   .   .

... let us attend ... to an article which has had its advocates among men of considerable liberality, the supposed propriety of political tests. 'Shall we have no federal oaths, no oaths of fidelity to the nation, the law and the republic? How in that case shall we distinguish, between the enemies, and the friends of freedom?'

Certainly there cannot be a method devised for this purpose, at once more iniquitous and ineffectual than a federal oath. What is the language that, in strictness of interpretation, belongs to the act of the legislature imposing this oath? To one party it says, 'We know that you are our friends; the oath, as it relates to you, we acknowledge to be superfluous; nevertheless you must take it, as a cover to our indirect purposes, in imposing it upon persons whose views are less unequivocal than yours.' To the other party it says, 'It is vehemently suspected that you are hostile to the cause in which we are engaged: this suspicion is either true or false; if false, we ought not to suspect you, and much less ought we to put you to this corrupting and nugatory purgation; if true, you will either candidly confess your difference, or dishonestly prevaricate: be candid, and we will indignantly banish you; be dishonest, and we will receive you as bosom friends.'

Those who say this however, promise too much. Duty and common sense oblige us to watch the man we suspect, even though he should swear he is innocent. Would not the same precautions, which we are still obliged to employ, to secure us against his duplicity, have sufficiently answered our purpose, without putting him to this purgation? Are there no methods, by which we can find, whether a man be the proper subject in whom to repose an important trust, without putting the

question to himself? Will not he who is so dangerous an enemy that we
cannot suffer him at large, discover his enmity by his conduct, without
reducing us to the painful necessity of tempting him to an act of prevarication? If he be so subtle a hypocrite that all our vigilance cannot
detect him, will he scruple to add to his other crimes the guilt of perjury?

.   .   .   .

Let us examine, . . . the federal oath of the French, proclaiming the
determination of the swearer, 'to be faithful to the nation, the law and the
king.' Fidelity to three several interests, which may, in various cases, be
placed in opposition to each other, will appear at first sight to be no very
reasonable engagement. The propriety of vowing fidelity to the king,
has already been brought to the trial, and received its condemnation.[1]
Fidelity to the law, is an engagement of so complicated a nature, as to
strike terror into every mind of serious reflection. It is impossible, that
a system of law, the composition of men, should ever be presented to
such a mind, that shall appear faultless. But, with respect to laws that
appear to me to be unjust, I am bound to every kind of hostility short of
open violence; I am bound to exert myself incessantly, in proportion to
the magnitude of the injustice, for their abolition. Fidelity to the nation,
is an engagement scarcely less equivocal. I have a paramount engagement, to the cause of justice, and the benefit of the human race. If the
nation undertake what is unjust, fidelity in that undertaking is a crime.
If it undertake what is just, it is my duty to promote its success, not because
I was born one of its citizens, but because such is the command of justice.

It may be alleged, with respect to the French federal oath, . . . that it
may be taken with a certain laxity of interpretation. When I swear
fidelity to the law, I may mean only, that there are certain parts of it that
I approve. When I swear fidelity to the nation, the law and the king, I
may mean, so far only, as these three authorities shall agree with each
other, and all of them agree with the general welfare of mankind. In a
word, the final result of this laxity of interpretation, explains the oath to
mean, 'I swear, that I believe it is my duty, to do everything that appears
to me to be just.' Who can look without indignation and regret, at
this prostitution of language? Who can think, without horror, of the
consequences, of the public and perpetual lesson of duplicity which is
thus read to mankind?

But, supposing there should be certain members of the community,
simple and uninstructed enough to conceive, that an oath contained some

[1] V. [iv and vi.]

real obligation, and did not leave the duty of the person to whom it was administered, precisely where it found it, what is the lesson that would be read to such members? They would listen, with horror, to the man, who endeavoured to persuade them, that they owed no fidelity to the nation, the law and the king, as to one who was instigating them to sacrilege. They would tell him that it was too late, and that they must not allow themselves to hear his arguments. They would perhaps have heard enough, before their alarm commenced, to make them look with envy on the happy state of this man, who was free to listen to the communications of others without terror, who could give a loose to his thoughts, and intrepidly follow the course of his enquiries wherever they led him. For themselves they had promised to think no more for the rest of their lives. Compliance indeed in this case is impossible; but will a vow of inviolable adherence to a certain constitution, have no effect in checking the vigour of their contemplations, and the elasticity of their minds?

.　　　.　　　.　　　.

CHAPTER V

OF OATHS

THE same arguments that prove the injustice of tests, may be applied universally to all oaths of duty and office. If I entered upon the office without an oath, what would be my duty? Can the oath that is imposed upon me make any alteration in my duty? If not, does not the very act of imposing it, by implication assert a falsehood? Will this falsehood have no injurious effect upon a majority of the persons concerned? What is the true criterion that I shall faithfully discharge the office that is conferred upon me? Surely my past life, not any protestations I may be compelled to make. If my life have been unimpeachable, this compulsion is an unmerited insult; if it have been otherwise, it is something worse.

.　　　.　　　.　　　.

Can there be a practice more pregnant with false morality, than that of administering oaths in a court of justice? The language it expressly holds is, 'You are not to be believed upon your mere word;' and there are few men, firm enough, resolutely to preserve themselves from contamination, when they are accustomed, upon the most solemn occasions, to be treated with contempt. To the unthinking it comes like a plenary indulgence to the occasional tampering with veracity in affairs of daily occurrence, that they are not upon their oath; and we may affirm, without risk of error, that there is no cause of insincerity, prevarication and falsehood more powerful, than that we are here considering. It treats veracity, in the scenes of ordinary life, as a thing not to be looked for. It takes for granted that no man, at least of plebeian rank, is to be credited upon his bare affirmation; and what it thus takes for granted, it has an irresistible tendency to produce.

Add to this, a feature that runs through all the abuses of political institution, it saps the very foundations of moral principle. Why is it that I am bound to be more especially careful of what I affirm in a court of justice? Because the subsistence, the honest reputation, or the life, of a fellow man, is there peculiarly at issue. All these genuine motives are, by the contrivance of human institution, thrown into shade, and we are expected to speak the truth, only because government demands it of us upon oath, and at the times in which government has thought proper, or recollected, to administer this oath. All attempts to strengthen the obligations of morality by fictitious and spurious motives, will, in the sequel, be found to have no tendency, but to relax them.

Men will never act, with that liberal justice, and conscious integrity, which are their highest ornament, till they come to understand what men are. He that contaminates his lips with an oath, must have been thoroughly fortified with previous moral instruction, if he be able afterwards to understand the beauty of an unconstrained and simple integrity. If our political institutors had been but half as judicious, in perceiving the manner in which excellence and worth were to be generated, as they have been ingenious and indefatigable in the means of depraving mankind, the world, instead of a slaughter-house, would have been a paradise.

Let us leave, for a moment, the general consideration of the principle of oaths, to reflect upon their particular structure, and the precise meaning of the term. They take for granted, in the first place, the existence of an invisible governor of the world, and the propriety of our addressing petitions to him, both which a man may deny, and yet continue a good member of society. What is the situation, in which the institution of which we treat, places this man? But we must not suffer ourselves to be stopped by trivial considerations.—Oaths are also so constructed, as to take for granted the religious system of the country whatever it may happen to be.

Now what are the words with which we are taught, in this instance, to address the creator whose existence we have thus recognized? 'So help me God, and the contents of his holy word.' It is the language of imprecation. I pray him to pour down his everlasting wrath and curse upon me, if I utter a lie.—It were to be wished that the name of that man had been recorded, who first invented this mode of binding men to veracity. He had surely himself very slight and contemptuous notions of the Supreme Being, who could thus tempt men to insult him, by braving his displeasure. If it be thought to be our duty to invoke his blessing, yet surely it must be a most hardened profaneness, that can thus be content to put all the calamity with which he is able to overwhelm us, to the test of one moment's rectitude or frailty.

CHAPTER VI

OF LIBELS

. . . . .

. . . it is necessary the truth should be told. How can this ever be done, if I be forbidden to speak upon more than one side of a question? . . . If we must always hear the praise of things as they are, and allow no man to urge an objection, we may be lulled into torpid tranquillity, but we can never be wise.

. . . . .

'Is it then to be supposed, that mankind will have the discernment and the justice, of their own accord, to reject the libel?' Yes; libels do not at present deceive mankind, from their intrinsic power, but from the restraint under which they labour. The man who, from his dungeon, is brought to the light of day, cannot accurately distinguish colours; but he that has suffered no confinement, feels no difficulty in the operation. Such is the state of mankind at present: they are not exercised to employ their judgement, and therefore they are deficient in judgement. The most improbable tale now makes a deep impression; but then men would be accustomed to speculate upon the possibilities of human action.

At first, it may be, if all restraint upon the freedom of writing and speech were removed, and men were encouraged to declare what they thought, as publicly as possible, every press would be burdened with an inundation of scandal. But the stories, by their very multiplicity, would defeat themselves. No one man, if the lie were successful, would become the object of universal persecution. In a short time, the reader, accustomed to the dissection of character, would acquire discrimination. He would either detect the imposition by its internal absurdity, or at least would attribute to the story no further weight, than that to which its evidence entitled it.

Libel, like every other human concern, would soon find its level, if it were delivered from the injurious interference of political institution. The libeller, that is, he who utters an unfounded calumny, either invents the story he tells, or delivers it with a degree of assurance, to which the evidence that has offered itself to him, is by no means entitled. In each case he would meet with his proper punishment in the judgement of the world. The consequences of his error would fall back upon himself. He would either pass for a malignant accuser, or for a rash and headlong censurer. . . .

.   .   .   .

CHAPTER VII

OF CONSTITUTIONS

A QUESTION intimately connected with the political superintendence of opinion, is presented to us, relative to a doctrine, which has lately been taught, upon the subject of constitutions. It has been said, 'that the laws of every regular state, naturally distribute themselves under two heads, fundamental and temporary; laws, the object of which is the distribution of political power, and directing the permanent forms according to which public business is to be conducted; and laws, the result of the deliberations of powers already constituted.' This distinction being established in the first instance, it has been inferred, 'that these laws are of very unequal importance, and that, of consequence, those of the first class, ought to be originated with much greater solemnity, and to be declared much less susceptible of variation, than those of the second.' The French national assembly of 1789, pushed this principle to the greatest extremity, and seemed desirous of providing every imaginable security for rendering the work they had formed immortal. It was not to be touched, upon any account, under the term of ten years; every alteration it was to receive must be recognized as necessary, by two successive national assemblies of the ordinary kind; after these formalities an assembly of revision was to be elected, and they to be forbidden to amend the constitution, in any other points, than those which had been previously marked out for their consideration.

It is easy to perceive that these precautions, are in direct hostility with the principles established in this work. 'Man and for ever!' was the motto of the labours of this assembly. Just broken loose from the thick darkness of an absolute monarchy, they assumed to prescribe lessons of wisdom to all future ages. They seem not so much as to have dreamed, of that purification of intellect, that climax of improvement, which may very probably be the destiny of posterity. The true state of man, as has been already said, is, not to have his opinions bound down in the fetters of an eternal quietism, but, flexible and unrestrained, to yield with facility to the impressions of accumulating observation and experience. That form of society will, of consequence, appear most eligible, which is least founded in a principle of permanence. But, if this view of the subject be just, the idea, of giving permanence to what is called the constitution of any government, and rendering one class of laws, under the appellation of fundamental, less susceptible of change than another, must be founded in misapprehension and error.

The error probably originally sprung, out of the forms of political monopoly, which we see established over the whole civilized world. Government could not justly flow, in the first instance, but from the choice of the people; or, perhaps more accurately speaking, ought to be adjusted in its provisions, to the prevailing apprehensions of equity and truth. But we see government at present administered, either in whole or in part, by a king and a body of noblesse; and we reasonably say, that the laws made by these authorities are one thing, and the laws from which they derived their existence another. Now this, and indeed every species of exclusive, institution, presents us with a dilemma, memorable in its nature, and hard of solution. If the prejudices of a nation are decisively favourable to a king or a body of noblesse, it seems impossible to say, that a king, or a body of noblesse, should not form part of their government. But then, on the other hand, the moment you admit this species of exclusive institution, you counteract the purpose for which it was admitted, and deprive the sentiments of the people of their genuine operation.

If we had never seen arbitrary and capricious forms of government, we should probably never have thought of cutting off certain laws from the code, under the name of constitutional. When we behold certain individuals, or bodies of men, exercising an exclusive superintendence over the affairs of a nation, we inevitably ask how they came by their authority, and the answer is, By the constitution. But, if we saw no power existing in the state but that of the people, having a body of representatives, and a certain number of official secretaries and clerks acting in their behalf, subject to their revisal, and renewable at their pleasure, the question, how the people came by this authority, would never have suggested itself.

.   .   .   .

CHAPTER VIII

OF NATIONAL EDUCATION

A MODE in which government has been accustomed to interfere, for the purpose of influencing opinion, is, by the superintendence it has, in a greater or less degree, exerted, in the article of education. It is worthy of observation, that the idea of this superintendence, has obtained the countenance of several of the zealous advocates of political reform. The question relative to its propriety or impropriety, is entitled, on that account, to the more deliberate examination.

The arguments in its favour have been already anticipated. 'Can it be justifiable in those persons, who are appointed to the functions of magistracy, and whose duty it is to consult for the public welfare, to neglect the cultivation of the infant mind, and to suffer its future excellence or depravity to be at the disposal of fortune? Is it possible for patriotism and the love of the public to be made the characteristic of a whole people, in any other way so successfully, as by rendering the early communication of these virtues a national concern? If the education of our youth be entirely confided to the prudence of their parents, or the accidental benevolence of private individuals, will it not be a necessary consequence, that some will be educated to virtue, others to vice, and others again entirely neglected?' To these considerations it has been added, 'That the maxim which has prevailed in the majority of civilized countries, that ignorance of the law is no apology for the breach of it, is in the highest degree iniquitous; and that government cannot justly punish us for our crimes when committed, unless it have forewarned us against their commission, which cannot be adequately done without something of the nature of public education.'

The propriety or impropriety of any project for this purpose, must be determined by the general consideration of its beneficial or injurious tendency. If the exertions of the magistrate in behalf of any system of instruction, will stand the test, as conducive to the public service, undoubtedly he cannot be justified in neglecting them. If, on the contrary, they conduce to injury, it is wrong and unjustifiable that they should be made.

The injuries that result from a system of national education, are, in the first place, that all public establishments include in them the idea of permanence. They endeavour, it may be, to secure and to diffuse whatever of advantage to society is already known, but they forget that more remains to be known. If they realized the most substantial benefits at the time of their introduction, they must inevitably [have] become less and less useful as they increased in duration. But to describe them as useless, is a very feeble expression of their demerits. They actively restrain the flights of mind, and fix it in the belief of exploded errors. It has frequently been observed of universities, and extensive establishments for the purpose of education, that the knowledge taught there, is a century behind the knowledge, which exists among the unshackled and unprejudiced members of the same political community. The moment any scheme of proceeding gains a permanent establishment, it becomes impressed, as one of its characteristic features, with an aversion to change. Some violent concussion may oblige its conductors to change an old system of philosophy for a system less obsolete; and they are then as pertinaciously attached to this second doctrine, as they were to the first. Real intellectual improvement demands, that mind should, as speedily as possible, be advanced to the height of knowledge already existing among the enlightened members of the community, and start from thence in the pursuit of further acquisitions. But public education has always expended its energies in the support of prejudice; it teaches its pupils, not the fortitude that shall bring every proposition to the test of examination, but the art of vindicating such tenets as may chance to be established. We study Aristotle, or Thomas Aquinas, or Bellarmine, or chief justice Coke, not that we may detect their errors, but that our minds may be fully impregnated with their absurdities. This feature runs through every species of public establishment; and, even in the petty institution of Sunday-schools, the chief lessons that are taught, are a superstitious veneration for the church of England, and to bow to every man in a handsome coat. All this is directly contrary to the true interests of mankind. All this must be unlearned, before we can begin to be wise.

It is the characteristic of mind to be capable of improvement. An individual surrenders the best attribute of man, the moment he resolves to adhere to certain fixed principles, for reasons not now present to his mind, but which formerly were.[1] The instant in which he shuts upon himself the career of enquiry, is the instant of his intellectual decease. He is no longer a man; he is the ghost of departed man. There can be no scheme more egregiously stamped with folly, than that of separating a tenet from the evidence upon which its validity depends. If I cease from the habit of being able to recall this evidence, my belief is no longer a perception, but a prejudice: it may influence me like a prejudice; but cannot animate me like a real apprehension of truth. The difference between the man thus guided, and the man that keeps his mind perpetually alive, is the difference between cowardice and fortitude. The man who is, in the best sense, an intellectual being, delights to recollect the reasons that have convinced him, to repeat them to others, that they may produce conviction in them, and stand more distinct and explicit in his own mind; and he adds to this a willingness to examine objections, because he takes no pride in consistent error. The man who is not capable of this salutary exercise, to what valuable purpose can he be employed? Hence it appears, that no vice can be more destructive, than that which teaches us to regard any judgement as final, and not open to review. The same principle that applies to individuals, applies to communities. There is no proposition, at present apprehended to be true, so valuable, as to justify the introduction of an establishment for the purpose of inculcating it on mankind. Refer them to reading, to conversation, to meditation; but teach them neither creeds nor catechisms, either moral or political.

Secondly, the idea of national education, is founded in an inattention to the nature of mind. Whatever each man does for himself, is done well; whatever his neighbours or his country undertake to do for him, is done ill. It is our wisdom to incite men to act for themselves, not to retain them in a state of perpetual pupillage. He that learns, because he desires to learn, will listen to the instructions he receives, and apprehend their meaning. He that teaches, because he desires to teach, will discharge his occupation with enthusiasm and energy. But the moment political institution undertakes to assign to every man his place, the functions of all will be discharged with supineness and indifference. Universities and expensive establishments have long been remarked for formal dullness. Civil policy has given me the power to appropriate my estate

[1] I. v, p. 46.

to certain theoretical purposes; but it is an idle presumption to think I can entail my views, as I can entail my fortune. Remove those obstacles, which prevent men from seeing, and which restrain them from pursuing, their real advantage; but do not absurdly undertake to relieve them from the activity which this pursuit requires. What I earn, what I acquire only because I desire to acquire it, I estimate at its true value; but what is thrust upon me, may make me indolent, but cannot make me respectable. It is an extreme folly, to endeavour to secure to others, independently of exertion on their part, the means of being happy.— This whole proposition of a national education, is founded upon a supposition which has been repeatedly refuted in this work, but which has recurred upon us in a thousand forms, that unpatronized truth is inadequate to the purpose of enlightening mankind.

Thirdly, the project of a national education ought uniformly to be discouraged, on account of its obvious alliance with national government. This is an alliance of a more formidable nature, than the old and much contested alliance of church and state. Before we put so powerful a machine under the direction of so ambiguous an agent, it behoves us to consider well what it is that we do. Government will not fail to employ it, to strengthen its hands, and perpetuate its institutions. If we could even suppose the agents of government not to propose to themselves an object, which will be apt to appear in their eyes, not merely innocent, but meritorious; the evil would not the less happen. Their views as institutors of a system of education, will not fail to be analogous to their views in their political capacity: the data upon which their conduct as statesmen, is vindicated, will be the data upon which their instructions are founded. It is not true that our youth ought to be instructed to venerate the constitution, however excellent; they should be led to venerate truth; and the constitution only so far as it corresponds with their uninfluenced deductions of truth. Had the scheme of a national education been adopted when despotism was most triumphant, it is not to be believed that it could have for ever stifled the voice of truth. But it would have been the most formidable and profound contrivance for that purpose, that imagination can suggest. Still, in the countries where liberty chiefly prevails, it is reasonably to be assumed that there are important errors, and a national education has the most direct tendency to perpetuate those errors, and to form all minds upon one model.

It is not easy to say whether the remark, 'that government cannot justly punish offenders, unless it have previously informed them what is virtue and what is offence,' be entitled to a separate answer. It is to be hoped that mankind will never have to learn so important a lesson, through so incompetent a channel. Government may reasonably and equitably presume, that men who live in society, know that enormous crimes are injurious to the public weal, without its being necessary to announce them as such, by laws, to be proclaimed by heralds, or expounded by curates. It has been alleged, that 'mere reason may teach me not to strike my neighbour; but will never forbid my sending a sack of wool from England, or printing the French constitution in Spain.' This objection leads to the true distinction upon the subject. All real crimes, that can be supposed to be the fit objects of judicial animadversion, are capable of being discerned without the teaching of law. All supposed crimes, not capable of being so discerned, are truly and unalterably placed beyond the cognizance of a sound criminal justice. It is true that my own understanding would never have told me that the exportation of wool was a crime: neither do I believe it is a crime, now that a law has been made affirming it to be such. It is a feeble and contemptible palliation of iniquitous punishments, to signify to mankind beforehand that you intend to inflict them. Men of a lofty and generous spirit would almost be tempted to exclaim; Destroy us if you please; but do not endeavour, by a national education, to destroy in our understandings the discernment of justice and injustice. The idea of such an education, or even perhaps of the necessity of a written law, would never have occurred, if government and jurisprudence had never attempted the arbitrary conversion of innocence into guilt.

CHAPTER IX

OF PENSIONS AND SALARIES

An article which deserves the maturest consideration, and by means of which political institution does not fail to produce the most important influence upon opinion, is that of the mode of rewarding public services. The mode which has obtained in all European countries, is that of pecuniary reward. He who is employed to act in behalf of the public, is recompensed with a salary. He who retires from that employment, is recompensed with a pension. The arguments in support of this system, are well known. It has been remarked, '. . . If one man, animated by the most disinterested motives, be permitted to serve the public upon these terms, another will assume the exterior of disinterestedness, as a step towards the gratification of a sinister ambition. If men be not openly and directly paid for the services they perform, we may rest assured, that they will pay themselves, by ways a thousand times more injurious. He who devotes himself to the public, ought to devote himself entire: he will therefore be injured in his personal fortune, and ought to be replaced. Add to this, that the servants of the public ought, by their appearance and mode of living, to command respect both from their countrymen, and from foreigners; and that this circumstance will require an expense, for which it is the office of their country to provide.'[1]

. . . .

. . . Surely it ought not to be the end of a good political institution, to increase our selfishness, instead of suffering it to dwindle and decay. If we pay an ample salary to him who is employed in the public service, how are we sure that he will not have more regard to the salary than to the public? If we pay a small salary, yet the very existence of such a payment, will oblige men to compare the work performed, and the reward bestowed; and all the consequence that will result, will be to drive the best men from the service of their country, a service, first degraded by being paid, and then paid with an ill-timed parsimony. Whether the salary be large or small, if a salary exist, many will desire the office for the sake of its appendage. Functions the most extensive in their consequences, will be converted into a trade. . . .

Another consideration of great weight in this instance is, that of the source from which salaries are derived: from the public revenue, from taxes imposed upon the community. The nature of taxation has perhaps seldom been sufficiently considered. By some persons it has been supposed that the superfluities of the community might be collected, and placed under the disposition of the representative or executive power. But this is a gross mistake. The superfluities of the rich are, for the most part, inaccessible to taxation; the burden falls, almost exclusively, upon the laborious and the poor. All wealth, in a state of civilized society, is the produce of human industry.[2] To be rich, is merely to possess a patent, entitling one man to dispose of the produce of another man's industry. Taxation therefore can no otherwise fall upon the rich, but so far as it operates to diminish their luxuries. But this it does in a very few instances, and in a very small degree. Its genuine operation is to impose a

---

[1] The substance of these arguments may be found in Burke's 'Speech on Economical Reform' [1780].

[2] VIII. ii.

new portion of labour, upon those whom labour has already plunged deep, in ignorance, degradation, and misery. The higher and governing part of the community, are like the lion who hunted in concert with the weaker beasts. The landed proprietor first takes a very disproportionate share of the produce to himself; the capitalist follows, and shows himself equally voracious. Both these classes, in the form in which they now appear, might, under a different mode of society, be dispensed with. Taxation comes in next, and lays a new burden, upon those who are bowed down to the earth already. Who is there, allowed the choice of an alternative, and possessing the spirit of a man, that would choose to be thus fed, with the hard-earned morsel that, through the medium of taxation, is wrested from the grip of the peasant?

Too much stress however is not to be laid upon this argument. There is no profession, there is perhaps no mode of life compatible with liberal and intellectual pursuits, that does not include in it a portion of iniquity. It is one of the evils of a corrupt state of society, that it forces the most enlightened and the most virtuous unwillingly to participate in its injustice. It would be weakness, and not magnanimity, that should teach us to view these things with a microscopical scrupulosity; and to refuse to be useful because no usefulness is pure. The most important objection to emoluments flowing from a public revenue, is built upon their tendency to corrupt the mind of the receiver, and the views of the spectators.

.   .   .   .   .

CHAPTER X

OF THE MODES OF DECIDING A QUESTION ON THE PART OF THE COMMUNITY

WHAT has been here said upon the subject of qualifications, naturally leads to a few observations upon the three principal modes of determining public questions and elections, by sortition, ballot and vote.

The idea of sortition was first introduced by the dictates of superstition. It was supposed that, when human reason piously acknowledged its insufficiency, the Gods, pleased with so unfeigned a homage, interfered to guide the decision. This imagination is now exploded. Every man who pretends to philosophy, will confess, that, wherever sortition is introduced, the decision is exclusively guided by the laws of impulse and gravitation.—Strictly speaking, we know of no such thing as contingence. But, so far as relates to the exercise of apprehension and judgement on the particular question to be determined, all decision by lot is the decision of contingence. The operations of impulse and gravitation, either proceed from a blind and unconscious principle; or, if they be the offspring of a superintending mind, it is mind executing general laws, not temporizing with every variation of human caprice.

All reference of public questions and elections to lot, includes in it one of two evils, moral imbecility or cowardice. There is no situation in which we can be placed, that has not its corresponding duties. There is no alternative that can be offered to our choice, that does not include in it a better and a worse. The idea of sortition therefore springs, either from an effeminacy that will not enquire, or a timidity that dares not pronounce its decision.

The path of virtue is simple and direct. The first attributes of a virtuous character, are a mind awake, and a quick and observant eye. A man of right dispositions will enquire out the lessons of duty. The man, on the contrary, who is spoiled by stupidity or superstition, will wait till these lessons are brought to him in a way that he cannot resist. A superficial survey will perhaps lead him to class a multitude of human transactions, among the things that are indifferent. But, if we be indefatigably benevolent, we shall, for the most part, find, even among things ordinarily so denominated, a reason for preference. He may well be concluded to have but a small share of moral principle, who easily dispenses himself from seeking the occasion to exercise it. Add to which, they are not trifles, but matters of serious import, that it has been customary to commit to the decision of lot.

But, supposing us to have a sentiment of preference, or a consciousness that to attain such a perception is our duty, if we afterwards desert it, this is the most contemptible cowardice. Nothing can be more unworthy, than a propensity to take refuge in indolence and neutrality, simply because we have not the courage to encounter the consequences of ingenuousness and sincerity.

Ballot is a mode of decision still more censurable than sortition. It is scarcely possible to conceive a political institution, that includes a more direct and explicit patronage of vice. It has been said, 'that ballot may in certain cases be necessary, to enable a man of a feeble character, to act with ease and independence, and to prevent bribery, corrupt influence and faction.' Hypocrisy is an ill remedy to apply to the cure of weakness.

A feeble and irresolute character might before be accidental; ballot is a contrivance to render it permanent, and to scatter its seeds over a wider surface. The true remedy for a want of constancy and public spirit, is to inspire firmness, not to inspire timidity. Sound and just conceptions, if communicated to the mind with perspicuity, may be expected to be a sufficient basis for virtue. To tell men that it is necessary they should form their decision by ballot, is to tell them that it is necessary they should be ashamed of their integrity.

If sortition taught us to desert our duty, ballot teaches us to draw a veil of concealment over our performance of it. It points out to us a method of acting unobserved. It incites us to make a mystery of our sentiments. If it did this in the most trivial article, it would not be easy to bring the mischief it would produce, within the limits of calculation. But it dictates this conduct in our most important concerns. It calls upon us to discharge our duty to the public, with the most virtuous constancy; but at the same time directs us to hide our discharge of it. One of the most beneficial principles in the structure of the material universe, will perhaps be found to be, its tendency to prevent our withdrawing ourselves from the consequences of our own actions. A political institution that should attempt to counteract this principle, would be the only true impiety. How can a man have the love of the public in his heart, without the dictates of that love flowing to his lips? When we direct men to act with secrecy, we direct them to act with frigidity. Virtue will always be an unusual spectacle among men, till they shall have learned to be at all times ready, to avow their actions, and assign the reasons upon which they are founded.

If then sortition and ballot be institutions pregnant with vice, it follows, that all social decisions should be made by open vote; that, wherever we have a function to discharge, we should reflect on the purpose for which it ought to be exercised; and that, whatever conduct we are persuaded to adopt, especially in affairs of general concern, should, most certainly in matters of routine and established practice, be adopted in the face of the world.

BOOK VII

OF CRIMES AND PUNISHMENTS

CHAPTER I

LIMITATIONS OF THE DOCTRINE OF PUNISHMENT WHICH RESULT FROM THE PRINCIPLES OF MORALITY

THE subject of punishment is perhaps the most fundamental in the science of politics. Men associated for the sake of mutual protection and benefit. It has already appeared, that the internal affairs of such associations are of an inexpressibly higher importance than their external.[1] It has appeared that the action of society, in conferring rewards, and superintending opinion, is of pernicious effect.[2] Hence it follows that government, or the action of society in its corporate capacity, can scarcely be of any utility, except so far as it is requisite for the suppression of force by force; for the prevention of the hostile attack of one member of the society, upon the person or property of another, which prevention is usually called by the name of criminal justice, or punishment.

Before we can properly judge of the necessity or urgency of this action of government, it will be of some importance to consider the precise import of the word punishment. I may employ force, to counteract the hostility that is actually committing on me. I may employ force, to compel any member of the society to occupy the post that I conceive most conducive to the general advantage, either in the mode of impressing soldiers and sailors, or by obliging a military officer, or a minister of state, to accept, or retain his appointment. I may put a valuable man to death for the common good, either because he is infected with a pestilential disease, or because some oracle has declared it essential to the public safety. None of these, though they consist in the exertion of force for some moral purpose, comes within the import of the word punishment. Punishment is also often used to signify, the voluntary infliction

<hr>

[1] V. xx.   [2] ... Book VI, throughout.

of evil upon a vicious being, not merely because the public advantage demands it, but because there is apprehended to be a certain fitness and propriety in the nature of things, that render suffering, abstractedly from the benefit to result, the suitable concomitant of vice.

The justice of punishment however, in this import of the word, can only be a deduction from the hypothesis of free will, if indeed that hypothesis will sufficiently support it; and must be false, if human actions are necessary. Mind, as was sufficiently apparent when we treated of that subject,[1] is an agent, in no other sense than matter is an agent. It operates and is operated upon, and the nature, the force and line of direction of the first, is exactly in proportion to the nature, force and line of direction of the second. Morality, in a rational and designing mind, is not essentially different from morality in an inanimate substance. . . .

. . . . .

. . . whether we enter philosophically into the principle of human actions, or merely analyse the ideas of rectitude and justice which have the universal consent of mankind, . . . in the refined and absolute sense in which that term has frequently been employed, there is no such thing as desert; in other words, . . . it cannot be just that we should inflict suffering on any man, except so far as it tends to good. Hence . . . punishment, in the last of the senses enumerated towards the beginning of this chapter, by no means accords with any sound principles of reasoning. It is right that I should inflict suffering, in every case where it can be clearly shown that such infliction will produce an overbalance of good. But this infliction bears no reference to the mere innocence or guilt of the person upon whom it is made. An innocent man is the proper subject of it, if it tend to good. A guilty man is the proper subject of it under no other point of view. To punish him, upon any hypothesis, for what is past and irrecoverable, and for the consideration of that only, must be ranked among the most pernicious exhibitions of an untutored barbarism. Every man upon whom discipline is employed, is to be considered as to the purpose of this discipline as innocent. The only sense of the word punishment, that can be supposed to be compatible with the principles of the present work, is that of pain inflicted on a person convicted of past injurious action, for the purpose of preventing future mischief.

It is of the utmost importance that we should bear these ideas constantly in mind, during our examination of the theory of punishment.

[1] IV. viii.

This theory would, in the past transactions of mankind, have been totally different, if they had divested themselves of the emotions of anger and resentment; if they had considered the man who torments another for what he has done, as upon a par with the child who beats the table; if they had conjured up to their imagination, and properly estimated, the man, who should shut up in prison and periodically torture some atrocious criminal, from the mere consideration of the abstract congruity of crime and punishment, without a possible benefit to others or to himself; if they had regarded punishment, as that which was to be regulated solely, by a dispassionate calculation of the future, without suffering the past, on its own account, for a moment to enter into the proceeding.

CHAPTER II

GENERAL DISADVANTAGES OF PUNISHMENT

HAVING thus endeavoured to show what denominations of punishment justice, and a sound idea of the nature of man, would invariably proscribe, it belongs to us, in the further prosecution of the subject, to consider merely that coercion, which it has been supposed right to employ, against persons convicted of past injurious action, for the purpose of preventing future mischief. And here we will, first, recollect what is the quantity of evil which accrues from all such coercion;[1] and secondly, examine the cogency of the various reasons by which it is recommended.[2]

.   .   .   .

No principle of moral science can be more obvious and fundamental, than that the motive by which we are induced to an action, constitutes an essential part of its character. This idea has perhaps sometimes been carried too far. A good motive is of little value, when it is not joined to a salutary exertion. But, without a good motive, the most extensively useful action that ever was performed, can contribute little to the improvement or honour of him that performs it. We owe him no respect, if he has been induced to perform it by ideas of personal advantage, or the influence of a bribe. It is, in some respects, worse, if the motive that governed him were the sentiment of fear. If we hold in any estimation the attributes of man, if we desire the improvement of our species, we

[1] [Ch. ii.]   [2] [Ch. iii.]

ought particularly to desire that they should be led in the path of useful-ness by generous and liberal considerations, that their obedience should be the obedience of the heart, and not that of a slave.

Nothing can be of higher importance to the improvement of the human mind, than that, whatever be the conduct we may be compelled to pursue, we should have distinct and accurate notions of the merits of every moral question in which we may be concerned. In all doubtful questions, there are but two criteria possible, the decisions of other men's wisdom, and the decisions of our own understanding. Which of these is conformable to the nature of man? Can we surrender our own under-standing? However we may strain after implicit faith, will not conscience in spite of ourselves whisper us, 'This decree is equitable, and this is founded in mistake?' Will there not be in the minds of the votaries of superstition, a perpetual dissatisfaction, a desire to believe what is dictated to them, accompanied with a want of that in which belief con-sists, evidence and conviction? If we could surrender our understanding, what sort of beings should we become?

The direct tendency of coercion is to set out understanding and our fears, our duty and our weakness, at variance with each other. Coercion first annihilates the understanding of the subject upon whom it is exer-cised, and then of him who employs it. Dressed in the supine prerogatives of a master, he is excused from cultivating the faculties of a man. What would not man have been, long before this, if the proudest of us had no hopes but in argument, if he knew of no resort beyond, if he were obliged to sharpen his faculties, and collect his powers, as the only means of effecting his purposes?

Let us reflect a little upon the species of influence, that coercion em-ploys. It avers to its victim that he must necessarily be in the wrong, because I am more vigorous or more cunning than he. Will vigour and cunning be always on the side of truth? It appeals to force, and represents superior strength as the standard of justice. . . .

.   .   .   .

Let us consider the effect that coercion produces upon the mind of him against whom it is employed. It cannot begin with convincing; it is no argument. It begins with producing the sensation of pain, and the sentiment of distaste. It begins with violently alienating the mind from the truth with which we wish it to be impressed. It includes in it a tacit confession of imbecility. If he who employs coercion against me could mould me to his purposes by argument, no doubt he would. He pretends to punish me, because his argument is strong; but he really punishes me, because his argument is weak.

CHAPTER III

OF THE PURPOSES OF PUNISHMENT

LET us proceed to consider the three principal ends that punishment proposes to itself, restraint, reformation and example. Under each of these heads the arguments on the affirmative side must be allowed to be cogent, not irresistible. Under each of them considerations will occur, that will oblige us to doubt universally of the propriety of punishment.

The first and most innocent of all the classes of coercion, is that which is employed in repelling actual force. This has but little to do with any species of political institution, but may nevertheless deserve to be first considered. In this case I am employed (suppose, for example, a drawn sword is pointed at my own breast or that of another, with threats of instant destruction) in preventing a mischief that seems about inevitably to ensue. In this case there appears to be no time for experiments. And yet, even here, a strict research will suggest to us important doubts. The powers of reason and truth are yet unfathomed. That truth which one man cannot communicate in less than a year, another can communicate in a fortnight. The shortest term may have an understanding commensurate to it. When Marius[1] said, with a stern look, and a commanding countenance, to the soldier, that was sent down into his dungeon to assassinate him, 'Wretch, have you the temerity to kill Marius!' and with these few words drove him to flight; it was, that the grandeur of the idea conceived in his own mind, made its way with irresistible force to the mind of his executioner. He had no arms for resistance; he had no vengeance to threaten; he was debilitated and deserted; it was by the force of sentiment only, that he disarmed his destroyer. If there were falsehood and prejudice mixed with the idea communicated, in this case, can we believe that truth is not still more powerful? It would be well for the human species, if they were all, in this respect, like Marius, all accustomed to place an intrepid confidence in the single energy of intellect. Who shall say what there is that would be impossible to men thus bold, and actuated only by the purest sentiments? Who shall say

---

[1] [Gaius Marius (157–86 B.C.), Roman general and consul.]

how far the whole species might be improved, did they cease to respect force in others, and did they refuse to employ it for themselves?

The difference however, between this species of coercion, and the species which usually bears the denomination of punishment, is obvious. Punishment is employed against an individual whose violence is over. He is, at present, engaged in no hostility, against the community, or any of its members. He is quietly pursuing, it may be, those occupations which are beneficial to himself, and injurious to none. Upon what pretence is this man to be the subject of violence?

For restraint. Restraint from what? 'From some future injury which it is to be feared he will commit.' This is the very argument which has been employed to justify the most execrable tyrannies. By what reasonings have the inquisition, the employment of spies, and the various kinds of public censure directed against opinion, been vindicated? By recollecting that there is an intimate connection between men's opinions and their conduct; that immoral sentiments lead, by a very probable consequence, to immoral actions. There is not more reason, in many cases at least, to apprehend that the man who has once committed robbery, will commit it again, than the man who has dissipated his property at the gaming table or who is accustomed to profess that, upon any emergency, he will not scruple to have recourse to this expedient. Nothing can be more obvious than that, whatever precautions may be allowable with respect to the future, justice will reluctantly class among these precautions a violence to be committed on my neighbour. Nor is it oftener unjust, than it is superfluous. Why not arm myself with vigilance and energy, instead of locking up every man whom my imagination may bid me fear, that I may spend my days in undisturbed inactivity? If communities, instead of aspiring, as they have hitherto done, to embrace a vast territory, and glut their vanity with ideas of empire, were contented with a small district, with a proviso of confederation in cases of necessity, every individual would then live under the public eye; and the disapprobation of his neighbours, a species of coercion, not derived from the caprice of men, but from the system of the universe, would inevitably oblige him, either to reform, or to emigrate.—The sum of the argument under this head is, that all punishment for the sake of restraint, is punishment upon suspicion, a species of punishment, the most abhorrent to reason, and arbitrary in its application, that can be devised.

The second object which punishment may be imagined to propose to itself, is reformation. We have already seen various objections that may be offered to it in this point of view. Coercion cannot convince, cannot conciliate, but on the contrary alienates the mind of him against whom it is employed. Coercion has nothing in common with reason, and therefore can have no proper tendency to the cultivation of virtue. It is true that reason is nothing more than a collation and comparison of various emotions and feelings; but they must be the feelings originally appropriate to the question, not those which an arbitrary will, stimulated by the possession of power, may annex to it. Reason is omnipotent: if my conduct be wrong, a very simple statement, flowing from a clear and comprehensive view, will make it appear to be such; nor is it probable that there is any perverseness that would persist in vice, in the face of all the recommendations with which virtue might be invested, and all the beauty in which it might be displayed.

But to this it may be answered, 'that this view of the subject may indeed be abstractedly true, but that it is not true relative to the present imperfection of human faculties. The grand requisite for the reformation and improvement of the human species, seems to consist in the rousing of the mind. It is for this reason that the school of adversity, has so often been considered as the school of virtue.[1] In an even course of easy and prosperous circumstances, the faculties sleep. But, when great and urgent occasion is presented, it should seem that the mind rises to the level of the occasion. Difficulties awaken vigour, and engender strength; and it will frequently happen that, the more you check and oppress me, the more will my faculties swell, till they burst all the obstacles of oppression.'

The opinion of the excellence of adversity, is built upon a very obvious mistake. If we divest ourselves of paradox and singularity, we shall perceive that adversity is a bad thing, but that there is something else that is worse. Mind can neither exist, nor be improved, without the reception of ideas. It will improve more in a calamitous, than a torpid state. A man will sometimes be found wiser at the end of his career, who has been treated with severity, than with neglect. But, because severity is one way of generating thought, it does not follow that it is the best.

It has already been shown that coercion, absolutely considered, is injustice. Can injustice be the best mode of disseminating principles of equity and reason? Oppression, exercised to a certain extent, is the most

---

[1] [At this point Godwin has a footnote reference to V. ii (omitted in this abridgement), where the theory in question is rejected for reasons similar to those which Godwin proceeds to use here. The earlier discussion was amplified by allusions to various historical characters.]

ruinous of all things. What is it but this, that has habituated mankind to so much ignorance and vice for so many thousand years? Is it probable, that that which has been thus terrible in its consequences, should, under any variation of circumstances, be made a source of eminent good? All coercion sours the mind. He that suffers it, is practically persuaded of the want of a philanthropy sufficiently enlarged, in those with whom he has intercourse. He feels that justice prevails only with great limitations, and that he cannot depend upon being treated with justice. The lesson which coercion reads to him is, 'Submit to force, and abjure reason. Be not directed by the convictions of your understanding, but by the basest part of your nature, the fear of personal pain, and a compulsory awe of the injustice of others.' It was thus Elizabeth of England and Frederick of Prussia were educated in the school of adversity. The way in which they profited by this discipline, was by finding resources in their own minds, enabling them to regard, with an unconquered spirit, the violence employed against them. Can this be the best mode of forming men to virtue? If it be, perhaps it is further requisite, that the coercion we use should be flagrantly unjust, since the improvement seems to lie, not in submission, but resistance.

But it is certain that truth is adequate to excite the mind, without the aid of adversity. By truth is here understood a just view of all the attractions of industry, knowledge and benevolence. If I apprehend the value of any pursuit, shall I not engage in it? If I apprehend it clearly, shall I not engage in it zealously? If you would awaken my mind in the most effectual manner, speak to the genuine and honourable feelings of my nature. For that purpose, thoroughly understand yourself that which you would recommend to me, impregnate your mind with its evidence, and speak from the clearness of your view, and the fullness of conviction. Were we accustomed to an education, in which truth was never neglected from indolence, or told in a way treacherous to its excellence, in which the preceptor subjected himself to the perpetual discipline of finding the way to communicate it with brevity and force, but without prejudice and acrimony, it cannot be believed, but that such an education, would be more effectual for the improvement of the mind, than all the modes of angry or benevolent coercion that ever were devised.

The last object which punishment proposes, is example. Had legislators confined their views to reformation and restraint, their exertions of power, though mistaken, would still have borne the stamp of humanity. But, the moment vengeance presented itself as a stimulus on the one side, or the exhibition of a terrible example on the other, no barbarity was thought too great. Ingenious cruelty was busied to find new means of torturing the victim, or of rendering the spectacle impressive and horrible.

It has long since been observed, that this system of policy constantly fails of its purpose. Further refinements in barbarity, produce a certain impression, so long as they are new; but this impression soon vanishes, and the whole scope of a gloomy invention is exhausted in vain.[1] The reason of this phenomenon, is that, whatever may be the force with which novelty strikes the imagination, the inherent nature of the situation speedily recurs, and asserts its indestructible empire. We feel the emergencies to which we are exposed, and we feel, or think we feel, the dictates of reason inciting us to their relief. Whatever ideas we form in opposition to the mandates of law, we draw, with sincerity, though it may be with some mixture of mistake, from the essential conditions of our existence. We compare them with the despotism which society exercises in its corporate capacity; and, the more frequent is our comparison, the greater are our murmurs and indignation against the injustice to which we are exposed. But indignation is not a sentiment that conciliates; barbarity possesses none of the attributes of persuasion. It may terrify; but it cannot produce in us candour and docility. Thus ulcerated with injustice, our distresses, our temptations, and all the eloquence of feeling present themselves again and again. Is it any wonder they should prove victorious?

Punishment for example, is liable to all the objections which are urged against punishment for restraint or reformation, and to certain other objections peculiar to itself. It is employed against a person not now in the commission of offence, and of whom we can only suspect that he ever will offend. It supersedes argument, reason and conviction, and requires us to think such a species of conduct our duty, because such is the good pleasure of our superiors, and because, as we are taught by the example in question, they will make us rue our stubbornness if we think otherwise. In addition to this it is to be remembered that, when I am made to suffer as an example to others, I am myself treated with supercilious neglect, as if I were totally incapable of feeling and morality. If you inflict pain upon me, you are either just or unjust. If you be just, it should seem necessary that there should be something in me that makes me the fit subject of pain, either absolute desert, which is absurd, or mischief I may be expected to perpetuate, or lastly, a tendency in what you do, to produce my reformation. If any of these be the reason why

[1] Beccaria, *Dei Delitti e delle Pene* [1764].

the suffering I undergo is just, then example is out of the question: it may be an incidental consequence of the procedure, but it forms no part of its principle. It must surely be a very inartificial and injudicious scheme for guiding the sentiments of mankind, to fix upon an individual as a subject of torture or death, respecting whom this treatment has no direct fitness, merely that we may bid others look on, and derive instruction from his misery. This argument will derive additional force from the reasonings of the following chapter.

CHAPTER IV

OF THE APPLICATION OF PUNISHMENT

A FURTHER consideration, calculated to show, not only the absurdity of punishment for example, but the iniquity of punishment in general, is, that delinquency and punishment are, in all cases, incommensurable. No standard of delinquency ever has been, or ever can be, discovered. No two crimes were ever alike; and therefore the reducing them, explicitly or implicitly, to general classes, which the very idea of example implies, is absurd. Nor is it less absurd, to attempt to proportion the degree of suffering to the degree of delinquency, when the latter can never be discovered. Let us endeavour to clear the truth of these propositions.

Man, like every other machine the operations of which can be made the object of our senses, may, in a certain sense, be affirmed to consist of two parts, the external and the internal. The form which his actions assume is one thing; the principle from which they flow is another. With the former it is possible we should be acquainted; respecting the latter there is no species of evidence that can adequately inform us. Shall we proportion the degree of suffering to the former or the latter, to the injury sustained by the community, or to the quantity of ill intention conceived by the offender? Some philosophers, sensible of the inscrutability of intention, have declared in favour of our attending to nothing but the injury sustained. The humane and benevolent Beccaria has treated this as a truth of the utmost importance, 'unfortunately neglected by the majority of political institutors, and preserved only in the dispassionate speculation of philosophers.'[1]

---

[1] [Godwin here includes as a footnote a quotation from *Dei Delitti e delle Pene* which can be translated as follows: 'This is one of those palpable truths which, by a marvellous

It is true that we may, in many instances, be tolerably informed respecting external actions, and that there will, at first sight, appear to be no great difficulty in reducing them to general rules. Murder, according to this system, suppose, will be the exertion of any species of action affecting my neighbour, so as that the consequences terminate in death. The difficulties of the magistrate are much abridged upon this principle, though they are by no means annihilated. It is well known how many subtle disquisitions, ludicrous or tragical according to the temper with which we view them, have been introduced to determine in each particular instance, whether the action were or were not the real occasion of the death. It never can be demonstratively ascertained.

But dismissing this difficulty, how complicated is the iniquity of treating all instances alike, in which one man has occasioned the death of another? Shall we abolish the imperfect distinctions, which the most odious tyrannies have hitherto thought themselves compelled to admit, between chance-medley, manslaughter and malice prepense? Shall we inflict on the man who, in endeavouring to save the life of a drowning fellow creature, oversets a boat, and occasions the death of a second, the same suffering, as on him who, from gloomy and vicious habits, is incited to the murder of his benefactor? In reality, the injury sustained by the community, is, by no means, the same in these two cases; the injury sustained by the community, is to be measured by the antisocial dispositions of the offender, and, if that were the right view of the subject, by the encouragement afforded to similar dispositions from his impunity. But this leads us at once, from the external action, to the unlimited consideration of the intention of the actor. The iniquity of the written laws of society, is of precisely the same nature, though not of so atrocious a degree, in the confusion they actually introduce between various intentions, as if this confusion were unlimited. One man shall commit murder, to remove a troublesome observer of his depraved dispositions, who will otherwise counteract and expose him to the world. A second, because he cannot bear the ingenuous sincerity with which he is told of his vices. A third, from his intolerable envy of superior merit. A fourth, because he knows that his adversary meditates an act pregnant with extensive mischief, and perceives no other mode by which its perpetration can be prevented. A fifth, in defence of his father's life or his daughter's chastity. Each of these men, except perhaps the last, may act, either from momentary impulse, or from any of the infinite shades

combination of circumstances, are not known with certainty except by a few thinkers from each nation and from each century.']

and degrees of deliberation. Would you award one individual punishment to all these varieties of action? Can a system that levels these inequalities, and confounds these differences, be productive of good? That
we may render men beneficent towards each other, shall we subvert
the very nature of right and wrong? Or is not this system, from whatever pretences introduced, calculated in the most powerful manner, to
produce general injury? Can there be a more flagrant injury, than to
inscribe, as we do in effect, upon our courts of judgement, 'This is the
Hall of Justice, in which the principles of right and wrong are daily and
systematically slighted, and offences of a thousand different magnitudes,
are confounded together, by the insolent supineness of the legislator, and
the unfeeling selfishness of those who have engrossed the produce of the
general labour to their particular emolument!'

But suppose, secondly, that we were to take the intention of the
offender, and the future injury to be apprehended, as the standard of
infliction. This would no doubt be a considerable improvement. This
would be the true mode of reconciling punishment and justice, if, for
reasons already assigned, they were not, in their own nature, incompatible. It is earnestly to be desired that this mode of administering
retribution should be seriously attempted. It is to be hoped, that men
will one day attempt to establish an accurate criterion, and not go on
for ever, as they have hitherto done, with a sovereign contempt of
equity and reason. This attempt would lead, by a very obvious process,
to the abolition of all punishment.

It would immediately lead to the abolition of all criminal law. An
enlightened and reasonable judicature would have recourse, in order to
decide upon the cause before them, to no code but the code of reason.
They would feel the absurdity of other men's teaching them what they
should think, and pretending to understand the case before it happened,
better than they who had all the circumstances under their inspection.
They would feel the absurdity of bringing every offence to be compared
with a certain number of measures previously invented, and compelling
it to agree with one of them. But we shall shortly have occasion to return
to this topic.[1]

The great advantage that would result, from men's determining to
govern themselves, in the suffering to be inflicted, by the motives of the
offender, and the future injury to be apprehended, would consist, in
their being taught how vain and presumptuous it is in them to attempt
to wield the rod of retribution. Who is it that, in his sober reason, will

[1] Ch. viii.

pretend to assign the motives that influenced me in any article of my conduct, and upon them to found a grave, perhaps a capital, penalty against me? The attempt would be iniquitous and absurd, even though the individual who was to judge me, had made the longest observation of my character, and been most intimately acquainted with the series of my actions. How often does a man deceive himself in the motives of his conduct, and assign to one principle, what, in reality, proceeded from another? Can we expect that a mere spectator should form a judgement sufficiently correct, when he who has all the sources of information in his hands, is nevertheless mistaken? Is it not to this hour a dispute among philosophers, whether I be capable of doing good to my neighbour for his own sake? 'To ascertain the intention of a man, it is necessary, to be precisely informed, of the actual impression of the objects upon his senses, and of the previous disposition of his mind, both of which vary in different persons, and even in the same person at different times, with a rapidity commensurate to the succession of ideas, passions and circumstances.'[1] Meanwhile the individuals, whose office it is to judge of this inscrutable mystery, are possessed of no previous knowledge, utter strangers to the person accused, and collecting their only materials from the information of two or three ignorant and prejudiced witnesses.

What a vast train of actual and possible motives enter into the history of a man, who has been incited to destroy the life of another? Can you tell me how much in these there was of apprehended justice, and how much of inordinate selfishness? how much of sudden passion, and how much of rooted depravity? how much of intolerable provocation, and how much of spontaneous wrong? how much of that sudden insanity which hurries the mind into a certain action by a sort of incontinence of nature, almost without any assignable motive, and how much of incurable habit? Consider the uncertainty of history. Do we not still dispute whether Cicero were more a vain or a virtuous man, whether the heroes of ancient Rome were impelled by vainglory or disinterested benevolence, whether Voltaire were the stain of his species, or their most generous and intrepid benefactor? Upon these subjects moderate men perpetually quote the impenetrableness of the human heart. Will moderate men pretend, that we have not an hundred times more evidence upon which to found our judgement in these cases, than in that of the

---

[1] [Godwin's footnote at this point quotes from Beccaria not only the sentences translated above but an additional sentence as well. This sentence can be translated as follows: 'It would therefore become necessary to formulate not only a particular legal code for each citizen, but a new law for every crime.']

man who was tried last week at the Old Bailey? This part of the subject will be put in a striking light, if we recollect the narratives that have been published by condemned criminals. In how different a light do they place the transactions that proved fatal to them, from the construction that was put upon them by their judges? And yet these narratives were written under the most awful circumstances, and many of them without the least hope of mitigating their fate, and with marks of the deepest sincerity. Who will say that the judge, with his slender pittance of information, was more competent to decide upon the motives, than the prisoner after the severest scrutiny of his own mind? How few are the trials which an humane and just man can read, terminating in a verdict of guilty, without feeling an uncontrollable repugnance against the verdict? If there be any sight more humiliating than all others, it is that of a miserable victim, acknowledging the justice of a sentence, against which every enlightened spectator exclaims with horror.

But this is not all. The motive, when ascertained, is a subordinate part of the question. The point, upon which only society can equitably animadvert, if it had any jurisdiction in the case, is a point, if possible, still more inscrutable than that of which we have been treating. A legal inquisition into the minds of men, considered by itself, all rational enquirers have agreed to condemn. What we want to ascertain is, not the intention of the offender, but the chance of his offending again. For this purpose we reasonably enquire first into his intention. But, when we have found this, our task is but begun. This is one of our materials, to enable us to calculate the probability of his repeating his offence, or being imitated by others. Was this an habitual state of his mind, or was it a crisis in his history likely to remain an unique? What effect has experience produced on him; or what likelihood is there, that the uneasiness and suffering that attend the perpetration of eminent wrong, may have worked a salutary change in his mind? Will he hereafter be placed in circumstances that shall impel him to the same enormity? Precaution is, in its own nature, a step in a high degree precarious. Precaution that consists in inflicting injury on another, will at all times be odious to an equitable mind. Meanwhile, be it observed, that all which has been said upon the uncertainty of crime, tends to aggravate the injustice of punishment for the sake of example. Since the crime upon which I animadvert in one man, can never be the same as the crime of another, it is as if I should award a grievous penalty against persons with one eye, to prevent any man in future from putting out his eyes by design.

One more argument, calculated to prove the absurdity of the attempt to proportion delinquency and suffering to each other, may be derived from the imperfection of evidence. The veracity of witnesses will, to an impartial spectator, be a subject of continual doubt. Their competence, so far as relates to just observation and accuracy of understanding, will be still more doubtful. Absolute impartiality it would be absurd to expect from them. How much will every word and every action come distorted, by the medium through which it is transmitted? . . .

But, supposing the external action, the first part of the question to be ascertained, we have next to discover through the same garbled and confused medium the intention. How few men should I choose to entrust with the drawing up a narrative of some delicate and interesting transaction of my life? How few, though, corporally speaking, they were witnesses of what was done, would justly describe my motives, and properly report and interpret my words? Yet, in an affair, that involves my life, my fame and future usefulness, I am obliged to trust to any vulgar and casual observer.

A man properly confident in the force of truth, would consider a public libel upon his character as a trivial misfortune. But a criminal trial in a court of justice, is inexpressibly different. Few men, thus circumstanced, can retain the necessary presence of mind, and freedom from embarrassment. But if they do, it is with a cold and unwilling ear that their tale is heard. If the crime charged against them be atrocious, they are half condemned in the passions of mankind, before their cause is brought to a trial. All that is interesting to them, is decided amidst the first burst of indignation; and it is well, if their story be impartially estimated, ten years after their body has mouldered in the grave. Why, if a considerable time elapse between the trial and the execution, do we find the severity of the public changed into compassion? For the same reason that a master, if he do not beat his slave in the moment of resentment, often feels a repugnance to the beating him at all. Not so much, perhaps, as is commonly supposed, from forgetfulness of the offence, as that the sentiments of reason have time to recur, and he feels, in a confused and indefinite manner, the injustice of punishment. Thus every consideration tends to show, that a man tried for a crime, is a poor deserted individual, with the whole force of the community conspiring his ruin. The culprit that escapes, however conscious of innocence, lifts up his hands with astonishment, and can scarcely believe his senses, having such mighty odds against him. It is easy for a man who desires to shake off an imputation under which he labours, to talk of being put on his trial; but no man ever seriously wished for this ordeal, who knew what a trial was.

CHAPTER V

OF PUNISHMENT CONSIDERED AS A TEMPORARY EXPEDIENT

THUS much for the general merits of punishment, considered as an instrument to be applied in the government of men. It is time that we should enquire into the apology which may be offered in its behalf, as a temporary expedient. No introduction seemed more proper to this enquiry, than such a review of the subject upon a comprehensive scale; that the reader might be inspired with a suitable repugnance against so pernicious a system, and prepared firmly to resist its admission, in all cases, where its necessity cannot be clearly demonstrated.

The arguments in favour of punishment as a temporary expedient are obvious. It may be alleged that, 'however suitable an entire immunity in this respect may be to the nature of mind absolutely considered, it is impracticable with regard to men as we now find them. The human species is at present infected with a thousand vices, the offspring of established injustice. They are full of factitious appetites and perverse habits: headstrong in evil, inveterate in selfishness, without sympathy and forbearance for the welfare of others. In time they may become accommodated to the lessons of reason; but at present they would be found deaf to her mandates, and eager to commit every species of injustice.'

One of the remarks that most irresistibly suggest themselves upon this statement is, that punishment has no proper tendency to prepare men for a state in which punishment shall cease. It were idle to expect, that force should begin to do that, which it is the office of truth to finish, should fit men, by severity and violence, to enter with more favourable auspices into the schools of reason.

But, to omit this gross misrepresentation in behalf of the supposed utility of punishment, it is of importance, in the first place, to observe, that there is a complete and unanswerable remedy, to those evils, the cure of which has hitherto been sought in punishment, that is within the reach of every community, whenever they shall be persuaded to adopt it. There is a state of society, the outline of which has been already sketched,[1] that, by the mere simplicity of its structure, would lead to the extermination of offence: a state, in which temptation would be almost unknown, truth brought down to the level of all apprehensions, and vice sufficiently checked, by the general discountenance, and sober condemnation of every spectator. Such are the consequences that might be expected to spring from an abolition of the craft and mystery of governing; while, on the other hand, the innumerable murders that are daily committed under the sanction of legal forms, are solely to be ascribed to the pernicious notion of an extensive territory; to the dreams of glory, empire and national greatness, which have hitherto proved the bane of the human species, without producing entire benefit and happiness to a single individual.

Another observation which this consideration immediately suggests, is, that it is not, as the objection supposed, by any means necessary, that mankind should pass through a state of purification, and be freed from the vicious propensities which ill-constituted governments have implanted, before they can be dismissed from the coercion to which they are at present subjected. Their state would indeed be hopeless, if it were necessary that the cure should be effected, before we were at liberty to discard those practices to which the disease owes its most alarming symptoms. But it is the characteristic of a well-formed society, not only to maintain in its members those virtues with which they are already imbued, but to extirpate their errors, and render them benevolent and just to each other. It frees us from the influence of those phantoms which before misled us, shows us our true advantage as consisting in independence and integrity, and binds us, by the general consent of our fellow citizens, to the dictates of reason, more strongly than with fetters of iron. It is not to the sound of intellectual health that the remedy so urgently addresses itself, as to those who are infected with diseases of the mind. The ill propensities of mankind no otherwise tend to postpone the abolition of coercion, than as they prevent them from perceiving the advantages of political simplicity. The moment in which they can be persuaded to adopt any rational plan for this abolition, is the moment in which the abolition ought to be effected.

A further consequence that may be deduced from the principles that have here been delivered, is that a coercion to be employed upon its own members, can, in no case, be the duty of the community. The community is always competent to change its institutions, and thus to extirpate offence in a way infinitely more rational and just than that of punishment.

[1] V. xxii, p. 217.

If, in this sense, punishment has been deemed necessary as a temporary expedient, the opinion admits of satisfactory refutation. Punishment can at no time, either permanently or provisionally, make part of any political system that is built upon the principles of reason. But, though, in this sense, punishment cannot be admitted, for so much as a temporary expedient, there is another sense in which it must be so admitted. Coercion, exercised in the name of the state upon its respective members, cannot be the duty of the community; but coercion may be the duty of individuals within the community. The duty of individuals, in their political capacity, is, in the first place, to endeavour to meliorate the state of society in which they exist, and to be indefatigable in detecting its imperfections. But, in the second place, it behoves them to recollect, that their efforts cannot be expected to meet with instant success, that the progress of knowledge has, in all cases, been gradual, and that their obligation to promote the welfare of society during the intermediate period, is certainly not less real, than their obligation to promote its future and permanent advantage. Even the future advantage cannot be effectually procured, if we be inattentive to the present security. But, as long as nations shall be so far mistaken, as to endure a complex government, and an extensive territory, coercion will be indispensably necessary to general security. It is therefore the duty of individuals to take an active share upon occasion, in so much coercion, and in such parts of the existing system, as shall be sufficient to counteract the growth of universal violence and tumult. It is unworthy of a rational enquirer to say, 'These things are necessary, but I am not obliged to take my share in them.' If they be necessary, they are necessary for the general welfare; of consequence, are virtuous, and what no just man will refuse to perform.

The duty of individuals is, in this respect, similar to the duty of independent communities, upon the subject of war. It is well known what has been the prevailing policy of princes under this head. Princes, especially the most active and enterprising among them, are seized with an inextinguishable rage for augmenting their dominions. The most innocent and inoffensive conduct on the part of their neighbours, will not, at all times, be a sufficient security against their ambition. They indeed seek to disguise their violence under plausible pretences; but it is well known that, where no such pretences occur, they are not, on that account, disposed to relinquish the pursuit. Let us imagine then a land of freemen invaded by one of these despots. What conduct does it behove them to adopt? We are not yet wise enough, to make the sword drop out of the hands of our oppressors, by the mere force of reason. Were we resolved, like Quakers, neither to oppose, nor, where it could be avoided, to submit to them, much bloodshed might perhaps be prevented: but a more lasting evil would result. They would fix garrisons in our country, and torment us with perpetual injustice. Supposing it were even granted, that, if the invaded nation should demean itself with unalterable constancy, the invaders would become tired of their fruitless usurpation, it would prove but little. At present we have to do, not with nations of philosophers, but with nations of men whose virtues are alloyed with weakness, fluctuation and inconstancy. At present it is our duty to consult, respecting the procedure which, to such nations, may be attended with the most favourable result. It is therefore proper, that we should choose the least calamitous mode, of obliging the enemy speedily to withdraw himself from our territories.

The case of individual defence is of the same nature. It does not appear, that any advantage can result from my forbearance, adequate to the disadvantages, of suffering my own life, or that of another, a peculiarly valuable member of the community, as it may happen, to become a prey to the first ruffian who inclines to destroy it. Forbearance, in this case, will be the conduct of a singular individual, and its effect may very probably be trifling. Hence it appears, that I ought to arrest the villain in the execution of his designs, though at the expense of a certain degree of coercion.

The case of an offender, who appears to be hardened in guilt, and to trade in the violation of social security, is clearly parallel to these. I ought to take up arms against the despot by whom my country is invaded, because my capacity does not enable me by arguments to prevail on him to desist, and because my countrymen will not preserve their intellectual independence in the midst of oppression. For the same reason I ought to take up arms against the domestic spoiler, because I am unable, either to persuade him to desist, or the community to adopt a just political institution, by means of which security might be maintained, consistently with the abolition of punishment.

To understand the full extent of this duty, it is incumbent upon us to remark, that anarchy as it is usually understood, and a well-conceived form of society without government, are exceedingly different from each other. If the government of Great Britain were dissolved tomorrow, unless that dissolution were the result of consistent and digested views of political truth previously disseminated among the inhabitants, it would be very far from leading to the abolition of violence. Individuals,

freed from the terrors by which they had been accustomed to be restrained, and not yet placed under the happier and more rational restraint
of public inspection, or convinced of the wisdom of reciprocal forbearance, would break out into acts of injustice, while other individuals,
who desired only that this irregularity should cease, would find themselves obliged to associate for its forcible suppression. We should have
all the evils and compulsory restraint attached to a regular government,
at the same time that we were deprived of that tranquillity and leisure
which are its only advantages.

It may not be useless in this place, to consider, more accurately than
we have hitherto done, the evils of anarchy. Such a review may afford
us a criterion by which to discern, as well the comparative value of
different institutions, as the precise degree of coercion which is required
for the exclusion of universal violence and tumult.

Anarchy, in its own nature, is an evil of short duration. The more
horrible are the mischiefs it inflicts, the more does it hasten to a close.
But it is nevertheless necessary that we should consider, both what is the
quantity of mischief it produces in a given period, and what is the scene
in which it promises to close. The first victim that is sacrificed at its
shrine, is personal security. Every man who has a secret foe, ought to
dread the dagger of that foe. There is no doubt that, in the worst anarchy,
multitudes of men will sleep in happy obscurity. But woe to him who,
by whatever means, excites the envy, the jealousy or the suspicion of his
neighbour! Unbridled ferocity instantly marks him for its prey. This is
indeed the principal evil of such a state, that the wisest, the brightest, the
most generous and bold, will often be most exposed to an immature fate.
In such a state we must bid farewell, to the patient lucubrations of the
philosopher, and the labour of the midnight oil. All is here, like the
society in which it exists, impatient and headlong. Mind will frequently
burst forth, but its appearance will be like the coruscations of the meteor,
not like the mild and equable illumination of the sun. Men, who start
forth into sudden energy, will resemble in temper the state that brought
them to this unlooked for greatness. They will be rigorous, unfeeling and
fierce; and their ungoverned passions will often not stop at equality,
but incite them to grasp at power.

With all these evils, we must not hastily conclude, that the mischiefs
of anarchy are worse than those which government is qualified to
produce. With respect to personal security, anarchy is perhaps a condition more deplorable than despotism;[1] but then it is to be considered,

---

[1] [Godwin's estimate of the relative worth of anarchy is noticeably lower in the third

that despotism is as perennial, as anarchy is transitory. Despotism, as it existed under the Roman emperors, marked out wealth for its victim, and the guilt of being rich never failed to convict the accused of every other crime. This despotism continued for centuries. Despotism, as it has existed in modern Europe, has been ever full of jealousy and intrigue, . . . He that dared utter a word against the tyrant, or endeavour to instruct his countrymen in their interests, was never secure that the next moment would not conduct him to a dungeon. . . . Nor was this all. An usurpation, that defied all the rules of justice, was obliged to purchase its own safety, by assisting tyranny through all its subordinate ranks. Hence the rights of nobility, of feudal vassalage, or primogeniture, of fines and inheritance. When the philosophy of law shall be properly understood, the true key to its spirit and history will probably be found, not, as some men have fondly imagined, in a desire to secure the happiness of mankind, but in the venal compact, by which superior tyrants have purchased the countenance and alliance of the inferior.

There is one point remaining in which anarchy and despotism are strongly contrasted with each other. Anarchy awakens thought, and diffuses energy and enterprise through the community, though it does not effect this in the best manner, as its fruits, forced into ripeness, must not be expected to have the vigorous stamina of true excellence. But, in despotism, mind is trampled into an equality of the most odious sort. Everything that promises greatness, is destined to fall under the exterminating hand of suspicion and envy. In despotism, there is no encouragement to excellence. Mind delights to expatiate in a field, where every species of distinction is within its reach. A scheme of policy, under which all men are fixed in classes, or levelled with the dust, affords it no encouragement to pursue its career. The inhabitants of countries in which despotism is complete, are frequently but a more vicious species of brutes. Oppression stimulates them to mischief and piracy, and superior force of mind often displays itself only, in deeper treachery, or more daring injustice.

One of the most interesting questions, in relation to anarchy, is that of the result in which it may be expected to terminate. The possibilities as to this termination, are as wide, as the various schemes of society which the human imagination can conceive. Anarchy may and has

edition than in the earlier ones. In the above passage, for example, in place of 'anarchy is perhaps a condition more deplorable than despotism', the first edition has: 'anarchy is certainly not worse than despotism', and the second edition reads: 'anarchy can scarcely be a much more deplorable state than despotism'.]

terminated in despotism; and, in that case, the introduction of anarchy will only serve to afflict us with variety of evils. It may lead to a modification of despotism, a milder and more equitable government than that which had gone before. It cannot immediately lead to the best form of society, since it necessarily leaves mankind in a state of ferment, which requires a strong hand to control, and a slow and wary process to tranquillize.[1]

The scene in which anarchy shall terminate, principally depends upon the state of mind by which it has been preceded. All mankind were in a state of anarchy, that is, without government, previously to their being in a state of policy. It would not be difficult to find, in the history of almost every country, a period of anarchy. The people of England were in a state of anarchy immediately before the Restoration. The Roman people were in a state of anarchy, at the moment of their secession to the Sacred Mountain.[2] Hence it follows that anarchy is neither so good nor so ill a thing in relation to its consequences, as it has sometimes been represented.[3]

Little good can be expected from any species of anarchy, that should subsist, for instance, among American savages. In order to anarchy being rendered a seed-plot of future justice, reflection and enquiry must have gone before, the regions of philosophy must have been penetrated, and political truth have opened her school to mankind. It is for this reason that the revolutions of the present age (for revolution is a species of anarchy), promise a more auspicious ultimate result, than the revolutions of any former period. For the same reason, the more anarchy can be held at bay, the more fortunate will it be for mankind. Falsehood may gain by precipitating the crisis; but a genuine and enlightened

---

[1] [The preceding sentence replaced the following five sentences which appeared in both earlier editions: 'And it does not seem impossible that it should lead to the best form of human society, that the most penetrating philosopher is able to conceive. Nay, it has something in it that suggests the likeness, a distorted and tremendous likeness, of true liberty. Anarchy has commonly been generated by the hatred of oppression. It is accompanied with a spirit of independence. It disengages men from prejudice and implicit faith, and in a certain degree incites them to an impartial scrutiny into the reason of their actions.']

[2] [A temporary migration of plebeians to a place outside Rome which was intended to secure concessions from the patricians.]

[3] [The first two editions continued: 'It is not reasonable to expect that a short period of anarchy should do the work of a long period of investigation and philosophy. When we say, that it disengages men from prejudice and implicit faith, this must be understood with much allowance. It tends to loosen the hold of these vermin upon the mind, but it does not instantly convert ordinary men into philosophers. Some prejudices, that were never fully incorporated with the intellectual habit, it destroys; but other prejudices it arms with fury, and converts into instruments of vengeance.']

philanthropy will wait, with unaltered patience, for the harvest of instruction. The arrival of that harvest may be slow, but it is perhaps infallible. If vigilance and wisdom be successful in their present opposition to anarchy, every benefit may ultimately be expected, untarnished with violence, and unstained with blood.

These observations are calculated to lead us to an accurate estimate of the mischiefs of anarchy, and, of consequence, to show the importance we are bound to attach to the exclusion of it. Government is frequently a source of peculiar evils; but an enlarged view will teach us to endure those evils, which experience seems to evince are inseparable, from the final benefit of mankind. From the savage state to the highest degree of civilization, the passage is long and arduous; and, if we aspire to the final result, we must submit to that portion of misery and vice, which necessarily fills the space between. If we would free ourselves from these inconveniences, unless our attempt be both skilful and cautious, we shall be in danger, by our impatience, of producing worse evils than those we would escape. Now it is the first principle of morality and justice, that directs us, where one of two evils is inevitable, to choose the least.[1] Of consequence, the wise and just man, being unable, as yet, to introduce the form of society which his understanding approves, will contribute to the support of so much coercion, as is necessary to exclude what is worse, anarchy.

If then constraint as the antagonist of constraint, must, in certain cases, and under temporary circumstances, be admitted, it is an interesting enquiry, to ascertain which of the three ends of punishment, already enumerated, must be selected, by the individuals by whom punishment is employed. And here it will be sufficient, very briefly to recollect the reasonings that have been stated under each of these heads.

It cannot be reformation. Reformation is improvement; and nothing can take place in a man worthy the name of improvement, otherwise than by an appeal to the unbiased judgement of his mind, and the essential feelings of his nature. If I would improve a man's character, who is there that knows not, that the only effectual mode is, by removing all extrinsic influences and incitements, by inducing him to observe, to

---

[1] [In the first two editions the preceding part of this paragraph reads: 'These observations are calculated to lead us to an accurate estimate of the mischiefs of anarchy, and prove that there are forms of coercion and government more injurious in their tendency than the absence of organization itself. They also prove that there are other forms of government which deserve in ordinary cases to be preferred to anarchy. Now it is incontrovertibly clear that, where one of two evils is inevitable, the wise and just man will choose the least.']

reason and enquire, by leading him to the forming a series of sentiments, that are truly his own, and not slavishly modelled upon the sentiments of another?

To conceive that compulsion and punishment are the proper means of reformation, is the sentiment of a barbarian; civilization and science are calculated to explode so ferocious an idea. It was once universally admitted and approved; it is now necessarily upon the decline.

Punishment must either ultimately succeed in imposing the sentiments it is employed to inculcate, upon the mind of the sufferer; or it must forcibly alienate him against them.

The last of these can never be the intention of its employer, or have a tendency to justify its application. If it were so, punishment ought to follow upon deviations from vice, not deviations from virtue. Yet to alienate the mind of the sufferer, from the individual that punishes, and from the sentiments he entertains, is perhaps the most common effect of punishment.

Let us suppose however, that its effect is of an opposite nature; that it produces obedience, and even a change of opinion. What sort of a being does it leave the man thus reformed? His opinions are not changed upon evidence. His conversion is the result of fear. Servility has operated that within him, which liberal enquiry and instruction were not able to do.

Punishment undoubtedly may change a man's behaviour. It may render his external conduct beneficial from injurious, though it is no very promising expedient for that purpose. But it cannot improve his sentiments, or lead him to the form of right proceeding but by the basest and most despicable motives. It leaves him a slave, devoted to an exclusive self-interest, and actuated by fear, the meanest of the selfish passions.

But it may be said, 'however strong may be the reasons I am able to communicate to a man in order to his reformation, he may be restless and impatient of expostulation, and of consequence render it necessary that I should retain him by force, till I can properly instil these reasons into his mind.' It must be remembered that the idea here, is not that of precaution, to prevent the mischiefs he might perpetrate, for that belongs to another of the three ends of punishment, that of restraint. But, separately from this idea, the argument is peculiarly weak. If the reasons I have to communicate be of an energetic and impressive nature, if they stand forward perspicuous and distinct in my own mind, it will be strange if they do not, at the outset, excite curiosity and attention in him to whom they are addressed. It is my duty to choose a proper season to communicate them, and not to betray the cause of justice by an ill-timed impatience. This prudence I should infallibly exercise, if my object were to obtain something interesting to myself; why should I be less quick-sighted when I purpose the benefit of another? It is a miserable way of preparing a man for conviction, to compel him by violence to hear an expostulation which he is eager to avoid.—These arguments prove, not that we should lose sight of reformation, if punishment for any other reason appear to be necessary; but that reformation cannot reasonably be made the object of punishment.

Punishment for the sake of example, is a theory that can never be justly maintained. The suffering proposed to be inflicted, considered absolutely, is either right or wrong. If it be right, it should be inflicted for its intrinsic recommendations. If it be wrong, what sort of example does it display? To do a thing for the sake of example, is, in other words, to do a thing today, in order to prove that I will do a similar thing tomorrow. This must always be a subordinate consideration. . . . He will display the best example, who carefully studies the principles of justice, and assiduously practises them. A better effect will be produced in human society by my conscientious adherence to them, than by my anxiety to create a specific expectation respecting my future conduct. . . . .

The third object of punishment according to the enumeration already made, is restraint. If punishment be, in any case, to be admitted, this is the only object it can reasonably propose to itself. The serious objections to which, even in this point of view, it is liable have been stated in another stage of the enquiry:[1] the amount of the necessity tending to supersede these objections, has also been considered.

The subject of this chapter is of great importance, in proportion to the length of time that may possibly elapse, before any considerable part of mankind shall be persuaded, to exchange the present complexity of political institution, for a mode which promises to supersede the necessity of punishment. It is highly unworthy of the cause of truth, to suppose that, during this interval, I have no active duties to perform, that I am not obliged to co-operate for the present welfare of the community, as well as for its future regeneration. The temporary obligation that arises out of this circumstance, exactly corresponds with what was formerly delivered on the subject of duty. Duty is the best possible application of a given power to the promotion of the general good.[2] But my power depends upon the disposition of the men by whom I am surrounded. If

[1] Ch. iii.   [2] II. iv.

I were enlisted in an army of cowards, it might be my duty to retreat, though, absolutely considered, it should have been the duty of the army to come to blows. Under every possible circumstance, it is my duty to advance the general good, by the best means which the circumstances under which I am placed will admit.

CHAPTER VI

SCALE OF PUNISHMENT

I T is time to proceed to the consideration of certain inferences that may be deduced from the theory of punishment which has now been delivered; nor can anything be of greater importance than these inferences will be found, to the virtue, the happiness and improvement of mankind.

And, first, it evidently follows that punishment is an act of painful necessity, inconsistent with the true character and genius of mind, the practice of which is temporarily imposed upon us by the corruption and ignorance that reign among mankind. Nothing can be more absurd, than to look to it as a source of improvement. . . . Nothing can be more unjust, than to have recourse to it, but upon the most unquestionable emergency. Instead of multiplying occasions of coercion, and applying it as the remedy of every moral evil, the true politician will anxiously confine it within the narrowest limits, and perpetually seek to diminish the occasions of its employment. There is but one reason which can, in any case, be admitted as its apology, and that is, where the allowing the offender to be at large shall be notoriously hazardous to public security.

Secondly, the consideration of restraint as the only justifiable ground of punishment, will furnish us with a simple and satisfactory criterion by which to measure the justice of the suffering inflicted.

.   .   .   .

To deprive an offender of his life in any manner, will appear to be unjust, as it seems always sufficiently practicable, without this, to prevent him from further offence. Privation of life, though by no means the greatest injury that can be inflicted, must always be considered as a very serious injury; since it puts a perpetual close upon the prospects of the sufferer, as to all the enjoyments, the virtues and the excellence of a human being.

... If there be any man whom it may be necessary, for the safety of the whole, to put under restraint, this circumstance is a powerful plea to the humanity and justice of those who conduct the affairs of the community, in his behalf. This is the man who most stands in need of their assistance. If they treated him with kindness, instead of supercilious and unfeeling neglect, if they made him understand with how much reluctance they had been induced to employ the force of the society against him, if they represented the true state of the case with calmness, perspicuity and benevolence, to his mind, if they employed those precautions, which an humane disposition would not fail to suggest, to keep from him the motives of corruption and obstinacy, his reformation would be almost infallible. These are the prospects to which his wants and his misfortunes powerfully entitle him; and it is from these prospects that the hand of the executioner cuts him off for ever.

.   .   .   .

The true reasons, in consequence of which these forlorn and deserted members of the community are brought to an ignominious death, are, first, the peculiar iniquity of the civil institutions of that community, and, secondly, the supineness and apathy of their superiors. In republican and simple forms of government, punishments are rare, and the punishment of death almost unknown. On the other hand, the more there is in any country of inequality and oppression, the more punishments are multiplied. The more the institutions of society contradict the genuine sentiments of the human mind, the more severely is it necessary to avenge their violation. ...

.   .   .   .

The justice of punishment is built upon this simple principle: Every man is bound to employ such means as shall suggest themselves, for preventing evils subversive of general security, it being first ascertained, either by experience or reasoning, that all milder methods are inadequate to the exigency of the case. The conclusion from this principle is, that we are bound, under certain urgent circumstances, to deprive the offender of the liberty he has abused. Further than this perhaps no circumstance can authorize us. He whose person is imprisoned (if that be the right kind of seclusion), cannot interrupt the peace of his fellow; and the infliction of further evil, when his power to injure is removed, is the wild and unauthorized dictate of vengeance and rage, the wanton sport of unquestioned superiority.

.   .   .   .

... there is one circumstance, by means of which restraint and reformation are closely connected. The person of the offender is to be restrained, as long as the public safety would be endangered by his liberation. But the public safety will cease to be endangered, as soon as his propensities and dispositions have undergone a change. The connection which thus results from the nature of things, renders it necessary, that, in deciding upon the species of restraint to be imposed, these circumstances be considered jointly, how the personal liberty of the offender may be least entrenched upon, and how his reformation may be best promoted.

The most common method pursued in depriving the offender of the liberty he has abused, is to erect a public jail, in which offenders of every description are thrust together, and left to form among themselves what species of society they can. Various circumstances contribute to imbue them with habits of indolence and vice, and to discourage industry; and no effort is made to remove or soften these circumstances. It cannot be necessary to expatiate upon the atrociousness of this system. Jails are, to a proverb, seminaries of vice; and he must be an uncommon proficient in the passion and the practice of injustice, or a man of sublime virtue, who does not come out of them a much worse man than he entered.

An active observer of mankind,[1] with the purest intentions, and who had paid a singular attention to this subject, was struck with the mischievous tendency of the reigning system, and called the attention of the public to a scheme of solitary imprisonment. But this, though free from the defects of the established mode, is liable to very weighty objections.

.   .   .   .   .

... To be virtuous, it is requisite that we should consider men, and their relation to each other. As a preliminary to this study, is it necessary that we should be shut out from the society of men? Shall we be most effectually formed to justice, benevolence and prudence in our intercourse with each other, in a state of solitude? Will not our selfish and unsocial dispositions be perpetually increased? What temptation has he to think of benevolence or justice, who has no opportunity to exercise it? The true soil in which atrocious crimes are found to germinate, is a gloomy and morose disposition. Will his heart become much either softened or expanded, who breathes the atmosphere of a dungeon? Surely it would be better in this respect to imitate the system of the universe, and, if we would teach justice and humanity, transplant those we would teach into a simple and reasonable state of society. Solitude,

---

[1] Mr. [John] Howard [1726–90].

absolutely considered, may instigate us to serve ourselves, but not to serve our neighbours. Solitude, imposed under too few limitations, may be a nursery for madmen and idiots, but not for useful members of society.

. . . .

CHAPTER VIII

OF LAW

. . . of great importance in the trial of offences, is . . . the method to be pursued by us in classing them, and the consequent apportioning the degree of animadversion to the cases that may arise. This article brings us to the direct consideration of law, which is, without doubt, one of the most important topics upon which human intellect can be employed. It is law, that has hitherto been regarded, in countries calling themselves civilized, as the standard, by which to measure all offences and irregularities that fall under public animadversion. Let us fairly investigate the merits of this choice.

The comparison which has presented itself, to those by whom the topic has been investigated, has hitherto been between law on one side, and the arbitrary will of a despot on the other. But if we would estimate truly the merits of law, we should first consider it, as it is in itself, and then, if necessary, search for the most eligible principle that may be substituted in its place.

It has been recommended, as 'affording information to the different members of the community, respecting the principles which will be adopted in deciding upon their actions.' It has been represented as the highest degree of iniquity, 'to try men by an *ex post facto* law, or indeed in any other manner, than by the letter of a law, formally made, and sufficiently promulgated.'

How far it will be safe altogether to annihilate this principle, we shall presently have occasion to enquire. It is obvious, at first sight, to remark, that it is of most importance, in a country where the system of jurisprudence is most capricious and absurd. If it be deemed criminal in any society to wear clothes of a particular texture, or buttons of a particular composition, it is unavoidable to exclaim, that it is high time the jurisprudence of that society should inform its members what are the fantastic rules by which they mean to proceed. But, if a society be contented with the rules of justice, and do not assume to itself the right of distorting or adding to those rules, there law is evidently a less necessary institution. The rules of justice would be more clearly and effectually taught, by an actual intercourse with human society, unrestrained by the fetters of prepossession, than they can be by catechisms and codes.[1]

One result of the institution of law, is, that the institution, once begun, can never be brought to a close. Edict is heaped upon edict, and volume upon volume. . . .

There is no maxim more clear than this, 'Every case is a rule to itself.' No action of any man, was ever the same as any other action, had ever the same degree of utility or injury. It should seem to be the business of justice, to distinguish the qualities of men, and not, which has hitherto been the practice, to confound them. But what has been the result of an attempt to do this in relation to law? As new cases occur, the law is perpetually found deficient. How should it be otherwise? Lawgivers have not the faculty of unlimited prescience, and cannot define that which is boundless. The alternative that remains, is, either to wrest the law to include a case which was never in the contemplation of its authors, or to make a new law to provide for this particular case. Much has been done in the first of these modes. The quibbles of lawyers, and the arts by which they refine and distort the sense of the law, are proverbial. But, though much is done, everything cannot be thus done. The abuse will sometimes be too palpable. Not to say, that the very education that enables the lawyer, when he is employed for the prosecutor, to find out offences the lawgiver never meant, enables him, when he is employed for the defendant, to discover subterfuges, that reduce the law to a nullity. It is therefore perpetually necessary to make new laws. These laws, in order to escape evasion, are frequently tedious, minute and circumlocutory. The volume in which justice records her prescriptions, is for ever increasing, and the world would not contain the books that might be written.

The consequence of the infinitude of law, is its uncertainty. This strikes at the principle upon which law is founded. Laws were made, to put an end to ambiguity, and that each man might know what he had to expect. How well have they answered this purpose? Let us instance in the article of property. Two men go to law for a certain estate. They would not go to law, if they had not both of them an opinion of their success. But we may suppose them partial in their own case. They would not continue to go to law, if they were not both promised success

[1] VI. viii.

by their lawyers. Law was made, that a plain man might know what he had to expect; and yet the most skilful practitioners differ about the event of my suit. It will sometimes happen, that the most celebrated pleader in the kingdom, or the first counsel in the service of the crown, shall assure me of infallible success, five minutes before another law-officer, styled the keeper of the king's conscience, by some unexpected juggle decides it against me. Would the issue have been equally uncertain, if I had had nothing to trust to, but the plain unperverted sense of a jury of my neighbours, founded in the ideas they entertained of general justice? Lawyers have absurdly maintained, that the expensiveness of law is necessary to prevent the unbounded multiplication of suits; but the true source of this multiplication is uncertainty. Men do not quarrel about that which is evident, but that which is obscure.

He that would study the laws of a country accustomed to legal security, must begin with the volumes of the statutes. He must add a strict enquiry into the common or unwritten law; and he ought to digress into the civil, the ecclesiastical and canon law. To understand the intention of the authors of a law, he must be acquainted with their characters and views, and with the various circumstances, to which it owed its rise, and by which it was modified while under deliberation. To understand the weight and interpretation that will be allowed to it in a court of justice, he must have studied the whole collection of records, decisions and precedents. Law was originally devised, that ordinary men might know what they had to expect; and there is not, at this day, a lawyer existing in Great Britain, vainglorious enough to pretend that he has mastered the code. Nor must it be forgotten that time and industry, even were they infinite, would not suffice. It is a labyrinth without end; it is a mass of contradictions that cannot be disentangled. Study will enable the lawyer to find in it plausible, perhaps unanswerable, arguments for any side of almost any question; but it would argue the utmost folly, to suppose, that the study of law can lead to knowledge and certainty.

A further consideration that will demonstrate the absurdity of law in its most general acceptation, is, that it is of the nature of prophecy. Its task is to describe what will be the actions of mankind, and to dictate decisions respecting them. Its merits, in this respect, have already been decided under the head of promises.[1] The language of such a procedure is, 'We are so wise, that we can draw no additional knowledge from circumstances as they occur; and we pledge ourselves that, if it be otherwise, the additional knowledge we acquire, shall produce no effect upon

[1] III. iii.

our conduct.' It is proper to observe, that this subject of law, may be considered, in some respects, as more properly belonging to the topic of the preceding book. Law tends, no less than creeds, catechisms and tests, to fix the human mind in a stagnant condition, and to substitute a principle of permanence, in the room of that unceasing progress which is the only salubrious element of mind. All the arguments therefore which were employed upon that occasion, may be applied to the subject now under consideration.

. . . .

From all these considerations we can scarcely hesitate to conclude universally, that law is an institution of the most pernicious tendency.

The subject will receive some additional elucidation, if we consider the perniciousness of law, in its immediate relation to those who practise it. If there ought to be no such thing as law, the profession of a lawyer is no doubt entitled to our disapprobation. A lawyer can scarcely fail to be a dishonest man. This is less a subject for censure, than for regret. Men are, in an eminent degree, the creatures of the circumstances under which they are placed. He that is habitually goaded by the incentives of vice, will not fail to be vicious. He that is perpetually conversant in quibbles, false colours and sophistry, cannot equally cultivate the generous emotions of the soul, and the nice discernment of rectitude. . . .

Let us however suppose, a circumstance which is perhaps altogether impossible, that a man shall be a perfectly honest lawyer. He is determined to plead no cause, that he does not believe to be just, and to employ no argument, that he does not apprehend to be solid. He designs, as far as his sphere extends, to strip law of its ambiguities, and to speak the manly language of reason. This man is, no doubt, highly respectable, so far as relates to himself; but it may be questioned whether he be not a more pernicious member of society, than the dishonest lawyer. The hopes of mankind in relation to their future progress, depend upon their observing the genuine effects of erroneous institutions. But this man is employed in softening and masking these effects. His conduct has a direct tendency to postpone the reign of sound policy, and to render mankind tranquil in the midst of imperfection and ignorance.

. . . .

The only principle which can be substituted in the room of law, is that of reason exercising an uncontrolled jurisdiction upon the circumstances of the case. To this principle no objection can arise on the score of wisdom. It is not to be supposed that there are not men now existing, whose intellectual accomplishments rise to the level of law. Law we sometimes call the wisdom of our ancestors. But this is a strange imposition. It was as frequently the dictate of their passion, of timidity, jealousy, a monopolizing spirit, and a lust of power that knew no bounds. Are we not obliged perpetually to revise and remodel this misnamed wisdom of our ancestors? to correct it by a detection of their ignorance, and a censure of their intolerance? But if men can be found among us, whose wisdom is equal to the wisdom of law, it will scarcely be maintained, that the truths they have to communicate, will be the worse, for having no authority, but that which they derive from the reasons that support them.

It may however be alleged that, '... Law may be supposed to have been constructed in the tranquil serenity of the soul, a suitable monitor, to check the inflamed mind, with which the recent memory of ills might induce us to proceed to the infliction of punishment.' This is the most considerable argument that can be adduced in favour of the prevailing system, and therefore deserves a mature examination.

. . . . .

. . . whatever inconveniences may arise from the passions of men, the introduction of fixed laws cannot be the genuine remedy. . . . Inexperience and zeal would prompt me to restrain my neighbour whenever he is acting wrong, and, by penalties and inconveniences designedly interposed, to cure him of his errors. But reason evinces the folly of this proceeding, and teaches me that, if he be not accustomed to depend upon the energies of intellect, he will never rise to the dignity of a rational being. As long as a man is held in the trammels of obedience, and habituated to look to some foreign guidance for the direction of his conduct, his understanding and the vigour of his mind will sleep. Do I desire to raise him to the energy of which he is capable? I must teach him to feel himself, to bow to no authority, to examine the principles he entertains, and render to his mind the reason of his conduct.

The habits which are thus salutary to the individual, will be equally salutary in the transactions of communities. Men are weak at present, because they have always been told they are weak, and must not be trusted with themselves. Take them out of their shackles, bid them enquire, reason and judge, and you will soon find them very different beings. Tell them that they have passions, are occasionally hasty, intemperate and injurious, but they must be trusted with themselves. Tell them that the mountains of parchment in which they have been hitherto entrenched, are fit only to impose upon ages of superstition and ignorance; that henceforth we will have no dependence but upon their spontaneous justice; that, if their passions be gigantic, they must rise with gigantic energy to subdue them; that, if their decrees be iniquitous, the iniquity shall be all their own. The effect of this disposition of things will soon be visible; mind will rise to the level of its situation; juries and umpires will be penetrated with the magnitude of the trust reposed in them.

．　　．　　．　　．

The juridical decisions that were made immediately after the abolition of law, would differ little from those during its empire. They would be the decisions of prejudice and habit. But habit, having lost the centre about which it revolved, would diminish in the regularity of its operations. Those to whom the arbitration of any question was entrusted, would frequently recollect, that the whole case was committed to their deliberation; and they could not fail occasionally to examine themselves, respecting the reason of those principles which had hitherto passed uncontroverted. Their understandings would grow enlarged, in proportion as they felt the importance of their trust, and the unbounded freedom of their investigation. Here then would commence an auspicious order of things, of which no understanding of man at present in existence can foretell the result, the dethronement of implicit faith, and the inauguration of reason and justice.

．　　．　　．　　．

An observation which cannot have escaped the reader in the perusal of this chapter, is, that law is merely relative to the exercise of political force, and must perish when the necessity for that force ceases, if the influence of truth do not still sooner extirpate it from the practice of mankind.

BOOK VIII

OF PROPERTY

CHAPTER I

PRELIMINARY OBSERVATIONS

THE subject of property is the keystone that completes the fabric of political justice. According as our ideas respecting it are crude or correct, they will enlighten us as to the consequences of a *simple form of society without government*, and remove the prejudices that attach us to complexity. There is nothing that more powerfully tends to distort our *judgement* and *opinions*, than erroneous notions concerning the goods of fortune. Finally, the period that must put an end to the system of *coercion* and *punishment*, is intimately connected with the circumstance of property's being placed upon an equitable basis.

. . . . .

The subject to which the doctrine of property relates, is, all those things which conduce, or may be conceived to conduce, to the benefit or pleasure of man, and which can no otherwise be applied to the use of one or more persons, than by a permanent or temporary exclusion of the rest of the species. Such things in particular are food, clothing, habitation and furniture.

Upon this subject two questions unavoidably arise. Who is the person entitled to the use of any particular article of this kind? Who is the person, in whose hands the preservation and distribution of any number of these articles, will be most justly and beneficially vested?

The answer to the first of these questions, is easy, upon the principles of the present work. Justice has been proved to be a rule applicable to all the concerns of man. It pronounces upon every case that can arise, and leaves nothing to the disposal of a momentary caprice.[1] There is not an

[1] II. ii.

article of the kinds above specified, which will not ultimately be the instrument of more benefit and happiness, in one individual mode of application, than in any other that can be devised. This is the application it ought to receive.

. . . Every man has a right to that, the exclusive possession of which being awarded to him, a greater sum of benefit or pleasure will result, than could have arisen from its being otherwise appropriated. This is the same principle as that just delivered, with a slight variation of form. . . .

Let us see how this principle will operate in the inferences it authorizes us to make. Human beings are partakers of a common nature; what conduces to the benefit or pleasure of one man, will conduce to the benefit or pleasure of another.[1] Hence it follows, upon the principles of equal and impartial justice, that the good things of the world are a common stock, upon which one man has as valid a title as another to draw for what he wants. It appears in this respect, as formerly it appeared in the case of our claim to the forbearance of each other,[2] that each man has a sphere, the limit and termination of which is marked out, by the equal sphere of his neighbour. I have a right to the means of subsistence; he has an equal right. I have a right to every pleasure I can participate without injury to myself or others; his title, in this respect is of similar extent.

This view of the subject will appear the more striking, if we pass in review the good things of the world. They may be divided into four classes; subsistence; the means of intellectual and moral improvement; unexpensive gratifications; and such gratifications, as are by no means essential to healthful and vigorous existence, and cannot be purchased but with considerable labour and industry. It is the last class principally that interposes an obstacle in the way of equal distribution. It will be matter of after-consideration how far and how many articles of this class would be admissible into the purest mode of social existence.[4] But, in the meantime, it is unavoidable to remark the inferiority of this class to the three preceding. Without it we may enjoy to a great extent, activity, contentment and cheerfulness. And in what manner are these seeming superfluities usually procured? By abridging multitudes of men, to a deplorable degree, in points of essential moment, that one man may be accommodated, with sumptuous yet, strictly considered, insignificant luxuries. . . .

[1] II. iii, p. 78.   [2] II. v, p. 89.   [3] Ch. vii.

To the forming a just estimate of costly gratifications, it is necessary, that we should abstract the direct pleasure, on the one hand, from the pleasure they afford us, only as instruments for satisfying our love of distinction. It must be admitted in every system of morality, . . . that, . . . we ought not to refuse any pleasure, except as it tends to the exclusion of some greater pleasure.[1] But it has already been shown,[2] that the difference in the pleasures of the palate, between a simple and wholesome diet on the one hand, and all the complexities of the most splendid table on the other, is so small, that few men would even think it worth the tedium that attends upon a change of services, if the pleasure of the palate were the only thing in question, and they had no spectator to admire their magnificence. . . . The same observation applies to the splendour of furniture, equipage and dress. . . .

. . . How many of these things would engage his attention, if he lived in a desert island, and had no spectator of his economy? If we survey the appendages of our persons, there is scarcely an article that is not in some respect an appeal to the goodwill of our neighbours, or a refuge against their contempt. It is for this that the merchant braves the perils of the ocean, and the mechanical inventor brings forth the treasures of his meditation. The soldier advances even to the cannon's mouth, and the statesman exposes himself to the rage of an indignant people, because he cannot bear to pass through life without distinction and esteem. Exclusively of certain higher motives which will hereafter be mentioned,[3] this is the purpose of all the great exertions of mankind. The man who has nothing to provide for but his animal wants, scarcely ever shakes off the lethargy of his mind; but the love of honour hurries us on to the most incredible achievements.

It must be admitted indeed, that the love of distinction appears, from experience and the past history of mankind, to have been their ruling passion. But the love of distinction is capable of different directions. At present, there is no more certain road to the general deference of mankind, than the exhibition of wealth. The poet, the wit, the orator, the saviour of his country, and the ornament of his species, may upon certain occasions be treated with neglect and biting contempt; but the man who possesses and disburses money in profusion, can scarcely fail to procure the attendance of the obsequious man and the flatterer. But let us conceive this erroneous and pernicious estimate of things to be reversed. Let us suppose the avaricious man, who is desirous of monopolizing the means of happiness, and the luxurious man, who expends without

---

[1] IV. xi, p. 185.   [2] I. v, pp. 48.   [3] Ch. vi.

limitation, in pampering his appetites, that which, in strict justice, is the right of another, to be contemplated with as much disapprobation, as they are now beheld by a mistaken world with deference and respect. Let us imagine the direct and unambiguous road to public esteem, to be the acquisition of talent, or the practice of virtue, the cultivation of some species of ingenuity, or the display of some generous and expansive sentiment; and that the persons who possess these talents, were as conspicuously treated with affection and esteem, as the wealthy are now treated with slavish attention. This is merely, in other words, to suppose good sense, and clear and correct perceptions, at some time to gain the ascendancy in the world. But it is plain that, under the reign of such sentiments, the allurements that now wait upon costly gratification, would be, for the most part, annihilated. If, through the spurious and incidental recommendations it derives from the love of distinction, it is now rendered, to many, a principal source of agreeable sensation, under a different state of opinion, it would, not merely be reduced to its intrinsic value in point of sensation, but, in addition to this, would be connected with ideas of injustice, unpopularity and dislike. . . .

. . . . .

The doctrine of the injustice of accumulated property, has been the foundation of all religious morality. Its most energetic teachers have been irresistibly led to assert the precise truth in this respect. . . . But, . . . the majority of its professors have been but too apt to treat the practice of justice, not as a debt, which it ought to be considered, but as an affair of spontaneous generosity and bounty.

The effect which is produced by this accommodating doctrine, is, to place the supply of our wants in the disposal of a few, enabling them to make a show of generosity with what is not truly their own, and to purchase the submission of the poor by the payment of a debt. Theirs is a system of clemency and charity, instead of a system of justice. It fills the rich with unreasonable pride, by the spurious denominations with which it decorates their acts; and the poor with servility, by leading them to regard the slender comforts they obtain, not as their incontrovertible due, but as the good pleasure and grace of their opulent neighbours.

CHAPTER II

PRINCIPLES OF PROPERTY

HAVING considered at large the question of the person entitled to the use of the means of benefit or pleasure, it is time that we proceed to the second question, of the person, in whose hands the preservation and distribution of any of these means, will be most justly and beneficially vested. . . .

. . . . .

Of property there are three degrees.

The first and simplest degree, is that of my permanent right in those things, the use of which being attributed to me, a greater sum of benefit or pleasure will result, than could have arisen from their being otherwise appropriated. It is of no consequence, in this case, how I came into possession of them, the only necessary conditions being, their superior usefulness to me, and that my title to them is such as is generally acquiesced in, by the community in which I live. Every man is unjust, who conducts himself in such a manner respecting these things, as to infringe, in any degree, upon my power of using them, at the time when the using them will be of real importance to me.

It has already appeared[1] that one of the most essential of the rights of man, is my right to the forbearance of others; not merely that they shall refrain from everything that may, by direct consequence, affect my life, or the possession of my powers, but that they shall refrain from usurping upon my understanding, and shall leave me a certain equal sphere for the exercise of my private judgement. This is necessary, because it is possible for them to be wrong, as well as for me to be so, because the exercise of the understanding is essential to the improvement of man, and because the pain and interruption I suffer, are as real, when they infringe, in my conception only, upon what is of importance to me, as if the infringement had been, in the utmost degree, palpable. Hence it follows, that no man may, in ordinary cases, make use of my apartment, furniture or garments, or of my food, in the way of barter or loan, without having first obtained my consent.

The second degree of property, is the empire to which every man is entitled, over the produce of his own industry, even that part of it the

---

[1] II. v and vi.

use of which ought not to be appropriated to himself. It has been repeatedly shown that all the rights of man which are of this description, are passive.[1] He has no right of option in the disposal of anything which may fall into his hands. Every shilling of his property, and even every, the minutest, exertion of his powers, have received their destination from the decrees of justice. He is only the steward. But still he is the steward. These things must be trusted to his award, checked only by the censorial power that is vested, in the general sense, and favourable or unfavourable opinion, of that portion of mankind among whom he resides. Man is changed, from the capable subject of illimitable excellence, into the vilest and most despicable thing that imagination can conceive, when he is restrained from acting upon the dictates of his understanding. All men cannot individually be entitled to exercise compulsion on each other, for this would produce universal anarchy. All men cannot collectively be entitled to exercise unbounded compulsion, for this would produce universal slavery: the interference of government, however impartially vested, is, no doubt, only to be resorted to, upon occasions of rare occurrence, and indispensable urgency.

It will readily be perceived, that this second species of property, is in a less rigorous sense fundamental, than the first. It is, in one point of view, a sort of usurpation. It vests in me the preservation and dispensing of that, which in point of complete and absolute right belongs to you.

The third degree of property, is that which occupies the most vigilant attention in the civilized states of Europe. It is a system, in whatever manner established, by which one man enters into the faculty of disposing of the produce of another man's industry. There is scarcely any species of wealth, expenditure or splendour, existing in any civilized country, that is not, in some way, produced, by the express manual labour, and corporeal industry, of the inhabitants of that country. The spontaneous productions of the earth are few, and contribute little to wealth, expenditure or splendour. Every man may calculate, in every glass of wine he drinks, and every ornament he annexes to his person, how many individuals have been condemned to slavery and sweat, incessant drudgery, unwholesome food, continual hardships, deplorable ignorance, and brutal insensibility, that he may be supplied with these luxuries. It is a gross imposition, that men are accustomed to put upon themselves, when they talk of the property bequeathed to them by their ancestors. The property is produced by the daily labour of men who are now in existence. All that their ancestors bequeathed to them, was a

[1] II. v.

mouldy patent, which they show, as a title to extort from their neighbours what the labour of those neighbours has produced.

It is clear therefore that the third species of property, is in direct contradiction to the second.

The most desirable state of human society would require, that the quantity of manual labour and corporeal industry to be exerted, and particularly that part of it which is not the uninfluenced choice of our own judgement, but is imposed upon each individual by the necessity of his affairs, should be reduced within as narrow limits as possible. For any man to enjoy the most trivial accommodation, while, at the same time, a similar accommodation is not accessible to every other member of the community, is, absolutely speaking, wrong. All refinements of luxury, all inventions that tend to give employment to a great number of labouring hands, are directly adverse to the propagation of happiness. Every additional tax that is laid on, every new channel that is opened for the expenditure of the public money, unless it be compensated (which is scarcely ever the case) by an equivalent deduction from the luxuries of the rich, is so much added to the general stock of ignorance, drudgery and hardship. The country gentleman who, by levelling an eminence, or introducing a sheet of water into his park, finds work for hundreds of industrious poor, is the enemy, and not, as has commonly been imagined, the friend, of his species.[1] Let us suppose that, in any country, there is now ten times as much industry and manual labour, as there was three centuries ago. Except so far as this is applied to maintain an increased population, it is expended in the more costly indulgences of the rich. Very little indeed is employed to increase the happiness or conveniences of the poor. They barely subsist at present, and they did as much at the remoter period of which we speak. Those who, by fraud or force, have usurped the power of buying and selling the labour of the great mass of the community, are sufficiently disposed to take care that they should never do more than subsist. An object of industry added to or taken from the general stock, produces a momentary difference, but things speedily fall back into their former state. If every labouring inhabitant of Great Britain were able and willing today to double the quantity of his industry, for a short time he would derive some advantage from the increased stock of commodities produced. But the rich would speedily discover the means of monopolizing this produce, as they had done the former. A small part of it only, could consist in commodities essential to the subsistence of man, or be fairly distributed through the

[1] [Cf. pp. 313-19.]

community. All that is luxury and superfluity, would increase the accommodations of the rich, and perhaps, by reducing the price of luxuries, augment the number of those to whom such accommodations were accessible. But it would afford no alleviation to the great mass of the community. Its more favoured members would give their inferiors no greater wages for twenty hours' labour, suppose, than they now do for ten.

What reason is there then that this species of property should be respected? Because, ill as the system is, it will perhaps be found, that it is better than any other, which, by any means, except those of reason, the love of distinction, or the love of justice, can be substituted in its place. It is not easy to say whether misery or absurdity would be most conspicuous, in a plan which should invite every man to seize, upon everything he conceived himself to want. If, by positive institution, the property of every man were equalized today, without a contemporary change in men's dispositions and sentiments, it would become unequal tomorrow. The same evils would spring up with a rapid growth; and we should have gained nothing, by a project, which, while it violated every man's habits, and many men's inclinations, would render thousands miserable. We have already shown,[1] and shall have occasion to show more at large,[2] how pernicious the consequences would be, if government were to take the whole permanently into their hands, and dispense to every man his daily bread. It may even be suspected that agrarian laws, and others of a similar tendency, which have been invented for the purpose of keeping down the spirit of accumulation, deserve to be regarded, as remedies, more pernicious, than the disease they are intended to cure.[3]

An interesting question suggests itself in this stage of the discussion. How far is the idea of property to be considered as the offspring of positive institution? The decision of this question, may prove extremely essential to the point upon which we are engaged. The regulation of property by positive laws, may be a very exceptionable means of reforming its present inequality, at the same time that an equal objection may by no means lie, against a proceeding, the object of which shall be merely to supersede positive laws, or such positive laws as are peculiarly exceptionable.

In pursuing this enquiry, it is necessary to institute a distinction, between such positive laws, or established practices (which are often found little less efficacious than laws), as are peculiar to certain ages and

[1] VI, viii, p. 237.   [2] Ch. viii.   [3] VI. i, p. 224.

countries, and such laws or practices, as are common to all civilized communities, and may therefore be perhaps interwoven with the existence of society.

The idea of property, or permanent empire, in those things which ought to be applied to our personal use, and still more in the produce of our industry, unavoidably suggests the idea of some species of law or practice by which it is guaranteed. Without this, property could not exist. Yet we have endeavoured to show, that the maintenance of these two kinds of property, is highly beneficial. Let us consider the consequences that grow out of this position.

Every man should be urged to the performance of his duty, as much as possible, by the instigations of reason alone.[1] Compulsion to be exercised by one human being over another, whether individually, or in the name of the community, if in any case to be resorted to, is at least to be resorted to only in cases of indispensable urgency. It is not therefore to be called in, for the purpose of causing one individual to exert a little more, or another a little less, of productive industry. Neither is it to be called in, for the purpose of causing the industrious individual to make the precise distribution of his produce which he ought to make. Hence it follows that, while the present erroneous opinions and prejudices respecting accumulation continue, actual accumulation will, in some degree, take place.

For, let it be observed that, not only no well-informed community will interfere with the quantity of any man's industry, or the disposal of its produce, but the members of every such well-informed community will exert themselves, to turn aside the purpose of any man who shall be inclined, to dictate to, or restrain, his neighbour in this respect.

The most destructive of all excesses, is that, where one man shall dictate to another, or undertake to compel him to do, or refrain from doing, anything (except, as was before stated, in cases of the most indispensable urgency), otherwise than with his own consent. Hence it follows that the distribution of wealth in every community, must be left to depend upon the sentiments of the individuals of that community. If, in any society, wealth be estimated at its true value, and accumulation and monopoly be regarded as the seals of mischief, injustice and dishonour, instead of being treated as titles to attention and deference, in that society the accommodations of human life will tend to their level, and the inequality of conditions will be destroyed.[2] A revolution of opinions is the only means of attaining to this inestimable benefit.

---

[1] II. vi; Book VII, *passim*.　　[2] Ch. i, p. 280.

Every attempt to effect this purpose by means of regulation, will probably be found ill conceived and abortive. Be this as it will, every attempt to correct the distribution of wealth by individual violence, is certainly to be regarded as hostile to the first principles of public security.

If one individual, by means of greater ingenuity or more indefatigable industry, obtain a greater proportion of the necessaries or conveniences of life than his neighbour, and, having obtained them, determine to convert them into the means of permanent inequality, this proceeding is not of a sort that it would be just or wise to undertake to repress by means of coercion. If, inequality being thus introduced, the poorer member of the community, shall be so depraved as to be willing, or so unfortunately circumstanced as to be driven, to make himself the hired servant or labourer of his richer neighbour, this probably is not an evil to be corrected by the interposition of government. But, when we have gained this step, it will be difficult to set bounds to the extent of accumulation in one man, or of poverty and wretchedness in another.

It has already appeared, that reason requires that no man shall endeavour, by individual violence, to correct this inequality. Reason would probably, in a well-ordered community, be sufficient to restrain men from the attempt so to correct it. Where society existed in the simplicity which has formerly been described,[1] accumulation itself would be restrained, by the very means that restrained depredation, the good sense of the community, and the inspection of all exercised upon all. Violence therefore would, on the one hand, have little to tempt it, as, on the other, it would be incessantly and irresistibly repressed.

But, if reason prove insufficient for this fundamental purpose, other means must doubtless be employed.[2] It is better that one man should suffer, than that the community should be destroyed. General security is one of those indispensable preliminaries, without which nothing good or excellent can be accomplished. It is therefore right that property, with all its inequalities, such as it is sanctioned by the general sense of the members of any state, and so long as that sanction continues unvaried should be defended, if need be, by means of coercion.

We have already endeavoured to show, that coercion would probably, in no case, be necessary, but for the injudicious magnitude and complication of political societies.[3] In a general and absolute sense therefore, it cannot be vindicated. But there are duties incumbent upon us, of a temporary and local nature; and we may occasionally be required, by the

[1] V. xxiv.   [2] VII. v.   [3] VII. v.

pressure of circumstances, to suspend and contravene principles, the most sound in their general nature.[1] Till men shall be persuaded to part with the ideas of a complicated government and an extensive territory, coercion will be necessary, as an expedient to counteract the most imminent evils. There are however various reasons, that would incline a just man to confine the province of coercion within the severest limits. It is never to be regarded but as a temporary expedient, the necessity of having recourse to which is deeply to be regretted. It is an expedient, protecting one injustice, the accumulation of property, for the sake of keeping out another evil, still more formidable and destructive. Lastly, it is to be considered that this injustice, the unequal distribution of property, the grasping and selfish spirit of individuals, is to be regarded as one of the original sources of government, and, as it rises in its excesses, is continually demanding and necessitating new injustice, new penalties, and new slavery.

Thus far then it should seem the system of coercion must be permitted to extend. We should set bounds to no man's accumulation. We should repress by wise and effectual, yet moderate and humane, penalties, all forcible invasion to be committed by one man upon the acquisitions of another. But it may be asked, are there not various laws or practices, established among civilized nations, which do not, like these we have described, stop at the toleration of unequal property, but which operate to its immediate encouragement, and to the rendering this inequality still wider and more oppressive?

What are we to conceive in this respect of the protection given to inheritance, and testamentary bequest? 'There is no merit in being born the son of a rich man, rather than of a poor one, that should justify us, in raising this man to affluence, and condemning that to invincible depression. Surely,' we might be apt to exclaim, 'it is enough to maintain men in their usurpation (for let it never be forgotten that accumulated property is usurpation), during the term of their lives. It is the most extravagant fiction, which would enlarge the empire of the proprietor beyond his natural existence, and enable him to dispose of events, when he is himself no longer in the world.'

The arguments however that may be offered, in favour of the protection given to inheritance and testamentary bequest, are more forcible, than might at first be imagined. We have attempted to show, that men ought to be protected, in the disposal of the property they have personally acquired; in expending it, in the necessaries they require, or the luxuries

[1] IV. vi. Appendix I.

in which they think proper to indulge; in transferring it, in such portions, as justice shall dictate, or their erroneous judgement suggest. To attempt therefore to take the disposal out of their hands, at the period of their decease, would be an abortive and pernicious project. If we prevented them from bestowing it in the open and explicit mode of bequest, we could not prevent them from transferring it before the close of their lives, and we should open a door to vexatious and perpetual litigation. Most persons would be inclined to bestow their property, after the period of their lives, upon their children or nearest relatives. Where therefore they have failed to express their sentiments in this respect, it is reasonable to presume what they would have been; and this disposal of the property on the part of the community, is the mildest, and therefore the most justifiable, interference. Where they have expressed a capricious partiality, this iniquity also is, in most cases, to be protected, because, for the reasons above assigned, it cannot be prevented, without exposing us to still greater iniquities.

But, though it may possibly be true, that inheritance, and the privilege of testation, are necessary consequences of the system of property, in a community the members of which are involved in prejudice and ignorance, it will not be difficult to find the instances, in every polished country of Europe, in which civil institution, instead of granting, to the inequalities of accumulation, only what could not prudently be withheld, has exerted itself, for the express purpose of rendering these inequalities greater and more oppressive. . . . We here distinctly recognize the policy of men who, having first gained a superiority, by means of the inevitable openings before cited, have made use of this superiority, for the purpose of conspiring to monopolize whatever their rapacity could seize, in direct opposition to every dictate of the general interest. These articles fall under the distinction, brought forward in the outset,[1] of laws or practices not common to all civilized communities, but peculiar to certain ages and countries.

It should seem therefore that these are institutions, the abolition of which is not to be entirely trusted to the silent hostility of opinion, but that they are to be abrogated by the express and positive decision of the community. For their abrogation, it is not necessary, that any new law or regulation should be promulgated, an operation which, to say the least, should always be regarded with extreme jealousy. Property, under every form it can assume, is upheld by the direct interference of institution; and that species which we at present contemplate, must inevitably

[1] pp. 285 f.

perish, the moment the protection of the state is withdrawn. Of the introduction of new regulations of whatever description it becomes the friend of man to be jealous; but we may allow ourselves to regard with a more friendly eye, a proceeding which consists merely in their abolition.

. . . .

There is another circumstance necessary to be stated, by way of qualification to the preceding conclusion. Evils often exist in a community, which, though mere excrescences at first, at length become so incorporated with the principle of social existence, that they cannot suddenly be separated, without the risk of involving the most dreadful calamities. . . . The inequalities of property perhaps constituted a state, through which it was at least necessary for us to pass, and which constituted the true original excitement to the unfolding the powers of the human mind.[1] . . . Yet, were they to be suddenly and instantly abolished, two evils would necessarily follow. First, the abrupt reduction of thousands to a condition, the reverse of that to which they had hitherto been accustomed, a condition, perhaps the most auspicious to human talent and felicity, but for which habit had wholly unfitted them, and which would be to them a continual source of dejection and suffering. It may be doubted, whether the genuine cause of reform, ever demands, that, in its name, we should sentence whole classes of men to wretchedness. Secondly, an attempt abruptly to abolish practices, which had originally no apology to plead for their introduction, would be attended with as dreadful convulsions, and as melancholy a series of public calamities, as an attack upon the first principles of society itself. All the reasonings therefore, which were formerly adduced under the head of revolutions,[2] are applicable to the present case.

Having now accomplished what was last proposed,[3] and endeavoured to ascertain in what particulars the present system of property is to be considered as the capricious offspring of positive institution, let us return to the point which led us to that enquiry, the question concerning the degree of respect to which property in general is entitled. And here it is only necessary that we should recollect the principle in which the doctrine of property is founded, the sacred and indefeasible right of private judgement. There are but two objects for which government can rationally be conceived to have been originated: first, as a treasury of public wisdom, by which individuals might, in all cases, with advantage be directed, and which might actively lead us, with greater certainty,

[1] Ch. vii.   [2] IV. ii.   [3] p. 285.

in the path of happiness: or, secondly, instead of being forward to act itself as an umpire, that the community might fill the humbler office of guardian of the rights of private judgement, and never interpose, but when one man appeared, in this respect, alarmingly to encroach upon another. All the arguments of this work have tended to show that the latter, and not the former, is the true end of civil institution. The first idea of property then, is a deduction from the right of private judgement; the first object of government, is the preservation of this right. Without permitting to every man, to a considerable degree, the exercise of his own discretion, there can be no independence, no improvement, no virtue and no happiness. This is a privilege in the highest degree sacred; for its maintenance, no exertions and sacrifices can be too great. Thus deep is the foundation of the doctrine of property. It is, in the last resort, the palladium of all that ought to be dear to us, and must never be approached but with awe and veneration. He that seeks to loosen the hold of this principle upon our minds, and that would lead us to sanction any exceptions to it without the most deliberate and impartial consideration, however right may be his intentions, is, in that instance, an enemy to the whole. A condition indispensably necessary to every species of excellence, is security. Unless I can foresee, in a considerable degree, the treatment I shall receive from my species, and am able to predict, to a certain extent, what will be the limits of their irregularity and caprice, I can engage in no valuable undertaking. Civil society maintains a greater proportion of security among men, than can be found in the savage state: this is one of the reasons why, under the shade of civil society, arts have been invented, sciences perfected, and the nature of man, in his individual and relative capacity, gradually developed.

·   ·   ·   ·

CHAPTER III

BENEFITS ATTENDANT ON A SYSTEM OF EQUALITY

HAVING seen the justice of an equal distribution of the good things of life, let us next proceed to consider, in detail, the benefits with which it would be attended. And here with grief it must be confessed, that, however great and extensive are the evils that are produced by monarchies and courts,[1] by the imposture of priests[2] and the iniquity of criminal laws,[3] all these are imbecile and impotent, compared with the evils that arise out of the established administration of property.

Its first effect is that we have already mentioned,[4] a sense of dependence. It is true that courts are mean-spirited, intriguing and servile, and that this disposition is transferred by contagion, from them, to all ranks of society. But accumulation brings home a servile and truckling spirit, by no circuitous method, to every house in the nation. Observe the pauper fawning with abject vileness upon his rich benefactor, speechless with sensations of gratitude, for having received that which he ought to have claimed, . . . with the spirit of a man discussing with a man, and resting his cause only on the justice of his claim. . . . Observe the tradesman, how he studies the passions of his customers, not to correct, but to pamper them, the vileness of his flattery and the systematical constancy with which he exaggerates the merit of his commodities. Observe the practices of a popular election, where the great mass are purchased by obsequiousness, by intemperance and bribery, or driven by unmanly threats of poverty and persecution. Indeed 'the age of chivalry is' not 'gone!'[5] The feudal spirit still survives, that reduced the great mass of mankind to the rank of slaves and cattle, for the service of a few.

· · · · ·

A second evil that arises out of the established administration of property, is the continual spectacle of injustice it exhibits. The effect of this consists, partly in the creation of wrong propensities, and partly in a hostility to right ones. There is nothing more pernicious to the human mind, than the love of opulence. Essentially active, when the original cravings of appetite have been satisfied, we necessarily fix on some object of pursuit, benevolent or personal, and, in the latter case, on the attainment of some excellence, or something which shall command the esteem and deference of others. Few propensities, absolutely considered, can be more valuable than this. But the established administration of property directs it into the channel of the acquisition of wealth. . . . In vain are sobriety, integrity and industry, in vain the sublimest powers of mind, and the most ardent benevolence, if their possessor be narrow in his circumstances. To acquire wealth and to display it, is therefore the universal passion. The whole structure of human society, is made a system of the narrowest selfishness. If the state of society were such, that self-love and benevolence were apparently reconciled as to their object, a man

[1] Book V.   [2] Book VI.   [3] Book VII.
[4] Ch. i, p. 281.   [5] Burke's *Reflections*.

might then set out with the desire of eminence, and yet become every day more generous and philanthropical in his views. But the passion we are here describing, is accustomed to be gratified at every step, by inhumanly trampling upon the interest of others. Wealth is acquired by overreaching our neighbour, and is spent in insulting him. The spectacle of injustice which the established administration of property exhibits, operates also in the way of hostility to right propensities. . . . It happens perhaps, during the period of education, that maxims of integrity and consistency are repeatedly enforced, and the preceptor gives no quarter to the base suggestions of selfishness and cunning. But how is the lesson that has been read to the pupil confounded and reversed, when he enters upon the scene of the world? If he ask, 'Why is this man honoured?' the ready answer is, 'Because he is rich.' If he enquire further, 'Why is he rich?' the answer, in most cases, is, 'From the accident of birth, or from a minute and sordid attention to the cares of gain.' Humanity weeps over the distresses of the peasantry in all civilized nations; and, when she turns, from this spectacle, to behold the luxury of their lords, gross, imperious and prodigal, her sensations certainly are not less acute. This spectacle is the school in which mankind have been educated. They have been accustomed to the sight of injustice, oppression and iniquity, till their feelings are made callous, and their understandings incapable of apprehending the principles of virtue.

. . . thirdly, . . . the established administration of property, is the true levelling system with respect to the human species, by as much as the cultivation of intellect is more valuable, and more characteristic of man, than the gratifications of vanity or appetite. Accumulated property treads the powers of thought in the dust, extinguishes the sparks of genius, and reduces the great mass of mankind to be immersed in sordid cares; beside depriving the rich, . . . of the most salubrious and effectual motives to activity. If superfluity were banished, the necessity for the greater part of the manual industry of mankind would be superseded; and the rest, being amicably shared among the active and vigorous members of the community, would be burdensome to none. . . .

From ideas of intellectual, let us turn to moral, improvement. And here it is obvious, that the great occasions of crime would be cut off forever.[1]

[1] I. iii.

The fruitful source of crimes consists in this circumstance, one man's possessing in abundance, that of which another man is destitute. We must change the nature of mind, before we can prevent it from being powerfully influenced by this circumstance, when brought strongly home to its perceptions by the nature of its situation. Man must cease to have senses, the pleasures of appetite and vanity must cease to gratify, before he can look on tamely at the monopoly of these pleasures. He must cease to have a sense of justice, before he can clearly and fully approve this mixed scene of superfluity and want. It is true, that the proper method of curing this inequality, is by reason and not by violence. But the immediate tendency of the established administration, is to persuade men that reason is impotent. The injustice of which they complain, is upheld by force; and they are too easily induced, by force to attempt its correction. All they endeavour, is the partial correction of an injustice, which education tells them is necessary, but more powerful reason affirms to be tyrannical.

Force grew out of monopoly. It might accidentally have occurred among savages, whose appetites exceeded their supply, or whose passions were inflamed by the presence of the object of their desire; but it would gradually have died away, as reason and civilization advanced. Accumulated property has fixed its empire; and henceforth all is an open contention, of the strength and cunning of one party, against the strength and cunning of the other. In this case, the violent and premature struggles of the necessitous, are undoubtedly an evil. They tend to defeat the very cause in the success of which they are most deeply interested; they tend to procrastinate the triumph of justice. But the true crime, in every instance, is in the selfish and partial propensities of men, thinking only of themselves, and despising the emolument of others; and, of these, the rich have their share.

The spirit of oppression, the spirit of servility, and the spirit of fraud, these are the immediate growth of the established administration of property. They are alike hostile to intellectual and moral improvement. The other vices of envy, malice and revenge, are their inseparable companions. In a state of society, where men lived in the midst of plenty, and where all shared alike the bounties of nature, these sentiments would inevitably expire. The narrow principle of selfishness, would vanish. No man being obliged to guard his little store, or provide, with anxiety and pain, for his restless wants, each would lose his individual existence, in the thought of the general good. No man would be an enemy to his neighbour, for they would have no subject of contention; and of consequence, philanthropy would resume the empire which reason assigns her. Mind would be delivered from her perpetual anxiety about corporal support, and free to expatiate in the field of thought which is congenial to her. Each would assist the enquiries of all.

.   .   .   .

CHAPTER IV

OBJECTION TO THIS SYSTEM FROM THE FRAILTY OF THE HUMAN MIND

.   .   .   .

EQUALITY of conditions, or, in other words, an equal admission to the means of improvement and pleasure, is a law rigorously enjoined upon mankind by the voice of justice. All other changes in society are good, only as they are fragments of this, or steps to its attainment. All other existing abuses are to be deprecated, only as they serve to increase and perpetuate the inequality of conditions.

We have however arrived at another truth not less evident than this. Equality of conditions cannot be produced by individual compulsion, and ought not to be produced by compulsion in the name of the whole. . . . There remain but two instruments for producing this volition, the illumination of the understanding and the love of distinction.

These instruments have commonly been supposed wholly inadequate to their object. . . . '. . . It is one thing to convince men, that a given conduct, on their part, would be most conducive to the general interest, and another to persuade them, actively to postpone, to considerations of general interest, every idea of personal ambition or pleasure. . . .'

. . . there is good reason to believe, though the human mind be un-questionably accessible to disinterested motives,[1] that virtue would be in most instances an impracticable refinement; were it not that self-love and social, however different in themselves, are found upon strict examination to prescribe the same system of conduct.

But this observation by no means removes the difficulty, intended to be suggested in the objection. 'Though frugality, moderation, and plainness, may be the joint dictate of these two authorities, yet it is the property of the human mind, to be swayed by things present, more than

[1] IV. x.

by things absent. In affairs of religion, we often find men indulging themselves in offences of small gratification, in spite of all the threats that can be held out to them of eternal damnation. It is in vain that, for the most part, you would preach the pleasures of abstinence amidst the profusion of a feast; or the unsubstantialness of fame and power, to him who is tortured with the goadings of ambition. The case is similar to that of the exacerbations of grief, the attempt to cure which by the consolations of philosophy, has been a source of inexhaustible ridicule.' The answer to these remarks has been anticipated.[1] The ridicule lies in supposing the endeavour to cure a man of his weakness, to consist in one phlegmatic and solitary expostulation, instead of conceiving it to be accompanied with the vigour of conscious truth, and the progressive regularity of a course of instruction.

. . . . .

Undoubtedly an apprehension of the demands of justice will be accompanied with a proportionate improvement of the mind in other respects, and a slow, but incessant, melioration of the institutions and practices of society. With this supposition, it could not however fail to happen, that, in proportion as the prejudices and ignorance of the great mass of society declined, the credit of wealth, and the reverent admiration with which it is now contemplated, must also decline. But, in proportion as it lost credit with the great mass of society, it would relax its hold upon the minds of those who possess it, or have the means of acquiring it. We have already seen,[2] that the great incitement to the acquisition of wealth, is the love of distinction. Suppose then that, instead of the false glare which wealth, through the present puerility of the human mind, reflects on its possessor, his conduct in amassing and monopolizing it, were seen in its true light. We should not then demand his punishment, but we should look on him as a man uninitiated in the plainest sentiments of reason. He would not be pointed at with the finger, or hooted as he passed along through the resorts of men, but he would be conscious that he was looked upon as the meanest of mankind. He would be incited to the same assiduity in hiding his acquisitions then, as he employs in displaying them now. He would be regarded with no terror, for his conduct would appear too absurd to excite imitation. Add to which, his acquisitions would be small, as the independent spirit and sound discretion of mankind, would allow but little chance of his being able to retain them in his service, as now, by generously rewarding them

[1] l. v. . . .   [2] VIII. i, p. 280.

with a part of the fruit of their own labours. Thus it appears, with irresistible probability, when the subject of wealth shall be understood, and correct ideas respecting it familiarized to the human mind, that the present disparity of conditions will subside, by a gradual and incessant progress, into its true level.

CHAPTER V

OBJECTION TO THIS SYSTEM FROM THE QUESTION OF PERMANENCE

... The inherent tendency of intellect is to improvement. If therefore this inherent tendency be suffered to operate, and no concussion of nature or inundation of barbarism arrest its course, the state of society we have been describing, must, at some time, arrive.

But it has frequently been said, 'that if an equality of conditions could be introduced today, it would be destroyed tomorrow. It is impossible to reduce the varieties of the human mind to such a uniformity, as this system demands. One man will be more industrious than another; one man will be provident and avaricious, and another dissipated and thoughtless. Misery and confusion would be the result of an attempt to equalize, in the first instance, and the old vices and monopolies would succeed, in the second. ...'

. . . . .

... there is a wide difference between the equality here spoken of, and the equality which has frequently constituted a subject of discussion among mankind. This is not an equality introduced by force, or maintained by the laws and regulations of a positive institution. It is not the result of accident, of the authority of a chief magistrate, or the over-earnest persuasion of a few enlightened thinkers; but is produced by the serious and deliberate conviction of the public at large. It is one thing, for men to be held to a certain system, by the force of laws, and the vigilance of those who administer them; and a thing entirely different, to be held by the firm and habitual persuasion of their own minds. ...
If the force of truth shall be strong enough, gradually to wean men from the most rooted habits, and to introduce a mode of society so remote from that which at present exists, it will also probably be strong enough, to hold them in the course they have commenced, and to prevent the

return of vices which have once been extirpated. This probability will be increased, if we recollect the two principles which must have led men into such a system of action; a stricter sense of justice, and a purer theory of happiness.

Equality of conditions cannot begin to assume a fixed appearance in human society, till the sentiment becomes deeply impressed, as well as widely diffused, that the genuine wants of any man, constitute his only just claim to the ultimate appropriation, and the consumption, of any species of commodity. . . . Men who are habituated to these views, can scarcely be tempted to monopolize; and the sense of the community respecting him who yields to the temptation, will be so decisive in its tenor, and unequivocal in its manifestation, as to afford small encouragement to perseverance or imitation.

A spontaneous equality of conditions, also implies a purer theory of happiness than has hitherto obtained. Men will cease to regard with complacence, the happiness that consists in splendour and ostentation, . . . They will cease to derive pleasure, from the empire to be possessed over others, or the base servility and terror with which they may address us. They will be contented, for the most part, with the means of healthful existence, and of unexpensive pleasure. They will find the highest gratification in promoting and contemplating the general happiness. . . .

CHAPTER VI

OBJECTION TO THIS SYSTEM FROM THE
ALLUREMENTS OF SLOTH

ANOTHER objection which has been urged against the system which counteracts the accumulation of property, is, 'that it would put an end to industry. . . . Once establish it as a principle in society, that no man is to apply to his personal use more than his necessities require; and every man will become indifferent to the exertions, which now call forth the energy of his faculties. . . .'

In reply to this objection, the reader must again be reminded, that the equality for which we are pleading, is an equality which would succeed to a state of great intellectual improvement. So bold a revolution cannot take place in human affairs, till the general mind has been highly cultivated. . . . Attempts, without this preparation, will be productive only of confusion. Their effect will be momentary, and a new and more barbarous inequality will succeed. Each man, with unaltered appetite, will watch the opportunity, to gratify his love of power or of distinction, by usurping on his inattentive neighbours.

.   .   .   .

When we talk of men's sinking into idleness, if they be not excited by the stimulus of gain, we seem to have little considered the motives that, at present, govern the human mind. We are deceived by the apparent mercenariness of mankind, and imagine that the accumulation of wealth is their great object. . . . There is, no doubt, a class in society, that is perpetually urged by hunger and need, and has no leisure for motives less gross and material. But is the class next above them less industrious than they? Will any man affirm, that the mind of the peasant is as far removed from inaction and sloth, as the mind of the general or the statesman, of the natural philosopher . . . or the poet, . . .

In reality, those by whom this reasoning has been urged, have mistaken the nature of their own objection. They did not suppose, that men could be roused into action only by the love of gain; but they conceived that, in a state of equality, men would have nothing to occupy their attention. . . .

.   .   .   .

CHAPTER VIII

OBJECTION TO THIS SYSTEM FROM THE INFLEXIBILITY OF ITS RESTRICTIONS

AN objection that has often been urged against a system of equality, is, 'that it is inconsistent with personal independence. Every man, according to this scheme, is a passive instrument in the hands of the community. He must eat and drink, and play and sleep, at the bidding of others. . . . Under the appearance of a perfect freedom from oppression and tyranny, he is in reality subjected to the most unlimited slavery.'

To understand the force of this objection it is necessary that we should distinguish two sorts of independence, one of which may be denominated natural, and the other moral. Natural independence, a freedom from all constraint, except that of reasons and inducements presented to the understanding, is of the utmost importance to the welfare and improvement of mind. Moral independence, on the contrary, is always injurious. The dependence, which is essential, in this respect, to the wholesome temperament of society, includes . . . a censure to be exercised by every individual over the actions of another, a promptness to enquire into and to judge them. Why should we shrink from this? What could be more beneficial, than for each man to derive assistance for correcting and moulding his conduct, from the perspicacity of his neighbours? The reason that this species of censure is at present exercised with illiberality, is, because it is exercised clandestinely, and because we submit to its operation with impatience and aversion. Moral independence is always injurious: for, as has abundantly appeared in the course of the present enquiry, there is no situation in which I can be placed, where it is not incumbent upon me to adopt a certain conduct in preference to all others, and, of consequence, where I shall not prove an ill member of society, if I act in any other than a particular manner. . . .

.   .   .   .

APPENDIX

OF CO-OPERATION, COHABITATION AND MARRIAGE

I T is a curious subject, to enquire into the due medium between individuality and concert. On the one hand, it is to be observed that human beings are formed for society. Without society, we shall probably be deprived of the most eminent enjoyments of which our nature is susceptible. . . . Our opinions, our tempers and our habits are modified by those of each other. This is by no means the mere operation of arguments and persuasives; it occurs in that insensible and gradual way, which no resolution can enable us wholly to counteract. He that would attempt to counteract it by insulating himself, will fall into a worse error than that which he seeks to avoid. He will divest himself of the character of a man, and be incapable of judging of his fellow men, or of reasoning upon human affairs.

On the other hand, individuality is of the very essence of intellectual excellence. He that resigns himself wholly to sympathy and imitation, can possess little of mental strength or accuracy. The system of his life is a species of sensual dereliction. . . . Mankind cannot be benefited by him.

He neither animates them to exertion, nor leads them forward to un-expected improvement. . . . The truly venerable, and the truly happy, must have the fortitude to maintain his individuality. If he indulge in the gratifications, and cultivate the feelings of man, he must at the same time be strenuous in following the train of his disquisitions, and exercising the powers of his understanding.

. . . It would be absurd to say that we are not capable of truth, of evidence and agreement. In these respects, so far as mind is in a state of progressive improvement, we are perpetually coming nearer to each other. But there are subjects about which we shall continually differ, and ought to differ. The ideas, associations and circumstances of each man, are properly his own; and it is a pernicious system that would lead us to require all men, however different their circumstances, to act by a precise general rule. Add to this, that, by the doctrine of progressive improvement, we shall always be erroneous, though we shall every day become less erroneous. The proper method for hastening the decline of error, and producing uniformity of judgement, is not, by brute force, by laws, or by imitation; but, on the contrary, by exciting every man to think for himself.

From these principles it appears, that everything that is usually under-stood by the term co-operation, is, in some degree, an evil. A man in solitude, is obliged to sacrifice or postpone the execution of his best thoughts, in compliance with his necessities, or his frailties. . . . It is still worse, when a man is also obliged to consult the convenience of others. If I be expected to eat or to work in conjunction with my neighbour, it must either be at a time most convenient to me, or to him, or to neither of us. We cannot be reduced to a clock-work uniformity.

Hence it follows that all supererogatory co-operation is carefully to be avoided, common labour and common meals. 'But what shall we say to a co-operation, that seems dictated by the nature of the work to be performed?' It ought to be diminished. . . . At present, to pull down a tree, to cut a canal, to navigate a vessel, require the labour of many. Will they always require the labour of many? When we recollect the com-plicated machines of human contrivance, various sorts of mills, of weaving engines, steam engines, are we not astonished at the com-pendium of labour they produce? Who shall say where this species of improvement must stop? . . .

The conclusion of the progress which has here been sketched, is something like a final close to the necessity of manual labour. . . .

. . . . .

Having ventured to state these hints and conjectures, let us endeavour to mark the limits of individuality. Every man that receives an impression from any external object, has the current of his own thoughts modified by force; and yet, without external impressions, we should be nothing. Every man that reads the composition of another, suffers the succession of his ideas to be, in a considerable degree, under the direction of his author. But it does not seem, as if this would ever form a sufficient objection against reading. . . . Conversation is a species of co-operation, one or the other party always yielding to have his ideas guided by the other: yet conversation, and the intercourse of mind with mind, seem to be the most fertile sources of improvement. It is here as it is with punishment. He that, in the gentlest manner, undertakes to reason another out of his vices, will probably occasion pain; but this species of punishment ought, upon no account, to be superseded.

Let not these views of the future individuality of man, be misapprehended, or overstrained. We ought to be able to do without one another. He is the most perfect man, to whom society is not a necessary of life, but a luxury, innocent and enviable, in which he joyfully indulges. . . .

Another article which belongs to the subject of co-operation, is cohabitation. The evils attendant on this practice, are obvious. In order to the human understanding's being successfully cultivated, it is necessary, that the intellectual operations of men should be independent of each other.[1] We should avoid such practices as are calculated to melt our opinions into a common mould. Cohabitation is also hostile to that fortitude, which should accustom a man, in his actions, as well as in his opinions, to judge for himself, and feel competent to the discharge of his own duties. Add to this, that it is absurd to expect the inclinations and wishes of two human beings to coincide, through any long period of time. To oblige them to act and to live together, is to subject them to some inevitable portion of thwarting, bickering and unhappiness. . . .

The subject of cohabitation is particularly interesting, as it includes in it the subject of marriage. It will therefore be proper to pursue the enquiry in greater detail. The evil of marriage, as it is practised in European countries, extends further than we have yet described. The method is, for a thoughtless and romantic youth of each sex, to come together, to see each other, for a few times, and under circumstances full of delusion, and then to vow eternal attachment. What is the consequence of this? In almost every instance they find themselves deceived.

[1] IV. iii, p. 140.

They are reduced to make the best of an irretrievable mistake. They are led to conceive it their wisest policy, to shut their eyes upon realities, happy, if, by any perversion of intellect, they can persuade themselves that they were right in their first crude opinion of each other. Thus the institution of marriage is made a system of fraud; and men who carefully mislead their judgements in the daily affair of their life, must be expected to have a crippled judgement in every other concern.

Add to this, that marriage, as now understood, is a monopoly, and the worst of monopolies. So long as two human beings are forbidden, by positive institution, to follow the dictates of their own mind, prejudice will be alive and vigorous. So long as I seek, by despotic and artificial means, to maintain my possession of a woman, I am guilty of the most odious selfishness. . . .

The abolition of the present system of marriage, appears to involve no evils. We are apt to represent that abolition to ourselves, as the harbinger of brutal lust and depravity. But it really happens, in this, as in other cases, that the positive laws which are made to restrain our vices, irritate and multiply them. Not to say, that the same sentiments of justice and happiness, which, in a state of equality, would destroy our relish for expensive gratifications, might be expected to decrease our inordinate appetites of every kind, and to lead us universally to prefer the pleasures of intellect to the pleasures of sense.

All these arguments are calculated to determine our judgement in favour of marriage as a salutary and respectable institution, but not of that species of marriage, in which there is no room for repentance, and to which liberty and hope are equally strangers.

. . . . .

CHAPTER IX

OBJECTION TO THIS SYSTEM FROM THE PRINCIPLE OF POPULATION[1]

. . . .

THE question of population, as it relates to the science of politics and society, is considerably curious. Several writers upon these topics, have treated it in a way calculated to produce a very gloomy impression, and have placed precautions to counteract the multiplication of the human

[1] [Cf. pp. 328 332.]

species, among the most important objects of civil prudence. These precautions appear to have occupied much attention in several ancient nations, among whom there prevailed a great solicitude, that the number of citizens in the state should suffer no augmentation. In modern times a contrary opinion has frequently obtained, and the populousness of a country has been said to constitute its true wealth and prosperity.

Perhaps however express precautions in either kind, are superfluous and nugatory. There is a principle in the nature of human society, by means of which everything seems to tend to its level, and to proceed in the most auspicious way, when least interfered with by the mode of regulation. In a certain stage of the social progress, population seems rapidly to increase; this appears to be the case in the United States of America. In a subsequent stage, it undergoes little change, either in the way of increase or diminution; this is the case in the more civilized countries of Europe. The number of inhabitants in a country will perhaps never be found, in the ordinary course of affairs, greatly to increase, beyond the facility of subsistence.

Nothing is more easy than to account for this circumstance. So long as there is a facility of subsistence, men will be encouraged to early marriages, and to a careful rearing of their children. . . . In such countries the wages of the labourer are high, for the number of labourers bears no proportion to the demand, and to the general spirit of enterprise. In many European countries, on the other hand, a large family has become a proverbial expression for an uncommon degree of poverty and wretchedness. The price of labour in any state, so long as the spirit of accumulation shall prevail, is an infallible barometer of the state of its population. It is impossible where the price of labour is greatly reduced, and an added population threatens a still further reduction, that men should not be considerably under the influence of fear, respecting an early marriage, and a numerous family.

.   .   .   .   .

CHAPTER X

REFLECTIONS

WE have now taken a general survey of the system of equality, and there remains only to state a few incidental remarks, with which it may be proper to wind up the subject.

No idea has excited greater horror in the minds of a multitude of persons, than that of the mischiefs that will ensue from the dissemination of what they call levelling principles. They believe 'that these principles will inevitably ferment in the minds of the vulgar, and that the attempt to carry them into execution will be attended with every species of calamity.' They represent to themselves 'the uninformed and uncivilized part of mankind, as let loose from restraint, and hurried into every kind of excess. Knowledge and taste, the improvements of intellect, the discoveries of sages, the beauties of poetry and art, are trampled under foot and extinguished by barbarians. . . .'

Whatever may be the abstract recommendations of the system of equality, we must not allow ourselves any such partiality upon a subject in which the welfare of the species is involved, as should induce us to shrink from a due attention to the ideas here exhibited. Massacre is the too possible attendant upon revolution, and massacre is perhaps the most hateful scene, . . . that any imagination can suggest. . . .

. . . it has sometimes been alleged by the friends of reform, 'that the advantages possessed by a system of liberty are so great, as to be worth purchasing at any price; that the evils of the most sanguinary revolution are temporary; that the vices of despotism, which few pens indeed have ventured to record in all their demerits, are scarcely less atrocious in the hour of their commission, and infinitely more terrible by their extent and duration; and finally, that the crimes perpetrated in a revolutionary movement, can in no just estimate be imputed to the innovators; that they were engendered by the preceding oppression, and ought to be regarded as the last struggles of expiring tyranny.'

But, . . . it must be recollected, that 'the benefits which innovation may seem to promise, are not to be regarded as certain. After all, it may not be utterly impossible, that the nature of man will always remain, for the most part, unaltered, and that he will be found incapable of that degree of knowledge and constancy, which seems essential to a liberal democracy or a pure equality. However cogent may be the arguments for the practicability of human improvement, is it then justifiable, upon the mere credit of predictions, to expose mankind to the greatest calamities? . . . Speculations therefore upon the new modes in which human affairs may be combined, different from any that occur in the history of past ages, may seem fitter to amuse men of acuteness and leisure, than to be depended on in deciding the dearest interests of mankind. Proceedings, the effects of which have been verified by experience, furnish a surer ground of dependence, than the most laboured reason can afford us in regard to schemes as yet untried.'

Undoubtedly in the views here detailed there is considerable force; and it would be well if persons, who are eager to effect abrupt changes in human society, would give them an attentive consideration. They do not however sufficiently apply to the question proposed to be examined. Our enquiry was not respecting revolution, but disquisition. We are not concerned to vindicate any species of violence; we do not assume that levelling principles are to be acted upon through the medium of force; we have simply affirmed that he who is persuaded of their truth, ought to endeavour to render them a subject of attention. To be convinced of this we have only to consider the enormous and unquestionable political evils that are daily before our eyes, and the probability there is that, by temperate investigation, these evils may be undermined, with little or no tumultuary concussion.[1] . . .

But there is another consideration worthy of serious attention in this place. Granting, for a moment, the utmost weight to the objections of those who remind us of the mischief of political experiments, it is proper to ask, Can we suppress discussion? Can we arrest the progress of the enquiring mind? If we can, it must be by the most unmitigated despotism. Intellect has a perpetual tendency to proceed. It cannot be held back, but by a power that counteracts its genuine tendency, through every moment of its existence. Tyrannical and sanguinary must be the measures employed for this purpose. Miserable and disgustful must be the scene they produce. Their result will be barbarism, ignorance, superstition, servility, hypocrisy. This is the alternative, so far as there is any alternative in their choice, to which those who are empowered to consult for the general welfare must inevitably resort, if the suppression of enquiry be the genuine dictate of public interest.

Such has been, for the most part, the policy of governments through every age of the world. . . .

In the meantime it ought not to be forgotten, that to say that a knowledge of political truth can be injurious to the true interests of mankind, is to affirm an express contradiction. Political truth is that science which teaches us to weigh in the balance of an accurate judgement, the different proceedings that may be adopted, for the purpose of giving welfare and prosperity to communities of men. The only way in which discussion can be a reasonable object of terror, is by its power of giving to falsehood, under certain circumstances, the speciousness of truth, or by that

[1] IV. ii.

partial propagation, the tendency of which is to intoxicate and mislead those understandings that, by an adequate instruction, would have been sobered and enlightened.

These considerations will scarcely permit us to doubt, that it is the duty of governments to maintain the most inflexible neutrality, and of individuals to publish the truths with which they appear to be acquainted. The more truth is discovered, the more it is known in its true dimensions, and not in parts, the less is it possible that it should coalesce with, or leave room for the effects of, error. . . .

The condition of the human species at the present hour is critical and alarming. We are not without grounds of reasonable hope, that the issue will be uncommonly beneficial. There is however much to apprehend, from the narrow views, and angry passions, of the contending parties. Every interval that can be gained, provided it is not an interval of torpor and indifference, is perhaps to be considered in the light of an advantage.

Meanwhile, in proportion as the just apprehensions of explosion shall increase, there are high duties incumbent upon every branch of the community.

First, upon those who are fitted to be precursors to their fellows in the discovery of truth.

They are bound to be active, indefatigable and disinterested. It is incumbent upon them to abstain from inflammatory language, and expressions of acrimony and resentment. . . . The lessons of liberty and equality are lessons of goodwill to all orders of men. They free the peasant from the iniquity that depresses his mind, and the privileged from the luxury and despotism by which he is corrupted. It is disgraceful to those who teach these lessons, if they stain their benignity, by showing that that benignity has not become the inmate of their hearts.

Nor is it less necessary that they should express themselves with explicitness and sincerity. No maxim can be more suspicious than that which teaches us to consult the temper of the times, and tell only as much as we imagine our contemporaries will be able to bear.[1] This practice is at present almost universal, and it will perhaps not be difficult to observe its pernicious effects. We retail and mangle truth. We impart it to our fellows, not with the liberal measure with which we have received it, but with such parsimony as our own miserable prudence may chance to prescribe. That we may deceive others with a tranquil

[1] III. vii, p. 127.

conscience, we begin with deceiving ourselves. We put shackles upon our minds, and dare not trust ourselves at large in the pursuit of truth. This practice seems to have been greatly promoted by the machinations of party, and the desire of one wise and adventurous leader to lead a troop of weak, timid and selfish adherents in his train. . . .

The dissimulation here censured, beside its ill effects upon him who practises it, and, by degrading and unnerving his character, upon society at large, has a particular ill consequence with respect to the point we are considering. It lays a mine, and prepares an explosion. This is the tendency of all unnatural restraint. The unfettered progress of investigation is perhaps always salutary. Its advances are gradual, and each step prepares the general mind for that which is to follow. They are sudden and unprepared, and therefore necessarily partial, emanations of truth, that have the greatest tendency to deprive men of their sobriety and self-command. Reserve in this respect is calculated, at once, to give a rugged and angry tone to the multitude, whenever they shall happen to discover what is thus concealed, and to mislead the depositaries of political power. It sooths them into false security, and prompts them to maintain an inauspicious obstinacy.

Having considered what it is that belongs in such a crisis to the enlightened and wise, let us next turn our attention to a very different class of society, the rich and great. And here, in the first place, it may be remarked, that it is a false calculation that leads us universally to despair of having these for the advocates of political justice. Mankind are not so miserably selfish, as satirists and courtiers have supposed. . . .

The rich and great are far from callous to views of general felicity, when such views are brought before them with that evidence and attraction of which they are susceptible. From one dreadful disadvantage their minds are free. They have not been soured with unrelenting tyranny, or narrowed by the perpetual pressure of distress. . . .

But let us suppose a considerable party of the rich and great to be actuated by no view but to their emolument and ease. It is not difficult to show them, that their interest in this sense will admit of no more than a temperate and yielding resistance. To such we may say: 'It is in vain for you to fight against truth. It is like endeavouring with the human hand to stop the inroad of the ocean. Be wise betimes. Seek your safety in concession. If you will not come over to the standard of political justice, temporize at least with an enemy whom you cannot overcome. . . .'

It will not be difficult to trace, in the progress of modern Europe from barbarism to refinement, a tendency towards the equalization of conditions. In the feudal times, as now in India and other parts of the world, men were born to a certain station, and it was nearly impossible for a peasant to rise to the rank of a noble. Except the nobles, there were no men that were rich; for commerce, either external or internal, had scarcely an existence. Commerce was one engine for throwing down this seemingly impregnable barrier, . . . Learning was another, and more powerful engine. In all ages of the church we see men of the basest origin rising to the highest eminence. Commerce proved that others could rise to wealth beside those who were cased in mail; but learning proved that the low-born were capable of surpassing their lords. . . .

. . . It is with morality in this respect as it is with politics. The progress is at first so slow as, for the most part, to elude the observation of mankind; nor can it be adequately perceived but by the contemplation and comparison of events during a considerable portion of time. After a certain interval, the scene is more fully unfolded, and the advances appear more rapid and decisive. . . .

.   .   .   .

One objection may perhaps be inferred from these considerations. 'If the inevitable progress of improvement insensibly lead towards equality, what need was there of proposing it as a specific object to men's consideration?' The answer to this objection is easy. The improvement in question consists in a knowledge of truth. But our knowledge will be very imperfect, so long as this great branch of universal justice fails to constitute a part of it. All truth is useful; can this truth, which is perhaps the most fundamental of all moral principles, be without its benefit? Whatever be the object towards which mind irresistibly advances, it is of no mean importance to us to have a distinct view of that object. Our advances will thus become accelerated. It is a well-known principle of morality, 'that he who proposes perfection to himself, though he will inevitably fall short of what he pursues, will make a more rapid progress, than he who is contented to aim only at what is imperfect.' The benefits to be derived in the interval from a view of equality as one of the great objects to which we are tending, are exceedingly conspicuous. Such a view will strongly conduce to make us disinterested now. It will teach us to look with contempt upon mercantile speculations, commercial prosperity, and the cares of gain. It will impress us with a just apprehension of what it is of which man is capable, and in which his perfection consists; and will fix our ambition and activity upon the worthiest objects. Intellect cannot arrive at any great and illustrious attainment, however much the nature of intellect may carry us towards it, without feeling some presages of its approach; and it is reasonable to believe that, the earlier these presages are introduced, and the more distinct they are made, the more auspicious will be the event.

THE END

APPENDIX

SELECTIONS FROM GODWIN'S OTHER WRITINGS

I

THE ENQUIRER[1]

OF AVARICE AND PROFUSION[2]

WHICH character deserves our preference, the man of avaricious habits, or of profuse ones? Which of the two conducts himself in the manner most beneficial to society? Which of the two is actuated by motives the most consonant to justice and virtue?

Riches and poverty are in some degree necessarily incidental to the social existence of man. There is no alternative, but that men must either have their portion of labour assigned them by the society at large, and the produce collected into a common stock; or that each man must be left to exert the portion of industry, and cultivate the habits of economy, to which his mind shall prompt him.

The first of these modes of existence deserves our fixed disapprobation.[3] It is a state of slavery and imbecility. It reduces the exertions of a human being to the level of a piece of mechanism, prompted by no personal motives, compensated and alleviated by no genuine passions. It puts an end to that independence and individuality, which are the genuine characteristics of an intellectual existence, and without which nothing eminently honourable, generous or delightful can in any degree subsist.

Inequality therefore being to a certain extent unavoidable, it is the province of justice and virtue to counteract the practical evils which inequality has a tendency to produce. It is certain that men will differ from each other in their degrees of industry and economy. But it is not less certain, that the wants of one man are similar to the wants of another, and that the same things will conduce to the improvement and happiness of each, except so far as either is corrupted by the oppressive and tyrannical condition of the society in which he is born. The nature of man requires, that each man should be trusted with a discretionary power. The principles of virtue require, that the advantages existing in any community should be equally administered; or that the inequalities

<hr>

[1] [Published 1797.]   [2] [Part II, Essay II.]   [3] *Political Justice*, VIII. ii.

which inevitably arise, should be repressed, and kept down within as narrow limits as possible.

Does the conduct of the avaricious man, or of the man of profusion, best contribute to this end?

.   .   .   .

Industry has been thought a pleasing spectacle. What more delightful than to see our provinces covered with corn, and our ports crowded with vessels? What more admirable than the products of human ingenuity? magnificent buildings, plentiful markets, immense cities? How innumerable the arts of the less favoured members of society to extort from the wealthy some portion of their riches? How many paths have been struck out for the acquisition of money? How various are the channels of our trade? . . . Is not this much better, than that the great mass of society should wear out a miserable existence in idleness and want?

It is thus that superficial observers have reasoned, and these have been termed the elements of political wisdom. It has been inferred, that the most commendable proceeding in a man of wealth, is to encourage the manufactures of his country, and to spend as large a portion of his property as possible in generating this beautiful spectacle of a multitude of human beings, industriously employed, well-fed, warmly clothed, cleanly and contented.

Another view of the subject which has led to the same conclusion is, that the wealth any man possesses is so much of pleasure and happiness, capable of being enjoyed, partly by himself, partly by others; that it is his duty to scatter the seeds of pleasure and happiness as widely as possible; and that it is more useful that he should exchange his superfluity for their labour, than that he should maintain them in idleness and dependence.

These views of the subject are both of them erroneous. Money is the representative and the means of exchange to real commodities; it is no real commodity itself. The wages of the labourer and the artisan have always been small; and, as long as the extreme inequality of conditions subsists, will always remain so. If the rich man would substantially relieve the burdens of the poor, exclusive of the improvement he may communicate to their understandings or their temper, it must be by taking upon himself a part of their labour, and not by setting them tasks. All other relief is partial and temporary.

Three or four hundred years ago in England, there was little of manufacture, and little comparatively of manual labour. Yet the great proprietors found then, as they find now, that they could not centre the employment of their wealth entirely in themselves; they could not devour to their own share all the corn and oxen and sheep they were pleased to call their property. There were not then commodities, decorations of their persons, their wives and their houses, sufficient to consume their superfluity. Those which existed, were cumbrous and durable, a legacy handed down from one generation to another; not as now, a perpetual drain for wealth and spur to industry. They generously therefore gave away what they could not expend, that it might not rot upon their hands. It was equitable however in their idea, that they should receive some compensation for their benefits. What they required of their beneficiaries, was that they should wear their liveries, and by their personal attendance contribute to the splendour of their lords.

It happened then, as it must always happen, that the lower orders of the community could not be entirely starved out of the world.

The commodities that substantially contribute to the subsistence of the human species, form a very short catalogue. They demand from us but a slender portion of industry. If these only were produced, and sufficiently produced, the species of man would be continued. If the labour necessarily required to produce them were equitably divided among the poor, and still more if it were equitably divided among all, each man's share of labour would be light, and his portion of leisure would be ample. There was a time, when this leisure would have been of small comparative value. It is to be hoped that the time will come, when it will be applied to the most important purposes. Those hours which are not required for the production of the necessaries of life, may be devoted to the cultivation of the understanding, the enlarging our stock of knowledge, the refining our taste, and thus opening to us new and more exquisite sources of enjoyment. It is not necessary that all our hours of leisure should be dedicated to intellectual pursuits; it is probable that the well-being of man would be best promoted by the production of some superfluities and luxuries, though certainly not of such as an ill-imagined and exclusive vanity now teaches us to admire; but there is no reason in the system of the universe or the nature of man, why an individual should be deprived of the means of intellectual cultivation.

It was perhaps necessary that a period of monopoly and oppression should subsist, before a period of cultivated equality could subsist. Savages perhaps would never have been excited to the discovery of truth and the invention of art, but by the narrow motives which such a period affords. But surely, after the savage state has ceased, and men have set out in the glorious career of discovery and invention, monopoly and oppression cannot be necessary to prevent them from returning to a state of barbarism. Thus much is certain, that a state of cultivated equality, is that state which, in speculation and theory, appears most consonant to the nature of man, and most conducive to the extensive diffusion of felicity.

It is reasonable therefore to take this state as a sort of polar star, in our speculations upon the tendency of human actions. Without entering into the question whether such a state can be realized in its utmost extent, we may venture to pronounce that mode of society best, which most nearly approaches this state. It is desirable that there should be, in any rank of society, as little as may be of that luxury, the object of which is to contribute to the spurious gratifications of vanity; that those who are least favoured with the gifts of fortune, should be condemned to the smallest practicable portion of compulsory labour; and that no man should be obliged to devote his life to the servitude of a galley-slave, and the ignorance of a beast.

How far does the conduct of the rich man who lives up to his fortune on the one hand, and of the avaricious man on the other, contribute to the placing of human beings in the condition in which they ought to be placed?

Every man who invents a new luxury, adds so much to the quantity of labour entailed on the lower orders of society. The same may be affirmed of every man who adds a new dish to his table, or who imposes a new tax upon the inhabitants of his country. It is a gross and ridiculous error to suppose that the rich pay for anything. There is no wealth in the world except this, the labour of man.[1] What is misnamed wealth, is merely a power vested in certain individuals by the institutions of society, to compel others to labour for their benefit. So much labour is requisite to produce the necessaries of life; so much more to produce those superfluities which at present exist in any country. Every new luxury is a new weight thrown into the scale. The poor are scarcely ever benefited by this. It adds a certain portion to the mass of their labour; but it adds nothing to their conveniences.[2] Their wages are not changed. They are paid no more now for the work of ten hours, than before for the work of eight. They support the burden; but they come in for no share of the fruit. If a rich man employ the poor in breaking up land and cultivating its useful productions, he may be their benefactor. But, if he employ them in erecting palaces, in sinking

---

[1] *Political Justice*, VIII, ii.   [2] Ibid.

canals, in laying out his parks, and modelling his pleasure-grounds, he will be found, when rightly considered, their enemy. He is adding to the weight of oppression, and the vast accumulation of labour, by which they are already sunk beneath the level of the brutes. His mistaken munificence spreads its baleful effects on every side; and he is entailing curses on men he never saw, and posterity yet unborn.

Such is the real tendency of the conduct of that so frequently applauded character, the rich man who lives up to his fortune. His houses, his gardens, his equipages, his horses, the luxury of his table, and the number of his servants, are so many articles that may assume the name of munificence, but that in reality are but added expedients for grinding the poor, and filling up the measure of human calamity. Let us see what is the tendency of the conduct of the avaricious man in this respect.

He recognizes, in his proceedings at least, if not as an article of his creed, that great principle of austere and immutable justice, that the claims of the rich man are no more extensive than those of the poor, to the sumptuousness and pamperings of human existence. He watches over his expenditure with unintermitted scrupulosity; and, though enabled to indulge himself in luxuries, he has the courage to practise an entire self-denial.

It may be alleged indeed that, if he do not consume his wealth upon himself, neither does he impart it to another; he carefully locks it up, and pertinaciously withholds it from general use. But this point does not seem to have been rightly understood. The true development and definition of the nature of wealth have not been applied to illustrate it. Wealth consists in this only, the commodities raised and fostered by human labour. But he locks up neither corn, nor oxen, nor clothes, nor houses. These things are used and consumed by his contemporaries, as truly and to as great an extent, as if he were a beggar. He is the lineal successor of those religious fanatics of former ages, who conveyed to their heirs all that they had, and took themselves an oath of voluntary poverty. If he mean to act as the enemy of mankind, he is wretchedly deceived. Like the dotard in Æsop's fables, when he examines his hoard, he will find that he has locked up nothing but pebbles and dirt.

His conduct is much less pernicious to mankind, and much more nearly conformable to the unalterable principles of justice, than that of the man who disburses his income in what has been termed, a liberal and spirited style. It remains to compare their motives, and to consider which of them has familiarized himself most truly with the principles of morality.

It is not to be supposed, when a man, like the person of splendour and magnificence, is found continually offending against the rights, and adding to the miseries, of mankind; and when it appears, in addition to this, that all his expenses are directed to the pampering his debauched appetites, or the indulging an ostentatious and arrogant temper;—It is not, I say, to be supposed in this case, that the man is actuated by very virtuous and commendable motives.

It would be idle to hold up the miser as a pattern of benevolence. But it will not perhaps be found an untenable position to say, that his mind is in the habit of frequently recurring to the best principles of morality. He strips the world of its gaudy plumage, and views it in its genuine colours. He estimates splendid equipages and costly attire, exactly, or nearly, at their true value. He feels with acute sensibility the folly of wasting the wealth of a province upon a meal. He knows that a man may be as alert, as vigorous, and as happy, whose food is the roots of the earth, and whose drink the running stream. He understands all this in the same sense and with the same perspicuity, as the profoundest philosopher.

It is true indeed that he exaggerates his principles, and applies them to points to which upon better examination they would not be found applicable. His system would not only drive out of the world that luxury, which unnerves and debases the men that practise it, and is the principal source of all the oppression, ignorance and guilt which infest the face of the earth: it is also inimical to those arts, by which life is improved, the understanding cultivated, and the taste refined. It would destroy painting, and music, and the splendour of public exhibitions. Literature itself would languish under its frigid empire. But our censure would be extensive indeed, if we condemned every enthusiast of any science or principle, who exaggerated its maxims.

After every deduction, it will still be found that the miser considers himself as a man, entitled to expend upon himself only what the wants of man require. He sees, and truly sees, the folly of profusion. It is this perception of the genuine principles of morality, it is this consciousness of unassailable truth, that support him in the system of conduct he has chosen. He perceives, when you endeavour to persuade him to alter his system, that your arguments are the arguments of sophistry and mis-representation. Were it not for this, he would not be able constantly to resist the force of expostulation and the shafts of ridicule. Were it not for this, he could not submit to the uniform practice of self-denial, and the general obloquy he encounters from a world of which he is comparatively the benefactor.

.   .   .   .

   This speculation upon the comparative merits of avarice and profusion, may perhaps be found to be of greater importance than at first sight might be imagined. It includes in it the first principles of morality, and of justice between man and man. It strikes at the root of a deception that has long been continued, and long proved a curse to all the civilized nations of the earth. It tends to familiarize the mind to those strict and severe principles of judging, without which our energy, as well as our usefulness, will lie in a very narrow compass. It contains the germs of a code of political science, and may perhaps be found intimately connected with the extensive diffusion of liberty and happiness.

II

THOUGHTS OCCASIONED BY THE PERUSAL OF DR. PARR'S SPITAL SERMON, PREACHED AT CHRIST CHURCH, APRIL 15, 1800[1]

. . . . .

... I WILL set out with transcribing a passage from the preface to a book, published by me in December 1799, and entitled, 'St. Leon: a Tale of the Sixteenth Century;' ...

'Some readers of my graver productions will perhaps, in perusing these little volumes, accuse me of inconsistency; the affections and charities of private life being everywhere in this publication a topic of the warmest eulogium, while in the *Enquiry Concerning Political Justice* they seemed to be treated with no degree of indulgence and favour. In answer to this objection all I think it necessary to say on the present occasion, is that, for more than four years, I have been anxious for opportunity and leisure to modify some of the earlier chapters of that work in conformity to the sentiments inculcated in this. Not that I see cause to make any change respecting the principle of justice, or anything else fundamental to the system there delivered; but that I apprehend domestic and private affections inseparable from the nature of man, and from what may be styled the culture of the heart, and am fully persuaded that they are not incompatible with a profound and active sense of justice in the mind of him that cherishes them. The way in which these seemingly jarring principles may be reconciled, is in part pointed out in a recent publication of mine (*Memoirs of the Author of a Vindication of the Rights of Woman*, ch. vi, p. 90. second edition), the words of which I will here therefore take the liberty to repeat. They are these:

' "A sound morality requires that *nothing human should be regarded by us as indifferent*;[2] but it is impossible we should not feel the strongest interest for those persons whom we know most intimately, and whose

---

[1] [In 1800 Samuel Parr delivered a virulent speech attacking various doctrines of the *Enquiry*. Godwin's response, bearing the above title, was published in 1801.]

[2] [Godwin's italicized clause appears to be based upon Terence's *Heautontimorumenos*, l. 77: 'I hold that nothing human is alien to me.']

welfare and sympathies are united to our own. True wisdom will recommend to us individual attachments; for with them our minds are more thoroughly maintained in activity and life than they can be under the privation of them, and it is better that man should be a living being, than a stock or a stone. True virtue will sanction this recommendation; since it is the object of virtue to produce happiness; and since the man who lives in the midst of domestic relations, will have many opportunities of conferring pleasure, minute in the detail, yet not trivial in the amount, without interfering with the purposes of general benevolence. Nay, by kindling his sensibility, and harmonizing his soul, they may be expected, if he is endowed with a liberal and manly spirit, to render him more prompt in the service of strangers and the public." [1]

Here is a full and explicit avowal of all I acknowledge or perceive to be erroneous upon this point in the *Enquiry Concerning Political Justice*; and this is the point, and the only point, which Dr. Parr, after he knew of my avowed purpose to introduce into it certain essential modifications, has attempted to refute, with such superciliousness of rebuke, and vehemence of invective. In fact it seems to me to be by a very nice shade that Dr. Parr and I differ upon this point: but this is not the first time in which the well-known maxim has been illustrated, that 'the smaller is the space by which a man is divided from you in opinion, with the more fury and intemperance will he often contend about it'.

I will now, first, attempt to ascertain the quantity of *pestilential and destructive* consequences which were like to have flowed from this error in my *Enquiry Concerning Political Justice*, 'for such offences I am charged withal;' and, secondly, I will enquire into the soundness of what Dr. Parr has 'heard remarked by persons well skilled in the tactics of controversy, that, after the surrender of so many outworks [as are contained in the point above specified], the citadel itself [the great purpose aimed at in the *Enquiry Concerning Political Justice*] is scarcely tenable.' [2]

In entering on the first of these questions it is right we should have a clear idea how far my admissions already recited militate with anything advanced in my original treatise. The idea of justice there contained is, that it is a rule requiring from us such an application of 'our talents, our understanding, our strength and our time,' [3] as shall, in the result, produce the greatest sum of pleasure, to the sum of those beings who are capable of enjoying the sensation of pleasure.—Now, if I divide my time into portions, and consider how the majority of the smaller portions may be

[1] *St. Leon*, Preface, p. viii.   [2] *Sermon*, p. 52. Godwin's brackets.
[3] *Political Justice*, II. ii, p. 75.

so employed, as most effectually to procure pleasure to others, nothing is more obvious, than that many of these portions cannot be employed so effectually in procuring pleasure, as to my immediate connections and familiars: he therefore who would be the best moral economist of his time, must employ much of it in seeking the advantage and content of those, with whom he has most frequent intercourse. Accordingly it is there maintained, that the external action recommended by this, and by the commonly received systems of morality, will in the generality of cases be the same, all the difference lying in this, that the motives exciting to action, upon the one principle, and the other, will be essentially different.

Here, according to my present admission, lies all the error of which I am conscious, in the original statement in the *Enquiry Concerning Political Justice*: I would now say that, 'in the generality of cases,' not only the external action, but the motive, ought to be nearly the same as in the commonly received systems of morality; that I ought not only, 'in ordinary cases, to provide for my wife and children, my brothers and relations, before I provide for strangers,'[1] but that it would be well that my doing so, should arise from the operation of those private and domestic affections, by which through all ages of the world the conduct of mankind has been excited and directed.

There is a distinction to be introduced here, . . . between the motive from which a virtuous action is to arise, and the criterion by which it is to be determined to be virtuous. The motives of human actions are feelings, or passions, or habits. Without feeling we cannot act at all; and without passion we cannot act greatly. But, when we proceed to ascertain whether our actions are entitled to the name of virtue, this can only be done by examining into their effects, by bridging them to a standard, and comparing them with a criterion.

I cannot be mistaken in affirming that Dr. Parr and I are agreed about this criterion. All the difference is that Dr. Parr is most inclined to call this criterion by the name of 'utility,' and that I have oftenest called it by the name of 'justice.' Nor is the difference here complete; since I have frequently used his name for it, though I believe he has never employed mine. We are agreed however, as I have said, in this interesting and leading proposition, that 'that action or principle which does not tend to produce a general overbalance of pleasurable sensation, is not virtuous.'

.   .   .   .   .

[1] p. 73

The human mind is so constituted, as to render our actions in almost every case much more the creatures of sentiment and affection, than of the understanding. We all of us have, twisted with our very natures, the principles of parental and filial affection, of love, attachment and friendship. I do therefore not think it the primordial duty of the moralist to draw forth all the powers of his wit in the recommendation of these.

Parental and filial affection, and the sentiments of love, attachment and friendship, are most admirable instruments in the execution of the purposes of virtue. But to each of them, in the great chart of a just moral conduct, must be assigned its sphere. They are all liable to excess. Each must be kept within its bounds, and have rigorous limits assigned it. I must take care not so to love, or so to obey my love to my parent or child, as to entrench upon an important and paramount public good.

Parental and filial affection, and the other principles above enumerated, are so far from composing the great topics by which the doctrine of virtue is to be taught, that they are the proper characteristics of a mind, which has as yet remained an utter stranger to doctrine. The most ignorant parent, whose lips were never refreshed from the well of knowledge, whose mind was never expanded by sympathy with the disinterested and illustrious dead, or by a generous anxiety for the welfare of distant climes and unborn ages, will scarcely ever fail to love his child. He will often love him so much, even though he should be an idiot, deformed and odious to the sight, or imbued with the basest and most hateful propensities, that he will perhaps rather consent that millions should perish, than that this miserable minion of his dotage should suffer a moment's displeasure. I do not regard a parent of this sort with any strong feeling of approbation.

Patriotism, or the love of our country, will frequently operate in a similar way. With the majority perhaps of the human species, a kind of selfish impulse of pride and vainglory, which assumes the form of patriotism, and represents to our imagination whatever is gained to our country as so much gained to our darling selves, leads to a spirit of hatred and all uncharitableness towards the countries around us. We rejoice in their oppression, and make a jubilee, venting our joy in a hundred forms of extravagance, when the bleeding carcasses of thousands of their miserable natives are strewed upon the plain. This sort of patriotism, in its simplest and most uninstructed exhibition, vents itself in uttering hisses, and perhaps casting stones at the unprotected foreigner as he passes along our streets. I do not regard a patriotism of this kind with much feeling of approbation.

A truly virtuous character is the combined result of regulated affections. These sentiments, of which scarcely any human being is destitute, and of which we have much more frequent occasion to observe the excess than the defect,—the cultivation of these sentiments, I say, does not appear to me the principal office of moral discipline. For, after all, though I admit that the assiduities we employ for our children ought to be, and must be, the result of private and domestic affections, yet it is not these affections that determine them to be virtuous. They must, as has been already said, be brought to a standard, and tried by a criterion of virtue.

This criterion has been above described, and it is not perhaps of the utmost importance whether we call it utility, or justice, or, more periphrastically, the production of the greatest general good, the greatest public sum of pleasurable sensation. Call it by what name you please, it will still be true that this is the law by which our actions must be tried. I must be attentive to the welfare of my child; because he is one in the great congregation of the family of the whole earth. I must be attentive to the welfare of my child; because I can in many portions of the never-ceasing current of human life, be conferring pleasure and benefit on him, when I cannot be directly employed in conferring benefit on others. I best understand his character and his wants; I possess a greater power of modelling his disposition and influencing his fortune; and, as was observed in *Political Justice*,[1] he is the individual, in the great 'distribution of the class needing superintendence and supply among the class capable of affording them,' whom it falls to my lot to protect and cherish.—I do not require that, when a man is employed in benefiting his child, he should constantly recollect the abstract principle of utility, but I do maintain that his actions in prosecuting that benefit are no further virtuous than in proportion as they square with that principle.

Considering the subject in this light, it appears to me to follow with irresistible evidence, that the crown of a virtuous character consists in a very frequent and a very energetic recollection of the criterion, by which all his actions are to be tried, 'whether they are of good, or whether they are of evil.' It is this point, and this point alone, that leads to the distinction between such a man, and a man of the most vulgar character, of a character the least entitled to our approbation. The person, who has been well instructed and accomplished in the great school of human excellence, has passions and affections like other men. But he is aware that all these affections tend to excess, and must be taught each to know its

[1] p. 73.

order and its sphere. He therefore continually holds in mind the principles by which their boundaries are to be fixed.

I should think such a man would be the more perfect, in proportion as he endeavoured to elevate philanthropy into a passion. There appears to me to be little danger on that side. That we are all of us the creatures of sensible impressions, is a great and momentous truth. Let a man then try, as much as he will, to cultivate a love for his species, we may, I conceive, be very secure that occasions enough will present themselves, to pull him down from his enthusiastic eminence, and remind him of his concerns as an individual.

.   .   .   .

In revising the question of Fenelon and the valet, in its relation to the sacredness, the beauty and utility of the domestic affections, three things are principally to be observed.

First, I will suppose that I save in preference, the life of the valet, who is my father, and in so doing entrench upon the principle of utility. Few persons even upon that supposition will be disposed severely to blame my conduct. We are accustomed and rightly accustomed, to consider every man in the aggregate, as a machine calculated to produce many benefits or many evils, and not to take his actions into our examination in a disjointed and separate manner. If, without pause or hesitation, I proceed to save the life of my father in preference to that of any human being, every man will respect in me the sentiment of filial affection, will acknowledge that the feeling by which I am governed is a feeling pregnant with a thousand good and commendable actions, and will confess, according to a trite, but expressive, phrase, that at least I have *my heart in the right place*, that I have within me those precious and inestimable materials out of which all virtuous and honourable deeds are made.

But, secondly, the consideration of the domestic affections, and their infinite importance to 'the culture of the heart,' does essentially modify the question of utility, and affect the application of the criterion of virtue. The action, viz., the saving of the life of Fenelon, is to be set against the habit, and it will come to be seriously considered, whether, in proportion to the inequality of the alternative proposed to my choice, it will contribute most to the mass of human happiness, that I should act upon the utility of the case separately taken, or should refuse to proceed in violation of a habit, which is fraught with a series of successive utilities.

Thirdly, it is proper to notice the deception which Dr. Parr and his coadjutors put upon themselves and others, in constantly supposing that, if the father is saved, this will be the effort of passion, but if Fenelon is saved, the act will arise only from cool, phlegmatic, arithmetical calculation. No great and honourable deed can be achieved, but from passion. If I save the life of Fenelon, unprompted to do so by an ardent love of the wondrous excellence of the man, and a sublime eagerness to achieve and secure the welfare and improvement of millions, I am a monster, unworthy of the appellation of a man, and the society of beings so 'fearfully and wonderfully made,' as men are.

.   .   .   .

The second thing I proposed, was to enquire into the soundness of what Dr. Parr has 'heard remarked by persons well-skilled in the tactics of controversy, that after the surrender of so many outworks (viz., the question of the private and domestic affections), the citadel itself (the great purpose aimed at in the *Enquiry Concerning Political Justice*)[1] is scarcely tenable.' Upon this point I shall be very short.

The great doctrine of the treatise in question is what I have there called (adopting a term I found, ready coined in the French language) the perfectibility, but what I would now wish to call, changing the term, without changing a particle of the meaning, the progressive nature of man, in knowledge, in virtuous propensities, and in social institutions.

Upon the face of the question it is not easy to see, how the admission of the private and domestic affections operates to put a period to the progress of human improvement. Our advances in knowledge, I believe it will be admitted, will not be materially and fatally interrupted by the due exercise of these affections.

Our improvement in virtuous propensities, is intimately connected with our improvement in knowledge. There is no condition of mind so favourable to the rank and poisonous vegetation of vice, as ignorance. It is only short-sightedness and folly which persuade men that, while they are overreaching and defrauding their neighbours, they are pro- moting their own interests. . . . The progress of knowledge will render familiar to every mind the criterion of virtue, or, in other words, this terrible doctrine of universal philanthropy. We shall be astonished to see in how many instances interests, supposed incompatible, perfectly coincide; shall find that what is good for you, is advantageous to me; that, while I educate my child judiciously for himself, I am rendering him a valuable acquisition to society; and that, by contributing to the

[1] [Godwin's parentheses.]

improvement of my countrymen, I am preparing for my child a society in which it will be desirable for him to live.

.   .   .   .

. . . I love to contemplate the yet unexpanded powers and capabilities of our nature, and to believe that they will one day be unfolded to the infinite advantage and happiness of the inhabitants of the globe. Long habit has so trained me to bow to the manifestations of truth wherever I recognize them, that, if arguments were presented to me sufficient to establish the uncomfortable doctrine of my antagonists, I would weigh, I would revolve them, and I hope I should not fail to submit to their authority. But, if my own doctrine is an error, and if I am fated to die in it, I cannot afflict myself greatly with the apprehension of a mistake, which cheers my solitude, which I carry with me into crowds, and which adds somewhat to the pleasure and peace of every day of my existence.

Respecting the point of the improvement of our social institutions, that cannot be fundamentally affected by any consideration to arise out of the domestic affections. Politics is nothing else, but one chapter extracted out of the great code of morality. While therefore the criterion of virtue remains unchanged, the conduct which ought to be held by states, by governments and subjects, and the principles of judicial proceeding between man and man will forever remain the same. In the *Enquiry Concerning Political Justice* it is endeavoured to be proved, that in morality each man is entitled to a certain sphere for the exercise of his discretion; that it is to be desired that in this sphere he should be directed by a free, an instructed and independent judgement; and that it is necessary for the improvement of mankind, that no man or body of men should entrench upon this sphere but in cases of the most irresistible urgency. The inference drawn from these particulars is, that the less government we had, and the fewer were the instances in which government interfered with the proceedings of individuals, consistently with the preservation of the social state, the better would it prove for the welfare and happiness of man. Nothing which has been admitted on the subject of the domestic affections, in the slightest degree interferes with these reasonings. As to the quantity of improvement which may from time to time be introduced into the social condition of man, and the extent to which the interferences of government may ultimately be proscribed, the decision of that question depends upon the degree in which the human species is susceptible of improvement in virtuous propensities.

.   .   .   .

The remainder of these pages shall be dedicated to an examination of so much of the reasoning in the *Essay on the Principle of Population*,[1] as has been supposed by some persons to be subversive of the favourite doctrine of the *Political Justice*, the progressive nature of man. . . .

·   ·   ·   ·

[After summarizing the main line of Malthus's argument, Godwin observes:] I do not attempt in the slightest degree to vitiate the great foundations of his theory. My undertaking confines itself to the task of repelling his conclusions.

I admit fully that the principle of population in the human species is in its own nature energetic and unlimited, and that the safety of the world can no otherwise be maintained, but by a constant and powerful check upon this principle. This idea demolishes at once many maxims which have been long and unsuspectedly received into the vulgar code of morality, such as, that it is the first duty of princes to watch for the multiplication of their subjects, and that a man or woman, who passes the term of life in a condition of celibacy, is to be considered as having failed to discharge one of the principal obligations they owe to the community. On the contrary it now appears to be rather the man who rears a numerous family, that has in some degree transgressed the consideration he owes to the public welfare. Population is always, as this author observes, in all old settled countries (putting out of our view the temporary occurrence of extraordinary calamities, which however may be expected to be rapidly repaired), in some degree of excess beyond the means of subsistence: there is constantly a smaller quantity of provisions, than would be requisite for the comfortable and vigorous support of all the inhabitants.

The checks upon population which are honoured with the patronage of the author of this Essay, are vice and misery. Here it is obvious to the remark of every man, that we can scarcely select checks which shall have a less seducing and agreeable appearance, or fewer intrinsic recommendations to plead in their behalf. Thus the author, in correspondence to the habitual fairness of his disquisitions, affords every advantage to such as shall feel disposed to enquire into the doctrine of substitutes.

Is it necessary that we should always preserve the precise portion of vice and misery which are now to be found in the world, under pain of being subjected to the most terrible calamities? The author very truly

[1] [Published by Thomas Malthus in 1798.]

says, that his inferences are in a state of open war against every 'extraordinary improvement in society.' . . .

To discover whether exactly the same proportions of vice and misery which now obtain, are requisite for the preservation of the great structure of human society, let us open our eyes to survey the records of ancient history, and to consider what is perhaps now taking place in different parts of the globe. One of the greatest evils which can infest political disquisition, is the imagination that what takes peace in the spot and period in which we live, is essential to the general regulation and well-being of mankind.

What was called the exposing of children prevailed to a very extensive degree in the ancient world. The same practice continues to this hour in China.

I know that the prejudices and habits of modern Europe are strongly in arms against this institution. I grant that it is very painful and repulsive to the imagination of persons educated as I and my countrymen have been. And I hope, and trust, that no such expedient will be necessary to be resorted to, in any state of society which shall ever be introduced in this or the surrounding countries.

Yet, if we compare it with misery and vice, the checks pleaded for in the *Essay on Population*, what shall we say? I contemplate my species with admiration and reverence. When I think of Socrates, Solon and Aristides among the Greeks, when I think of Fabricius, Cincinnatus and Cicero among the Romans, above all, when I think of Milton, Shakespeare, Bacon and Burke, and when I reflect on the faculties and capacities everywhere, in different degrees, inherent in the human form, I am obliged to confess,—that I know not of how extraordinary productions the mysterious principle to which we owe our existence is capable, but that my imagination is able to represent to itself nothing more illustrious and excellent than man. But it is not man, such as I frequently see him, that excites much of my veneration. I know that the majority of those I see, are corrupt, low-minded, besotted, prepared for degradation and vice, and with scarcely any vestige about them of their high destination. Their hold therefore is rather upon my compassion and general benevolence, than upon my esteem. Neither do I regard a new-born child with any superstitious reverence. If the alternative were complete, I had rather such a child should perish in the first hour of its existence, than that a man should spend seventy years of life in a state of misery and vice. I know that the globe of earth affords room for only a certain number of human beings to be trained to any degree of perfection; and I had rather witness the existence of a thousand such beings, than a million of millions of creatures, burdensome to themselves, and contemptible to each other.

.   .   .   .

... the exposing of children is in its own nature an expedient perfectly adequate to the end for which it has been cited.

This was the expedient resorted to by the ancients and the Chinese as a check upon the principle of population. Other expedients may be found in the descriptions and records of other parts of the world. In the island of Ceylon for example, it appears to be a part of the common law of the country, that no woman shall be a mother before she is thirty, ...

I have not introduced these particulars, as seeming to me necessary to the solution of the difficulty proposed. It was just however to give a comprehensive, though compendious, view of the subject. This catalogue might be further enlarged.

It is right however that, in addition to these particulars, we should hypothetically take into the account, the resources of the human mind; the inventions and discoveries with which almost every period of literature and refinement is pregnant, rendering familiar and obvious to every understanding, what previously to such discoveries presumption and ignorance had pronounced to be impossible; and the vast multitude of such discoveries which may be expected, before we arrive at the chance of making experiment of a state of equality and universal benevolence. Were it not for the impression which the ingenuousness of this author and some of his readers has made upon me, I should certainly have pronounced, that a man must be strangely indifferent or averse to schemes of extraordinary improvement in society, who made this a conclusive argument against them, that, when they were realized, they might peradventure be of no permanence and duration.

.   .   .   .

It is ... worthy of our attention to enquire, respecting such a country as England, where, according to the majority of political calculators, population has long been at a stand, by what checks it is kept down within the limits it is found to observe.

One of the checks continually operating is, that great numbers of the children who are born in this country, are half destroyed by neglect and improper food, and that, after pining away a few weeks, or a year or two of existence, they perish miserably without any chance of approaching maturity. The parents, in many classes of the community, scarcely able to maintain themselves in life, if they provide food in sufficient quantity for their children, can at least pay no attention to its being properly adapted to their age or constitution. . . . This is undoubtedly a sufficient check upon increasing population. But there is nothing in this which any political reasoner will recommend to imitation. This is probably the principal of those checks arising from misery and vice, which the writer of the treatise before us had in his contemplation.

Another check upon increasing population which operates very powerfully and extensively in the country we inhabit, is that sentiment, whether virtue, prudence or pride, which continually restrains the universality and frequent repetition of the marriage contract. Early marriages in this country between a grown up boy and girl are of uncommon occurrence. Every one, possessed in the most ordinary degree of the gift of foresight, deliberates long before he engages in so momentous a transaction. He asks himself again and again how he shall be able to subsist the offspring of his union. I am persuaded it very rarely happens in England that a marriage takes place, without this question having first undergone a repeated examination. There is a very numerous class in every great town, clerks to merchants and lawyers, journeymen in shops, and others, who either never marry, or refrain from marriage till they have risen through the different gradations of their station to that degree of comparative opulence, which they think authorizes them to take upon themselves the burden of a family. It is needless to remark that, where marriage takes place at a later period of life, the progeny may be expected to be less numerous. If the check from virtue, prudence or pride operates less in the lower classes of life than in the class last described, it is that the members of those classes are rendered desperate by the oppression under which they groan; they have no character of prudence or reflection to support, and they have nothing of that pride, arising from what is called the decent and respectable appearance a man makes among his neighbours, which should enable them to suppress the first sallies of passion, and the effervescence of a warm constitution.

Let us apply these remarks to that condition of society, which forms the only important question between me and the author of the *Essay on Population*, a condition of society in which a great degree of equality and an ardent spirit of benevolence are assumed to prevail. We have found that, in the community in which we live, one of the great operative checks upon an increasing population arises from virtue, prudence or pride. Will there be less of virtue, prudence and honourable pride in such a condition of society, than there is at present? It is true, the ill consequences of a numerous family will not come so coarsely home to each man's individual interest, as they do at present. It is true, a man in such a state of society might say, If my children cannot subsist at my expense, let them subsist at the expense of my neighbour. But it is not in the human character to reason after this manner in such a situation. The more men are raised above poverty and a life of expedients, the more decency will prevail in their conduct, and sobriety in their sentiments. Where every one has a character, no one will be willing to distinguish himself by headstrong imprudence. Where a man possesses every reasonable means of pleasure and happiness, he will not be in a hurry to destroy his own tranquillity or that of others by thoughtless excess.

·   ·   ·   ·

I do not imagine that I have here exhausted the subject which the author of the *Essay on Population* has led me to consider. I will not pretend that I have so linked together my arguments, and in such manner fenced them against uncertainty and exception, as to have made out an absolute demonstration that we have nothing to fear, from that source of ruin with which this writer menaces us. But I think, to say the least, I have collected such strong presumptions, as may well lead us to believe, that there is no imminent danger to be apprehended from that side. I trust I have put down such hints of what must be in the highest degree gratifying to every lover of virtue and of man, as to convince the majority of impartial readers, that there is no such 'obstacle in the way to any extraordinary improvement in society,' as should oblige us to sit down for ever under the whole mass of existing moral evils, and to deprecate every generous attempt to improve the condition of mankind, as leading, under specious appearances, to the reality of great and intolerable mischief.

·   ·   ·   ·

III

THOUGHTS ON MAN[1]

ESSAY XI

OF SELF-LOVE AND BENEVOLENCE

N o question has more memorably exercised the ingenuity of men who have speculated upon the structure of the human mind, than that of the motives by which we are actuated in our intercourse with our fellow-creatures. . . .

.   .   .   .

Locke is the philosopher, who, in writing on Human Understanding, has specially delivered the doctrine, that uneasiness is the cause which determines the will, and urges us to act. He says,[2] 'The motive we have for continuing in the same state, is only the present satisfaction we feel in it; the motive to change is always some uneasiness: nothing setting us upon the change of state, or upon any new action, but some uneasiness. This is the great motive that works on the mind.'

It is not my concern to enquire, whether Locke by this statement meant to assert that self-love is the only principle of human action. It has at any rate been taken to express the doctrine which I here propose to refute.

And, in the first place, I say, that, if our business is to discover the consideration entertained by the mind which induces us to act, this tells us nothing. It is like the case of the Indian philosopher,[3] who, being asked what it was that kept the earth in its place, answered, that it was supported by an elephant, and that elephant again rested on a tortoise. He must be endowed with a slender portion of curiosity, who, being told that uneasiness is that which spurs on the mind to act, shall rest satisfied with this explanation, and does not proceed to enquire, what makes us uneasy?

An explanation like this is no more instructive, than it would be, if, when we saw a man walking, or grasping a sword or a bludgeon, and

---

[1] [Published 1831.]   [2] *An Essay Concerning Human Understanding*, II. xxi. 29.
[3] Locke, II. xiii. 19.

we enquired into the cause of this phenomenon, any one should inform us that he walks, because he has feet, and he grasps, because he has hands.

I could not commodiously give to my thoughts their present form, unless I had been previously furnished with pens and paper. But it would be absurd to say, that my being furnished with pens and paper, is the cause of my writing this Essay. . .

The advocates of self-love have, very inartificially and unjustly, substituted the abstract definition of a voluntary agent, and made that stand for the motive by which he is prompted to act. It is true, that we cannot act without the impulse of desire or uneasiness; but we do not think of that desire and uneasiness; and it is the thing upon which the mind is fixed that constitutes our motive. In the boundless variety of the acts, passions and pursuits of human beings, it is absurd on the face of it to say that we are all governed by one motive, and that, however dissimilar are the ends we pursue, all this dissimilarity is the fruit of a single cause.

One man chooses travelling, another ambition, a third study, a fourth voluptuousness and a mistress. Why do these men take so different courses?

Because one is partial to new scenes, new buildings, new manners, and the study of character. Because a second is attracted by the contemplation of wealth and power. Because a third feels a decided preference for the works of Homer, or Shakespeare, or Bacon, or Euclid. Because a fourth finds nothing calculated to stir his mind in comparison with female beauty, female allurements, or expensive living.

Each of these finds the qualities he likes, intrinsically in the thing he chooses. . . . The cause of these differences is, that each man has an individual internal structure, directing his partialities, one man to one thing, and another to another.

.   .   .   .

. . . the benevolent man is an individual who finds a peculiar delight in contemplating the contentment, the peace and heart's ease of other men, and sympathizes in no ordinary degree with their sufferings. He rejoices in the existence and diffusion of human happiness, though he should not have had the smallest share in giving birth to the thing he loves. It is because such are his tastes, and what above all things he prefers, that he afterwards becomes distinguished by the benevolence of his conduct.

The reflex act of the mind, which these new philosophers put forward as the solution of all human pursuits, rarely presents itself but to the speculative enquirer in his closet. The savage never dreams of it. The active man, engaged in the busy scenes of life, thinks little, and on rare occasions of himself, but much, and in a manner for ever, of the objects of his pursuit.

.   .   .   .

The doctrine of the modern philosophers on this point, is in many ways imbecile and unsound. It is inauspicious to their creed, that the reflex act of the mind is purely the affair of experience. Why did the liberal-minded man perform his first act of benevolence? The answer of these persons ought to be, because the recollection of a generous deed is a source of the truest delight. But there is an absurdity on the face of this solution. We do not experimentally know the delight which attends the recollection of a generous deed, till a generous deed has been performed by us. We do not learn these things from books. And least of all is this solution to the purpose, when the business is to find a solution that suits the human mind universally, the unlearned as well as the learned, the savage as well as the sage. And surely it is inconsistent with all sound reasoning, to represent that as the sole spring of our benevolent actions, which by the very terms will not fit the first benevolent act in which any man engaged.

The advocates of the doctrine of 'self-love the source of all our actions,' are still more puzzled, when the case set before them is that of the man, who flies, at an instant's warning, to save the life of the child who has fallen into the river, . . . This man, as might be illustrated in a thousand instances, treats his own existence as unworthy of notice, and exposes it to multiplied risks to effect the object to which he devotes himself.

They are obliged to say, that this man anticipates the joy he will feel in the recollection of a noble act, and the cutting and intolerable pain he will experience in the consciousness that a human being has perished, whom it was in his power to save. It is in vain that we tell them that, without a moment's consideration, he tore off his clothes, or plunged into the stream with his clothes on, . . . Still they tell us, that he recollected what compunctious visitings would be his lot if he remained supine— he felt the sharpest uneasiness at sight of the accident before him, and it was to get rid of that uneasiness, and not for the smallest regard to the unhappy being he has been the means to save, that he entered on the hazardous undertaking.

Uneasiness, the knowledge of what inwardly passes in the mind, is a thing not in the slightest degree adverted to but in an interval of leisure. No; the man here spoken of thinks of nothing but the object immediately before his eyes; he adverts not at all to himself; he acts only with an undeveloped, confused and hurried consciousness that he may be of some use, and may avert the instantly impending calamity. He has scarcely even so much reflection as amounts to this.

·   ·   ·   ·

What is the true explanation of these determinations of the human will? Is it, that the person, thus consigning himself to death, loved nothing but himself, regarded only the pleasure he might reap, or the uneasiness he was eager to avoid? Or, is it, that he had arrived at the exalted point of self-oblivion, and that his whole soul was penetrated and engrossed with the love of those for whom he conceived so exalted a partiality?

·   ·   ·   ·

ESSAY XII

OF THE LIBERTY OF HUMAN ACTIONS

THE question, which has been attended with so long and obstinate debates, concerning the metaphysical doctrines of liberty and necessity, and the freedom of human actions, is not even yet finally and satisfactorily settled.

The negative is made out by an argument which seems to amount to demonstration, that every event requires a cause, a cause why it is as it is and not otherwise, that the human will is guided by motives, and is consequently always ruled by the strongest motive, and that we can never choose anything, either without a motive of preference, or in the way of following the weaker, and deserting the stronger motive.[1]

Why is it then that disbelief or doubt should still subsist in a question so fully decided?

For the same reason that compels us to reject many other demonstrations. The human mind is so constituted as to oblige us, if not theoretically, at least practically, to reject demonstration, and adhere to our senses.

The case is thus in the great question of the non-existence of an external world, or of matter. However much the understanding may be satisfied

[1] *Political Justice*, IV. vii.

of the truth of the proposition by the arguments of Berkeley and others, we no sooner go out into actual life, than we become convinced, in spite of our previous scepticism or unbelief, of the real existence of the table, the chair, and the objects around us, and of the permanence and reality of the persons, both body and mind, with whom we have intercourse. . . .

But there is a great difference between the question of a material world, and the question of liberty and necessity. The most strenuous Berkeleian can never say, that there is any contradiction or impossibility in the existence of matter. All that he can consistently and soberly maintain is, that, if the material world exists, we can never perceive it, and that our sensations, and trains of impressions and thinking go on wholly independent of that existence.

But the question of the freedom of human actions is totally of another class. To say that in our choice we reject the stronger motive, and that we choose a thing merely because we choose it, is sheer nonsense and absurdity; and whoever with a sound understanding will fix his mind upon the state of the question will perceive its impossibility.

In the meantime it is not less true, that every man, the necessarian as well as his opponent, acts on the assumption of human liberty, and can never for a moment, when he enters into the scenes of real life, divest himself of this persuasion.

Let us take separately into our consideration the laws of matter and of mind. We acknowledge generally in both an established order of antecedents and consequents, or of causes and effects. This is the sole foundation of human prudence and of all morality. It is because we foresee that certain effects will follow from a certain mode of conduct, that we act in one way rather than another. . . .

Yet, at the same time that we admit of a regular series of cause and effect in the operations both of matter and mind, we never fail, in our reflections upon each, to ascribe to them an essential difference. In the laws by which a falling body descends to the earth, and by which the planets are retained in their orbits, in a word, in all that relates to inanimate nature, we readily assent to the existence of absolute laws, so that, when we have once ascertained the fundamental principles of astronomy and physics, we rely with perfect assurance upon the invariable operation of these laws, yesterday, today, and for ever. . . .

But we believe, or, more accurately speaking, we feel, that it is otherwise in the universe of mind. Whoever attentively observes the phenomena of thinking and sentient beings, will be convinced, that men and animals are under the influence of motives, that we are subject to the predominance of the passions, of love and hatred, of desire and aversion, of sorrow and joy, and that the elections we make are regulated by impressions supplied to us by these passions. But we are fully penetrated with the notion, that mind is an arbiter, that it sits on its throne, and decides, as an absolute prince, this way or that; in short, that, while inanimate nature proceeds passively in an eternal chain of cause and effect, mind is endowed with an initiating power, and forms its deter-minations by an inherent and indefeasible prerogative.

. . . I am fully persuaded, as far as the powers of my understanding can carry me, that the phenomena of mind are governed by laws altogether as inevitable as the phenomena of matter, and that the decisions of our will are always in obedience to the impulse of the strongest motive.

The consequences of the principle implanted in our nature, by which men of every creed, when they descend into the scene of busy life, pro-nounce themselves and their fellow-mortals to be free agents, are sufficiently memorable.

From hence there springs what we call conscience in man, and a sense of praise or blame due to ourselves and others for the actions we perform.

. . . our moral sentiments are all involved with, and take their rise in, the delusive sense of liberty. It is in this that is contained the peculiar force of the terms virtue, duty, guilt and desert. We never pronounce these words without thinking of the action to which they refer, as that which might or might not be done, and therefore unequivocally approve or disapprove in ourselves and others. A virtuous man, as the term is understood by all, as soon as we are led to observe upon those qualities, and the exhibition of those qualities in actual life, which con-stitute our nature, is a man who, being in full possession of the freedom of human action, is engaged in doing those things which a sound judgement of the tendencies of what we do pronounces to be good.

Duty is a term that can scarcely be said to have a meaning, except that which it derives from the delusive sense of liberty. According to the creed of the necessarian, it expresses that mode of action on the part of the individual, which constitutes the best possible application of his capacity to the general benefit.[1] In the meantime, if we confine ourselves

---

[1] *Political Justice*, II. iv.

to this definition, it may as well be taken to describe the best application of a knife, or any other implement proceeding from the hands of the manufacturer, as of the powers of a human being. But we surely have a very different idea in our minds, when we employ the term duty. It is not agreeable to the use of language that we should use this term, except we speak of a being in the exercise of volition.

Duty then means that which may justly be required of a human creature in the possession of liberty of action. It includes in its proper sense the conception of the empire of will, the notion that mind is an arbiter, that it sits on its throne, and decides, as an absolute prince, this way or that.

. . . .

A multitude of terms instantly occur to us, the application of which is limited in the same manner as the term duty is limited: such are, to owe, obligation, debt, bond, right, claim, sin, crime, guilt, merit and desert. Even reward and punishment, however they may be intelligible when used merely in the sense of motives employed, have in general acceptation a sense peculiarly derived from the supposed freedom of the human will.

The mode therefore in which the advocates of the doctrine of necessity have universally talked and written, is one of the most memorable examples of the hallucination of the human intellect. They have at all times recommended that we should translate the phrases in which we usually express ourselves on the hypothesis of liberty, into the phraseology of necessity, that we should talk no other language than that which is in correspondence with the severest philosophy, and that we should exert ourselves to expel all fallacious notions and delusions so much as from our recollection. They did not perceive what a wide devastation and destruction they were proposing of all the terms and phrases that are in use in the communications between man and man in actual life.—They might as well have recommended that we should rigorously bear in mind on the ordinary occasions of life, that there is no such thing as colour, that which we ordinarily call by that name having no existence in external objects, but belonging only to our way of perceiving them.

. . . .

There is an old axiom of philosophy, which counsels us to 'think with the learned, and talk with the vulgar;' and the practical application of this axiom runs through the whole scene of human affairs. Thus the most learned astronomer talks of the rising and setting of the sun, and forgets in his ordinary discourse that the earth is not for ever at rest, and does not constitute the centre of the universe. Thus, however we reason respecting the attributes of inanimate matter and the nature of sensation, it never occurs to us, when occupied with the affairs of actual life, that there is no heat in fire, and no colour in the rainbow.

In like manner, when we contemplate the acts of ourselves and our neighbours, we can never divest ourselves of the delusive sense of the liberty of human actions, of the sentiment of conscience, of the feelings of love and hatred, the impulses of praise and blame, and the notions of virtue, duty, obligation, right, claim, guilt, merit and desert. And it has sufficiently appeared in the course of this Essay, that it is not desirable that we should do so. They are these ideas to which the world we live in is indebted for its crowning glory and greatest lustre. . . .

But, though the doctrine of the necessity of human actions can never form the rule of our intercourse with others, it will still have its use. It will moderate our excesses, and point out to us that middle path of judgement which the soundest philosophy inculcates. We shall learn, according to the apostolic precept, to 'be angry, and sin not, neither let the sun go down upon our wrath.' We shall make of our fellow-men neither idols to worship, nor demons to be regarded with horror and execration. We shall think of them, as of players, 'that strut and fret their hour upon the stage, and then are heard no more.' We shall 'weep, as though we wept not, and rejoice, as though we rejoiced not, seeing that the fashion of this world passeth away.' And, most of all, we shall view with pity, even with sympathy, the men whose frailties we behold, or by whom crimes are perpetrated, satisfied that they are parts of one great machine, and, like ourselves, are driven forward by impulses over which they have no real control.

INDEX

abstraction, 64–6, 146, 154 f., 160.
accumulation of wealth, 284–8, 313–19.
action, 35, 41, 94, 161, 169, 253, 273.
   voluntary and involuntary, 28, 39–60, 118, 164 f., 167.
Addison, Joseph, 18 n.
addresses, political, 101 f., 221, 224.
adversity, 250 f.
Æsop, 317.
Agincourt, war of Cressy and, 21.
agrarian laws, 285.
Alexander, 21, 85.
alphabet, 66.
America, United States of, xii, 3, 265, 304.
anarchy, xxix, 22, 262–6, 283.
appetite, 47, 50, 54; see desire.
Aquinas, St. Thomas, 236.
Aristides, 329.
aristocracy, 40, 61, 142 f., 200 f., 203 f., 210 f., 234.
Aristotle, 236.
artisan, 100, 163.
assemblies, representative, 102, 204 f., 219–21.
associations, political, 139–41.
Athens, 204.
atoms, 32.
Attila, 57.
authority, 88, 93, 122, 130.
   kinds of, xxvii–xxix, 121.
   political, xxx–xxxi, 67 f., 98 f., 100–2, 112–16, 124 f., 218, 221 f., 224–6, 235.
avarice, 53, 86, 180 f., 280 f., 313, 317–19.

Bacchus, 21.
Bacon, Francis, 329, 334.
ballot, 241–3; see election.
Beccaria, Cesare, 252 n., 253, 256 n.
Becket, St. Thomas à, 82.
Bellarmine, St. Robert, 236.
benevolence, xxii–xxiii, 67, 71, 81, 133, 151, 169; see disinterestedness.
   and self-love, 179–84, 292 f., 333–6.
   highest form of pleasure, xvii, 50, 145 f., 188 f.
benevolent man, xvii–xx, 188 f.
Bentham, Jeremy, xiii.

Berkeley, George, 27 n., 337.
birth, man's nature at, 34.
blame, how understood by necessitarians, 174.
body, 32, 58; see matter.
books, 57, 141.
bribery, 152.
Burke, Edmund, xi, 22 n., 65 n., 87, 208 n., 240 n., 292 n., 329.

Caesar, Julius, 21.
Caligula, Gaius Caesar, 100.
Cambyses, 21.
capacity, human, 58, 80 f., 148–50, 268.
   and virtue, 80 f., 83 f., 148 f., 170.
capital punishment, 26, 120, 269 f.
Cato, 147.
causation, 31, 34, 59, 85, 158–65, 168 f., 174–9, 190, 333 f., 336–8.
Ceylon, 330.
chain of events, 31, 34, 84, 104, 165, 168 f., 174, 190.
chance, 162 f., 168, 242.
character, 27–38, 46, 93 f., 121 f., 161, 324.
   influence of government upon, 27 f., 37 f., 199 f., 203 f., 224–6.
charity, 74, 281; see philanthropy.
Charles I, 21.
China, 330.
church, habit of attending, 45.
Cicero, 153, 256, 329.
Cincinnatus, 329.
circulation of blood caused by thought, 179.
Clark, Samuel, 167 n.
classes, 209, 290, 299, 330 f.
clergy, 61, 93, 226–8.
climate, 51, 60–2.
coercion, 95 f., 118, 121, 249, 269, 278, 286 f., 295; see force, punishment, violence.
   evils of, 217, 247 f., 250 f.
   necessity of, 116, 134 f., 261, 287 f.
cohabitation, 302.
Coke, Edward, 236.
Coleridge, Samuel Taylor, xii.
commerce, 196, 210, 309, 314.
communication, 55–7, 141, 146 f., 267 f.

PRINTED IN GREAT BRITAIN
AT THE UNIVERSITY PRESS, OXFORD
BY VIVIAN RIDLER
PRINTER TO THE UNIVERSITY